K

CLIMATE CHANGE IN THE 21ST CENTURY

Climate Change in the 21st Century

STEWART J. COHEN

with

MELISSA W. WADDELL

McGill-Queen's University Press
Montreal & Kingston · London · Ithaca

Legal deposit fourth quarter 2009
Bibliothèque nationale du Québec

Printed in Canada on acid-free paper that is 100% ancient forest free
(100% post-consumer recycled), processed chlorine free

McGill-Queen's University Press acknowledges the support of the
Canada Council for the Arts for our publishing program. We also
acknowledge the financial support of the Government of Canada
through the Book Publishing Industry Development Program (BPIDP)
for our publishing activities.

Library and Archives Canada Cataloguing in Publication

Cohen, Stewart J. (Stewart Jay), 1953–
  Climate change in the 21st century / Stewart J. Cohen; with
Melissa W. Waddell.

  Includes bibliographical references and index.
  ISBN 978-0-7735-3326-4 (bnd)
  ISBN 978-0-7735-3327-1 (pbk)

  1. Climatic changes. 2. Global warming. I. Waddell, Melissa W. II. Title.

QC903.C57 2009   304.2'5   C2009-901543-9

This book was typeset by Interscript in 10.5/13 Sabon.

Contents

Tables and Figures

Preface

In 1997, I began teaching a graduate course on human-induced climate change, popularly known as global warming, at the University of British Columbia. The idea was to offer a broad introduction on climate change to an interdisciplinary student audience with the hope that some of the students would become interested in pursuing a research topic on some aspect of global warming. I also saw this course as an important learning opportunity for me.

As a climatologist/geographer by training, my initial approach to global warming was to apply traditional tools from climatology and to report on the quantitative results of some model simulations. I was looking at potential implications for water resources in the North American Great Lakes and was quite concerned about the large changes in water balance that emerged from these simulations. When my results were published in 1985, reaction was swift. I found myself invited to many conferences in Canada and the United States to discuss them. I came in contact with many different perspectives from engineering, community health, national and international policy, and economics. I felt that there was a great deal of interest being expressed in the technical aspects of global warming impacts. Momentum was building towards a wider effort to create a global-warming policy framework.

I had the opportunity to work on the organizing committee for a major international conference in Toronto in 1988. This was the World Meteorological Organization – United Nations Environment Programme (WMO-UNEP) conference The Changing Atmosphere: Implications for Global Security, later known simply as the Toronto Conference. Such gatherings are commonplace today, but in 1988, global warming was still unknown to most people and governments. Through the leadership of Howard Ferguson and Gordon MacKay, from Environment Canada, and an international advisory board, a deliberate effort was made to seek out people who could offer a wide range of expertise from the natural and social sciences, technology and governance, and developed and developing countries. This conference was definitely not about climate science alone. Being exposed to this "global village" chatter taught me that if global-warming policy was to cover such breadth, research and teaching had to as well.

Since that landmark event, I have pursued research activities that have focused on interdisciplinary team building as a means towards increasing our understanding of the regional implications of global warming. The case studies I have undertaken have often brought regional development concerns directly into the climate change dialogue being initiated by researchers. These concerns have included water rights, governance of resource harvesting, land use planning, and management of renewable resources and parks. Global warming is gradually entering into regional discourses on long-term planning and management of climate-sensitive resources, as well as on energy demand from transportation, industry, and communities. Ultimately, this should lead to a more explicit linkage of climate change policy and sustainable development.

Global warming is discussed in the education system as well. I've been invited to do guest lectures on global-warming topics in university classes in civil engineering, environmental studies, geography, education, and sociology of the environment, but it is difficult to find university courses devoted solely to the subject of human-induced climate change. When I decided to offer a climate change course at the University of British Columbia, I found that I was gathering reference materials from many different sources, including reports of the Intergovernmental Panel on Climate Change (IPCC), numerous journal articles and government reports, and a growing number of books and materials from the grey literature (documents that were not subjected to external peer review before publication), but there was no single source that I could use to anchor the teaching curriculum for a cross-disciplinary audience. So, after several years of teaching the climate change course, I submitted a proposal to the government of Canada's Science Horizons program to find a science writer to assist me in translating class lectures into chapters, which would form a reference that could be used for teaching purposes. Thus in 2004, I began my writing and editing partnership with Melissa Waddell. This collaboration between researcher and science writer follows the model of the well-known book *The Genesis Strategy*, by Stephen Schneider, with Lynne Mesirow, published in 1976.

Another source of inspiration has been *Climate Affairs* (2003) by Michael Glantz. Dr Glantz has been a champion of multidisciplinary collaboration on climate change for many years, producing not only books and articles but also an international newsletter, *Network Newsletter,* published from 1985 to 2005. Its purpose was to connect disparate research and policy interests in climate issues, in order to create, in effect, a global learning community around this difficult and challenging problem.

Finally, I have benefitted from my participation in several IPCC activities, beginning with my contribution to *Preliminary Guidelines for Assessing Impacts of Climate Change* (1992). My involvement has continued throughout the last sixteen years, including serving as a lead author for the recently published Fourth Assessment Report, *Climate Change 2007: Impacts, Adaptation and Vulnerability.* The awarding of the 2007 Nobel Peace Prize to the IPCC is an important indicator of the increasing appreciation for clear communication on climate change, and I feel very proud to have been a small part of this international effort in shared learning.

This book is meant to contribute to creating a learning community around global warming. It is not designed to be a synthesis of all the literature. Other publications do that. What it tries to do is to open various windows of knowledge by looking at some of the basic ideas of each. The climate scientist, biologist, economist, and ethicist approach climate change using different tools and fundamental ways of framing problems. It is to be hoped that this book captures some of these perspectives in a way that will provide the reader with an appreciation of the many dimensions of global warming.

Stewart J. Cohen

Acknowledgments

This book originated from a series of lectures offered in a graduate course entitled Climate Change in the 21st Century at the University of British Columbia. The course has been listed both by the Resource Management and Environment Studies Program at the Institute for Resources, Environment and Sustainability and by the Department of Geography. We would like to express our appreciation to the University for its support of this course and to Professor John Robinson for his helpful advice during the first year the course was offered, back in 1997.

We would like to acknowledge the students participating in the fall 2004 class who made it possible for us to try out some new ideas: Matthew Asplin, Brad Badelt, Sarah Burch, Fred Ghatala, Stacy Langsdale, Aynslie Ogden, Pascal Poudenx, Simone Rousseau, Shingo Takahashi, and guest speakers Tony Lemprière and Eric Mazzi.

The transformation of course lectures to book chapters has been a challenging and rewarding process for both of us. We would like to thank the Science Horizons program of the government of Canada, Les Lavkulich and Leslie Stephenson for assisting with the application to this program, and Don MacIver, director of the Adaptation & Impacts Research Division (AIRD) of Environment Canada, for supporting our collaborative work on the creation of this book. Our thanks also go to Tina Neale and Robin Bing Rong of AIRD for their assistance. However, any judgments expressed in these pages are those of the authors and not necessarily those of the Government of Canada or the University of British Columbia.

We have drawn on a wide range of materials for this publication. We are grateful to many individuals for their assistance in obtaining illustrative material: Nigel Arnell, Joe Alcamo, Elaine Barrow, Anne-Marie Brinkmann, Ian Burton, Tim Carter, Allan Carroll, Renate Christ,

Caroline Davis, Rob de Löe, Raymond Desjardins, Suraje Dessai, David Flanders, Philippe Gachon, Steve Glover, Alan Hamlet, Clair Hanson, Bryan Hanssen, Ann Henderson-Sellers, Deborah Herbert, John Houghton, Hao Le, Bo Lim, Marco Jannsen, Catrinus Jepma, Mick Kelly, Werner Kurz, Neil Leary, Bernhard Lehner, Michael Mann, Larry McDaniel, Karen McNeill, Linda Mearns, Martin Middelburg, Mohan Munasinghe, Denise Neilsen, Tim Oke, Hermann Ott, Martin Parry, Andy Pitman, Norah Pritchard, Milka Radojevic, Cynthia Rosenzweig, Michael Quick, John Robinson, Daniel Scott, P.R. Shukla, Brian Simpson, Fiona Smith, Dagmar Schröter, Gilles Sommeria, Michel St Martin, Melinda Tignor, Ferenc Toth, Kimberley van Alphen, Angelika Wirtz, Gary Yohe, and others whom we may have inadvertently omitted. We also acknowledge assistance from Joel Smith regarding figure 6.11, and some very useful suggestions from Livia Bizikova, Sarah Burch, and John Robinson regarding figure 9.10, and from Tom Peterson, and Roger Pulwarty regarding figure 10.12. We would like to thank the anonymous reviewers of this book for their many substantive and helpful comments and the staff at McGill-Queen's University Press for their support of this publication.

Finally, we would like to express our deep gratitude to our families for their personal support and encouragement of our career endeavours – Nanci, Genna, Andrew, and David Cohen; Peter, Linda, and Cheryl Waddell; and Dwayne Ashman.

Stewart J. Cohen
Melissa W. Waddell

Websites

Australian Government Department of Climate Change. http://www.climatechange.gov.au

Carbon Dioxide Information Analysis Centre. http://cdiac.esd.ornl.gov/home.html

Climate Research Unit at the University of East Anglia. http://www.cru.uea.ac.uk/cru/cru.htm

Columbia Basin Trust–Climate Change. http://www.cbt.org/initiatives/climatechange

Earth System Science Partnership. http://www.essp.org

Government of Canada Canadian Climate Change Scenarios Network. http://www.cccsn.ca

Government of Canada Climate Impacts & Adaptation Program. http://www.adaptation.nrcan.gc.ca

Government of Canada ECOACTION. http://www.ecoaction.gc.ca

The Integrated Assessment Society. http://www.tias-web.info/

International Emissions Trading Association. http://www.ieta.org

International Human Dimensions Programme on Global Environmental Change. http://ihdp.unu.edu

Intergovernmental Panel on Climate Change (IPCC). http://www.ipcc.ch

International Institute for Sustainable Development. http://www.iisd.org

IPCC Data Distribution Centre. http://ipcc-ddc.cru.uea.ac.uk

Joint Implementation Quarterly (JIN Foundation, Groningen, the Netherlands). http://www.jiqweb.org

Kimball's Biology Pages. http://users.rcn.com/jkimball.ma.ultranet/BiologyPages

Network Newsletter (Institute for the Study of Society and the Environment, National Centre for Atmospheric Research, Boulder, CO). http://www.isse.ucar.edu

NOAA Earth System Research Lab Global Monitoring Division. http://
    www.esrl.noaa.gov/gmd/ccgg/trends/
Northern Climate Exchange. http://www.taiga.net/nce
Postdam Institute for Climate Impact Research. http://www.
    pik-postdam.de
Tiempo Climate Cyberlibrary. International Institute for Environment
    and Development, London, England, University of East Anglia,
    Norwich, England, and Stockholm Environment Institute. http://
    www.tiempocyberclimate.org
United Kingdom Climate Impacts Programme. http://www.ukcip.org.uk
United Nations Convention on Biological Diversity. http://www.cbd.int
United Nations Environment Program. http://www.unep.ch
United Nations Framework Convention on Climate Change. http://
    www.unfccc.int
United States Climate Change Science Program. http://www.
    climatescience.gov
Weart, S. 2004. *The Discovery of Global Warming.* http://www.aip.org/
    history/climate/
World Meteorological Organization. http://www.wmo.int
Worldwatch Institute. http://www.worldwatch.org

Abbreviations

ACIA	Arctic Climate Impact Assessment
AGCM	Atmospheric general circulation model
AGGG	Advisory Group on Greenhouse Gases
AIACC	assessments of impacts and adaptations to climate Change in multiple regions and sectors (see Leary et al., 2008a, b)
AIJ	activities implemented jointly (pilot projects established in anticipation of ratification of the Kyoto Protocol and implementation of JI)
ALSIS	a land surface scheme tested in model inter-comparison of evaporation and river flow simulations (see Wood et al. 1998)
AIM	Asia Integrated Model (Kainuma et al. 2003)
AMIP	atmospheric model intercomparison project (see Gates et al. 1999)
AMSD	linkage between climate change adaptation and mitigation, and sustainable development (see Bizikova et al. 2007)
AOGCM	atmosphere-ocean general circulation model
AR4	Fourth Assessment Report of IPCC
ATEAM	Advanced Terrestrial Ecosystem Analysis and Modelling Study (Metzger et al. 2006)
ATP	ability to pay
BASE	a land surface scheme tested in model inter-comparison of evaporation and river flow simulations (see Wood et al. 1998)
BATS	a land surface scheme tested in model inter-comparison of evaporation and river flow simulations (see Wood et al. 1998)

BEST	a land surface scheme tested in model intercomparison of soil moisture simulations (see Henderson-Sellers 1996; Pitman et al. 1999)
BGC	a land surface scheme tested in model intercomparison of soil moisture simulations (see Henderson-Sellers 1996; Pitman et al. 1999)
BIOME2	a land surface scheme tested in model intercomparison of soil moisture simulations (see Henderson-Sellers 1996; Pitman et al. 1999)
BMRC	Bureau of Meteorology Research Centre, Melbourne Australia (see Gates et al. 1999)
BUCK	a land surface scheme tested in model inter-comparison of evaporation and river flow simulations (see Wood et al. 1998)
BUCKET	a land surface scheme tested in model intercomparison of soil moisture simulations (see Henderson-Sellers 1996; Pitman et al. 1999)
C3	plants, including many trees and some important agricultural crops (such as rice, wheat, and soybeans) that produce a three-carbon compound during photosynthesis
C4	plants, mainly of tropical origins (such as sugar cane, maize, and grasses) that produce a four-carbon compound during photosynthesis
CAM	crassulacean acid metabolism plants, primarily desert plants, that incorporate both C3 and C4 carbon cycling pathways
CAPS	a land surface scheme tested in model inter-comparison of evaporation and river flow simulations (see Wood et al. 1998)
CBA	cost-benefit analysis
CBD	Convention on Biological Diversity
CDM	clean development mechanism
CENTURY	a land surface scheme tested in model intercomparison of soil moisture simulations (see Henderson-Sellers 1996; Pitman et al. 1999)
CER	Certified Emission Reduction credits
CFC	chlorofluorocarbons
CGCM	Canadian general circulation model
CH_4	methane
CLASS	a land surface scheme tested in model intercomparison of soil moisture, evaporation, and river flow simulations (see

	Henderson-Sellers 1996; Wood et al. 1998; Pitman et al. 1999)
CMIP	Coupled Model Intercomparison Program (see Covey et al. 2004)
CNRM	Centre National de Recherches Météorologiques, Toulouse, France (see Gates et al. 1999)
CO$_2$	carbon dioxide
COOL	Climate OptiOns for the Long term (see van de Kerkhof 2004)
COP	Conference of the Parties to the UN Framework Convention on Climate Change
CRCM	Canadian Regional Climate Model
CSIRO9	a land surface scheme tested in model intercomparison of soil moisture simulations (see Henderson-Sellers 1996; Pitman et al. 1999)
DC	developed countries
DERF	dynamic extended range forecasting, GFDL, Princeton, NJ (see Gates et al. 1999)
DNM	Department of Numerical Mathematics, Moscow Russia (see Gates et al. 1999)
EERE	everything else remains equal
EIT	economies in transition (generally refers to countries in Eastern Europe formerly in the Warsaw Pact, and the former Soviet Union)
ENSO	El Niño – Southern Oscillation
ERU	emission reduction unit
ET	emissions trading
EU	European Union
GCM	general circulation model
GDP	gross domestic product
GEF	Global Environmental Facility
GFDL	Geophysical Fluid Dynamics Laboratory, Princeton, NJ
GHG	greenhouse gas (carbon dioxide, methane, nitrous oxide, water vapour)
GISS	Goddard Institute for Space Studies, New York
GPP	gross primary production of carbon through photosynthesis, a process by which plants take carbon dioxide to build carbohydrates, while releasing oxygen back to the atmosphere
GWP	global warming potential

Gt	gigatonnes (10^{15} grams)
HadCM	Hadley Centre climate model
IA	integrated assessment
IAM	integrated assessment model
IAP94	a land surface scheme tested in model inter-comparison of evaporation and river flow simulations (see Wood et al. 1998)
ICAM	Integrated Climate Assessment Model (Morgan and Dowlatabadi 1996)
ICSU	International Council of Scientific Unions
IETA	International Emissions Trading Association
IGY	International Geophysical Year
IMAGE	Integrated Model for Assessing the Greenhouse Effect (Alcamo 1994)
IPCC	Intergovernmental Panel on Climate Change
ISBA	a land surface scheme tested in model inter-comparison of soil moisture, evaporation, and river flow simulations (see Henderson-Sellers 1996; Wood et al. 1998; Pitman et al. 1999)
IS92	greenhouse gas emission scenarios developed by the IPCC in 1992; there are six scenarios, labelled IS92a through IS92f
JI	joint implementation
JUSCANZ	coalition of countries sharing information within the UNFCCC negotiations: Japan, United States, Canada, Australia, and New Zealand
JUSSCANNZ	expanded group of countries following from JUSCANZ: Japan, United States, Switzerland, Canada, Australia, Norway, and New Zealand
LAPS	a land surface scheme tested in model inter-comparison of soil moisture simulations (see Henderson-Sellers 1996; Pitman et al. 1999)
LDC	least developed countries
LINK	program established in the United Kingdom for climate scenario delivery
LMD	Laboratoire de Météorologie Dynamique, Paris (see Gates et al. 1999)
LULUCF	Land Use, Land Use Change, and Forestry (IPCC report)
MBIS	Mackenzie Basin Impact Study (Cohen 1997a)

MDG	Millennium Development Goals
MEA	Millennium Ecosystem Assessment
MOP	Meeting of the Parties of the Kyoto Protocol
MOSAIC	a land surface scheme tested in model inter-comparison of evaporation and river flow simulations (see Wood et al. 1998)
MPI	Max Planck Institute for Meteorology, Hamburg (see Gates et al. 1999)
Mt	megatonnes (10^{12} grams)
NAS	National Academy of Sciences (US)
NCAR	National Center for Atmospheric research, Boulder, CO
NCEP	a land surface scheme tested in model inter-comparison of evaporation and river flow simulations (see Wood et al. 1998)
NIC	newly industrialized countries (from Ott et al. 2004)
NPP	net primary production of carbon, which is the remainder of GPP less the energy lost through respiration
NRL	Naval Research Laboratory, Monterey, CA (see Gates et al. 1999)
NSIDC	National Snow and Ice Data Center, University of Colorado
N_2O	nitrous oxide
OECD	Organization of Economic Cooperation and Development
PAA	partial allocated amount (related to carbon emissions trading)
PAR	participatory action research
PDO	Pacific Decadal Oscillation
PIA	participatory integrated assessment
PILPS	Project for Inter-comparison of Land-surface Parameterisation Schemes (see Henderson-Sellers 1996; Pitman et al. 1999)
PLACE	a land surface scheme tested in model inter-comparison of soil moisture, evaporation, and river flow simulations (see Henderson-Sellers 1996; Wood et al. 1998; Pitman et al. 1999)
ppm	parts per million
PPP	purchasing power parity
QELRC	quantified emission limitation or reduction commitment
QELRO	quantified emission limitation or reduction obligation

RCM	regional climate model
RIDC	rapidly industrializing developing countries (from Ott et al. 2004)
RIVM	National Institute of Public Health and the Environment, The Netherlands
SAR	Second Assessment Report of IPCC
SBSTA	Subsidiary Body for Scientific and Technological Advice (supporting the UNFCCC)
SBI	Subsidiary Body for Implementation (supporting the UNFCCC)
SCBD	Secretariat for the Convention on Biological Diversity
SECHIBA2	a land surface scheme tested in model inter-comparison of soil moisture simulations (see Henderson-Sellers 1996; Pitman et al. 1999)
SEWAB	a land surface scheme tested in model inter-comparison of evaporation and river flow simulations (see Wood et al. 1998)
SMIC	Study of Man's Impact on Climate (1971)
SPM	Summary for Policymakers for various documents published by IPCC
SPONSOR	a land surface scheme tested in model inter-comparison of evaporation and river flow simulations (see Wood et al. 1998)
SRES	Special Report on Emission Scenarios (IPCC); scenario families are labeled A1 – global convergence with rapid economic growth (including three A1 groups: A1B (balance of energy sources), A1T (non-fossil energy sources), A1FI (fossil-intensive), A2 (heterogeneous world), B1 (global convergence with emphasis on sustainability), and B2 (local solutions to sustainability)
SSIB	a land surface scheme tested in model inter-comparison of soil moisture, evaporation, and river flow simulations (see Henderson-Sellers 1996; Wood et al. 1998; Pitman et al. 1999)
SUNGEN	model produced by University of Albany, State University of New York–Albany, and NCAR, Boulder CO (see Gates et al. 1999)
SWAP	a land surface scheme tested in model inter-comparison of evaporation and river flow simulations (see Wood et al. 1998)

TAR	Third Assessment Report of IPCC
TARGETS	Tool to Assess Regional and Global Environmental and Health Targets for Sustainability (Rotmans and de Vries 1997)
TIAS	The Integrated Assessment Society
TPES	total primary energy supply
UBC	University of British Columbia
UKCIP	United Kingdom Climate Impacts Program
UNFCCC	United Nations Framework Convention on Climate Change
UNEP	United Nations Environment Programme
UNCED	United Nations Conference on Environment and Development, which took place in Rio de Janeiro in 1992, also known as the Earth Summit
USD	US dollars
VIC	a land surface scheme tested in model inter-comparison of soil moisture simulations (see Henderson-Sellers 1996; Wood et al. 1998; Pitman et al. 1999)
VOSL	value of a statistical life
W	watts (unit of power, or energy per second, expressed as kilograms meter^2 second^{-3})
WaterGAP	integrated global water model (Lehner et al. 2006)
WMO	World Meteorological Organization
WRE	emissions scenarios developed by Wigley, Richels, and Edmonds (1996)
WTP	willingness to pay
WTA	willingness to accept
YONU	Yonsei University, Seoul, South Korea (see Gates et al. 1999)
2xCO$_2$	a climate scenario that assumes a doubling of average carbon dioxide concentrations compared with conditions before the onset of the Industrial Revolution

CLIMATE CHANGE IN THE 21ST CENTURY

1

The Many Dimensions of Climate Change in the Twenty-first Century

Is the world getting warmer? Is this warming a result of human activities? Could this human-induced global warming lead to dangerous interference with the atmosphere? If the answer to these questions is yes, then what is the best way to respond? These questions are complex. Indeed, there are many related questions that confound us and attract our attention to the inadvertent effects of human activity on the world's climate. What forces are driving human development to affect the atmosphere in this way? How will these developments evolve in the coming decades? Is there a single dangerous level of warming for the earth? If not, what are the various dangerous warming levels for different regions, ecosystems, and peoples, and why are they different? What is the best way to reduce inadvertent human interference with the atmosphere so that this interference does not become dangerous? And if reduction of human interference is not enough on its own, what is the best way to reduce vulnerability or exposure? Or alternatively, what is the best way to increase regional and national capabilities to adapt to potentially damaging effects of warming?

Simple answers have been, and continue to be, elusive. There is a profound recognition of the enormous magnitude of this challenge and that it is of a global scale requiring a major international effort. This challenge is confounded by the uncertainties inherent in our collective knowledge of global warming. However, the fact that questions about climate change are being asked by scientists and concerned citizens around the world indicates the seriousness of the world-wide interest in global warming. This is true regardless of whether there is unanimous agreement that humans are warming the climate and whether this issue is just as important as, or more important than, solving other global challenges, such as poverty and conflict.

Furthermore these problems that exist on a global scale may interact. Climate change, for example, could exacerbate existing and emerging stresses on world food production and water supplies and threaten species and ecosystems that are already endangered. But opportunities could also emerge from the two-way interaction between sustainable development policy and climate policy (Swart, Robinson, and Cohen 2003). Rather than expecting policy from one discourse to independently solve such global problems, perhaps we should recognize that there are several arenas of research and debate that could bring us closer to reducing these various risks.

Many books, research papers, technical reports, and editorials have been written about global warming or human-induced (anthropogenic) climate change. They include major international assessments provided by the Intergovernmental Panel on Climate Change (IPCC), which are broad reviews of the research literature on climate science, impacts and adaptation, and the mitigation of greenhouse gas (GHG) emissions. Other publications offer perspectives on key aspects of global warming, such as the discovery of human-induced warming by climate science (e.g., Weart 2004), potential future impacts on food production (e.g., Rosenzweig and Hillel 1998), and analyses of the international policy response embodied in the United Nations Framework Convention on Climate Change (UNFCCC) and the associated Kyoto Protocol (e.g., Oberthür and Ott 1999; Victor 2001).

This growing body of literature offers specialized discourse on a wide range of topics from climate modelling to carbon cycle research, impacts assessment, emission reduction technologies, and climate policy. The IPCC has recognized the need for the integration and synthesis of this literature in order to address the many cross-cutting aspects of climate change (e.g., IPCC 2001a, 2007e). There have also been introductory texts, or primers, on climate change (e.g., Houghton 2004) and multi-authored volumes that seek to describe connections between the various aspects of climate change (e.g., Griffin 2003; Coward and Weaver 2004).

The objectives of this book are to explore various aspects of the climate change issue by illustrating some of the fundamental ideas and research approaches that underlie the thinking of climate scientists, impacts researchers, and policy analysts, and to do this from a generalist's perspective. The idea is to broadly cover many topics in order to sketch some of the cross-linkages between the physical, biological, and social aspects of climate change. This is an attempt to provide a resource for teaching about the many dimensions of climate change, a "Global Warming 101" whose purpose is to fill an empty niche in the climate change literature. Drawing on the idea of "climate affairs," an approach to looking at climate issues through its human context, an approach that incorporates many lenses, including climate science, impacts, politics, policy, law, economics, and ethics (Glantz 2003), this book seeks to discuss the specific case of anthropogenic (or human-induced) climate change (global warming) by exploring its many physical and human dimensions and linkages with global development challenges. While development may be causing the problem in the first place, it may also provide direction towards a sustainable solution.

A primer or teaching resource should include definitions of terms, descriptions of concepts, and examples. Doing so requires a series of discussions that focus on the fundamental ideas offered from these various components, rather than an inventory of research results. Other sources, particularly the assessments of the IPCC, are available to provide and continuously update these inventories. This book focuses on how these various concepts contribute to the global warming narrative as it continues to evolve.

The terms "global warming," "climate change," and "human-induced, or anthropogenic, climate change" have been used interchangeably in the literature. Climate change is traditionally defined as "a significant change in the climatic state … in the course of a certain time interval, where the means are taken over a period of a decade or longer" (Geer 1996, 42). This definition does not distinguish between natural and anthropogenic climate change. The IPCC uses the term "climate change" to refer to a change that can result from both natural and anthropogenic causes (IPCC 2001a), but it also notes that the UNFCCC uses this term to define human-induced change. Houghton (2004) refers to global warming as the result of increased concentrations of greenhouse gases but also uses the term "climate change" in a similar manner. In the chapters to follow, we will generally use that term as the UNFCCC has done, but supplemented by other descriptors, depending on the subject being discussed.

Our review of climate change starts with an overview of the history of anthropogenic climate change research. The pioneering studies of nineteenth- and early-twentieth-century scientists identified how gaseous emissions from human activities could lead to a change in global temperature. First, it was observed that carbon dioxide (CO_2) was increasing in the atmosphere as a result of human activity, including fossil

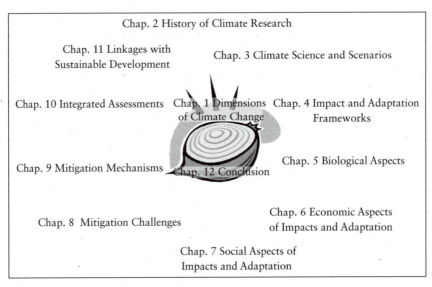

Figure 1.1   The many dimensions of climate change

fuel consumption and deforestation. Scientists measured changes in the chemistry of the atmosphere, and a few individuals within the atmospheric-science community postulated that human activity might change the CO_2 balance of the planet. They decided that they needed to calculate or model how these kinds of changes might affect the atmosphere and the global climate.

By working through this relationship between changes in atmospheric chemistry and the atmosphere itself, these investigators produced a number of scenarios of changes in climate and changes in ocean levels, leading other scientists to describe potential impacts of these changes. Those scientists suggested that the impacts could be fairly serious, which, in turn, later prompted others to think about different kinds of responses, ranging from adaptation to the reduction of GHG emissions. Some of these responses were based on new or emerging technologies, while others depended more on changes in governance, attitudes about quality of life, or alternative paths of development. Our vision of this chain of research as layers of a metaphorical onion is reflected in the structure of this book and sketched in figure 1.1.

We begin with an overview of early scientific research on GHG emissions and subsequent changes in atmospheric concentrations of these gases. In chapters 2 and 3, GHG emissions are described in terms of net emissions of carbon: "net" emissions because while carbon is getting into the atmosphere as a result of the burning of oil, gas, and coal, as well as deforestation and other human activities, not all of it is staying there. Some of it is leaving as it gets absorbed by the ocean and landscape systems in what have become known as carbon sinks. Although there is still a lot of uncertainty about the strength of these sinks (which include forest sinks, soil sinks, and ocean sinks), it is nevertheless acknowledged that they do exist and that they are reducing the cumulative uptake of carbon emissions by the atmosphere. In chapters 3, 8, and 9 we will see, therefore, that it is not a simple linear step from observations of human burning of fossil fuels to calculations of present and future GHG concentrations. One cannot make those calculations without accounting for the fact that the natural sinks may be changing over time and, in particular, that they may change in the future either because of climatic and ecological changes or because of deliberate human actions influenced by climate policy.

Determining GHG concentrations allows atmospheric scientists to model the specific effects on the earth's radiation budget and therefore on its climate. The models of the climate can be used to see what happens to a number of different atmospheric constituents, including temperature, precipitation, and so on (chapter 3). These scenarios then become input into a range of other kinds of tools, for example, tools that simulate stream flow (hydrological models), food production (crop yield models for specific crops like wheat or corn or grass), forest growth, or changes in human health (the spread of malaria, say). But here, too, it's not a simple question of what the impacts model tells us. We might be able to determine something about ecological effects, but what happens to communities or economies? We need another range of tools to assess the various human dimensions of climate change, and chapter 4 introduces the broad challenges of undertaking impacts research, including scenario-based approaches, which differ from traditional studies of impacts of observed climatic events. Chapters 5 and 6 provide an overview of some of the approaches used in determining biological and economic impacts.

There is a lot of criticism of the climate science part of the chain, but there is also a huge amount of uncertainty associated with determining the effects on the social side, such as the costs of impacts and the costs (and possible benefits) of a response. It could be argued that the uncertainties regarding the ecological and economic impacts are even more serious than the uncertainties in climate science. But even if we were to get to a consensus on what the damages would be and what the values of various interested parties (governments, indigenous peoples, businesses, non-government advocates, and others) would be, we would still be faced with a question about what constitutes an appropriate response to the damages. Chapter 7 provides an outline of the social aspects of climate change impacts and the emerging discourse on adaptation.

Chapters 8 and 9 review the various emission reduction measures that have been launched by the Kyoto process. There are debates now about whether responses to climate change should be done in a top-down manner, say from national governments, or through a multilateral consensus-based policy instrument, like the Kyoto Protocol, or whether various public sector, private sector, or individual entities ought to be free to choose their own response measures. In other words, proponents of individual actions might suggest that if individual companies or countries are encouraged to respond in their own way through market forces or other non-regulatory, voluntary measures, they will become efficient in their own way. Some constituencies would prefer to avoid being involved in a multilateral process like Kyoto; they would argue that individual, economically driven measures will encourage innovative approaches to creating efficiencies in energy consumption and production. Again, one can argue about the politics of that position, but in the current debate on climate policy, while some constituencies advocate individual action, others continue to support the global, multilateral Kyoto Protocol and anticipated post-Kyoto dialogue and activities.

The complexity of the climate change challenge, with its linkages from science to governance, has led a number of investigators to try novel interdisciplinary approaches to studying the implications of climate change and of climate change policy alternatives. Some of these approaches have attempted to be integrative, as they seek to capture some of the synergies between causal elements. Chapter 10 outlines some integrated assessment models, as well as some participatory versions of integrated assessments.

As we move towards the critical question of climate policy, as part of the larger question of alternatives for the development of global resources, we then encounter questions about responsibilities and equity. Chapter 11 focuses on bringing the climate change question into this context. We consider equity to include both the rights between the current generation and future generations (intergenerational equity) and the rights between the lesser developed "south" and the more developed "north" (international equity). One can imagine that a global dialogue on equity would involve a huge array of people, cultures, disciplinary backgrounds, incomes, histories, and so on, and, indeed, such a dialogue has emerged from concerns about climate change. How did this happen? There are other global concerns, such as concerns about desertification, biodiversity, and species extinction, not to mention trade or global security. Yet climate change has attracted wide attention and visibility, either in its own right, or because of its implications for these other issues.

Two other chapters complement the chapters described above. Chapter 2 provides a brief review of the historical development of the idea of human-induced climate change and of how this idea evolved from scientific discourse into a broader policy context. Chapter 12 completes the chain by reviewing the linkages between the various components and by looking ahead to what may become a new level of activity on climate change.

In recent years, there has been a significant increase in the public visibility of the global-warming issue. If the 2007 "Live Earth" event, organized by Al Gore, is any indication, human-induced climate change has struck a chord among people throughout the world. What we have now is a phenomenon that has taken off way beyond what the initial messengers from the atmospheric sciences could ever have dreamed was possible. At different times during the last century, Aarhenius (1896), Callendar (1938, cited in Weart 2004), Keeling (1960, cited in Weart 2004), the *Report of the Study of Man's Impact on Climate* (SMIC 1971), and others, raised the global warming alarm, because they concluded that the global mean temperature was going to increase as a result of increasing emissions of CO_2. Now, at the beginning of the twenty-first century, global warming is beginning to merge with other concerns, leading into a global debate on environment, development, and international equity. With the awarding of the 2007 Nobel Peace Prize to the IPCC and Al Gore, global warming has now been recognized as a global security concern as well.

2

The History of Climate Change Research from the 1820s

INTRODUCTION

It is common knowledge today that the composition of the atmosphere is changing. Concentrations of carbon dioxide (CO_2), methane (CH_4), nitrous oxide (N_2O), and other greenhouse gases (GHGs) have increased as a result of human activities such as the combustion of fossil fuels for industry, transportation, and basic energy needs and the alteration of landscapes for food and timber production or mining. The discovery of the increasing trend in GHG concentrations was a relatively recent event, having been initially documented in 1960 by Charles Keeling at his observatory in Mauna Loa, in Hawaii (Keeling 1960, cited in Weart 2004). However, Keeling was not the first to notice such a trend. Others had suggested years earlier that increasing human activity was gradually changing the atmosphere, and potentially the earth's temperature. Though this research effort was small at first, it has become a well-organized international endeavour, supported both by national governments and by agencies of the United Nations.

How did this begin? What prompted a few individuals during the late nineteenth and early twentieth centuries to suggest the connection between human activity and climate change? Once there was widespread awareness of this connection, how did the idea of human-induced climate change emerge from the scientific community and enter into the international policy realm? And what role has the media played in influencing the public perception of the uncertainty of climate change?

PIONEER STUDIES OF ANTHROPOGENIC CLIMATE CHANGE, FROM THE 1820S TO THE 1930S

The modern climate change debate can be traced back almost two hundred years to the beginnings of the Industrial Revolution. In the 1820s,

Jean-Baptiste Fourier began discussing the interaction between radiation from the sun and atmospheric gases, followed a few decades later by John Tyndall's studies of the absorption of infrared radiation by water vapour and CO_2 (Budyko 1982; Houghton 2004; Weart 2004). By the end of the nineteenth century, more scientists had become interested in atmospheric processes and long-term fluctuations in climate. One such scientist was Svante Aarhenius, a Swedish physicist, who wrote a paper in 1896 titled *On the Influence of Carbonic Acid*. At that time, CO_2 was referred to as carbonic acid, and it was recognized that if it was emitted into the atmosphere in large amounts, it could change the absorption of terrestrial long-wave energy by the atmosphere. This energy would then be re-transmitted to the earth's surface. Without the aid of computers or calculators, Aarhenius determined a potential warming rate that is only slightly higher than estimates from recent model-based simulations. He calculated that a doubling of the atmospheric concentration of CO_2 would increase the global average temperature by 5°C to 6°C (Aarhenius 1896), while current estimates range from an increase of 1.5°C to 4.5°C (Cubasch and Meehl 2001).

Aarhenius wasn't the only one interested in this issue. In the years following his 1896 publication, the issue of increasing atmospheric CO_2 was discussed more frequently within the atmospheric science and physics communities. Weart (2004) details the early studies of climate variability, climate change, and the interplay of natural forces and human forcing resulting from increasing CO_2 and deforestation. Weart's bibliography for the 1890s to 1930s includes the works of Thomas Chamberlin, Edward Brückner, and Guy Stewart Callendar. Chamberlin (1897, cited in Weart 2004) suggested that CO_2 could fluctuate over geological time scales. Brückner (1915, cited in Weart 2004) was interested in short-term climate variability and its implications for society. He paid considerable attention to the possible impact of deforestation on climate (Stehr, von Storch, and Flügel 1995). Callendar returned to Aarhenius' thesis of future warming from modern increases in CO_2 and suggested a warming of 2°C from a doubling of CO_2 (Callendar 1938, cited in Weart 2004). Budyko (1982) also devoted considerable attention to Callendar's work, suggesting that he was the first to clearly articulate the global-warming theory.

Although Brückner felt that it was important to communicate his concerns to the public (Stehr, von Storch, and Flügel 1995), much of this early dialogue remained within the confines of the atmospheric-science research community. For other researchers and interested lay-persons, there were still many uncertainties associated with long-term climate change, as well as with potential short-term changes in CO_2 concentrations and with the role of oceans and forests as carbon sinks. Weart (2004) points out that although global average temperature was rising during this time, researchers in the atmospheric sciences were not connecting this increase to CO_2 emissions. The prevailing view was that water vapour would absorb the same long-wave radiation as CO_2 and that the ocean would absorb most of the CO_2 from fossil fuel emissions, thereby preventing a rapid build-up of CO_2 in the atmosphere.

THE BROADENING OF THE CLIMATE CHANGE RESEARCH EFFORT, FROM THE 1950S TO THE 1970S

Global temperature increases that were observed through the 1940s gave way to a slight cooling trend during the 1960s and 1970s, even though CO_2 concentrations continued to increase. At that time a few people (e.g., Ponte 1976, cited in Weart 2004) even talked about ice-age scenarios! Skeptics pointed to this cooling trend and questioned why Earth wasn't warming up in the late 1960s. They also questioned whether there really was a direct relationship between GHG concentrations and climate change. It was often asked how natural and anthropogenic forces were interacting to influence climate change, a point that will be discussed further in chapter 3.

The emergence of a clear trend in increasing atmospheric CO_2 concentrations from Keeling's observations at Mauna Loa (Keeling 1960, cited in Weart 2004) brought visibility and attention back to Callendar's concerns that the oceans would not absorb the additional CO_2 from fossil fuel emissions (Weart 2004). As well, Revelle and Suess (1957, cited in Weart 2004) had been discussing both the possibility of human activities altering the chemical composition of the atmosphere and the relative strengths of various sinks for CO_2 (particularly the oceans), which would affect the rate of increase of atmospheric CO_2.

Keeling's work was part of a larger global effort known as the International Geophysical Year (IGY), which Jäger and O'Riordan (1996) identify as the beginning of the expanded global discourse on human-induced climate change (figure 2.1). IGY and post-IGY efforts during the 1950s and 1960s led to a major review of the implications of human activities for the global climate, a review organized as the Study of Man's Impact on Climate (SMIC 1971). Although it was not focused exclusively on the idea that increased CO_2 could lead to a warmer climate, that idea did feature prominently in it. Among the sources cited in the review was Machta

International Geophysical Year
1957–58
Early general circulation models
1960–65
UN Conference on the Human Environment (Stockholm)
1972
First World Climate Conference
1979
Villach Conferences (WMO, UNEP, ICSU)
1980–85
Advisory Group on Greenhouse Gases
1987–88
World Conference on Changing Atmosphere (Toronto)
1988
Intergovernmental Panel on Climate Change (IPCC)
First Assessment Report,
1990
UN Framework Convention on Climate Change (UNFCCC)
1992
First Conference of the Parties (COP-1)
1995
COP-3: Kyoto Protocol
1997
Kyoto Protocol Ratified
2005
Stern Review, IPCC Fourth Assessment Report
2007

Figure 2.1   The history of climate change science and politics.
Source: Adapted and updated from Jäger and O'Riordan (1996)

(1971, cited in SMIC 1971), who predicted that CO_2 concentrations would increase from 320 ppm to 365–385 ppm by 2000.

The SMIC also looked at tropospheric ozone, stratospheric ozone, and deliberate attempts at weather modification from cloud seeding. Acid rain, which was to become a major environmental concern in the 1970s and 1980s, was not directly identified within this study. However, sulphur dioxide was recognized as a principal air pollutant that could be transformed into sulphuric acid in the atmosphere. Eventually, policy regulations aimed at aerosol emission reduction would provide a template for future climate change policy initiatives.

In 1975, global CO_2 emissions were estimated to be around 4.5 giga-tonnes (Gt) per year, representing a doubling of annual emission rates since 1957, the year Keeling established his monitoring site at Mauna Loa. Following the 1975 estimate, a number of investigators offered predictions of annual emissions to 2100, assuming different rates of growth of energy consumption. These predictions varied considerably, but in general, CO_2 emissions were expected to increase to around 40 Gt by 2050, declining to 20 Gt by 2100 as a result of an expected depletion of fossil fuel reserves (Kellogg and Schware 1981).

While energy studies and projections of CO_2 were attracting much attention during this period, atmospheric scientists began to take advantage of advances in computer capabilities. The first experiments with computer-based simulations of global climate were performed, including an early attempt to create a coupled atmosphere-ocean model (Manabe and Bryan 1969, cited in Weart 2004). These early versions of atmospheric circulation models, later known as general circulation models (GCMs), did not include ocean heat transport or moving sea ice, nor did they represent terrestrial vegetation or clouds in a sophisticated way. There were also limitations resulting from the lack of high-speed computing capabilities. At the time, it was noted that a climate model grid size of 250 x 250 km would require 960 hours of machine time for a 1–year integration of the atmosphere and ocean models (SMIC 1971). For a grid size of 500 x 500 km, the processing time could be reduced to 120 hours. Consequently modellers were forced to represent the earth's landscapes with very large grid sizes, resulting in a very coarse resolution of the world map.

The results of these experiments suggested that increasing CO_2 concentrations in the atmosphere would lead to global warming but that these modelling limitations represented a significant barrier to accurate predictions of climate change. Much of this scientific discourse did not yet attract much attention outside the scientific community. SMIC (1971) did see the potential climate changes resulting from atmospheric CO_2 increases as an important research challenge that required urgent study and offered a number of specific recommendations for model improvement. Indeed, SMIC (1971) foresaw the day when such models would be used for climate change studies: "When a realistic model of the joint ocean-atmosphere system is completely formulated, one can then test the possibility of climatic change due to human activity. For example, one can evaluate the climatic change resulting from a change in CO_2 content in the atmosphere by comparing the climates of two models with different CO_2 contents" (145).

Just as model predictions were becoming important during the 1970s, so too was the need for more climate impacts literature. The desertification in the Sahel region of Africa during the 1968–73 drought raised concerns about changing climate patterns and their potential effect on food supplies. Before the formation of the IPCC in 1988, there was no regular mechanism for assessing climate-related literature. However, during the 1960s and 1970s, individual authors did begin to write on climate issues, addressing the growing questions about climate variability, climate change, and linkages with human activity.

Schneider and Mesirow's (1976) review, *The Genesis Strategy*, focused on the need to reduce vulnerability to climatic extremes, but they avoided making any strong statements about the direction of future climate change. At this time, in addition to the publications supporting the idea of global warming, some publications, such as Ponte's *The Cooling* (1976), were specifically promoting the idea of an oncoming Ice Age. However, the atmospheric research community failed to reach a consensus about a particular direction of temperature and climate change. Indeed, there was no evidence of any real consensus during the early to mid-1970s regarding future changes in climate (Kellogg 1987; Peterson et al. 2008). A survey of temperature trends to 2000 conducted by US-based researchers in 1975 (National Defense University 1978) concluded that opinion was equally divided between modest warming and modest cooling, within 0.5°C of prevailing averages, with a majority favouring little or no change (±0.2°C). However, there were signs that scientists in several countries (Australia, Canada, and the United States) were seriously considering the potential for warming. From 1975 to 1977 national science bodies in those countries published reports that outlined their concerns (Hecht and Tirpak 1995). At the same time, after years of effort, Manabe and colleagues published their GCM simulation results, the first climate change scenario based on a doubling of CO_2 concentrations, referred to as $2xCO_2$ (in particular, Manabe and Wetherald 1975, cited in Budyko 1982). Over the next decade, various modelling groups produced a number of these $2xCO_2$ scenarios.

Returning to the case of the Sahel drought and its ensuing impacts, a number of investigators were suggesting that desertification and the associated food supply shortages were more likely the result of bad land management than of climatic variability (Slater and Levin 1981). Because of the seasonal rainfall patterns in the region, nomadic herders had developed permanent communities following the introduction of deep-tube well technology. Herders kept their livestock near these wells, which eventually led to overgrazing, reduced vegetation cover, and ultimately a widespread loss of livestock. Investigators argued that human activity on the ground, rather than any shift in climate, had created the desertification problem (Glantz 1976; Garcia 1981), which became a standard example of how a new technology that initially offered to improve conditions for livestock herders eventually developed into a liability instead.

The Sahel case represented an early attempt at climate impact assessment. Such a study generally focused on extreme events (such as droughts) as triggers for a climate-related disaster. The assessment's purpose was to sort out the causal mechanisms of the disaster, to determine the roles of human decision making and of natural factors, and to see whether the two elements worked in tandem to create the problem or whether human decisions actually created new vulnerabilities to climatic events.

Did this then mean that the prevailing view of climate impacts researchers was that the root cause of damage and disaster was bad management decision making, rather than climate change? The decline in rainfall in the Sahel was quite dramatic during the 1970s (see Lamb 1982), and perhaps under conditions that had prevailed during the previous several decades, local ecosystems could have absorbed the effects of changing patterns of livestock management and governance. At this time, however, a threshold was crossed because of the simultaneous effects of humans and the shifting Sahelian climate. Aside from the implications for Sahel countries directly, this case also raised awareness of the need for an increased effort at climate impact assessment, an effort that would expand during the 1980s to incorporate both the lessons learned from historic events, such as cases from the natural-hazards literature (for example Burton, Kates, and White 1978), and also from the potential implications of scenarios of future climate changes.

Climate change modelling efforts were also about to expand. Following Manabe's lead, by 1980 the Goddard Institute for Space Studies and Oregon State University were almost ready to produce their own simulations of future climate change. At this time, the US National Academy of Sciences convened a research board to assess climate change resulting from increasing CO_2 concentrations in the atmosphere. It concluded that a doubling would lead to a warming of 1.5°C–4.5°C (NAS 1979).

This convergence of awareness of the importance of climate to the world's ecosystems and peoples and the looming challenge of increasing CO_2 concentrations in the atmosphere led the World Meteorological Organization (WMO) to organize the World Climate Conference in 1979.

Participants expressed strong concerns about the potential implications of increasing CO_2. One result was the creation of the WMO's World Climate Program, which, in collaboration with the United Nations Environment Program (UNEP), was to assess the social and economic impacts of climatic variability and change. As a sign of things to come, the subsequent report (Kellogg and Schware 1981) outlined the dilemma of climatologists being unable to make predictions about future climate change, thereby hampering other studies that could have focused on societal responses. Their proposed solution was to create sets of climate scenarios from GCM simulations or reconstructions of past warm climates.

THE GROWTH OF SCENARIO-BASED RESEARCH IN THE 1980s

Clearly, the research efforts during the 1960s and 1970s established the foundation for several distinct research efforts related to human-induced climate change, including

1 scenarios of energy futures and associated CO_2 emissions,
2 simulations of global climate patterns with GCMs,
3 studies of impacts of recent and historic climatic events, and
4 assessments of adaptation experiences.

The early 1970s had witnessed the Sahel drought, as we have seen, as well as a drought-induced crop failure in the Soviet Union, and the collapse of the Peruvian anchovy fishery caused by El Niño. At the beginning of the 1980s, additional assessments of observed climate events were being published (e.g., an assessment of the 1982–83 El Niño by Glantz, Katz, and Krenz 1987; Glantz 1996) but there was little previous experience with studies of impacts of future scenarios of climate change, since climate-modelling groups had not yet considered the data needs of impacts researchers. However, there was still a growing sense of urgency about climate-related failures in food production, which would ultimately pave the way for scenario-based impacts studies. Global food production was perceived as vulnerable to climate variability, even though knowledge of climate and food interactions was seen as "very incomplete" because it was not possible, according to Hare (1981, 11), "to specify the impact of climate on the largest economic scales – those of international trade, of the commodity markets, and of national economic policies."

Hare went on to raise concerns about widespread indifference among economists and policy-makers, despite the best efforts of natural scientists: "We [natural scientists] desire to export our convictions, but the buyers are reluctant" (14). He suggested two possible reasons for this indifference: (1) because climate impacts are often buffered by trade and relief efforts, identifying the role of climate in the food system is hindered by non-linearities and time lags in response; and (2) in developing countries, technological, social, and political changes have fundamentally altered climate-society relationships and perceptions of risk.

During the early 1980s, the challenge for impacts researchers was to distinguish natural environmental influences from the social ones. Increased interest in the role of climate in historical events (e.g., Smith and Parry 1981; Wigley, Ingram, and Farmer 1981) led to a re-examination of its potential role in current affairs, particularly regarding food production (e.g., Slater and Levin 1981; Lamb 1982). But the impacts research community was beginning to look beyond applications only to historical events. They needed to inventory the range of assessment methods and to establish climate impact assessments as a multi-disciplinary research endeavour with a potential for long-term methodological development, similar to what was happening with climate models. Examples of applications of various analytic tools from different fields, such as agriculture, fisheries, and hydrology, were being documented as part of a growing effort to establish a discourse on the practice of climate impact assessment. A major review of interdisciplinary approaches and integrated assessment models led to the publication of a multi-authored volume on impacts methodology (Kates, Ausubel, and Berberian 1985). The review included two examples of socio-economic assessments of future climate change: a 1975 study of global cooling and a 1983 report on global warming (see Farhar-Pilgrim 1985).

Meanwhile, climate scientists were accelerating their efforts in climate modelling and applying such models to the CO_2 question. A follow-up assessment by the US National Academy of Sciences (NAS 1982) concluded that there was no reason to alter the main conclusions of the 1979 report (NAS 1979) regarding the amount of warming that would result from a doubling of CO_2 concentrations. The conclusions were based on new simulations produced by three climate-modelling groups in the United States: the Geophysical Fluid Dynamics Lab (led by Manabe), the Goddard Institute for Space Studies (led by Hansen), and Oregon State University (led by Gates and Schlesinger). Their simulations also showed increases in global precipitation.

The 1979 report also documented the possible role of aerosols and the relative warming potentials of various trace gases. For example, a doubling of CH_4 and N_2O would result in an increase of 0.3°C and 0.6°C respectively, while CO_2 doubling alone would account for an increase of 2.9°C (Lacis et al. 1981).

Modelling uncertainties were described in considerable detail, particularly for clouds (e.g., uncertainties concerning cloud optical properties), sea ice, and the role of the oceans. In addition, NAS (1982, 18–24) reviewed "dissenting inferences" (forerunners of the climate change skeptics), including inferences by Newell and Dopplick (1979, 1981), Idso (1980, 1981), and Lindzen, Hou, and Farrell (1982), who all suggested a relatively small sensitivity of climate to changes in CO_2. NAS (1982) concluded that these suggestions were based on incomplete methods or observations. This scientific debate continued throughout the 1980s and worked its way into the political debates associated with the UN climate change initiatives of the 1990s.

The NAS reports and other publications led to efforts to communicate scientific concerns to policy-makers: a number of publications emerged from Europe and North America in the early 1980s as part of these efforts. They were tapping into an emerging interest in interactions between climate and energy production and consumption (e.g., Bach, Pankrath, and Williams 1980; Clark 1982). However, the publication of *Can We Delay a Greenhouse Warming* by the US Environmental Protection Agency (Seidel and Keyes 1983) drew a direct connection between climate and energy policy and expressed the effects of energy policy alternatives in terms of the date that the world would warm by 2°C. This report assumed that this warming would occur by 2045 in the absence of a policy response. It concluded that a ban on coal and shale oil could delay this warming until 2065, while fossil fuel taxes would have little effect.

This entry of climate change into mainstream politics led to a series of international conferences organized by the United Nations. A conference in Villach, Austria, in 1985 produced a report that declared a consensus on the main scientific aspects of human-induced climate change, including the role of CH_4 and other trace gases, and that also requested an international policy response (WMO 1986). The initial response was a request by the UNEP to the United States asking for technical, political, and financial support (Hecht and Tirpak 1995). What emerged was a proposal for an intergovernmental mechanism to conduct a government-led scientific assessment of all aspects of climate change. The WMO and the UNEP would later establish the Intergovernmental Panel on Climate Change (IPCC).

While this discussion was under way, Canada organized the 1988 Toronto Conference (WMO 1989), the first major international gathering of researchers, policy-makers, and non-governmental organizations to make global warming its principal focus. The conference statement included a call for a 20 percent reduction in GHG emissions from 1988 levels by 2005 (WMO 1989, 296–7), a goal that was later to be known as the Toronto target. It also called for

1 "a comprehensive global convention as a framework for protocols on the protection of the atmosphere" (WMO 1989, 297),
2 the creation of a "World Atmosphere Fund, financed in part by a levy on the fossil fuel consumption of industrialized countries," for the transfer of fuel-efficient technologies (298), and
3 "support for the work of the [IPCC] to conduct continuing assessments of scientific results, and to initiate [intergovernmental] discussion on responses" (298).

INTERGOVERNMENTAL PANEL ON CLIMATE CHANGE (IPCC)

In 1986, the UNEP, the WMO, and the International Council of Scientific Unions (ICSU) set up the Advisory Group on Greenhouse Gases (AGGG). Agrawala (1998a) describes the AGGG as a small panel of international experts who helped to organize some workshops leading up to the Toronto Conference in 1988. At the same time, the UNEP asked the United States (see the preceding section) to communicate with the WMO to coordinate an intergovernmental mechanism with the UNEP. Agrawala (1998a) concludes that the main reason for the growth in support for the IPCC was the leadership of the UNEP director Mustafa Tolba, coupled with the lack of a clear mandate and support for the AGGG, the desire of the United States government to work through an intergovernmental process (for various political reasons), and the recognition that any assessment of climate change had to go far beyond the science of climate change.

At the first IPCC plenary in 1988, delegates agreed to establish three working groups that would operate in parallel to each other. Working Group I was to focus on the science of climate change, and this has continued to be its mandate up to the present time. Working Group II was identified as the impacts and adaptation group, although it also took on the assessment of the technological aspects of mitigation options as part of the IPCC Second Assessment (Watson, Zinyowera, and Moss 1995). For subsequent reports, mitigation became the purview of Working Group III, which had originally started with a focus on response strategies, evolving to a review of the economic and social dimensions of mitigation for the Second Assessment (Bruce, Lee, and Haites 1996), and then to a more complete assessment of mitigation in the Third Assessment (Metz et al. 2001).

The challenge for the IPCC has been to be both scientifically sound and politically acceptable. It achieves the former by attracting leading scientists from many disciplines and backgrounds to participate as authors and reviewers and by establishing an extensive process of peer review by governments and non-governmental researchers and organizations. Agrawala (1998b) describes the history of the establishment of the IPCC process of review and notes how quickly the IPCC achieved international visibility in the media, as well as among governments and non-government interests.

At the time of the 1992 meeting of the United Nations Conference on Environment & Development (UNCED), also known as the Earth Summit, in Rio de Janeiro, the IPCC's first report had to be seen as acceptable by delegates if this work was to aid in deliberations for a possible climate convention. Following the Rio event, stricter procedures were put in place, not only to ensure the integrity of the review process but also to broaden participation in the assessment by developing-country experts.

The UNCED meeting was crucial for the climate change issue. After the 1988 Toronto Conference, negotiators began drafting language for the UN Framework Convention on Climate Change (UNFCCC), which was to be presented for debate at UNCED, along with the Conventions on Desertification and Biodiversity. The ratification of the UNFCCC in 1994 would not have occurred without the learning opportunities provided by the IPCC process (Agrawala 1998b).

Political acceptability required the production of policy-makers' summaries, which would be subject to line-by-line approval at plenary sessions of the relevant IPCC working groups. This political process was designed to achieve global credibility among governments and to prevent the IPCC from earning a reputation for activism (Agrawala 1998b). This does not mean that the IPCC's scientific integrity was or could be undermined by political forces with particular interests (e.g., fossil fuel interests or environmental interests), but even so, the IPCC has clearly influenced the negotiations around climate policy. Its statements about the discernible human influence on the climate, for example, have lent considerable urgency to the negotiations. Its status as a legitimate voice on climate change has been unmatched by any supporting mechanisms for other global-scale issues, such as desertification and biodiversity. In other words, IPCC assessments have provided the impetus for keeping the policy negotiations alive.

As part of its assessment mandate, the IPCC has taken on some complex and controversial questions about climate change. Although they may be initially defined as value-neutral science questions, it turns out that they have important social, economic, and, therefore, political dimensions. Two examples noted by Jäger and O'Riordan (1996) are (1) the global-warming potential (GWP) of various GHGs and (2) the value of social and economic damage arising from climate change impacts.

In one of its initial reports (Houghton, Callander, and Varney 1992), the IPCC produced a table showing the equivalent radiative forcings of each gas (the net change in downward radiation minus upward radiation due to a change in, for example, the concentration of methane) compared with CO_2 and identified their sources. This comparison included point source emissions from burning of fossil fuels, as well as the effects of deforestation, primarily in tropical regions. The GWP is expressed as an index, with CO_2 assigned the value of 1.0 and the values of all other gases scaled relative to CO_2, accounting for both differences in radiative forcing and lifetime in the atmosphere. CH_4, for example, was estimated to have a GWP of 35 for the first twenty years, and 11 over one hundred years, though this value continues to be adjusted with each assessment (see chapter 3). The values for CH_4 mean that the warming effect of CH_4 was 35 times that of CO_2 for the first twenty years after emission, and 11 times that of CO_2 when averaged over one hundred years. Jäger and O'Riordan (1996) point out that the implications of this calculation for developing countries is that it increased the amount of blame attributed to tropical deforestation, which is a major problem that includes illegal logging in countries with weak enforcement of forestry laws (Christy et al. 2007). Reducing emissions would require something different from what would be needed for developed-country industrial sources. This problem is discussed further in chapters 7, 8, 9, and 11.

The choice of method for quantification of economic damages, already a challenge for economists, was a controversial one for the IPCC Second Assessment (Bruce, Lee, and Haites 1996). Potential mortality effects were converted to monetary figures by estimating the value of a statistical life (VOSL) on the basis of the incomes of various countries and the theoretical willingness to pay for a reduction of climate-related risks. Jäger and O'Riordan (1996) note that this method led to complaints from developing countries that damages to their peoples were being undervalued (see chapter 6).

The IPCC's role as the great filter of all climate change information has been challenged by a group of scientists and political interests who have been labelled as "climate skeptics." Their science-related complaints focus on IPCC statements about climate science and related data and methods. However, Oberthür and Ott (1999) note that since the IPCC's role is to assess peer-reviewed work, it can arrive at consensual statements on matters of science while still taking into account any peer-reviewed work published by dissenters.

All IPCC publications (on science, impacts, response, technical matters, and so on) are subjected to several rounds of peer review. The IPCC manages this process, but the reviewers are generally not members of author teams and are external to the IPCC. In addition, the quality of IPCC assessments of climate science has been tested through reviews undertaken by other scientific bodies, such as the US National Academy of Sciences (NAS 2001). These reviews have agreed with IPCC conclusions about the evidence for human modification of the climate (Oreskes 2004). On matters other than climate science (e.g., impacts and adaptation), the IPCC is dealing with even greater complexity because of the interdisciplinary nature of climate-ecosystem and climate-society linkages, as well as the difficulties in projecting the effectiveness of climate-policy responses. Although these aspects of the assessments have been reviewed by the IPCC through similar processes, they have not been subjected to sweeping reviews by external bodies.

The initial visibility of the IPCC climate science assessments (Working Group I) may have resulted from its more persuasive arguments about the state of the climate itself. Working Group I authors did not have to address matters of human behaviour and so had a clearer foundation for assigning high or low levels of confidence to their conclusions about temperature trends, precipitation scenarios, and the influence of GHG emissions on climate.

It is also important to mention that during the First and Second Assessments of 1990–96, Working Groups II and III had more difficulties in providing information that was connected to the latest findings of climate scientists, because of the time lag between the generation of climate scenarios and their application by other researchers (Jäger and O'Riordan 1996). Subsequent reports have shown that this lag has been somewhat reduced, particularly since the IPCC has facilitated the generation and distribution of updated GHG emissions scenarios and their use by climate modelling groups to construct new climate change scenarios from various climate models (Carter et al. 2000). This result was achieved through the creation of the IPCC Data Distribution Center and publication of the Special Report on Emission Scenarios (SRES) (Nakicenovic and Swart 2000). Increased research activity within developing countries will further reduce the time lag.

Since IPCC findings were being transmitted to negotiators of the UNFCCC, attention has been drawn not only to the science component but also to assessments of response options, including special reports on sinks (Watson et al. 2000b) and technology transfer (Metz et al. 2000). As a result, the IPCC, as a recognized source of information, was and continues to be a substantial influence on the negotiating process without indicating any political opinions or value judgments.

THE UNITED NATIONS FRAMEWORK CONVENTION ON CLIMATE CHANGE (UNFCCC) AND THE CONFERENCE OF THE PARTIES (COPS)

With the ratification of the UNFCCC in 1994, signatories became Parties to the Convention. A key element of the UNFCCC was its stated objective, outlined in Article 2:

> The ultimate objective of this Convention and any related legal instruments that the Conference of the Parties may adopt is to achieve, in accordance with the relevant provisions of the Convention, stabilization of greenhouse gas concentrations in the atmosphere at a level that would prevent dangerous anthropogenic interference with the climate system. Such a level should be achieved within a time frame sufficient to allow ecosystems to adapt naturally to climate change, to ensure that food is not threatened and to enable economic development to proceed in a sustainable manner (UNEP 1994, 6)

The inclusion of the words "stabilization" and "dangerous" in Article 2 has had significant implications for research and policy negotiations. Stabilization of GHG concentrations requires more than stabilization of

GHG emissions (Houghton 2004). Various levels of stabilization can be defined by science, and the particular level that is defined will have its own implications for the setting of GHG emission reduction targets (this problem is discussed further in chapter 8). Moreover, defining the level of dangerous climate change is a challenge that cannot be addressed solely by science, economics, or other fields of study. Ultimately, a value judgment is required, a judgment dependent on many factors, such as the current and anticipated levels of climate-related exposure and risk and their underlying human dimensions that are regionally unique. For example, the amount of sea level rise considered dangerous in the Maldives and Thailand might be manageable in Portugal and Japan because of differences in coastal elevations, as well as in their governments' capacities to provide and maintain flood defenses, to organize evacuations, or to implement resettlement. (This problem will be expanded on in chapters 7, 8, 9, and 11.)

Article 4 of the UNFCCC, which concerned the issue of commitments, was also important. Parties had to commit themselves to provide inventories of GHG emission sources and sinks and information on national programs, to cooperate on technology transfer and adaptation, and to promote sustainable development (UNEP, 1994).

The UNFCCC also initiated an annual series of open meetings known as the Conference of the Parties (COPs). COPs have become major international events attracting senior representatives of governments, with many side events promoting various scientific and political aspects of climate change. The first COP, COP-1, was held in Berlin in 1995. COP-3, held in Kyoto in 1997, resulted in the drafting of the Kyoto Protocol, which was finally ratified in November 2004. Subsequent COPs have led to agreements (or "accords") on adaptation and funding mechanisms. (These agreements will be discussed in chapters 8 and 9.) Considering all its achievements, Grubb, Vrolijk, and Brack (1999) conclude that the UNFCCC was able to provide a set of principles and to establish the institutional and procedural basis upon which the next steps could be taken.

Figure 2.1 illustrates the chronology of events leading up to the UNFCCC and the initiation of the COP negotiating process. Note that a separate advisory process composed of two subsidiary bodies was established to support the negotiations. The mandates of the Subsidiary Body on Scientific and Technical Advice (SBSTA) and of the Subsidiary Body on Instruments (SBI) differed from the mandate of IPCC (see chapter 8).

GHG SCENARIOS

The development of scenarios with changing GHG emission rates played a role in the historical evolution of the dialogue on climate change that has been as important and as visible as the climate-modelling component itself. Chapters 3, 8, and 11 will discuss the scientific aspects of the development of these scenarios and their application within GCMs and subsequent use in impacts research. Human-induced climate change is perceived as a problem if the implications for ecosystems and societies are negative, but also if radiative forcing owing to GHG emissions is seen as continuing to increase. If GHG concentrations were already stabilizing or decreasing the problem would be less urgent, but recent GHG emissions trends are showing no signs of stabilizing but are increasing dramatically (figure 2.2). But how should future GHG emissions and concentrations be defined?

The construction of GHG emission scenarios has evolved from a simple exercise of extrapolation of past trends, known as business-as-usual trends, or assumptions of linear or percentage growth (such as a 1 percent increase per year), to more sophisticated exercises of story development. The emergence of the IPCC has facilitated the development of these scenarios by encouraging the global networking of researchers from many disciplines who cooperate on scenario construction.

During the 1980s, GCM simulations and subsequent impacts studies were generally based on the $2xCO_2$ scenario, that is, the instantaneous doubling of CO_2 concentrations compared with pre-industrial concentrations, though here too, there was inconsistent treatment of what $1xCO_2$ was (ranging from 280 ppm to 315 ppm). Since there was no organized system of climate scenario delivery to impacts researchers, a number of ad hoc arrangements were made. For example, in Canada during the 1980s and early 1990s, Environment Canada served as an informal distribution centre providing climate model outputs from its first generation GCM to impacts researchers. In the United States, the National Center for Atmospheric Research (NCAR) provided a similar function for model outputs provided by US-based climate modeling groups. This was a new experience for climate modellers, climate science organizations (both national and international), and users of these data sets. Eventually, the learning from these early applications led to a more organized system of scenario development and delivery during the 1990s, beginning with the LINK program established in the United Kingdom in 1991

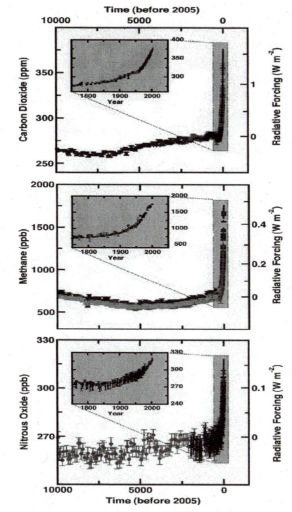

Figure 2.2 Trends in greenhouse gas concentrations.
Source: IPCC (2007c), fig. SPM-1. Reprinted with permission of IPCC

(Viner and Hulme 1994). LINK has provided instruction to users of scenario data sets, as well as workshops that have brought together climate modellers, climate data managers, and various researchers who want to apply scenario data sets to studies of climate change impacts and adaptation. LINK has also maintained web-based access to data sets and has continued to update these data sets as newer model outputs become available (the data sets are accessible through the University of East Anglia website – see the list of websites at the beginning of this book).

Initially, by convention, impacts researchers were informally instructed to assume that a doubling of CO_2 concentrations ($2xCO_2$) would be reached in the 2050s. Making this assumption was clearly a temporary expedient. Researchers recognized that the assumption was unrealistic since GHG concentrations were not going to suddenly increase in this fashion. However, climate modellers followed this convention because it was easier to do so than to construct scenarios based on "transient" changes. "Transient change" refers to continuous incremental change over time. Thus a transient simulation would show results for every day, month, or year in a continuous time series over a projection of fifty or one hundred years or more (for example, a transient simulation could be the scenario of a 1 percent increase in CO_2 concentrations per year or a more complex narrative, such as one of the SRES series, in which rates of change may vary over time). An equilibrium simulation would show only a new average condition, such as a new average temperature for a year or a winter season, or for 25 January. The completion of the first transient simulations by three groups in the United States (Hansen et al. 1988; Washington and Meehl 1989; Stouffer, Manabe, and Bryan 1989; all three cited in Bretherton, Bryan, and Woods 1990) soon led to transient simulations produced by other groups. They were generally based on an assumed increase in CO_2 concentrations of 1 percent per year.

In 1989, the newly formed IPCC asked an expert group to prepare a set of scenarios of global emissions of CO_2, CH_4, N_2O, and other trace gases, scenarios that were included in the 1990 assessment, later known as the IPCC First Assessment Report. In 1991, this initial set was revised, and the IS92 series was generated (Leggett, Pepper, and Swart 1992). This series became the standard for climate model simulations and subsequent use by the impacts research community throughout the mid-1990s, though the use of $2xCO_2$ could still be seen in publications in the late 1990s as well. Following the release of the Second Assessment Report in 1995–96, criticism of the IS92 series (see Grubb, Vrolijk, and Brack 1999) led the IPCC to broaden the process of scenario, or story, development, ultimately leading to publication of new scenarios in the Special Report on Emission Scenarios, or SRES (see the discussion of emission scenarios in chapter 3). SRES has now become the new standard for climate scenarios and impacts studies.

The move from 2xCO$_2$ to IS92 and now to SRES has been part of the process of building an interdisciplinary research community around the climate change issue. The SRES expert group created their storylines by incorporating global population forecasts, energy supply forecasts, updates on deforestation rates, and the potential impacts of other policy initiatives, such as the Montreal Protocol (concerning substances that deplete the stratospheric ozone layer). The IS92 scenarios explicitly excluded development of new climate policy initiatives (Leggett, Pepper, and Swart 1992), and this practice has continued with the SRES as well (Nakicenovic and Swart 2000). While IS92 scenarios were variants on published United Nations or World Bank population and economic-growth forecasts, the SRES storylines were based on a wider range of global development possibilities, from a "fortress-world" story of multinational empires to a more sustainable world of highly efficient energy and industrial systems supported by a well-integrated global trading network. The authors avoided putting descriptive labels on these scenarios, identifying them only with "A" and "B" markers, with variants constructed within each (see chapter 11).

Although the IPCC does not do new research directly, this process of networking and facilitation has been important in creating new opportunities for research by other parties. The creation of the IS92 and SRES scenarios and subsequent conversion to climate change scenarios (Carter et al. 2000) would probably not have occurred without the influence of the IPCC.

KYOTO PROTOCOL

The ratification of the UNFCCC in 1994 was recognized as establishing a framework for a general approach to climate change. There were statements of concern on the need to protect the climate system, but it was also recognized that various parties had unique needs and circumstances that would have to be accounted for in any specific arrangement. Details about the implementation of mechanisms for slowing the growth of GHG emissions and concentrations would also be needed so that stabilization could be achieved.

The IPCC Second Assessment Report concluded that there was a "discernible human influence on the climate" (Santer et al. 1995, 439) On the basis of this conclusion, the COPs brought together political leaders to consider policy options. One of these, COP-3, set the stage for the debate about and drafting of what is now known as the Kyoto Protocol.

By 1997, 167 countries and the European Union had ratified the UN-FCCC (Grubb, Vrolijk, and Brack 1999). The IPCC, as well as the SBSTA and the SBI, were creating dialogue and generating information. The Global Environmental Facility (GEF) had been established as the financing agency. COP-1 had already selected a mechanism for a pilot phase of activities to be undertaken among developed-countries with developing country partners. This mechanism, which was later to become Joint Implementation, as described in the Kyoto Protocol, will be discussed further in chapters 8 and 9. COP-1 also produced the Berlin Mandate, which stated that there needed to be a strengthening of commitments from developed countries, which were identified as Annex 1 parties by the UNFCCC. The Ad-Hoc Group on the Berlin Mandate began a series of meetings among various parties to negotiate commitments and mechanisms. This process was to be completed in 1997 with a view to adopting the results at COP-3. Oberthür and Ott (1999) provide details about these negotiations.

The COP-3 event was the climax of many months of negotiations within the Berlin Mandate process. Most developed countries had already declared their positions on GHG emission targets and related commitments (Canada was an important exception). However, many substantive issues had not yet been settled before the Kyoto meeting began in early December 1997. These issues included the technical aspects of targets, the potential role of sinks, the role of developing countries, and the treatment of non-compliance. Oberthür and Ott (1999) describe in great detail the diplomatic activities that took place before and during COP-3, including the Ministerial Segment of 8–11 December 1997. After an intense session of what was described as negotiation-by-exhaustion, the Kyoto Protocol, complete with mechanisms and targets, was signed on 11 December 1997. This launched debates at the domestic level in countries throughout the world.

Finally, with ratification by Russia in November 2004, the protocol had enough support from Annex 1 parties to come into force in February 2005. As a result, the Kyoto mechanisms, including sinks and emissions trading, became available to all parties to the protocol. In addition, a mechanism supporting adaptation, the Adaptation Fund, also became available. The fund was not part of the original protocol but was crafted as part of the 2001 Marrakech Accords (COP-7) and was finally adopted at COP-11 in November 2005 (Schipper 2006). The performance of these mechanisms will be evaluated during the first Commitment Period, 2008–12. As of October 2007, 190 countries plus the European Union have ratified the UNFCCC, while 176 countries, including India and China, have ratified the Kyoto Protocol. At COP-13, in December 2007, Australia announced that it would also ratify Kyoto. Because the United States has continued to remain outside the protocol, they lack an incentive to utilize Kyoto's policy instruments (see chapters 8 and 9).

ROLE OF MASS MEDIA

Climate change has become a topic of interest for the mass media. For most people, knowledge about climate change comes through this source, rather than through direct contact with researchers (Corbett and Durfee 2004). Research on media coverage of climate change has focused on the accuracy of media coverage of climate change science, as well as on the political aspects of domestic and international negotiations concerning policy measures. One issue, for example, is the portrayal of uncertainty of the occurrence of climate change.

Media coverage in the United States appears to be shifting from interviews with researchers to interviews with politicians and interest groups. This shift is part of an increasing focus on controversy rather than on incremental advances in climate science. Gelbspan (1997) has documented how certain groups opposed to reductions in fossil fuel consumption have used the mass media to promote their view that theories of anthropogenic climate change are very uncertain and that any policy measure dealing with climate change, such as mandatory cuts in GHG emissions, should not be undertaken. Corbett and Durfee (2004) cite a number of studies and polls to suggest that this focus on controversy has contributed to the perception in the United States that the science of global warming is uncertain. Their own experimental study which employed a series of hypothetical (or alternative) stories on the thinning of Antarctic ice confirms this generalization. They found that while the inclusion of context in media stories increased perceptions of certainty, the inclusion of controversy reduced perceptions of certainty and that the media tended to focus on controversy at the expense of context.

Boykoff and Boykoff (2004) raise another interesting question of whether the normal media process of balanced reporting (presenting multiple perspectives on an issue) results in a divergence of public and scientific discourse on climate change such that the result is biased media coverage or "informational bias." Boykoff and Boykoff suggest that it is the combination of the need for journalistic balance and the newly emerging preferential relationships between the media and certain individuals or representatives of particular advocacy organizations that could contribute to this informational bias. In order to measure this bias, Boykoff and Boykoff sampled press coverage by four major US newspapers during 1988–2002, and found that balanced accounts of anthropogenic contributions to warming, which give equal coverage to proponents and skeptics, accounted for more than half the published stories. One-third of the stories were oriented towards anthropogenic causes, but they still presented both sides. The rest of the stories were split between exclusive coverage of anthropogenic causes and scepticism about such causes. This orientation towards balance differed from the reporting of climate change science by the IPCC, which indicated a strong consensus about the role of anthropogenic forcing in the current climate, as well as the climate of the future. Boykoff and Boykoff (2004) conclude that the minority, skeptical view has been given higher visibility than is warranted by the prevailing scientific discourse.

This is not to say that it will be easy to deal with the many challenges associated with communicating climate change issues in a way that expresses the urgency of the problem while still accurately describing the current state of knowledge. Moser and Dilling (2004) note that inattention to and inaction on climate change occurs for several reasons:

1 climate change is seen as a "creeping" long-term problem, which can be difficult to pay attention to in the short term;
2 climate change is complex, and there are real scientific uncertainties;
3 humans have a limited attention span and are more likely to focus on short-term issues; and
4 it is difficult to communicate seriousness and urgency without it sounding like fear-mongering.

They suggest that communication should focus on topics with the greatest scientific certainty, highlighting options for effective response and broadening the range of communicators beyond climate scientists to include people from other educational and professional backgrounds.

DISCUSSION

This brief history of the climate change issue has outlined the progression from scientific theory to international policy. Ratification of the Kyoto Protocol is certainly not the end of the diplomatic process, however. Negotiations have already begun on post-2012 arrangements.

The speed at which Kyoto was ratified is quite remarkable. There were several catalysts influencing the process. In particular, the publication of the first GCM simulations of future climate in the late 1970s, combined with technological advances in computing power and communications, which enabled new information to be distributed rapidly, with follow-up by other research groups and interested parties concerned about environment issues, were especially prominent. The networking function of the UN bodies, including the IPCC, also helped to make the possible connections between science and policy more visible.

Uncertainties remain in the science, not only regarding future climate change but also with respect to future GHG emissions, impacts on ecosystems and societies, and the future performance of the Kyoto mechanisms. Many of these uncertainties relate to the difficulties in anticipating the future behaviour of individuals, markets, businesses, and countries. In the following chapters, we will describe a number of these difficulties, as well as the contexts for the varying perspectives and forms of knowledge that contribute to the many dimensions of global warming.

3

The Atmospheric Science Aspects
of Climate Change

INTRODUCTION

This chapter begins with basic information about climate systems and the carbon cycle and then moves on to discuss how we can see early signals of a particular scenario developing in observed climate patterns and trends. This is followed by a discussion of long-term and short-term signal detection.

What methods are used to detect early signals of human-induced change in observed recent climate patterns and trends? Short-term signal detection, which looks at the trends of temperature and rainfall over several years to decades, seeks to answer whether humans are affecting the climate today or whether we are still in essentially a natural climate. Long-term signal detection, which looks at the trends of temperature and rainfall over decades to centuries, seeks to answer whether recent climate trends are different from conditions during the distant past. These are not easy tasks, and they have become sources of controversy within the climate science community.

The discussion of signal detection is followed by a review of climate models, including GCMs. The review provides a general description of the structure of the models and of how they have evolved from the AGCM, which is the atmospheric general circulation model, to the AOGCM, which is the atmosphere-ocean global climate model. During this evolution, the models grew from being simple and one-dimensional to being three-dimensional and inclusive of oceans, land surfaces, and dynamic processes. However, many problems still remain.

Radiative forcing is one crucial issue that will be discussed, because it drives so much of the climate modelling process. As previously noted in chapter 2, radiative forcing is the net change of downward radiation minus upward radiation due to a change in a constituent of the atmosphere, such as the concentration of CO_2 or CH_4. Besides GHGs, there are other elements to consider, such as aerosols, soot, and changes in the output of the sun. If we can't achieve consensus on how much additional energy the GHGs are trapping in the atmosphere, then this uncertainty would influence subsequent steps in the climate modelling process. Because changes in radiative forcing represent a very important input to the entire climate-model simulation of future climate change, any errors in determining radiative forcing will affect all aspects of climate scenarios.

We'll also examine the problem of spatial resolution (i.e., the problem of how much of the surface the model can "see") and the difficulties in accurately representing clouds. If the various GCMs produce different patterns of cloud formation, then they will produce different precipitation scenarios for the same location and change in GHG emissions.

Another important issue is the modelling of soil moisture, which is expressed in terms of moisture accumulation in the soil, moisture movement within the soil, and usage of the moisture in the soil. Soil moisture is represented by what is known as the "bucket," which is a metaphor for the collection of water in a column of soil. Variations in the assumed bucket structure among the climate models has implications for the resulting climate model scenarios, such as temperature changes, and their use in impacts studies.

To produce climate change scenarios, it is also necessary to understand what emissions scenarios are being applied. We'll revisit the discussion we began in chapter 2 about emissions scenarios by discussing their evolution from equilibrium to transient scenarios. We'll then examine the applicability of these emissions scenarios to future warming predictions today.

With this understanding of how emissions scenarios work, we'll then look at other ways of creating climate change scenarios without applying emissions scenarios, particularly analogues (climate indicators of a past event applied to the future) and arbitrary (or hypothetical) cases, which were more in vogue in the 1980s and early 1990s than they are now. At present, impacts researchers almost exclusively use GCM-based scenarios linked with emissions scenarios, and we'll discuss why this is the case.

THE ENERGY BALANCE AND THE GLOBAL
CLIMATE SYSTEM

We begin by considering the radiation, or energy, balance of the atmosphere. Physics tells us that the hotter the radiating body, the shorter the wavelength of emission. As a result, the sun, which is, of course, very hot, emits energy in short wavelengths (around 0.5 microns). When this shortwave radiation enters the earth's atmosphere, some of it passes through it to the earth's surface. The earth absorbs it and then reradiates it outward. The earth is, of course, not nearly as hot as the sun, so the earth emits this energy at longer thermal infrared wavelengths (ranging from 8 to 13 microns, including certain wavelengths that can be transmitted through the atmosphere to space, otherwise known as the atmospheric window). The fact that the wavelengths are different and that water vapour, CO_2, and other constituents of the atmosphere can absorb longwave energy (figure 3.1) while still being relatively transparent to shortwave radiation results in a natural warming of the earth. Therein lies one of the fundamental aspects of the greenhouse effect. Indeed, some commentators have argued that there is actually greater absorption of the far infrared wavelengths (above 15 microns) by water vapour than is indicated here (Harries 1996).

Energy from the sun is transformed from light to heat energy by different mechanisms: radiation, conduction, and convection. Radiation is emitted at different wavelengths, depending on the temperature of the radiating body (see above). Conduction refers to heat passing through a substance, such as water, metal, air, or soil. Air is not a good conductor of heat, but conduction is important for heat transfer into the ground. Convection describes heat transfer through circulation of fluids and gases. This includes sensible heat, which is heat transfer by the rising and mixing of warmed air, and latent heat (heat that we cannot feel), which enables water to be converted to water vapour by evaporation, or ice to be converted to water by melting. Conversely, condensation and freezing would result in the release of latent heat. These changes between vapour, liquid water, and ice are collectively referred to as phase changes of water, and in each case, there is a transfer of energy (Barry and Chorley 1982). When vegetation is also considered, the transpiration of water vapour by plants combined with evaporation, known as evapotranspiration, provides a measurement of the net transfer of the energy required to change liquid water to vapour over a vegetated landscape.

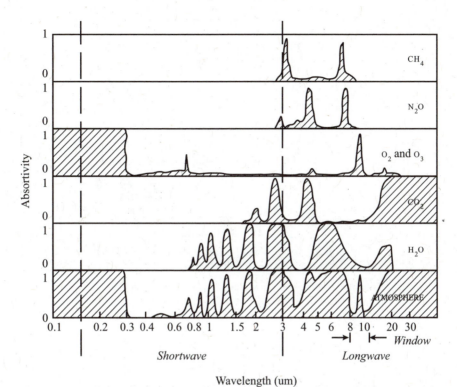

Figure 3.1   Absorption of radiation at various wavelengths by trace gases and by the atmosphere as a whole.
Source: Oke (1978), after Fleagle and Businger (1963). Reprinted with permission of Tim Oke

Incoming and outgoing transmission of energy between the earth and space represents a fundamental component of the earth's climate. The difference between energy reaching the earth and what is re-emitted to the atmosphere and eventually to space is part of an energy cycle that is in balance at the global scale. This balance is important for both atmospheric and ecosystem functions.

Figure 3.2 illustrates this energy balance. It can be used to follow the energy from the sun as it gets transformed from shortwave to longwave after absorption by the earth's surface. The top of the atmosphere receives 342 watts (w) per square meter of solar radiation, of which about half passes through the atmosphere to be absorbed by the earth's surface, while the rest is reflected by clouds and atmospheric constituents

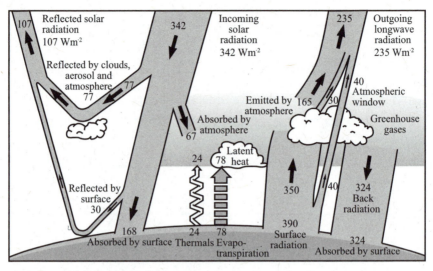

Figure 3.2   Global energy balance, in watts per square metre (Wm⁻²).
Source: Kiehl and Trenberth (1997). Reprinted with permission of the American Meteorological Society

(such as particulates), and also by aerosols (see the next section). Some longwave energy emitted from the surface escapes to space through the atmospheric window, which is a small-wavelength interval in the thermal infrared wavelengths for which the atmosphere is transparent.

Land surfaces and oceans absorb about 168 w per square meter of the incoming solar energy and use it to heat the land and the air and to evapotranspire water. These processes transform the energy from shortwave to longwave energy. Evapotranspiration, which is the process by which water becomes a vapour, accounts for 78 w per square meter of energy in the form of latent heat. The process of heating the air also requires energy in the form of sensible heat.

Some of the incoming solar energy is also reflected by the surface of the earth. The technical name for reflectivity is "albedo." Surface reflection varies depending on the type of surface. For example, forests, grass-covered plains, bare ground, deserts, and ice do not have the same albedo. Ice has a very high albedo, while a dark tropical forest has a very low one. Overall, about 30 w per square meter of the original 342 w per square meter, or about 10 percent of the energy, is reflected by the earth's surface. The total of the atmospheric reflections and the surface reflections is around 107 w per square meter, and the total amount of energy lost from the earth is 235 w per square meter. How do these energy transformations and the energy balance present a challenge for climate modellers?

First, regarding the climate system itself, modellers have to account for the energy balance and variations in land and water surfaces. Early in the evolution of the modelling process, the first and simplest models were based solely on the link between the sun and an assumed two-dimensional flat earth. As climate modellers began attempting to mimic reality more closely, they had to account both for the fact that the earth is not actually flat and for the fact that it is not completely terrestrial. Our planet is mostly ocean, but the ocean is not all open water: some of it is ice. On land, there are mountains and different kinds of vegetation. Some areas are deserts or semi-arid grasslands, while others are forested. Sub-arctic regions include the transition between forest and tundra, and some land areas are covered by glaciers and snow. Finally, because humans have significantly altered some areas through deforestation, reforestation, and urban development, climate models must find a way to account for large changes in land cover and land use over space and time. All these factors will affect the modelling of the climate system and must be accounted for by the modellers.

The marine aspect of the climate system includes interactions between the atmosphere and the ice, as well as between the atmosphere and the ocean. Modelling these interactions requires what the modellers call the coupling of atmospheric and oceanic processes, which includes the coupling of the ocean and ice, as well as the coupling of the ocean and the atmosphere, since the ocean is not static. This modelling is carried out through mathematical expressions. The old models assumed that the ocean was an unmoving slab because it was easy to model that way, but in fact, of course, oceans are not unmoving slabs: ocean currents transport heat, and they do so in a very non-linear way. Climate models need to mimic these currents in order to accurately depict heat distribution around the earth.

Land-atmosphere linkages can be simpler to model than ocean-atmosphere linkages simply because the land is not moving. However, a model still has to account for topography, which affects wind patterns, as well as temperature and moisture parameters. These factors are tremendously complex to include in a global-scale model. And later in this chapter, when discussing resolution, we will consider why it is so difficult for a climate modeller to capture some of the smaller-scale circulation features, such as rain shadow effects. In a model with low spatial resolution, the mountains will not look like mountains. They will look like giant blocks, because the grid cells will be so large.

Topography affects the hydrological cycle, which also needs to be included in climate models. Clouds are very difficult to model, as will be seen later in this chapter, and model projections of changes in clouds are highly uncertain. In addition, at some locations with complex climate patterns, such as Vancouver, British Columbia, there can be a 30 percent difference in rainfall between adjacent weather stations. Such intricacies cannot be captured at the scale of a global climate model.

THE GLOBAL CARBON CYCLE

In order to understand how GHG emissions can increase global temperature, it is necessary to examine the global cycling of carbon. Parallel to the global energy budget there is a global carbon budget (figure 3.3) in which the units of measurement are gigatonnes (Gt) of carbon. The atmospheric reservoir of carbon is estimated to be about 750 Gt. It should be noted that this measurement is not the same as the measurement of concentrations of CO_2 in ppm. The current atmospheric concentration of CO_2 is actually about 385 ppm (as of 2007; see WMO, 2008), which has been directly measured from observation sites in Mauna Loa (Hawaii), Alert (Nunavut), and elsewhere.

While the atmosphere must retain some energy in order to maintain surface temperature conditions that are suitable for human survival, increasing CO_2 concentrations in the atmosphere can re-radiate longwave energy back to the surface, as well as absorb energy that may otherwise have been lost to space. Thus, if GHG concentrations continue to increase, the outward loss of radiation will gradually diminish, resulting in more energy being available to increase air temperatures.

Because there are very large carbon pools in the earth's vegetation and in the soil, it is necessary to account for the relatively small exchanges of carbon that occur with the atmosphere. Changes in land use – historically, the clearing of forests – emit more CO_2 than is being absorbed by new vegetation. As a result, about 1 Gt of carbon is lost annually to the atmosphere from the soils and vegetation. Figure 3.3 also identifies primary production, which in this case refers to the conversion of energy by terrestrial and aquatic organisms (e.g., plants, algae, plankton) into carbohydrates, such as sugars. Primary production uses CO_2 through photosynthesis and is opposed by respiration, which releases CO_2. Because primary production and respiration are approximately in balance, they do not contribute significantly to atmospheric CO_2 concentrations.

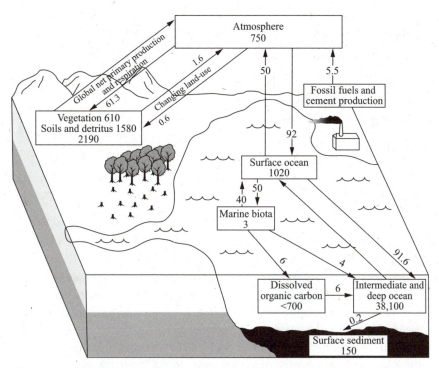

Figure 3.3   Global carbon budget, in gigatonnes (Gt).
Source: Schimel et al. (1995). Reprinted with permission of IPCC

On the other hand, human activities such as fossil fuel consumption, cement manufacturing, and land use changes are significant sources of carbon that emit large amounts of CO_2 into the atmosphere, although not all the CO_2 that they produce actually remains there, because the oceans act as sinks that can absorb a lot of it. Once those sinks are full, however, the atmospheric sink absorbs the rest. Fossil fuel emissions and cement production emissions, which have grown considerably since 1995, when they were estimated to be about 5.5 Gt per year (Prentice 2001), are thus increasing CO_2 concentrations in the atmosphere.

Other important by-products of human activity are aerosols. Aerosol emissions have the opposite effect of CO_2 emissions in that they reflect shortwave radiation, which potentially produces a slight cooling effect. Natural sources of particulates, such as volcanic eruptions, can have more significant cooling effects, as has been shown for the 1880s (Lamb 1982). These effects tend to be of limited duration since the volcanic materials remain in the atmosphere for only a short time before settling back down to the earth.

Table 3.1
Summary of Changes in the Global Carbon Budget, in Gigatonnes

	1980s	1990s	2000–5
Atmospheric increase	3.3 ± 0.1	3.2 ± 0.1	4.1 0.1
Fossil carbon dioxide emissions	5.4 ± 0.3	6.4 ± 0.4	7.2 ± 0.3
Net ocean-to-atmosphere flux	−1.8 ± 0.8	−2.2 ± 0.4	−2.2 ± 0.5
Net land-to-atmosphere flux	−0.3 ± 0.9	−1.0 ± 0.6	−0.9 ± 0.6
Partitioned as follows			
Land use change flux	1.4	1.6	
	(0.4 to 2.3)	(0.5 to 2.7)	NA
Residual land sink	−1.7	−2.6	
	(−3.4 to 0.2)	(−4.3 to −0.9)	NA

Source: IPCC (2007d).

Just how much of this CO_2 is being absorbed through ocean sinks? And how much CO_2 actually stays in the atmosphere? And how much of it is being absorbed somewhere else? There has been considerable discussion about the ocean as a carbon sink; figure 3.3 illustrates the different reservoirs and transfer points for carbon. The intermediate and deep oceans are actually huge reservoirs. Even the surface ocean reservoir is almost comparable to soils. Table 3.1 indicates an ocean sink of 2.2 petagrams (10^{15} grams or one gigatonne (Gt)) per year. That is, there are two more gigatonnes of CO_2 absorbed by the surface ocean than it emits to the atmosphere. Note that a negative number indicates that the flux is in the opposite direction. For example, a negative ocean-atmosphere flux indicates that carbon is being transferred from the atmosphere to the ocean. Since the ocean is such an impressive sink, there have even been some suggestions that somehow one could deliberately manipulate this property to manage it as a carbon sink. However, ethical issues, as well as scientific uncertainties, are associated with this idea.

Table 3.1 also shows an atmospheric increase of 3.3 Gt per year from 1980 to 1989. This atmospheric increase of 3.3 Gt per year was derived from subtracting the ocean sinks absorption of 2.0 Gt per year and land-atmosphere fluxes of 0.2 Gt per year from the net carbon emissions of 5.5 Gt.

In the IPCC Third Assessment Report of 2001, the 1980s sinks estimates were updated. Although they reflected a change of only 0.1 Gt (Prentice 2001), as shown in table 3.1, there was evidence to suggest that global emissions had increased by about 20 percent in the 1990s – a relatively large increase in emissions. Despite this increase, no significant change in the annual rate of increase in atmospheric concentrations of CO_2 was observed. The atmospheric carbon uptake had not changed, but why? The land-atmosphere flux estimate appeared to show that the natural sink had compensated quite substantially for the increase in emissions. This raises interesting questions. Are we seeing forests adapting to a higher CO_2 environment naturally by taking up more CO_2 and increasing their photosynthesis rates? And is that going to be a naturally occurring mechanism as we move into the 400 ppm and 450 ppm CO_2 worlds? Recent updates reported by the IPCC in 2007 indicate that global emission rates during 2000–5 have increased by a further 0.8 Gt of carbon, an increase of 15 percent since the 1990s. Unlike what was observed during the 1990s, this additional carbon has accumulated in the atmosphere itself. The land-atmosphere and ocean-atmosphere fluxes have not increased (in other words, they have not become more negative). Consequently, the terrestrial and marine sinks have not taken up the additional carbon, suggesting that carbon sequestration rates may be reaching their limit, or that land use change, particularly deforestation, may be accelerating (IPCC 2007d; Denman et al. 2007).

SIGNAL DETECTION

An important question for climate science, as well as for anyone interested in human-induced climate change, is whether the warming over the past century is attributable only to natural variability or whether increases in GHGs have already begun to affect the climate. The IPCC has concluded that the balance of evidence supports the hypothesis that the human signal can be detected in recent observed climate patterns (Mitchell and Karoly 2001).

One of the key sources of evidence for long-term natural and human-induced climate signals is paleoclimatology, which focuses on climatic evidence obtained from vegetation, soil, ice, and historical structures and documents. Paleoclimatology is very important because it allows us to extend records back before the establishment of monitoring stations with meteorological instruments. In most countries, there are instrumental records only for the twentieth century, and even they are problematic because of station movement, inconsistent use of instruments, and the potential growth in urban heat islands. And although it is possible to take a subset of those stations and be fairly satisfied that the instrumental record represents climate patterns accurately, this record is still quite brief. But by using evidence from tree rings, ice cores, or pollen analysis, paleoclimatology can extend the climate record much farther back.

Figure 3.4 summarizes the results of several studies that have reconstructed temperature records for the past eighteen hundred years. Some of these records are not global data sets but are described as northern-hemisphere or extratropical records. The lack of global coverage for these temperature trends, as well as the statistical methodology used, has attracted some criticism (McIntyre and McKitrick 2003, 2005), and future research may reveal some regional differences in long-term trends that would affect the overall global trend. Recent studies illustrate such regional variations in long-term trends, but as more of these data sets become available, analyses of the overall global trend show an increase in temperature during the twentieth century (including up to 2004) beyond any increases that have been estimated for the past millennium (Jones and Mann 2004; Moberg et al. 2005).

While there is considerable variation between the records, there is a consensus that in the 1880s, an increasing trend in temperatures emerged that resulted by the 1980s in temperature conditions that had not been observed for any period of the last millennium. Note that the 0.0 on the vertical axis of figure 3.4 represents the 1961–90 temperature average. In figures like this, rather than using the numerical value of the 1961–90 temperature average, which would be around 15°C, the researcher represents the 1961–90 temperature average as the zero line. Consequently, any curve plotted below that line indicates that the value at a particular time is cooler than this 1961–90 temperature average. And similarly, any value above that line represents conditions warmer than that average. For most of the last millennium, temperatures were 0.2°C to 0.5°C cooler than this 1961–90 northern-hemisphere temperature average. By contrast, the consensus among the studies represented in figure 3.4 is that, at least in the last millennium, temperatures in the last several years have never been so warm.

The global temperature trends described above exhibit increases and decreases that suggest the existence of natural cycles of varying lengths. The causes of these cycles vary from relatively short-term periodic fluctuations in solar output (including sunspot cycles) to longer-term effects of changes in the earth's orbit around the sun (such as variations in earth-sun distance and the angle of the tilt of the polar axis). These variations lead to changes in surface heating and subsequently, to variations in atmospheric circulation patterns (such as the locations of large semi-permanent high-pressure

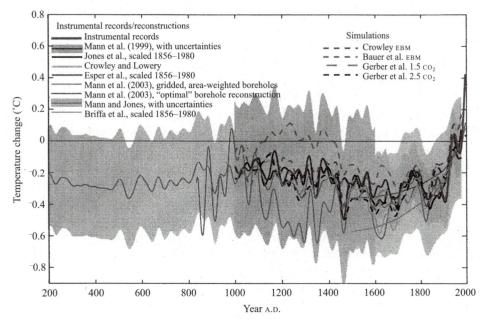

Figure 3.4   Past global temperatures estimated from proxy records. Individual reconstructions are indicated for the following studies: Bauer et al. (2003), Briffa et al. (2001), Crowley (2000), Crowley and Lowery (2000), Esper et al. (2002), Gerber et al. (2003), Jones et al. (1998), Mann, Bradley, and Hughes (1999), Mann, Rutherford, et al. (2003), Mann and Jones (2003).
Source: Mann, Ammann, et al. (2003). Graphic courtesy of Michael Mann. Copyright: American Geophysical Union

systems) that alter surface wind and precipitation patterns (Lamb 1982). Obviously, any attempt to detect the signal of anthropogenic influences on global climate needs to take prevailing natural cycles into account. This is why long-term climate records are needed and why proxy data sources are such an important complement to relatively short-term instrumental records.

Some researchers are concerned that modern instrumental stations in growing urban areas are not measuring real climate change but just the growth of urban heat islands, which arise when the urban landscape, with its concrete buildings, industries, and automobiles, creates an artificially warmer environment than in surrounding rural areas (Oke 1987). Investigators interested in tracking global climate trends have paid considerable attention to this problem and have endeavoured to avoid it by creating data sets that include only rural stations, discarding those that would be affected by an urban heat island (Folland and Karl 2001). Peterson et al. (1999) compared a specially selected set of rural stations where no major population growth was occurring around them with selected stations comprising the full global data set that is being used to construct global trends. Their study showed that both data sets revealed trends that are basically the same. Note that this study does not address the question of the causes of the climate trends but only assesses whether the stations in the data sets are measuring trends that are representative of the globe as a whole or whether they are merely measuring urban heat island effects. The results appear to show that some confidence can be placed in the global data set.

Another highly contentious question is whether the surface temperature of the globe is really representative of global climate trends. Some critics have argued that if we are to really understand what is happening with temperature trends, we must assess satellite records, rather than surface temperature trends, because satellites monitor a whole atmosphere column and not just conditions at an individual weather station where the thermometer is located (Christy, Spencer, and Braswell 2000). Houghton (2004) summarizes recent observed differences between surface records, balloon measurements, and satellite data from a microwave instrument known as a microwave sounding unit. The surface records show a warming since 1979 that is 0.13°C greater than the warming revealed by the other two sources. The differences are not completely understood, however. Increasing GHG does lead to cooling at higher elevations, and the satellite and balloon observations may be including these higher elevations in their data sets. Others have noted that satellite orbits change over time, and if they do, then the satellite's field of view will vary too, as will the magnitude of the air column it measures temperature for.

Another approach to signal detection uses GCMs. A coupled atmosphere-ocean GCM has been used in an experiment to see if it could replicate the observed global temperature trend on the basis of radiative forcing from natural and anthropogenic sources. Two sets of model simulations are shown in figure 3.5. Both panels show observed global temperatures and the timing of major volcanic eruptions (Santa Maria, Agung, El Chicon, and Pinatubo), which emitted volcanic aerosols, leading to short-term cooling. The bottom panel shows a series of model simulations using only natural forcing and compares with the observed global temperature trend of the last 100 years. This experiment showed that temperatures

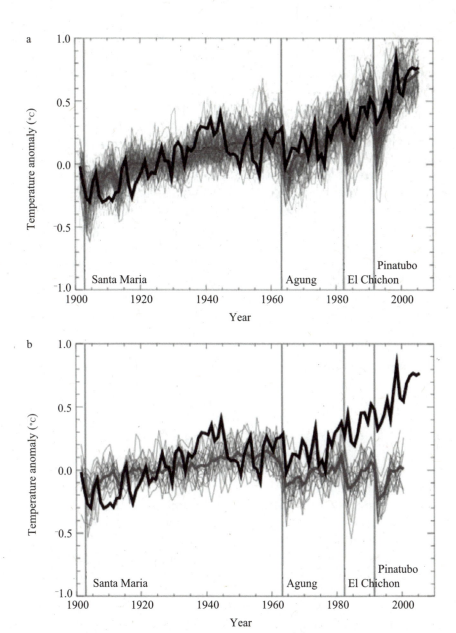

Figure 3.5   Observed (black line) and model-simulated (grey line) global mean surface temperature anomalies, with anthropogenic and natural forcings together (*top*), and natural forcing only (*bottom*). Year indicated for major volcanic eruptions (Santa Maria, Agung, El Chichon, and Pinatubo).
Source: Hegerl et al. (2007), figure 9.5. Reprinted with permission of IPCC

were over-predicted for the early 1900s and then under-predicted for the period since about the late 1970s. This case demonstrates that a climate model simulation without anthropogenic GHG forcing produces temperatures that are below what has been observed in the last thirty years. What natural sources of radiative forcing are included in this type of simulation? In the short term, things like small alterations in the solar output are included, because the solar constant actually varies over time. Major volcanic injections, if they occur, are also included. Long-term variations in the earth's orbit, however, are not considered.

The top panel shows a series of simulations that include both anthropogenic GHG and natural forcings. A more accurate picture of the trend in temperature over time is achieved. Thus, a model without increasing GHG cannot replicate current temperature trends; the influence of increasing CO_2 must be included. The results from including the interplay of both natural and anthropogenic GHG forcings has led climate modellers to argue that because their models cannot replicate current observed temperatures unless CO_2 forcing is included, they have evidence that the current climate trend is no longer completely natural. Current atmospheric concentrations of CO_2 are 385 ppm, which represents an increase of about a third since the Industrial Revolution. In the context of the $2xCO_2$ scenario described earlier, this is the equivalent of a $1^1/_3$ CO_2 scenario.

ATMOSPHERE-OCEAN GLOBAL CLIMATE MODELS (AOGCMS)

We move now to a discussion of the evolution of climate models. In the 1970s, the climate models included only the atmosphere but not ocean-heat transport: climate modellers simply prescribed a value for ocean-heat transport, rather than using a value from the outcome of a model. Ocean-heat transport was finally being included in climate models by the 1990s. The models were now called atmosphere-ocean global climate models (AOGCMS), since they were coupled, or mathematically linked, ocean models and atmospheric models. AOGCMS thus represented all physical processes that drive climate patterns over space and time (figure 3.6).

More recently, modellers have thought of somehow incorporating dynamic vegetation processes. While this task would be difficult, it would allow changes in forests to be observed in the simulation, instead of forests remaining unchanged over the life of the model run. If a forest was ten years old at the start of the model run, as it progressed through age

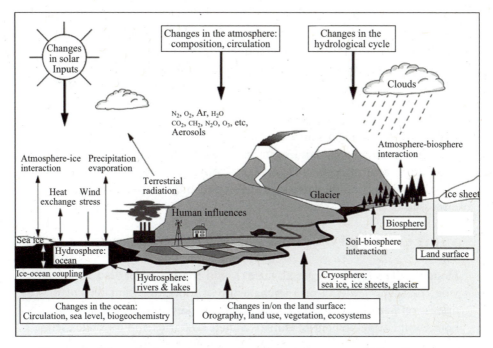

Figure 3.6   Schematic of a GCM representing all physical processes driving climate patterns.
Source: Baede et al. (2001). Reprinted with permission of IPCC

twenty years, thirty years, and forty, changes in its canopy height, CO_2 flux, and other attributes could be observed. In addition, the incorporation of vegetation processes provides additional information on surface-atmosphere feedbacks in terms of latent heat flux and evapotranspiration (see discussions by Bonan 2002).

The current effort in global climate model development now incorporates thirty-four GCMs (McAvaney et al. 2001). This illustrates the worldwide effort in this research area. A number of countries, such as Canada, the United States, Australia, the United Kingdom, France, Germany, Japan, China, and others, have made investments to try to create global-scale climate models. Each country has developed its own model and differences do exist between them.

Another school of climate modelling has also been trying since the late 1980s to produce regional climate models. They attempt to model smaller regions in much detail, rather than trying to model the entire globe in less detail. A number of groups (Giorgi and Hewitson 2001) have produced some promising results, but they have not yet advanced to the point where data sets are readily available for applications in impacts research worldwide. These models have to simulate processes for different layers above the ground and the ocean and for layers below the ocean surface, as well as within the root zones of vegetation, which is not an easy task. Climate models have consequently become more and more complicated over time. In the mid-1970s they were just simple atmospheric physics models, but now they have progressed to include the atmosphere, land surfaces, oceans, aerosols, carbon cycles, vegetation, atmospheric chemistry, and other processes. However, climate modelling is not without difficulties: some of the challenges are discussed in the next section.

CHALLENGES FOR CLIMATE MODEL DEVELOPMENT

Houghton (2004), Giorgi et al. (2001), and McAvaney et al. 2001) provide considerable detail on the challenge of modelling climate. For our discussion here, I would like to highlight four key sources of uncertainty both for the development of climate change scenarios and for their use in impacts research and policy analyses, namely, radiative forcing, model resolution, clouds and precipitation, and the land-surface bucket.

Radiative Forcing

Radiative forcing is important because it is the driver behind the science community's argument that the world will warm up as a result of increasing atmospheric CO_2 and other GHGs. A range of studies have looked at these individual atmospheric constituents and have tried to determine how much energy each constituent is actually absorbing or reflecting. CO_2 is the single biggest contributor to positive radiative forcing (figure 3.7). That is, as CO_2 concentrations have increased since 1750 from 280 ppm to 380 ppm, an additional 1.5 w per square meter of energy has been continuously trapped in the atmosphere. In other words, the additional 100 ppm of CO_2 has resulted in the 1.5 w per square meter increase in radiative forcing in 2005. Similarly, the increase in CH_4 concentrations from 650 ppb to 1950 ppb has resulted in the absorption of another 0.5 w per square meter, and N_2O and halocarbons absorb a little more energy than CH_4 alone. There is also some additional forcing from ozone in the troposphere, the lowest region of the atmosphere. This is not stratospheric ozone but the combination of hot

Radiative Forcing Terms

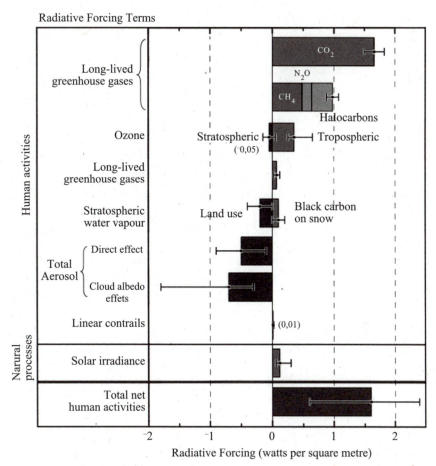

Figure 3.7 Annual mean radiative forcing in 2005, compared with 1750. "Black carbon on snow" refers to soot and other by-products of fossil fuel burning that settle on snow-covered areas, reducing their albedo. "Linear contrails" refers to condensation trails created by aircraft exhaust.
Source: Forster et al. (2007, Working Group I, FAQ 2.1, figure 2). Reprinted with permission of IPCC

air, humidity, and the by-products of automobile exhaust, which produces what is known as smog. Smog and potentially a little of the black carbon that comes out of fossil fuels also contribute to positive radiative forcing. The total positive radiative forcing estimated for the period from 1750 to the present is between 2.5 and 3 W per square meter (Ramaswamy 2001). Since the solar constant is around 1360 W per square meter (Barry and Chorley 1982), the positive contribution of historic increases in GHGs represents less than a 0.2 percent addition to the sun's energy that is already reaching the earth's atmosphere. Projected radiative forcing for the year 2100 compared with 2000 would be an additional 2 to 7 W per square meter, covering the range of GHG emissions scenarios.

There are also negative contributors to radiative forcing. Changes in stratospheric ozone can actually produce a partial cooling effect. Sulphate aerosols can lead to cooling, but the IPCC has indicated that the level of scientific understanding of sulphates is pretty low. The same is true of other kinds of tropospheric aerosols. They could have no impact, or they could have on impact similar to all the GHGs. The effects of tropospheric aerosols are very uncertain. It is also known that the solar "constant" is not in fact constant but that it can fluctuate. The solar output may even be greater now than it was in the past.

Together, all these contributors to radiative forcing have perhaps produced an additional 2 W per square meter of GHG emissions historically, increasing by as much as 7 W per square meter by 2100. How significant is this additional 2 W per square meter, or even 9 W per square meter? To put this small addition of radiant energy into context, consider this energy as being in a column of air above the land, but including the underlying land surface area. The energy that comes from the sun drives all the climatic processes that exist, including the heating of the air, the heating of the ground, the evapotranspiration of water, and the movement of the air (wind). Because there is a balance in this column of air between the incoming radiative forcing of the sun and the losses and the transformations that occur outwards from the earth, the earth's atmosphere will not heat up too much or cool down too much. But if there was an additional 2 W per square meter added to this column of air every second of every year, what would happen? The energy could be used to heat more air, evapotranspire more water, or heat more land. It is therefore apparent that if this column of air was expanded to the size of the earth's atmosphere, the additional amount of energy would become significant.

While 2 to 9 W per square meter may not initially seem like a significant addition to the atmosphere, further examination proves that it is. This small addition to the energy balance led to the negotiation of the United Nations Framework Convention on Climate Change (UNFCCC). There were, of course, many steps between the point of scientifically stating the amount of additional energy retention in the atmosphere and negotiating the UNFCCC. Because of the impact these numbers have had, a lot of attention has been directed towards them. Are they actually

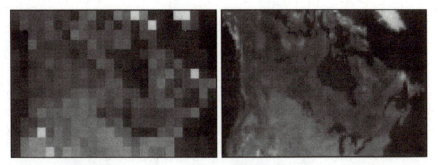

Figure 3.8   Representation of North America in a GCM with 3.75° latitude x 3.75° longitude resolution (*left*), and a RCM with 0.5° latitude x 0.5° longitude resolution (*right*). Graphic courtesy of Hao Le

correct? And most importantly, because the overall magnitude and direction of radiative forcing is the input into GCMs that drives the scenarios of the future, can the uncertainties associated with these numbers be reduced?

Model Resolution

Resolution varies among GCMs and poses a challenge for modellers. But what exactly does "resolution" mean? Figure 3.8 illustrates the difference between coarse resolution and fine resolution for North America. Imagine a map of North America that is out of focus (left) where it is possible to identify the Atlantic Ocean, Hudson Bay, and the Pacific Ocean but for which the other features are more difficult to see. Now compare this with the fine resolution map (right), and more details appear. The new map then begins to look like what it is supposed to. Not only do we see the oceans, but we can even point out some of the larger lakes, such as the Great Lakes, Great Slave Lake, and Great Bear Lake. The differences in topography are discernible as well. The first map is an illustration of coarse resolution, whereas the second map is an illustration of fine resolution. Whether modellers will ever get to very fine resolutions for a GCM is uncertain, but the hope is that regional climate models (RCMs) will produce this kind of resolution.

What does an individual data point from a global climate model represent? How much land and/or water surface area would be in a single data point? As mentioned previously, not all GCMs are created equal, and they therefore all use different resolutions. Most GCMs currently have resolutions around 3.5° latitude by 3.5° longitude, which is equivalent to

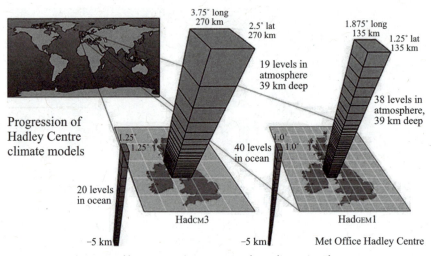

Figure 3.9   Schematic of how a GCM represents a three-dimensional space.
Source: © British Crown copyright 2007, the Met Office. Graphic courtesy of the Met Office

400 km x 400 km in the mid-latitudes. This means that one grid cell would represent 160,000 km². This would also apply to layers of the ocean and the upper atmosphere. Figure 3.9 illustrates the difference in resolution between two models produced by the Hadley Centre in the United Kingdom. The coarse-scaled AOGCM, an older model named HadCM3, has much larger grid sizes than the newer model, named HADGEM1. Smaller grid sizes enable the modeller to provide a more detailed landscape, including variations in elevation and land cover within relatively small regions. It is also easier to explicitly include a larger number of lakes, many of which cannot be seen in the coarse-scaled models. These finer details should improve the results of model simulations of many climate indicators, such as precipitation and soil moisture. Also, the additional number of layers in the upper atmosphere and ocean offers a better opportunity to model clouds and variations in horizontal and vertical transport of heat. The choice of resolution therefore has implications for the accuracy of climate predictions.

Modellers need to include changes in land features, elevation, and vegetation and to incorporate changes in the composition of the atmosphere, but coarser resolutions do not differentiate between these features very well. The atmosphere has to be divided into different layers because what is happening near the ground is different from what is happening at higher elevations. Some models use only a few layers, while others use up to thirty layers. The higher the resolution, the better a model can represent clouds at different elevations, which is important for climate predictions.

As for the resolution of the ocean surfaces and depths, different models again exhibit a wide range of grid sizes. Modellers have to specify the percentage of each grid that is land or ocean. They also have to specify a number to represent the grid's reflectivity, as well as its vegetation (forest, grass, desert, and so on). When a grid is very big, it starts to encompass land, ocean, and possibly ice, and it then becomes difficult to say that the result is very accurate. This is a big dilemma that modellers have to contend with.

One might ask why modellers do not simply add more grids to create a finer resolution surface for their GCMs. Unfortunately, doing so begins to challenge computer capabilities for processing such large data sets. For current GCM resolutions, the largest supercomputers in the world are required to run the models. To get predictions for a hundred or more years of simulation, if it took the computer a day to process one day of simulation, we would not live to see the result. Aggregation through using larger grid sizes allows the GCM to simulate a single day in just a few minutes, but when the grid is divided further, the time required to compute the simulation increases by much more than a few minutes.

When the resolution for a GCM is coarse, then not only are there problems in the representation of land surface features, but there are significant implications for the resulting temperature and moisture parameters in a particular grid. For example, each of the large grids becomes represented by a single elevation value, which in a global climate sense could be acceptable as far as temperature is concerned. Such generalized values, however, have already been demonstrated to be inaccurate with respect to rainfall (for example, see figure 3.10). In addition, land cover patterns are distorted as a result of using coarser resolution. For example, much of the Florida panhandle would be represented as completely ocean, while all of James Bay would be represented as completely land, simply because of where the GCM's grid boundaries happen to be. These problems are difficult to resolve, but in the absence of any feasible global-scale alternatives, some modellers are looking at regional climate models (RCMs) as potential solutions.

An RCM is created by embedding a model of a smaller region within a GCM, making the GCM the boundary condition. In other words, the larger-scale estimates of temperature, precipitation, cloud, and other factors are all defined by what the larger model dictates, but the additional

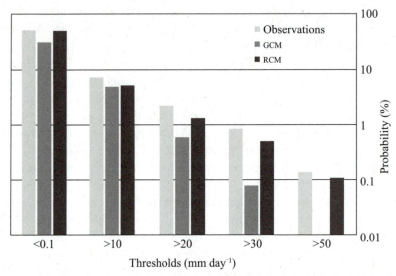

Figure 3.10   Example of simulations showing the probability of winter days in the Alps with different thresholds of daily rainfall, as observed, simulated by a 300 km resolution GCM, and simulated by a 50 km resolution RCM.
Source: Houghton (2004). Reprinted with permission of the Met Office, John Houghton, and Cambridge University Press

calculations, through a process known as downscaling, can account for a much finer topography. Lakes, mountains, and valleys become visible, but the results depend on whatever scale the external model was set at to begin with (Houghton 2004). In the long run, the RCM research groups are trying to make the RCM model windows as big as possible. In Canada, for example, Environment Canada and the Ouranos Consortium have produced the Canadian Regional Climate Model, which provides model simulations for North America (Plummer et al. 2006). Focusing on one country is the compromise between creating fine-resolution scenario data sets for certain regions of the world and not having any.

How does the difference between RCM and GCM simulations affect climate impacts studies? An interesting example from the American Midwest looked at outcomes for a particular crop yield study (Mearns et al. 1999). The yield differences resulting from the GCM and RCM simulations for the EPIC corn yield model are shown in figure 3.11. The GCM used was the CSIRO model, and the RCM was the RegCM, which was run using the larger-scale conditions already simulated by the CSIRO GCM. This means that both sets of corn yield estimates were obtained using the

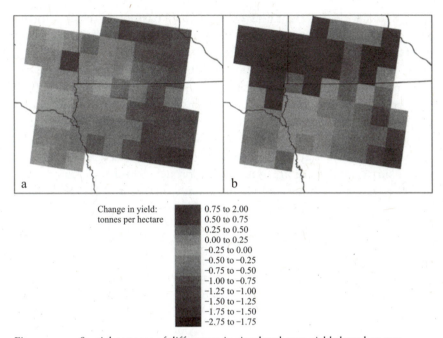

Change in yield:
tonnes per hectare

0.75 to 2.00
0.50 to 0.75
0.25 to 0.50
0.00 to 0.25
−0.25 to 0.00
−0.50 to −0.25
−0.75 to −0.50
−1.00 to −0.75
−1.25 to −1.00
−1.50 to −1.25
−1.75 to −1.50
−2.75 to −1.75

Figure 3.11   Spatial patterns of differences in simulated corn yields based on two
different climate change scenarios for northwest Iowa and surrounding states;
(a) course-resolution GCM and (b) fine-resolution RCM.
Source: Mearns et al. (1999). Graphic courtesy of Linda Mearns and Larry McDaniel

same GCM and the same crop yield model. The only difference lay in the
resolution of the GCM outputs that were applied to the crop yield model.
Results in the map on the left are from the GCM in its original coarse resolution (a). On the right, an RCM of finer resolution (b) was embedded
in the coarse GCM. Under coarse resolution, there is a crop yield loss in
the eastern part of the study area and a crop yield gain in the west. Under fine resolution, however, there were large yield increases in the
north. The same global climate model and the same GHG emission scenario were used both times: the only difference was that the second
model used the regional outputs.

How much of an improvement is achieved by using an RCM? The RCM
can give a better picture than would be given by a coarse resolution for
this part of the North American map. The implications for the ability of
impacts researchers to arrive at a damage report are huge. Impacts researchers are consumers of climate model outputs, and they need some
guidance on which ones should be used. Perhaps the preference would be

for fine resolution, but right now we lack a firm basis upon which to make a judgment. In the meantime, the accuracy of GCM results is tested by comparing simulated current climate patterns with observed climate patterns, because one cannot test the accuracy of simulations of future climate patterns. For now, modellers compare many GCM simulations for the same GHG emission scenarios, in order to see if there is some consensus. As more RCMs are developed, a similar process of inter-model comparison will emerge.

There are other ways to create scenarious with finer resolution besides using RCMs: there are statistical approaches and topographic approaches as well. While each one has its advantages and disadvantages, there is no consensus on the best method to use.

Clouds and Precipitation

Clouds and their resulting precipitation patterns are influenced by humidity, atmospheric stability, and wind direction. These influences, in turn, are affected by location, topography, vegetation, surface (land or water) temperatures, and the amount of condensation nuclei (natural or anthropogenic) in the atmosphere. Figure 3.12 illustrates that improvements in modelling technologies have not resolved various uncertainties associated with modelling clouds. Indeed, there is no consensus among the various models illustrated. The solid line labelled OBS (for "observed") shows current observed cloud distributions by latitude from satellite records. These observations show relatively high amounts of cloud directly over the equator and lower amounts in the tropics and in the northern hemisphere, where there are some arid climates, such as the Sahara Desert. When assessing model outputs for future cloud distributions, GCM researchers look to see if the outputs for the current climate match current satellite observations. Unfortunately, there is little agreement. In many locations, and especially in the southern hemisphere, the models underestimate current cloud cover. Many models also underestimate the real cloud cover in the tropics, but then overestimate it in the high latitudes, particularly for the southern hemisphere. Although it does not appear that these models were able to accurately simulate cloudiness, the results from this 1999 comparison actually represented an improvement over earlier simulations, especially in the mid-latitudes. The benefit of inter-model comparison is that it offers an important learning experience that can enable modellers to find ways to improve their models. This particular example from the Atmospheric Model Intercomparison Project, or AMIP (Gates et al. 1999), which included

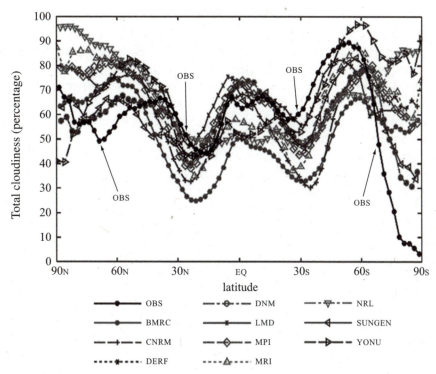

Figure 3.12 Comparison of zonally averaged December-February cloudiness simulated by ten GCMs, compared with observed data (indicated by "OBS") from the International Satellite Cloud Climatology Project. BMRC = Bureau of Meteorology Research Centre, Melbourne, Australia; CNRM = Centre National de Recherches Météorologiques, Toulouse, France; DERF = Dynamic Extended Range Forecasting, GFDL, Princeton, NJ; DNM = Department of Numerical Mathematics, Moscow, Russia; LMD = Laboratoire de Météorologie Dynamique, Paris; MPI = Max Planck Institute for Meteorology, Hamburg, Germany; MRI = Meteorological Research Institute, Tsukuba, Japan; NRL = Naval Research Laboratory, Monterey, CA; SUNGEN = model produced by University of Albany, State University of New York–Albany, NCAR, Boulder, CO; YONU = Yonsei University, Seoul, South Korea.
Source: Gates et al. (1999). Adapted from graphic provided by the American Meteorological Society

models with specified (or pre-set) ocean conditions, laid the groundwork for the Coupled Model Intercomparison Project, or CMIP, which assessed newer models with dynamic oceans, meaning that ocean conditions were not pre-set before model simulations were carried out (Covey et al. 2004). Coordination of common model experiments supported by a central archive for model results provided a long-term learning opportunity for the development of coupled atmosphere-ocean models.

Because it is very difficult to accurately predict cloud cover and because different GCMs therefore make different cloud pattern predictions, the precipitation results from various GCMs also differ. Consequently, for the same GHG emissions scenario, there could be different precipitation scenarios for each of the GCMs, including differences in projected directions of change.

Figure 3.13 (upper panel) shows precipitation scenarios for British Columbia produced from two different GCMs. The CGCM2 maps are from the Canadian GCM, version 2. The HadCM3 maps are from the UK-based Hadley climate model, version 3. The precipitation scenarios are for different time slices, labelled in the figure as the 2020s (2010–39), 2050s (2040–69), and the 2080s (2070–99). In each succeeding time slice, CO_2 concentrations have continued to increase. So, in the Canadian GCM, there is a small increase in the 2020s for southwest British Columbia, which increases further over time. In the Hadley model, there is an initial decrease, which is maintained until near the end of the time frame, when it then increases slightly. In the northeast part of the province, the Hadley model predicts an extremely wet scenario, but the Canadian model predicts only a slightly wet scenario. These differences illustrate that even if they use a common location and a common GHG emission scenario, different climate models can produce very different precipitation scenarios.

GCMs can also produce different temperature predictions because the temperature estimate obtained from a climate model is not divorced from the precipitation estimate. If a model tends to be too dry in its estimates during the summer, then the model will probably overestimate summer temperatures. If the model tends to be too wet in its estimates, then the model will probably underestimate temperatures. Fortunately, there tends to be less of a discrepancy between models in the case of temperature predictions (figure 3.13, lower panel). Both the CGCM2 and the HadCM3 models for British Columbia show approximately the same scenarios of change. Initially, there is virtually no change in temperature, up to the 2020s. Warming begins to emerge sooner in the Canadian model than in the Hadley model, and by the 2080s, the Canadian model shows warmer conditions than the Hadley model. Thus, both models indicate warming, but the Canadian model predicts warmer temperatures than the Hadley model. The Hadley model's relatively wetter precipitation predictions are likely the reason why that model predicts temperatures that are not nearly as warm as the Canadian model's predictions.

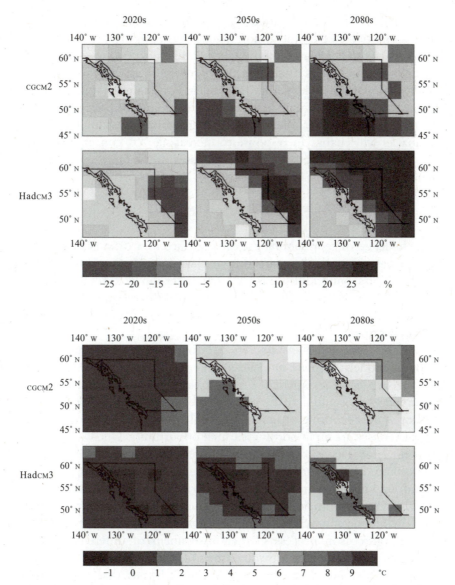

Figure 3.13 Representation of projected changes in precipitation (*upper panel*) and temperature (*lower panel*) in British Columbia, Canada, for two GCMs.
Source: Graphic courtesy of Elaine Barrow

The effects of different cloud types on the amount of radiation absorbed and reflected by the atmosphere are also important. These kinds of feedbacks depend on cloud height, cloud thickness, the size of the particles within clouds (including the presence of ice crystals), and the amount of water vapour within the clouds. For example, it is estimated that cloud radiative forcing increases as the amount of precipitable water increases. However, there is no consensus on how cloud radiative feedbacks will change in response to increasing CO_2 concentrations in the atmosphere, and this is one of the causes of the large spread in climate model sensitivity (Stocker 2001).

The Land-Surface "Bucket"

The challenge of representing the land surface in a GCM is made difficult in part because there are different ways of representing what a "bucket" of ground looks like and how water moves through it. To illustrate this, it is instructive to look at model intercomparison studies by Henderson-Sellers (1996) and Pitman et al. (1999) on soil moisture bucket routines.

Model intercomparisons are very helpful in assisting scientists in developing models. Climate modellers make these comparisons as part of the ongoing learning experience. Some observers are concerned that intercomparisons could actually result in a consensus on the wrong solution or in an anchoring of modelling results that may be incorrect, but these exercises are an important learning opportunity. One way to think of them is as raising the floor, rather than as racing to the bottom. There should be a professional standard across the modelling community around how climate models are constructed, so that the best way to model clouds and other aspects of the climate system can be found. The work by Henderson-Sellers (1996) and Pitman et al. (1999) followed a similar comparison process in their assessment of different ways of modelling water movement through the soil.

Figure 3.14 shows the different bucket schemes that were tested (Henderson-Sellers 1996) and illustrates the features that make all these buckets so different. The first thing to notice is that different numbers of soil layers are assumed in each model. Subsequent comparisons of a larger set of models (Pitman et al. 1999) indicate that models also have different numbers of canopy layers. Any models that do not assume the presence of one or more canopy layers above the ground would not be able to treat the interception of precipitation by plant leaves or needles. Other features that vary between buckets are the number of soil layers

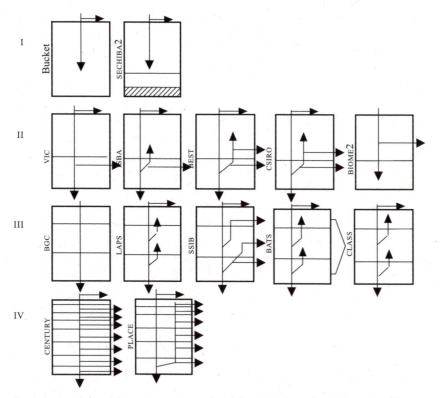

Figure 3.14   Schematic representations of runoff and drainage for land surface schemes in different soil moisture bucket models. I = single-layer models; II = two-layer models; III = three-layer models; IV = multi-layer models. For model names, see list of abbreviations and acronyms.
Source: Henderson-Sellers (1996). Reprinted with permission of Ann Henderson-Sellers and Elsevier Limited

(represented in the figure by horizontal lines), soil layer depths, and the variation in the sub-models that are used. For example, within the field of microclimatology, several models are available to estimate evapotranspiration, soil and air temperature, and soil moisture (see Pitman et al. 1999 for more information). To understand why different bucket schemes produce different results for the same site at the same time, it is important to appreciate that these schemes have different structures and theoretical foundations, which explains why there is no consensus among model results.

At the simplest conceptual level, a bucket of soil has only one large layer. Some water flows on the surface as runoff, while the rest is absorbed straight into the ground, without any horizontal movement in the soil. This process is referred to as infiltration, a concept that is very easy to model but that is also very unrealistic. Another relatively simple version of the bucket is the single-layer model with a defined bottom, below which water does not penetrate. Water from the surface infiltrates to a certain depth (represented by the arrow), but then goes no further. In the two-layer models, the water can move in both layers and may actually come back up towards the surface, as water is withdrawn by plants. One example of a two-layer model is the variable infiltration capacity (VIC) model. The bucket used for that model includes some run-off, and the rest of the water infiltrates down to a lower layer. Water can also move horizontally, and some of it can also percolate down to a deeper layer to become groundwater. However, water does not move back towards the surface in this model.

Other two-layer buckets are more complex. With the BEST model, water can move horizontally in both layers and can be drawn by plant roots back up to the surface. In three-layer models, water can move in three layers, and in multi-layer models, such as CENTURY and PLACE, it can move in up to eight layers. With each addition of a layer to the soil, the model grows bigger and more complex.

In Henderson-Sellers' (1996) intercomparison, all the bucket schemes were tested using the same climatic and soil conditions. One indicator for comparison between models was how the amount of energy used to heat the air, which is called sensible heat, compared with the amount of energy used to evapotranspire water (known as latent heat). This comparison draws on information from the energy budget that we discussed earlier in this chapter. After short-wave solar energy is lost as a result of reflection and scattering by the atmosphere and the earth's surface, the remaining net radiation will be used primarily for sensible heat or latent heat. If the model predicts too much moisture for a particular case, then not enough energy will be left to heat the air to the correct temperature, and the model will then underestimate the temperature. But if there is not enough moisture, there will be too much energy left to heat the air, and the model will overestimate temperature. These possibilities illustrate how simulation errors in one aspect of climate may affect another.

Henderson-Sellers compared a range of soil moisture bucket routines in the same location, and organized a model intercomparison workshop at Macquarie University in Sydney, Australia. Figure 3.15 shows the comparison of latent and sensible heat from these tests. The BEST and CSIRO9 models show latent heat flux around 60 W per square meter, compared with sensible heat flux around 20 W per square meter. The

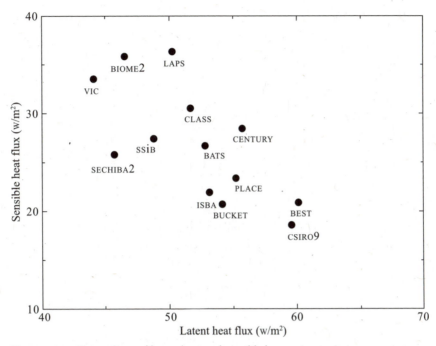

Figure 3.15 Comparison of latent heat and sensible heat estimates in watts per square metre (Wm⁻²).

Source: Henderson-Sellers (1996). Reprinted with permission of Ann Henderson-Sellers and Elsevier Limited

ratio of sensible heat flux to latent heat flux is thus about 1:3. The VIC model shows a sensible heat flux of about 35 W per square meter and a latent heat flux of about 45 W per square meter, which is a ratio of 4:5. These results illustrate that different soil moisture buckets will obtain different results even if the same location is modelled. And of course, if any of these buckets were embedded in a GCM, they would also likely affect temperature and moisture simulations.

Several years after the original model intercomparison, Pitman et al. (1999) continued to compare the models for two different sites: a forest site and a grass site (figure 3.16). And again, as in figure 3.15, the ratios between the amount of latent heat flux and the amount of sensible heat flux can be compared. Results for the forest site indicate that sensible heat flux is between 10 and 20 W per square metre and that latent heat flux is around 110 to 130 W per square metre. Thus, the ratio of sensible heat flux to latent heat flux is around 1:6 for this forest site. This ratio suggests that in a healthy forest canopy during the growing season, most

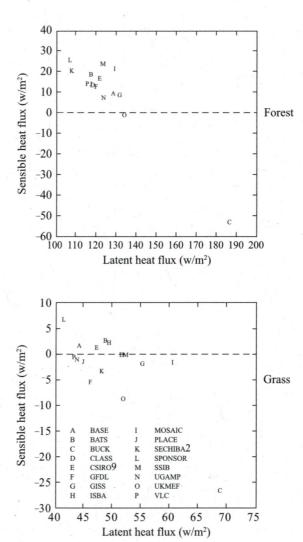

Figure 3.16 (*left*)

Figure 3.16   Comparison of latent heat and sensible heat estimates for a forest and a grass site (*left*), in watts per square metre (wm⁻²), and root zone soil water (mm) for different models at a forest site (*right*). For model names, see list of abbreviations and acronyms.

Source: Pitman et al. (1999). Reprinted with permission of Andy Pitman and Springer Science and Business Media

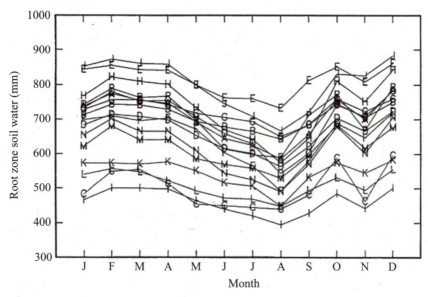

Figure 3.16 (*right*)

of the energy will be used to evapotranspire water, and only a small amount will be used to heat the air. In the case of the grass site, both fluxes are of smaller magnitude. For some bucket schemes, however, sensible heat flux is actually negative, which means that instead of energy being used to heat the air, there is actually some cooling, with perhaps some energy flux directed at the underlying soil. Thus, very different energy balance situations are represented by the various buckets for the same site and time.

Overall, this experiment reveals more disagreement among the models for the grass site than for the forest site. One particular model, the BUCK model, labelled "c," which lacked an overlying plant canopy, even showed results that were drastically different from the others. In other words, bucket c was a complete outlier for both sites. Nevertheless, one would hope that these kinds of tests would eventually lead to some consensus about the best structure for the buckets.

The right-hand panel in figure 3.16, also from Pitman et al. (1999), shows model results for root zone soil moisture that vary from a low of 500 mm of water in the root zone to a high of 800 mm for the same location and time. The importance of these differences emerges when GCMs are used directly for computations of regional-scale surface runoff and evapotranspiration, as Wood et al. (1998) illustrate in a case study

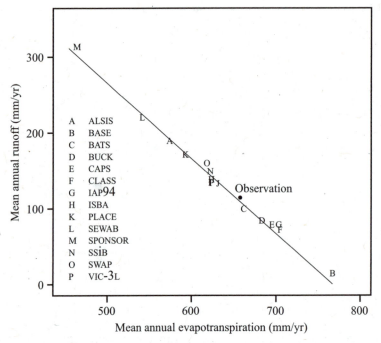

Figure 3.17   Comparison of runoff and evapotranspiration for Arkansas–Red River system, 1980–86. For model names, see list of abbreviations and acronyms.
Source: Wood et al. (1998). Reprinted with permission from Elsevier Limited

of the Arkansas–Red River system (figure 3.17). Some buckets result in an overprediction of runoff by 50 percent or more, while others underpredict runoff, which leads to overestimates of evapotranspiration.

Summary of Climate Model Issues

In this section, we have examined several challenges for climate models, including radiative forcing, model resolution, clouds and precipitation, and the land surface bucket.

Downscaling can be achieved in a simple or a complex manner. It would be easy to take just a few grid points, retrieve the grid values for a climate parameter (such as temperature), draw isolines (lines of equal value) between the grid points, and to insert estimated values between the points, but this procedure is likely to result in very large errors, especially where the region of interest includes complex terrain, such as mountain ranges. Statistical methods are available for downscaling, methods in which large-scale climate variables can be correlated with regional or local variables. However, this approach depends on the availability of local data, and it is difficult to know how well a statistical relationship based on observations would apply to a changed climate.

Downscaling with RCMs appears to show some promise, but it must be remembered that RCMs depend on the global-scale climate models they are embedded in. If a GCM has errors in representing physical processes within an individual grid, the RCM will not overcome these errors. But since the RCM may have a resolution of 50 km, say, compared with the GCM resolution of 300 km or more, an RCM can represent more detailed climate patterns and account for the topography masked by the larger GCM grid.

Precipitation projections will continue to be very uncertain until a better way is found to represent clouds, not only the formation of different types of clouds but also the distribution of clouds over space and time. The applications of different land surface bucket schemes have resulted in different estimates of soil moisture and energy budgets and, ultimately, of surface runoff following rain and snowmelt events. Many of the schemes tested by Pitman et al. (1999) underpredicted soil moisture during the growing season. There are big differences in how well these schemes perform under different surfaces. Also, the tests did not account for CO_2 enrichment. This topic will be explored further in chapter 5, but for now it should be noted that CO_2 enrichment can significantly affect water use by plants, which will then affect the performance of the land surface buckets.

It is important to note that these inter-model comparisons laid the ground for more recent efforts to improve the way various climate processes are modelled. Land surface models have been upgraded in recent years, with improvements to the representation of runoff and soil moisture (Randall et al. 2007). This is, however, a long-term learning process, and there will continue to be challenges in being able to better incorporate land surface processes and other considerations in the next generation of climate models.

EMISSION SCENARIOS

In order for climate modellers to produce scenarios of future human-induced climate change, they need input from the energy community that describes how emissions may change in the future. Initially, in the 1980s, climate modellers did not use emissions scenarios. Instead, they

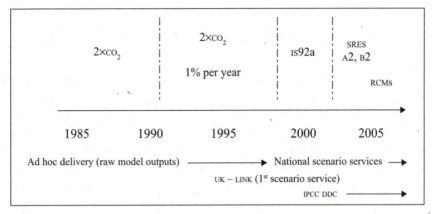

Figure 3.18   Evolution of climate change scenarios and scenario delivery. UK-LINK refers to climate scenario program at the University of East Anglia in the United Kingdom. IPCC DDC is the Data Distribution Center of the IPCC

used what were known as equilibrium scenarios. A step change in CO_2 concentration was assumed to take place sometime in the future, so that after concentrations had been held constant for a time at a level representing pre–Industrial Revolution conditions (around 300 ppm), there would be a sudden change to another concentration, often a doubling to around 600 ppm. The GCM would then simulate climate conditions for a hundred years at 600 ppm. These $2\times CO_2$ equilibrium scenarios represented the state of the art during the 1980s. Until about 1993, any impacts studies using GCM simulations were based on them, even though they did not actually represent the way that the atmosphere was expected to change. But they did provide the easiest way to model the changes at that time.

Figure 3.18 illustrates the transition of scenarios from the 1980s to the present. In the 1990s, transient scenarios became available. Climate modellers wanted to produce a time series, rather than a static period average, so they assumed a gradual change in emissions over time. This change was initially somewhat arbitrary and was usually set at a 1 percent increase in CO_2 per year. These transient scenarios could still have been wrong, of course, but they were at least closer to a more realistic representation of future changes in CO_2 concentrations. Recent observations at Mauna Loa indicate that concentrations are increasing at annual rates up to 0.7 percent, a percentage that is higher than observed annual increases during the 1960s and 1970s (data available at http://www.esrl.noaa.gov/gmd/ccgg/trends/).

Within transient scenarios there was a difference between cold-start and warm-start scenarios. With cold-start transient scenarios, the modeller would record all the information from the beginning of the simulation. Consequently, the scenario was not yet simulating the current climate before the start of the simulation with increased radiative forcing. With a warm start, the model would already have been running for many years, in order to simulate the current climate first. At this point, the emissions scenario would be inserted, thereby gradually changing the radiative forcing as the concentration of GHGs increased. Models with warm starts are more difficult, because the model must be run for a longer period, which requires a lot more computer time. However, warm start modelling is still becoming the standard practice.

Nowadays, there are emissions scenarios based on assumptions of economic growth or other development storylines. Thus, instead of assuming an arbitrary 1 percent increase of CO_2 concentrations per year, modellers follow an emissions scenario path based on one of these storylines. The first GHG emissions scenarios were in the IS92 series, which was shortly followed by the SRES series (Nakicenovic and Swart 2000). As climate modelling has evolved, the standard practice has now become one in which simulations use warm starts and emissions scenarios like those in SRES. The equilibrium experiments and incremental 1 percent CO_2 increases per year are no longer offered as scenarios: the storylines for these new GHG emissions scenarios are a little more sophisticated. We return to them in more detail in chapters 8 and 11, but because they are important in both climate science and climate impacts research, we will take an introductory look at them now.

Very different approaches are used to construct these two different sets of scenarios (Nakicenovic and Swart 2000). The IS92 scenarios were based on projections in population growth originating from the World Bank or the United Nations. They assumed an economic growth rate that was parallel to population growth, as well as to the energy supply scenarios (e.g., the availability of oil, gas, and nuclear power). IS92 included an emission reduction policy, but not a climate change policy. Since IS92 predates the Kyoto Protocol, it could not have anticipated what a climate change policy like Kyoto would contain.

Several years later, a different approach was taken in creating the SRES scenarios. They were generated from a set of stories that described the relationships between market forces and political forces that drive emissions. At first glance, the SRES scenarios do not look very different from the IS92 scenarios. Upon further examination, however, it becomes

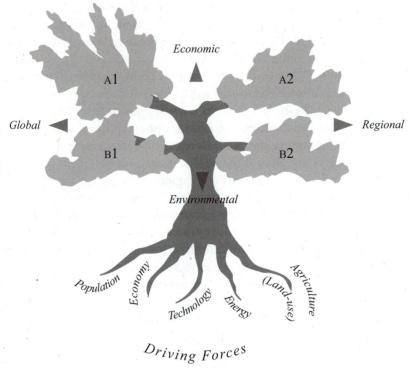

Figure 3.19   SRES storylines.
Source: Nakicenovic and Swart (2000). Reprinted with permission of IPCC

apparent that the scenarios differ in the way they were created and in the trajectory the emissions projections follow. In other words, the IS92 scenarios look more like straight-line extrapolations, but the SRES scenarios look more complex, with increasing and decreasing trends. The scenarios differ because SRES incorporates stories of economic and social changes for large regions of the world and IS92 does not. However, SRES scenarios still provide a highly aggregated view, as was the case with IS92, and the SRES stories still do not include any specific climate change policy.

Figure 3.19 illustrates the SRES storylines. The A2 family represents the regional economic imperatives (the economy is more important than the environment), while the B2 family represents the regional environmental imperatives (an environment-economy balance). Both the A1 and the B1 families are more globally oriented (see chapters 8 and 11). What first resulted from those storylines was a series of CO_2 emissions scenarios, with the worst cases being one of the A1 global imperatives (Fossil Fuel Intensive – A1FI) and one of the A2 regional economic imperatives. They both predicted CO_2 emissions of 30 Gt per year by 2100, compared to the current annual emission rate of 6 Gt per year. In contrast to these worst cases are the B1 imperatives, which apply a global approach or vision of sustainability, including increased efficiency and more use of renewable energy and other low-emission energy sources. This imperative predicts a future world with CO_2 emissions that are almost the same as what they are now, without the implementation of a specific climate policy. The IS92 scenarios, or the business-as-usual scenarios from ten years ago, lie somewhere in the middle, between these worst and best cases.

After deciding on which emissions scenario to use in a model run, an energy modeller converts an emission to an atmospheric concentration, which is done in cooperation with the atmospheric modellers. This conversion produces future estimates of CO_2 concentrations, which are in turn converted into radiative forcing estimates and then used as inputs into GCMs, to produce climate change scenarios. Differences in the climate predictions arise from the large differences in CO_2 concentrations between scenarios. Emission concentrations range from 500 ppm for the B1 case to about 950 ppm in the A1FI case.

Figure 3.20 shows all the SRES simulations, as well as projections for a scenario of constant concentrations at 2000 level. There is a huge range of possible emissions futures that do not reflect possible climate policy measures or the uncertainty of climate models. These emissions scenarios are related to uncertainties in predicting future development paths worldwide.

The global-warming issue has created a global marketplace for GHG-based climate scenarios. It is understood that they need to be simple enough to obtain so that impacts researchers, policy analysts, and other non-climate researchers can use the scenarios to look at issues like adaptation, impacts, vulnerability, and mitigation. The scenarios themselves, however, must make sense from a climate perspective. Arbitrary temperature and precipitation numbers cannot be used if they make no sense to the climatologist. Best practice would suggest that a scenario should be chosen from within a range of projections that have been established through recognized scientific activities and review. It is unlikely that an impact study will be based on a 10°C global-warming scenario, because this scenario has not been produced. The worst case for the globe as a whole, A1FI, is up to 6°C warmer by 2100. An

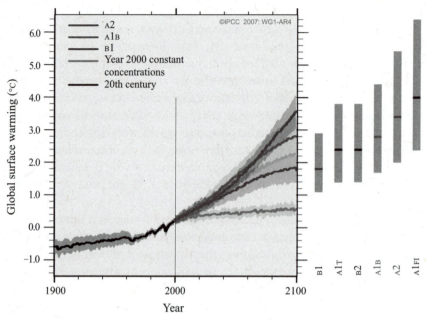

Figure 3.20   Global temperature scenarios. The vertical bars show the range of projected temperature changes for climate model simulations for the indicated SRES scenario. See figure 3.19. A1T = A1 world with application of advanced technologies with reduced carbon emissions. A1B = A1 world with balance of fossil fuel and advanced technologies. A1FI = A1 world with fossil-intensive technologies.
Source: IPCC (2007c). Reprinted with permission of IPCC

impacts researcher can arbitrarily choose which climate models and emission scenarios to use, but the existing range should serve as the boundary for this selection. Current practice tends towards selecting both a high-and a low-emission scenario, so that the researcher is able to describe uncertainties in terms of impacts, not just temperature.

THE ALTERNATIVE CLIMATE CHANGE SCENARIOS

It is important to remember that climate models produce climate information based on the changes in emissions derived from the emissions scenarios that they consume. A climate model does not produce an emissions scenario. The climate model requires the emissions scenario in order to produce a climate scenario. Different sets of researchers with different sets of data inputs produce GHG emissions scenarios, and their simulation outputs are measured in gigatonnes. The climate modellers then have to determine how this change in the concentration of CO_2 in the atmosphere will affect the climate. The key input here is radiative forcing, and the choice of GHG emissions scenarios is one of several key challenges for climate modellers.

Consumers of climate model information are likely to want information that is similar to what would be available from a typical weather station. A climate model could provide this information for intervals as small as a few minutes, but the amount of data would be enormous. A simple approach for using GCM outputs is to use monthly anomalies (or differences) from a base case in a climate scenarios database and then to add it to observed data from a local station.

In recent years, the GCM-based scenarios have become the most popular ones for predicting future climates. Now, however, there are new choices to make besides the traditional approach of simple interpolation based on the original outputs of the GCMs. There is the option of statistical downscaling (Wilby and Wigley 1997), as well as the option of using RCMs. It is also possible to do some work directly from an assumption about global mean annual temperature change. However, given the needs of regional- (and national-) scale planners and decision makers, there will probably be a growing demand for RCM outputs for regional impact and policy studies.

Other types of scenarios besides GCMs may be used to predict future climates. Figure 3.21 lists the range of scenario types, including methods used in some of the older impact studies from the 1980s, that are available to predict future climates. One method is to construct analogue cases, which are based on paleoclimatic reconstructions or historical observations. Another method is to construct arbitrary, or synthetic, scenarios.

Parry and Carter (1988) provide an example of a spatial analogue for Saskatchewan, Canada. A region with a current climate that would perhaps look like Saskatchewan's climate fifty years from now might be found farther to the southeast, in the central United States. Let us say that the climate statistics from there represent Saskatchewan's climate in the 2050s. Can a crop study be done using this spatial analogue data set? This method might be of some value, but when the same method was applied to European locations, the analogue for Iceland was northern Scotland, and Leningrad's (now St. Petersburg) future climate was assumed to be similar to the climate of a region near the Black Sea. One problem was that the landscapes in the analogue regions were quite different and included large areas of ocean.

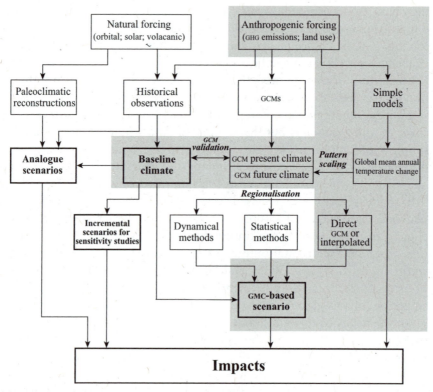

Figure 3.21   Types of climate change scenarios, including sources of data.
Source: Mearns et al. (2001). Reprinted with permission IPCC

Temporal analogues can also include paleoclimate evidence from some fairly warm periods, such as 6000 years BP (before present), which is known as the Climatic Optimum. At that time the earth was probably warmer than it is today. However, the value of paleoclimatic evidence for current predictions is limited because past climatic shifts were not caused by human-induced increases in GHGs, and also unfortunately, paleoclimatology cannot yet provide the resolution needed for regional studies. Furthermore, the quality of the reconstructions is uncertain, and in general, the best data, which come from the fairly recent past, are at the low end of the range of projected warming.

There is, however, a very well-known and important impacts study that was based on an analogue scenario of the North American Dust Bowl of the 1930s. The MINK study (the acronym stands for Missouri, Iowa, Nebraska, and Kansas: Rosenberg 1993) assessed how a Dust

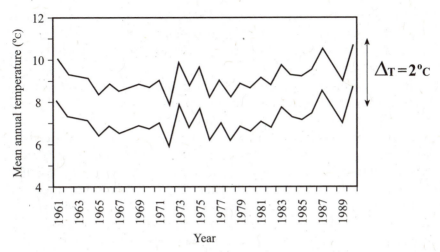

Figure 3.22   Constructing an incremental scenario of a warming of 2°C

Bowl climate would affect the MINK region in the future. Could this warm, dry period be an analogue of future warming? And what would that mean for agricultural production and forestry? In Nebraska in the 1930s the average temperature was 1°C warmer than the current average. In Kansas, it was 0.9°C warmer. What made the Dust Bowl event so important was that the climate was very dry, with reductions in precipitation of about 20 percent for Nebraska and Kansas over the period. In their study, Rosenberg's team could actually compute detailed indicators, like the Palmer drought severity index, because there was a lot of climate information available at the time.

So the advantage of using analogues is that detailed data sets that are physically plausible can be obtained. It is recognized, however, that the Dust Bowl did not result from human-induced GHGs, and generally most of these kinds of climatic deviations from mean conditions are not nearly as large as the ones the climate models have predicted for the future. In general, climatologists would argue that the Dust Bowl scenario is not an analogue, because the forcing was natural and what will change climate in the future is a mixture of both GHG emissions and natural forcings. However, this case does offer a useful experience for impacts research.

Figure 3.22 shows an example of an incremental scenario. The lower line indicates the temperature record for a particular station. To generate a 2°C warming scenario, a modeller would simply add 2°C to each value in the temperature record. The upper line in the figure would then represent a +2°C scenario. This approach results in a future scenario with the same kind of sensitivity and variability that the historical record has, and it can be used to test impact models that concern food, water, fish, or forestry. The advantage of sensitivity scenarios is, of course, that they are very simple, but the disadvantages are that they are quite arbitrary, potentially quite unrealistic, and inconsistent with known uncertainty ranges.

An example of the use of arbitrary, or synthetic, cases is provided by Rosenzweig et al. (1996). This example is about changes in orange yields for four locations in the United States: Los Angeles, Miami, Daytona Beach, and Bakersfield. The study tested how the model of Valencia orange yields responds in different parts of the United States to increases in temperature ranging from 1 to 5°C and to increases in CO_2 concentrations ranging from present concentration levels to an almost doubled concentration level. CO_2 was included because of the issues surrounding the effects of CO_2 enrichment on crop yields which include potential changes in crop water use efficiency, crop yield and nutrient value of crop biomass (see chapter 5). In this case orange yields were projected to increase at higher levels of CO_2 concentration but would decrease with elevation of temperature.

CHOOSING A SCENARIO

From the earlier discussion of GCMs and the problems associated with analogue cases and incremental cases, it can be seen that perhaps GCMs are the best option for predicting future climate scenarios. However, there are still problems with these models. They are not accurate at the regional scale, especially with precipitation simulations. As well, different GCMs give different climate information, making it difficult to express a high level of confidence in the results. While it is expensive to run many climate change experiments using many different scenarios, it is prudent to use more than one, so as to offer some indication of the range of potential impacts projections.

How does one choose a climate change scenario? Global-scale patterns show some similarities, such as high latitude warming being greater than tropical warming throughout the twenty-first century (figure 3.23). But regional-scale patterns can show large differences between scenarios. One suggestion is to look at the range of possible scenarios that are available in the region of interest. These scenarios can be shown in a scatterplot (figure 3.24). From this range of scenarios for

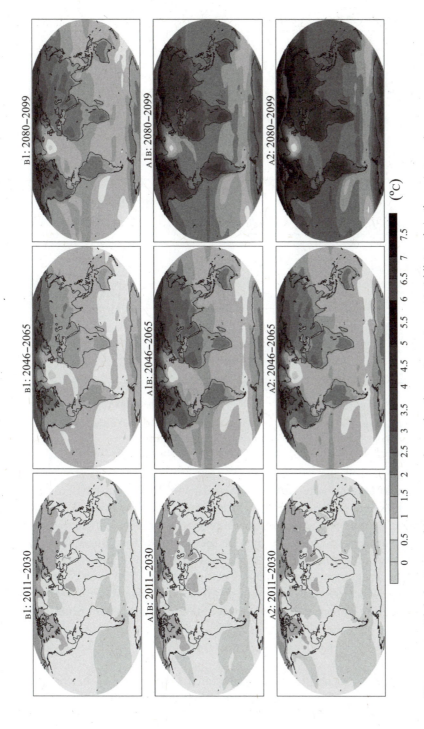

Figure 3.23 Global patterns of temperature change for the B1 (upper), A1B (middle) and A2 (lower) scenarios.
Source: Meehl et al. (2007). Reprinted with permission from IPCC

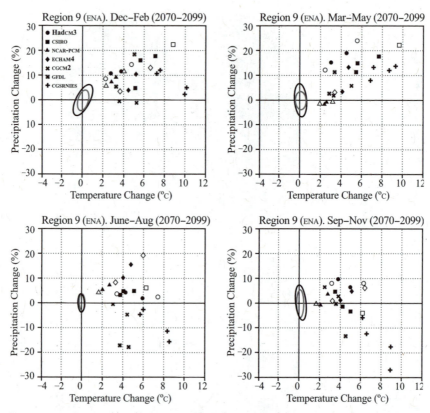

Figure 3.24   Scatterplots showing GCM-based scenarios for eastern North America
(ENA). For model names, see list of abbreviations and acronyms.
Source: Ruosteenoja et al. (2003). Reprinted with permission from Tim Carter

a particular location, one can then choose a subset of scenarios that represent the range of the larger set. For example, one can choose a warm, dry case, a cooler, wet case, and perhaps one representing median conditions. The impacts cases can then be presented for this range. Adding to this selection are scenarios produced by RCMs. An example from the Canadian RCM, CRCM4.1, is shown in figure 3.25. This is still a relatively new information product, but it offers a higher-resolution data set for application in regional-scale impact and adaptation assessments.

DISCUSSION

This chapter has described the current state of knowledge of the climate science aspects of global warming, including what is known about the

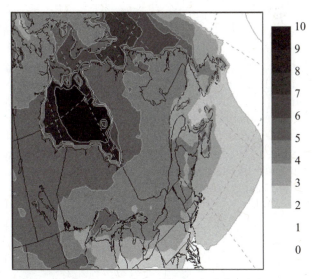

Figure 3.25   Regional scenario of projected change in daily minimum temperature for December-February for eastern Canada, 2041–70, from the Canadian Regional Climate Model, CRCM 4.1.1. The CRCM time series has been generated and supplied by Ouranos Climate Simulations Team. The map has been produced by the Canadian Climate Change Scenarios Network, Environment Canada. Graphic provided by Philippe Gachon and Milka Radojevic

effects of GHGs on the atmosphere, uncertainties regarding climate models, and uncertainties concerning projections of future GHG emissions. The key issues here are the estimate of radiative forcing, the importance of radiative forcing in determining temperature, and the role of different GHGs, including water vapour, in this forcing, as well as the potential cooling effect of sulphates. Because there is less certainty about the effect of sulphates, the focus is still mostly on CO_2, CH_4, and other GHGs, the radiative forcing these GHGs produce, and how this forcing drives climate change.

There does at least seem to be a strong consensus that observed climate trends have been affected by GHGs already, so that the climate is no longer entirely natural. But few scientists would attribute any particular climatic event, such as a drought or a heat wave (or a severe storm), to global warming alone. There is also a consensus that at present there are no alternatives to using GCMs to predict future climate change, although at some point, RCMs will be more useful for regional-scale studies. For now, however, the uncertainties concerning precipitation, clouds, and downscaling must be recognized in the development of scenarios.

The models and the climate predictions also depend on what the energy-modelling community can say about emissions. But because there is a wide range of emissions scenarios, climate scenarios will continue to diverge, regardless of any potential convergence in climate modelling. This problem will affect the results of any impacts studies and any attempts to come up with a climate change damage report and adaptation or mitigation assessments. It is therefore imperative that while climate and emissions scenarios continue to be developed, impact studies are carried out using a range of possible scenarios, so that researchers and modellers can learn of the sensitivity of watersheds, ecosystems, health systems, and national economies to global warming.

4

Impact and Adaptation Assessment Frameworks

INTRODUCTION

In chapter 3 we saw how atmospheric science provides a picture of past climate trends and future scenarios of human-induced climate change. This information is important because it provides a context for studying the range of climate conditions encountered by past and present societies and for trying to understand how different the future climate may become. But if we want to understand the implications of this change for ecosystems and societies of the future, climate information alone is insufficient. We need to use other forms of knowledge in order to construct a clearer picture of what climate change may mean to the future of our world. In particular, we need to consider the issues of climate-related vulnerability, the potential impacts of climate change scenarios, and the challenges and opportunities of adapting to climate change.

The next four chapters, including this one, cover various aspects of climate change impacts and vulnerability, and of adaptation to those impacts. These subjects are very complex because knowledge from many disciplines is required to assess these factors. Climate scientists can produce pictures of future climates, as we have seen, but those pictures do not also automatically produce a damage scenario report. Knowledge of the climate science aspects of climate change does not easily translate into a clear definition of *dangerous* climate change for ecosystems and economic systems. What level of warming would be safe? Would a warming of 3°c be dangerous for all peoples, or only for some? As we explore this aspect of climate change more deeply, it becomes apparent that defining dangerous climate change is not simply about biological effects or physical effects, because these effects are imposed on societies and communities, which are all in different stages of development. It has been a challenge to see this kind of research effort move towards some sense of interdisciplinary maturity. While we have been seeing some encouraging signs, there are still challenges ahead.

Before examining specific impacts in chapters 5, 6, and 7, let us first consider the impacts research challenge. Box 4.1 provides some brief descriptions of key terms used to describe impacts and adaptation. The assessment of potential damages from projected climate change needs to consider local conditions, including environmental, economic, and social contexts. A climate change impact is a consequence or effect of climate change and may be defined as a change of state resulting from a particular set of new climate statistics (such as higher winter temperatures or lower summer rainfall), but quantifying this change of state will depend, in part, on the current state. For example, the impact of a climate change scenario on corn production, water supplies, fish stocks, transportation, or the incidence of malaria will be influenced by current conditions of production, infrastructure, management, and governance. These conditions vary because of biophysical and socio-economic factors that are unique to each location, thereby creating different situations of risk, opportunity, exposure, vulnerability, and capacity to respond (or "adapt") to change.

The severity of climate impacts is a function of both the climatic event and the level of vulnerability (Kates et al. 1985; Smit and Pilifosova 2001; Glantz 2003). Response strategies can include increasing resilience to climate stresses and improving local capabilities to make good choices (Kellogg and Schware 1981; Kelly and Adger 2000; Lim et al. 2004). Climate impact and adaptation assessment is therefore about more than just the influence of climate. The assessment process is unique (compared with environmental or social-impact assessments) in that it focuses on determining the relative importance of climate variability and change, both with and without adaptation, compared with other factors. The consideration of various factors related to climate change (ecosystem, economic, and social factors) is therefore an explicit part of this process (see chapters 5, 6, and 7).

Next there is the important step of linking the impact assessment process with information about projected climate change. How are outputs from global climate models used to determine the potential effects of climate change scenarios on food, water, ecosystems, economies, places, or peoples? Some generic methodological issues are involved. However, specific applications of climate scenario data sets are challenging for

Box 4.1   Climate Change Impacts and Adaptation Terminology

Adaptation. The act of adjusting practices, processes, or structures of
   systems to projected or actual changes in climate.
Adaptive Capacity. The ability of a system to adjust to climate
   change, variability, and extremes, so as to moderate potential damages, take advantage of opportunities, or cope with consequences.

- Determinants: The internal availability or status of economic resources, equity, information and skills, infrastructure, institutions,
  and technology, etc.
- Levels: The specificity with which adaptive capacity can be dis-
  cused or compared, from systems levels (laws, accountability,
  property rights, markets, etc.) to institutional levels (corporate
  governance, staff, etc.) to individual levels (performance monitoring, skill development, etc.).

Coping Range. The variation in climatic stimuli that a natural or
   human system can absorb without undergoing significant impacts.
Exposure. The nature and degree to which a system is unprotected
   from the effects of changes in climate.
Impact. The consequences or effects of climate change on natural
   and human systems.
Resilience. The ability of a system to recover from the effects of
   climate change; the amount of change a system can withstand
   without changing state.
Sensitivity. The degree to which a system will respond to a change in
   climatic conditions.
Vulnerability. The extent to which climate change may damage or
   harm a system; a function of exposure, sensitivity, and adaptive
   capacity; a component of climate-related risk that is not covered
   by available coping mechanisms and/or adaptation.

Sources: McCarthy et al. (2001a); Lim et al. (2004); Smit and Pilo-
fosova (2003).

individual disciplines because answering these questions tests each discipline's modelling capability. Taking a model or, for that matter, any analytical tool outside its range of calibration and applying it to a climate change problem is not an easy task for many disciplines. And when looking at the social and economic aspects of this problem, the researcher finds that there are already difficulties in predicting the future behaviour of markets, peoples, and governments, even without considering climate change. How can we think about predicting the future with a changed climate when this change is superimposed on other environmental and developmental changes that are occurring?

Of particular interest is the complex topic of adaptation. Adaptation includes both purposeful and planned responses to climate change, as well as reactive responses to recent extreme events, which can provide some insight into the adaptation process. Adaptation is not simply a technical issue of whether the existing engineering or the existing economic infrastructure can incorporate climate change into ongoing operations. Regions and countries differ in their ability to prepare for or respond to a change in climate that is outside their historic experience. The differences may be reflected in the way they deal with extreme events, and their capabilities may change in the future as economies and governments change (see chapters 7 and 11).

It is important to remember that impacts and adaptations are assessed within a policy context. Article 2 of the United Nations Framework Convention on Climate Change (UNFCCC) establishes that the purpose of the convention is to "prevent dangerous anthropogenic interference with the climate system." It is difficult to quantitatively define what constitutes "dangerous" interference, but as we saw in the discussion of the UNFCCC in chapter 2, the convention specifically mentions indicators that would be taken into account when defining dangerous interference. It is assumed that determining the amount of warming (or greenhouse gas concentration) needed to reach a dangerous condition requires researchers to consider the role of existing and future vulnerabilities and adaptation choices. These are local/regional factors: global-scale indicators may hide important details. Global-scale greenhouse gas concentrations are assessed, as we have seen, in terms of future scenarios of climate change, including projections of temperature, precipitation, and sea levels. These projections provide an opportunity to assess different scenarios of emissions growth and policy-related emissions reduction in an aggregated sense, in which global indicators, such as runoff or malaria potential become proxies for indicators of damage to ecosystems and societies. However, the scale is different for the impacts and adaptation assessments themselves, which by necessity incorporate complex local/regional relationships between climate and place. Scaling up from local/regional cases to global assessments of economic and ecologic damage is a very challenging undertaking (as will be seen in chapters 6, 7, and 11).

Organizing the Assessment

Unlike climate science, which can draw on a lengthy history of scholarship within the atmospheric and oceanic sciences, climate change impacts and adaptation research is a relatively new endeavour. One publication in this area, *Climate Impact and Adaptation Assessment* (Parry and Carter 1998), attempts to be a recipe book, in that it lists a series of steps to take to pursue impacts and adaptation research in an organized manner.

The general challenge of climate change is to consider how it will affect different things, what kind of responses may ensue, and how these responses may change established relationships between climate and place. Any planned or reactive form of adaptation will affect this relationship directly, and any GHG mitigation that occurs may create other feedbacks and alter the pattern of climate change itself over space and time. However, development paths themselves may also change the relationship between climate and place. Population growth, land use modifications, technological changes, shifts in international trade, and an evolution (or revolution) in governance can alter how climate-sensitive resources are managed, what techniques are used for resource exploitation, and where communities, large and small, can grow.

Many uncertainties are associated with impacts and adaptation studies. Figure 4.1 illustrates how uncertainty can explode from the initial projections of future emissions, which can lead to various carbon cycle responses, different global climate sensitivities, and regional climate change scenarios, and then to a range of possible impacts. It is easy to feel overwhelmed by cascading uncertainties and to question why anyone would bother to try doing an impacts and adaptation assessment. But nevertheless, there is a growing body of literature on climate change impacts and adaptation, because investigators are beginning to draw some boundaries around the problem; within manageable limits, it is to be hoped.

The impacts research community rarely becomes directly engaged in considering the uncertainties of the climate models themselves. The

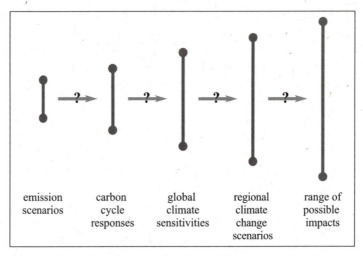

Figure 4.1   The uncertainty explosion.
Source: Ahmad et al. (2001). Reprinted with permission of IPCC

climate science community has its own scientific debate on such issues (see chapter 3). As a consumer of climate information, the impacts community is trying to use whatever tools it has to translate climate change scenarios into a different form of knowledge, one that is meaningful to resource managers, communities, investors, governments, and various other interests.

Let us consider three questions:

1 *What if?* In a scenario of climate change, what kinds of impacts may occur? Without absolute certainty regarding future climate conditions, can a damage scenario report be provided?
2 *So what?* Does the damage scenario make a difference? Since the scenario is presented to interested parties (sometimes referred to as stakeholders; see chapter 7) such as irrigation purveyors, municipal planners, or engineers, the dialogue can turn to whether the impacts scenario makes a difference to their vision of the future. They all include planning matters in their jobs, and they worry about the future being different from the present. Current planning processes may consider population growth or changes in important industries or market conditions. The climate change impacts scenario represents a new set of climate statistics translated into a physical impact.
3 *What can be done?* What adaptation measures should be considered? If climate change scenarios can be translated into parameters that are

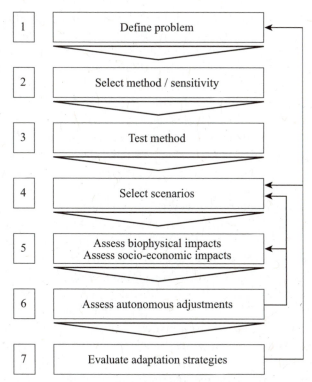

Figure 4.2   Stepwise approach for organizing impacts and adaptation studies.
Source: Parry and Carter (1998). Reprinted with permission from Martin Parry and Tim Carter, and Eathscan

relevant to stakeholders in their planning context, then it should be possible to start a dialogue about adaptation measures that might be different from the ones included in their initial planning scenario.

Parry and Carter's (1998) book offers a stepwise program for organizing impact and adaptation assessments (figure 4.2). Defining the problem is an obvious first step, but there are different schools of thought about who defines the problem and whose problem is to be considered. Assuming the problem is defined, the next step is to choose the methods to be used. For water resources, there are many different hydrologic models. For agriculture, there are different crop models. And there are alternative methods of epidemiological assessments, economic analyses, and modelling catastrophic risks.

Once a method is selected, it has to be tested in some way, and then the climate change scenarios must be selected. The initial biophysical impacts can then be assessed and a social and economic study of the implications of these changes for a particular place or economic activity can be done, a study that would include any reactive or autonomous adjustments that may occur. Once the adjustments are accounted for, we can start talking about purposeful adaptation strategies (see chapter 7).

The initial cases from the early 1980s tended to be purely desk studies. Investigators would apply simple scenarios of temperature and precipitation changes to an analytical tool such as corn or wheat yield models or water budget models for lakes. For example, the scenario temperatures would be applied to the corn model, and the corn model simulation would provide the projected future corn yield at that temperature: this was a simple study of impacts. However, other investigators began to think about what would happen if the assessment could incorporate both climate and other factors, such as population growth, at the same time.

Over the last two decades, several different approaches have been tried. One approach, initiated by the climate community itself, is sometimes referred to as a direct, or top-down, approach, also known as the scenario approach. The first step is to assemble information on climate, climate variation, and climate-sensitive indicators from the activity or place of interest. For agriculture, this step would begin with information on specific crops and the individual farm or farm enterprise, and it would then perhaps scale up to regional agricultural production. This step would be complemented (or followed) by an assessment of adaptive responses at the enterprise level, linked with the policy level. This approach would thus be initiated as a futures-focused study, with the first step being the assembling of climate and crop yield information. After the initial impact scenarios were completed, they could be used to facilitate a dialogue on future response options. If the scenarios were outside the range of experience of local practitioners and planners, a review of current vulnerabilities and operations might ensue, in order to see what modifications, if any, might be needed to reduce scenario-related exposure and risk.

An updated version of this approach is described in Willows and Connell (2003) as part of the UK Climate Impacts Programme (UKCIP). One interesting component of the UKCIP approach is the idea of tiered risk assessment. A first-tier preliminary screening of climate change impact and adaptation risk provides a structure for obtaining climate and non-climate information that is relevant to the exposure unit or location of interest. This is followed by a second-tier qualitative risk assessment and, if possible, by a third-tier quantitative risk assessment.

An alternative is what has been called the bottom-up approach to climate impact and adaptation assessment. The first step focuses on questions about the regional variations in sensitivity to current climatic variability. For example, can we understand what makes wheat and corn yields fluctuate under current conditions? What conditions create a good year for wheat and a bad year for wheat, and why does that happen? What is the current status of the infrastructure supporting wheat and corn? What are the current vulnerabilities at the individual-enterprise level or for large production activities or agro-ecosystems? At a later stage, there would be an analysis of climatic change scenarios and their associated implications. The choreography of this approach differs from the top-down model in that it begins with the present and assesses current vulnerabilities first, by finding out from people in the region how this drought or that flood or this heat or cold spell affects them today, before considering future climate variations and scenarios.

The bottom-up approach began with current climate-related sensitivity and vulnerability as the themes. It has recently evolved to more explicitly incorporate the social issues that underlie local-scale vulnerabilities to climate (Dessai and Hulme 2004), following what is sometimes called the vulnerability approach. In this framework, the bottom-up choreography begins by determining vulnerabilities and risk management issues, before turning to estimating changing risk resulting from top-down scenarios of climate change (figure 4.3).

The next question concerns the capacity of a particular location to respond to a risk, its adaptive capacity (see box 4.1 and chapter 7). This question is not simply about the physical capability of, say, a structure made of concrete such as a seawall. It's about education levels, income levels, governance, institutional capabilities, and many other components that determine whether a region is or is not ready to deal with a new risk. Once these capabilities are determined, then an actual risk management strategy can be planned. Under current conditions, different communities manage risks in different ways, but in a changed climate, because some of those risks may have changed, the current risk management strategy might have to be modified.

Regardless of which approach is used in assessing impacts, various questions need to be asked about adaptation. What are the objectives of an adaptation strategy? Is it to reduce exposure, to take advantage of an opportunity, or to manage risk? These objectives may all sound the same, but in fact they are not necessarily the same. And as in the case of defining the problem, these questions, hide further problems: Who

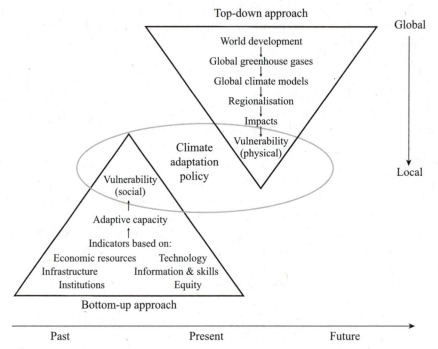

Figure 4.3 Approaches used to inform climate adaptation policy.
Source: Dessai and Hulme (2003, 2004). Reprinted with permission from Suraje Dessai and Earthscan

defines the objectives? Does the climate impacts researcher do so, or are the objectives supposed to emerge from a larger dialogue, and how would this process work?

Assuming that an agreed set of objectives has been defined, we must then identify the potential impacts that emerged from the previous set of steps, and also the range of available response options, including any constraints that may hamper their implementation. Can we find a way to quantify how these adaptation options may actually perform under scenario conditions, and how can such an assessment then be incorporated into the overall planning and development process? It is not easy to jump to that step directly from a climate change assessment. The planning authority or government must handle many other issues as well, and other goals or objectives may have greater weight. A particular adaptation strategy may meet those other goals or objectives, but it may not. In that case, what trade-offs are involved in adapting to climate change, compared to doing something else? And then, after answering all these questions, perhaps at the end, there could be recommendations. Thus, although this appears to be a simple linear approach, it is in fact only the beginning of a process that is likely to be more complex and that will involve identifying a number of steps that will be required to link global climate change with regional planning and decision making.

Climate science has an important role to play in looking at current vulnerabilities, current risks, and future risks. Other forms of knowledge are also important, including local indigenous knowledge, which is sometimes referred to as traditional environmental knowledge: TK, or TEK (Johnson 1992). In many places, there are people who have lived traditional resource-based lifestyles for many centuries, people such as the Inuit and Saami in the Arctic and indigenous tribes in the tropics. The question that therefore arises is, how can knowledge obtained from a traditional lifestyle be merged with knowledge that has been obtained from Western-based and Western-sanctioned research?

CHALLENGES FOR IMPACT
AND ADAPTATION ASSESSMENT

Although it may be possible to define a choreography of steps for an impacts and adaptation assessment, the result would not be a linear process. When few cared about climate change, dialogue on this issue was largely confined to the research community. But now, at the beginning of the twenty-first century, this issue has been so visible in the media and in the public education system that most people have at least heard about climate change (see chapter 2 for a discussion about climate change in the media). As a result, initiating an impacts and adaptation assessment now requires dialogue with a wide range of stakeholders or actors – or however one can characterize people who are not professional researchers. Stakeholders represent an important knowledge resource. They know their systems and communities intimately, and they know the trade-offs that are frequently involved in managing climate-sensitive systems to meet multiple objectives. Defining the problem has to involve a dialogue between a number of different parties, and dialogue should be about more than one-way information flow or outreach. Dialogue can, and should, be an opportunity for shared learning (see chapter 10).

A second problem has to do with scaling. In chapter 3, we discussed the difficulties in scaling down from a global climate to a regional climate. Difficulties also arise when researchers try to translate global or regional climate scenarios into, say, corn yields in Nebraska or salmon counts in the North Pacific. Those kinds of downscaling problems are tremendous, not just for the climate community but also for resource managers and planners considering how a particular location is going to develop. Climate change occurs over a moving human target, so we can not avoid talking about the human dimensions as well. This problem has not received nearly as much attention as the climate change scenarios, but there will eventually need to be an effort to combine climate change scenarios and development scenarios (see chapters 10 and 11).

The third problem has to do with tools. How should they be chosen? Biologists and agronomists know that there are different ways to model crop yields. Hydrologists have developed a wide range of hydrology models. The scale and the resolution of available data will create important problems that will depend on whether the analytical tool is physically based or empirically based. In addition to the tools already mentioned, there are also economic models, decision support tools (such as those developed for engineering), and qualitative methods, including content analysis and dialogue processes (such as focus groups).

Finally, linking research with policy decisions creates a challenge. If communities, industries, and governments are going to adapt to climate change, adaptation has to be a part of a policy process. Otherwise, it is highly unlikely that proactive (planned) adaptation to climate change will occur. Who will accept and implement an adaptation proposal? There must be a way to determine how to make adaptation to climate change politically and socially acceptable to the very individuals who will have to adapt. This problem is very different from the challenge of reducing emissions of GHGs. Emissions reduction or mitigation measures often, though not always, focus on a technological fix, such as designing a hybrid car or making carbon a tradeable commodity (see chapters 8 and 9). It is unlikely that a global-scale adaptation instrument could be developed that could be applied throughout the world. A multitude of different actors in thousands of different communities are going to consider climate change adaptation measures, and decisions will be made in the context of specific places and conditions of development (see chapters 7 and 10).

Figure 4.4 illustrates the scale problem. The lightly shaded rectangle represents the typical size and timing of a big El Niño–Southern Oscillation (or ENSO) event similar to the 1982–83 event (see Glantz 1996). The effects of an El Niño can extend over months and years, and even up to a decade, by prolonging or exacerbating climatic extremes like drought in some regions. The darker shaded rectangle in the figure shows the extent of a short-term disruptive event like the drought in the United Kingdom in 1995, which was shorter in time and more local in scale than an El Niño event. The scales of the 1995 drought and the 1982–83 El Niño

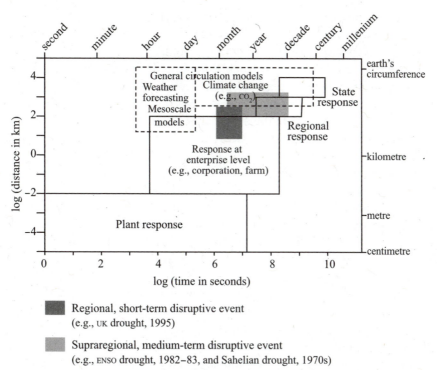

Figure 4.4 The mismatch in time and space scales between observed extreme climatic events, the present-day ability to project climate changes, and the responses to such changes. Dashed lines indicate projections; solid lines, responses. Shaded areas represent examples of two different scales of disruptive climatic events: a country-level drought (dark grey = the UK in 1995) and supraregional effects (light grey = ENSO-related floods and droughts or the 1970s Sahelian drought).
Source: Parry and Carter (1998). Reprinted with permission from Martin Parry and Tim Carter, and Earthscan

event overlap to some degree. But now, superimpose these two events on both the scales of businesses and governments and the scales of the modelled climate change phenomena. GCMs can provide information at very large spatial scales, and their climate change projections can extend from a decade to a century or more. The spatial and temporal data needed for impact and adaptation assessments of observed extreme events can be provided from available weather and climate information, but the spatial and temporal data needed for climate change impacts assessments and adaptation assessments are different from the simulated data that is available from GCM-based scenarios. However, this gap may soon be filled by RCMs if their reliability can be demonstrated.

The responses of actors such as national governments to extreme events (such as floods or droughts) tend to be at a larger scale than the individual events themselves, and they can be consistent with climate change time and space scales (such as long-term changes in drought statistics). In other words, extreme events often convince governments to initiate adaptive measures in other locations that may be exposed to similar events. For example, in the aftermath of Hurricane Hazel's impact on Toronto, Ontario, in 1954 – an event that included floods that killed eighty-one people – the government of Ontario amended its Conservation Authorities Act to enable an authority to acquire lands for recreation and conservation purposes and to regulate that land for the safety of the community. Flood control programs were initiated first by the Metropolitan Toronto Conservation Authority and subsequently by other authorities throughout Ontario (Toronto and Region Conservation Authority 2004). Smaller-scale responses can also take place, in individual communities or watersheds; regional governments could serve as suitable partners to work with and to discuss adaptation to events of this kind.

Individual actors can be significantly affected by both climate change and individual weather events, such as a major drought, and they will look for specific options that could become part of a longer-term policy. A biologist studying plant responses would argue that such biological responses are typically very short-term, extending to perhaps a month or a season, and since individual plants are very small, it is difficult for a biologist to scale up from plant responses to climate change anomalies and global policy issues. Biologists may face substantial difficulties scaling up, whereas climate modellers encounter a scaling-down problem. Thus, the human dimensions of impacts and adaptation incorporate multiple scales with multiple actors.

The above example, which provides a snapshot of the space-time continuum, illustrates the non-trivial challenge of scale. Another concern is that future impacts and adaptations will not occur over a fixed baseline. Climate change will occur concurrently with elections, technological changes, population growth, trading re-alignments, and so on. Case studies of impacts from the 1980s tended to assume that nothing but the climate would change. Now suppose that we define a likely development path (or plausible scenario), for some particular place and commodity, like corn in the US Midwest. And also suppose that we can predict improvements in corn technology and associated yield increases. With technological improvements, the climate-related impact on corn production, which previously would have been portrayed as causing a big loss, would perhaps now cause only a small loss.

If we could not only include the anticipated future technological change but also assess the implications of an adaptation measure of some kind, then different results would be predicted again. Maybe the corn industry would respond proactively to develop more drought-tolerant seeds or to push for expansion of irrigation to places where it was not currently available, reducing some of the impacts even further. This hypothetical example suggests a slightly smaller impact, once we have accounted for purposeful adaptation and ongoing development. Note, however, that this example does not include the possible side effects of choosing a particular adaptation measure, such as an expansion of irrigated agriculture creating additional pressure on water resources. Will the water be available to support the expansion without hindering the achievement of other water-related objectives, such as maintaining ecosystems?

Finally, it is important to remember that climate change is not only about changes in mean conditions. Frequencies of extreme events may change because of changes in the mean or the variance of the climate or because of changes in both. A modest change in the mean could therefore lead to a relatively large change in the frequency of an extreme event (figure 4.5). If changes in frequency provide an indication of changes in the probability of an event of a particular impact or consequence, then it becomes possible to identify changes in risk. This can be written as the equation risk = consequence x probability. Information on consequence emerges from the scenario impacts or damage assessment. Probability may be difficult to determine because the total population of possible scenario outcomes is not known. The use of scatterplots can provide at least some practical indication of the range of possible outcomes.

Thus ideally, an impacts researcher would try to incorporate all these factors; but doing so would be very difficult in practice. Ultimately, the goal would be to move away from the simplifying assumption that everything else remains equal, towards the notion that the ground is moving under our feet while the atmosphere is changing over our heads.

THE SCENARIO APPROACH VERSUS
THE VULNERABILITY APPROACH

We began the discussion of impacts and adaptation assessments by outlining two general approaches. One, labelled as the scenario approach (also referred to as the top-down approach), begins an assessment with an analysis of future impacts and uses this analysis to initiate a broad dialogue on impacts and adaptation. The alternative, vulnerability approach (also referred to as the bottom-up approach) begins with an

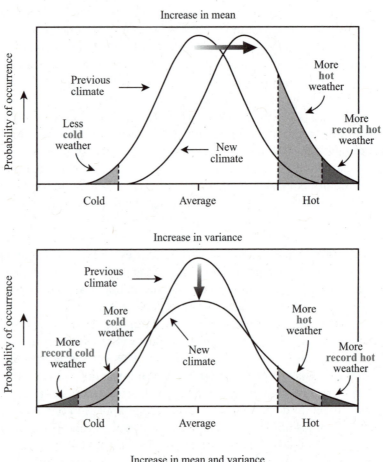

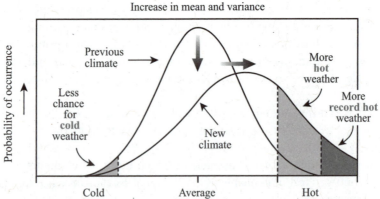

Figure 4.5   Changes in the probability of extreme temperature because of changes in the mean and the variance of temperature.
Source: Folland et al. (2001). Reprinted with permission from IPCC

Table 4.1.
Comparison of Vulnerability-First and Scenario-First Approaches for Assessment
of Climate Change Impacts, Vulnerability and Adaptation

Vulnerability-First	*Scenario-First*
Identify current vulnerabilities	Identify scenario-based impacts
Assess current management	Estimate projected changes in risks
Estimate projected changes in risks	Identify projected changes in vulnerabilities
Assess adaptive capacity for projected risks	Assess adaptive capacity for projected risks
Identify modifications to management	Identify modifications to management

assessment of current problems related to recent and ongoing exposure
to climate events. Table 4.1 illustrates the two approaches. Given that
both approaches include steps that focus on vulnerability and scenarios,
we have labelled them here as vulnerability-first and scenario-first.

The choice of choreography, that is, the choice of how impact and adaptation assessments are organized, depends on the local context, including
local awareness of climate-related trends and issues. The researcher must
determine whether the region under study has little awareness of climate
change and little practical experience with climate change studies and
whether it is highly vulnerable to current climate extremes, such as
droughts and floods. Is it likely to be a less-developed region or country? If
it is, it may indeed require an assessment that begins by asking basic fundamental questions. What are its specific vulnerabilities? Why do floods,
for example, create greater economic loss and loss of life than in neigh-
bouring regions? The example of tropical storm Jeanne in 2004 illustrates
the differences in vulnerability between Haiti, which experienced substantial loss of life, and Florida, which did not. Also, an assessment of current
risks can eventually lead to an assessment of future scenarios and adaptation, as the capacity for impact assessment improves with experience.

Some regions, most likely developed regions or regions that are well
aware of the climate change issue, such as many small island states or rapidly industrializing countries such as China, already understand their vulnerabilities to currently observed climatic variations and extremes. Under
the right circumstances, they may be quite willing to jump directly into a
scenario discussion. One example is King County, Washington, in the
United States. The county government organized a climate change conference in 2005 which led to the development of a guidebook on preparing
for climate change, with the specific objective of providing a framework for
developing adaptation plans in the face of expected future impacts (Snover
et al. 2007). The initial focus on future scenarios consists of scoping the

expected local impacts using available information sources, and organizing a local effort at identifying relevant planning areas. This would be followed by a climate resiliency study, including a re-examination of current plans and management strategies and current vulnerabilities (see chapter 7). But, obviously, since the future is still to come, there are no performance records on trial. Thus, the mandate of a climate change scenario-based assessment is very different from the mandate of an inquiry into current management performance when dealing with recent extreme events. Other mechanisms, available either through national governments or international agencies, already exist for such post-mortems. The scenario approach offers a forward-looking exercise in shared learning. If the future "what if" can be defined for the specific conditions of the region of interest, then this approach enables the dialogue to move directly into assessments of changing risks and an evaluation of adaptation strategies. Whatever choreography is chosen, there are elements common to both types of approaches. Each approach can be forward-looking, account for vulnerabilities, and incorporate local knowledge and perspectives. The only difference is whether the assessment begins with a future scenario or with the present.

This kind of debate has tended to be categorized in other ways. For instance, it might be assumed that in a scenario approach, only scientists define the problem and that they fail to engage stakeholders (hence the label of top-down). Perhaps in the 1980s, when scenario studies were just beginning, this assumption was accurate, but not anymore. Best practice in impacts and adaptation assessments is evolving to the point that it is unlikely that a climate change impact study could be initiated and funded without including a clear process of stakeholder engagement, regardless of whether a vulnerability or a scenario approach was used. The key consideration is the context within which the assessment is to be undertaken, a context which is continuing to evolve through learning and experience (Füssel and Klein 2006). An alternative label, therefore, could be decision-driven, indicating that the shared learning process is being initiated by the specifics of the problem being addressed and that there are variants on how this could be carried out.

Before deciding on the choreography of the assessment, some advance preparation is required, including a review of background documents produced by local authorities and informal interviews with local interests. Some questions to be considered include

• Has there been any previous climate-related research in this location? Did this effort include any local investigators?

- Has climate change been included in any local (routine) planning documents?
- Has the site experienced any recent extreme events, and was it able to cope on its own or was outside assistance required?
- Are any major development initiatives being considered? Is climate change being included in any proposals or planning documents?

Impacts and adaptation studies are enhanced by stakeholder acceptance and cooperation (see chapter 7). Either choreography may be applicable, but since climate change is a long-term problem in which the past may not be the only or the best guide to the future, our view is that scenarios represent an excellent opportunity to begin a rewarding learning experience and that there are situations where scenarios would be a good first step in the process. Assessments of future scenarios can also lead researchers and local partners to realize that current practices may need to be re-examined and current vulnerabilities reconsidered.

DISCUSSION

What is the value of the labels top-down and bottom-up? Perhaps they are useful when identifying the initiator of impacts and adaptation studies, but in climate change research, researchers, not local practitioners, have initiated both scenario and vulnerability studies. In other words, these studies, with only a few exceptions, have been top-down. One of these exceptions is the community-based initiative organized by the Columbia Basin Trust in British Columbia, Canada (described at http://www.cbt.org). This is a unique effort resulting from experiences with scenario-based studies, combined with local knowledge and regional dialogue, that has led to the trust's program to promote the development of community-based adaptation plans. In this case, a bottom-up effort has been initiated because of awareness raised by previous top down research efforts.

Impacts and adaptation research methodologies are evolving and becoming more multi-disciplinary in character. Labels such as top-down and bottom-up are not very helpful for categorizing different study methodologies, and we will not use them in the remaining chapters of this book. And since many new impacts and adaptation research initiatives contain both scenario and vulnerability components, it may be more relevant in a historical context to refer to older studies as first-generation and to newer ones as second-generation, as is now the case with GCMs.

5

Ecosystem Processes and Climate Change

INTRODUCTION

Climate change is projected to have significant implications for ecosystems ranging from changes in ecosystem function to changes in commercial enterprises in agriculture and forestry. In addition, the potential for carbon sequestration, or the management of biological and geological reservoirs for increased storage of carbon, as a policy response has created a growing demand for information on CO_2 enrichment of vegetation and its direct effects on plant growth.

As was the case in chapter 3, the approach we take for this topic is from a generalist's perspective, opening a window on the study of biology, which is an important component of the study of climate change. More detailed information can be obtained from Watson, Zinyowera, and Moss (1995) and McCarthy et al. (2001a). In addition, Rosenzweig and Hillel (1998) provide an overview of impacts on agriculture, including a detailed discussion of relevant biological processes.

BACKGROUND

We begin with some definitions of terms from the Intergovernmental Panel on Climate Change (IPCC) that are used to describe ecosystem functions (see McCarthy et al. 2001a). Gross primary production (GPP) denotes the total uptake of carbon by vegetation through photosynthesis. Net primary production (NPP) is the rate of accumulation of carbon by vegetation after losses from plant respiration and other plant functions are taken into account. Carbon is an important building block for plants, and the excitement about additional CO_2 in the atmosphere (also referred to as CO_2 enrichment) is that it can represent an additional nutrient source for plants. It has been postulated that plants will benefit from CO_2 enrichment because they will photosynthesize more and their GPP will increase (Rosenzweig and Hillel 1998). If that was to occur, plants could grow faster and accumulate more biomass at higher temperatures without requiring additional water. Some have suggested that crops and trees would benefit from a higher concentration of CO_2 and this could offset any potential losses in yield due to higher temperatures alone. Research has shown, however, that this is not always the case (Ainsworth and Long 2005; Long et al. 2006; Tubiello et al. 2007). This problem will be discussed shortly.

Carbon storage in the vegetation and in the soil can support mechanisms that enable a particular site to act as a carbon sink, removing GHGs from the atmosphere. Other sites, however, may be a source of carbon, in that there is transport (or a flux) of carbon going to the atmosphere from a particular land surface. This can happen particularly in some wetland and peatland areas where emissions may be in the form of methane (CH_4). Since a sink is a plot of land where, on a net basis, plants pull more carbon out of the atmosphere than they release, many view rapidly growing forest sites, such as poplar plantations, as valuable carbon sinks because of their very high photosynthetic rates and therefore their very high consumption of CO_2. We will discuss the policy aspects of sinks further in chapters 8 and 9, but for now we will limit our discussion to the biological aspects only.

Some plant canopies produce a considerable volume of leaves. The leaf area index is a measure of this biomass. A leaf area index of 1 means that there is enough leaf matter to cover the area below the plant canopy with just one layer. For a thick canopy, the leaf area index could be 5, 6, 10, or more. Any change in biomass has implications for carbon sequestration. In addition, there are potential implications for crop and timber yield, although yield changes will also depend on changes in nutrient or fibre content matter, which does not result exclusively from biomass changes alone.

PLANT COMMUNITIES, ECOSYSTEMS, AND BIODIVERSITY

The following sections of this chapter will consider the effects of climate change and increased CO_2 concentrations on plants and other living organisms. Organisms also, of course, interact with other organisms, and a study of ecological systems provides an understanding of their dependencies and interactions. Ecology has been described as the study of the "web of life" within ecosystems ranging from very small spatial scales to global scales. The impacts of climate change and increased CO_2 concentrations can lead to a cascade of effects within individual ecosystems, as well as across many ecosystems, but it is difficult to predict the extent of such impacts, including related adaptations.

Kirschbaum et al. (1995) review a number of key components of ecological processes:

- *The Niche.* Organisms have preferred places or habitats in which to live; a niche encompasses environmental conditions in which the organism could potentially grow and reproduce if it were subject to no competition or other effects from other species. Climate change may cause the distribution of suitable habitats to change.
- *Competition.* Organisms compete with each other for light, nutrients, food, and space. Climate change and increased CO_2 concentrations may alter the competitive balance between species at various sites.
- *Herbivory.* Insect herbivores may be affected by changes in plant growth resulting from temperature/moisture changes, as well as by the side effects of increased CO_2 concentrations, which are likely to alter the ratio of carbon to nitrogen in plant tissue. As herbivores seek to maintain their nitrogen requirements, they may consume more plant tissue, and some plants may in turn develop defence mechanisms. Insect population cycles may also change.
- *Community.* A community has been described either as a collection of individual species or as an integrated assemblage of interacting species. It is difficult to generalize how climate change could affect communities, since communities are always changing (i.e., through succession) in response to natural climatic variability and various disturbances (such as fire or species invasions).
- *Migration.* Climatic zones suitable for particular ecosystems have been referred to as ecoclimatic zones (or biogeoclimatic zones). Any spatial shift in these zones will place existing species and communities in a different climate zone from the one that prevailed when they were established. Past species migration rates are estimated to be much less than what will take place as a result of the anticipated shift in climate zones. Future migration rates will depend on human interventions in landscape patterns and on any direct human interventions in species dispersal (for example, establishing plantations) that may occur.

Beyond the consideration of individual ecosystems is the notion that throughout the planet there is considerable biological diversity of living organisms from all sources, including terrestrial, marine, and other aquatic ecosystems. Biodiversity for a particular location is determined by (a) the mean climate and its variability; (b) the availability of resources (energy, water, nutrients, and so on); (c) the disturbance regime (severe weather, landslides, and so on); (d) dispersal opportunities or barriers; (e) the original mix of species; (f) the intensity of interactions between species, for example, through competition and predation; and (g) reproduction and possible future changes in genetic structure (Secretariat of the Convention on Biological Diversity 2003). Past climate changes have altered plant and animal communities, and it is expected that future climate changes will also be important drivers of ecosystem changes, along with other drivers associated with human activity, such as pollution and changes in land use (Millennium Ecosystem Assessment 2005).

The link between climate change and biodiversity has important implications for policy. The Convention on Biological Diversity (CBD) originated at the 1992 Earth Summit, the same event that produced the United Nations Framework Convention on Climate Change (UNFCCC). Scientific and policy considerations are leading to joint discussions on how best to integrate the efforts to deal with biodiversity and climate change (Secretariat of the Convention on Biological Diversity 2003). The discussions are important because of the potential side effects of proposed climate policy measures for biodiversity, such as the use of forest plantations for the production of biofuels and for enhancing the absorption of carbon from the atmosphere (see chapters 8 and 9).

GENERAL PLANT RESPONSES TO CHANGING CO_2 AND TEMPERATURE

If CO_2 concentrations continue to increase during the twenty-first century, plants will be affected simultaneously by changing CO_2 levels and by climate change. In order to determine the implications of these combined changes, it is important to understand how plants currently respond to variations in environmental conditions.

In an environment of increasing CO_2, plant responses will be affected by changes in resources, including nitrogen and water (figure 5.1). The upper left panel of figure 5.1 compares photosynthesis rates under different resource conditions. If the plant is already starving for nitrogen, additional CO_2 will not provide as much benefit as it would if nitrogen was not limited. The middle left panel shows changes in root-shoot ratios. When a root-shoot ratio increases, the plant is expanding its root

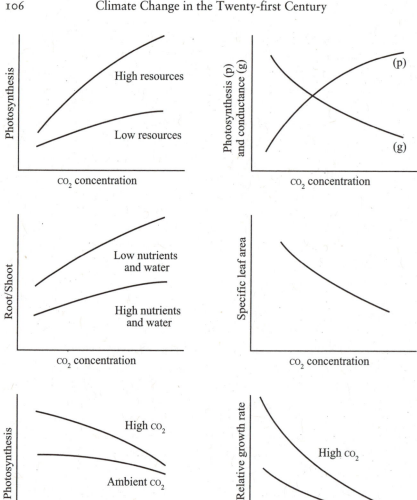

Figure 5.1   Responses of plants to CO_2 concentration.
Source: Rosenzweig and Hillel (1998). Reprinted with permission from Cynthia Rosenzweig

system to look for more nutrients underground, rather than expanding surface biomass. In a situation with low nutrients and water, additional CO_2 will thus lead to a very substantial increase in the root-shoot ratio. Under conditions of abundant nutrients and water, however, plants tend to spend more time growing biomass on the surface than they spend increasing their root system.

In general, in a high-CO_2 world, photosynthesis rates are initially much higher than in a low-CO_2 world, but they eventually decline to near ambient (or current) conditions. The same is true of relative growth rates. Stomatal conductance (an indicator of how long stomata, tiny openings on plant leaves, are open so that transpiration can occur) decreases at higher CO_2 concentrations, leading to increased water use efficiency, while photosynthesis rates increase. Eventually, these changes level off. Initial enhancement of growth may decline or disappear with time. Specific leaf area decreases, often due to decreased nitrogen concentration (Bazzaz 1990). These are broad generalizations, however, and not all plants will respond in exactly the same manner to additional CO_2 in the atmosphere. Responses will depend on whether they are what is called C3 or C4 plants, terminology that will be discussed in the next section.

Just like CO_2, temperature is also very important for plants, because they have an optimum temperature range where growth can occur. At the maximum temperature threshold, there is an immediate decline in growth. In a warm climate, a temperature increase can have negative implications, while in cooler climates, some warming can create advantages, because growth can begin earlier in the growing season. Growth responses to temperature, however, vary from plant to plant.

C3 and C4 Plants and their Responses to Changing CO_2 and Temperature

Biologists have identified three different kinds of carbon-cycling processes in vegetation, which they have used to categorize plants as C3, C4, or CAM. Most plants are either C3 or C4. C4 plants are likely to be found in habitats with high daytime temperatures and intense sunlight. Examples are corn (maize) and sugarcane. C3 plants are found in cooler or more humid habitats; examples include wheat, rice, soybeans, and mid-latitude trees. C3 and C4 plants react differently to elevated levels of CO_2, and of particular interest is the potential fertilization effect of increased atmospheric concentrations of CO_2 and the implications of this increase for plant growth, crop yield, and plant succession.

The CAM (crassulacean acid metabolism) plants, which are primarily succulent or desert plants (such as cacti and pineapple), incorporate both C3 and C4 carbon cycling as part of their adaptation to conditions of high daytime temperatures and low soil moisture. Carbon cycling in CAM plants follows C4 pathways at night and C3 pathways during the day (Kimball 2005). Because of this pattern, we will address only the issues relating to C3 and C4 plants, and not to CAM plants.

The first product of C3 plants during photosynthesis is a three-carbon compound called 3-phosphoglyceric acid; hence the term "C3 plants." Similarly, the first product of C4 plants during photosynthesis is a four-carbon compound called oxaloacetate; hence the term "C4 plants."

As mentioned, plants vary in their responses to changing CO_2, partly because they use different mechanisms for photosynthesis, the process by which they fix CO_2 from the air in order to build carbohydrates and release oxygen as a by-product. Photorespiration is the opposite process to photosynthesis, in that CO_2 is released from the plant when the atmospheric CO_2 concentrations are low. Photorespiration "causes C3 crops (such as wheat, rice, and soybeans) to exhibit lower rates of net photosynthesis than do C4 crops such as maize at current CO_2 levels ... because in C4 plants loss to photorespiration is minimal" (Rosenzweig and Hillel 1998, 72). This happens because C4 plants are able to concentrate CO_2 in their photosynthetic pathways, whereas C3 plants cannot. C4 plants are therefore more efficient at photosynthesizing than C3 plants under present CO_2 levels. However, this difference in photosynthetic rates is not maintained as CO_2 levels increase, in which case C4 plants lose their competitive edge, because they are likely to be less affected by an increase in CO_2 than C3 plants. When CO_2 levels increase, photorespiration is minimized for C3 plants, and photosynthesis rates can be maximized. This results in C3 plants photosynthesizing at higher rates than C4 plants at higher CO_2 levels.

Figure 5.2 compares the effects of increased atmospheric CO_2 concentrations on wheat, a C3 plant, and maize, a C4 plant. As CO_2 concentrations increase above current levels (beyond 400 ppm), the photosynthetic rate of wheat actually becomes higher than that of maize. The rate for maize levels off because it is unable to gain any additional advantage from CO_2 concentrations above the current ambient concentration. This exemplifies the need to carefully assess the effects of rising CO_2 levels on the ability of particular plants to photosynthesize, and therefore to grow and survive.

Generally speaking, as the temperature increases, so will the photosynthetic rates of plants. This increase obviously cannot continue indefinitely, however, and after a plant's threshold temperature is reached, it will cease to photosynthesize. This too, also points to the need to understand the effects of rising temperature on the ability of individual plant species to photosynthesize, and therefore to grow and survive. A related question

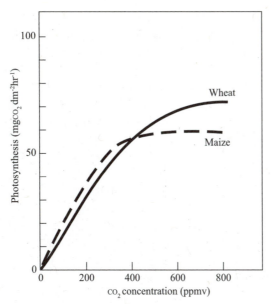

Figure 5.2 Effect of atmospheric CO_2 concentration on rate of photosynthesis of maize and wheat (milligrams of CO_2 per square decametre of leaf area per hour, or $mgCO_2$ dm^{-2} hr^{-1}) in controlled-environment experiments.
Source: Rosenzweig and Hillel (1998). Reprinted with permission from Cynthia Rosenzweig

concerns the effects of increasing temperature and increasing CO_2 on plants. The interaction between increasing CO_2 and increasing temperature is complex, and no single result can be predicted. In the orange yield study described in chapter 3, varied results were obtained for oranges grown at different temperatures and atmospheric CO_2 concentrations.

CO_2 Enrichment and the Effects on Plant Communities

When looking at how CO_2 enrichment affects plants, researchers need to consider more than just the individual plants, since plants grow in communities and compete for space, light, and nutrients. Bazzaz (1998) offers an example of the effects of CO_2 enrichment on plant communities in tropical forests. Figure 5.3 shows the photosynthetic responses to ambient and elevated CO_2 of four pioneer tree species in the nettle family found in rainforest in Mexico, relatively small in height, but all having slightly different structures and architectures. The top panel shows that under current conditions, three species (*Cecropia, Myriocarpa,* and

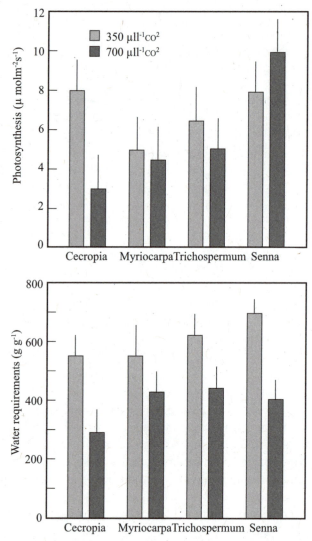

Figure 5.3   The photosynthetic response in one-millionth of a mole (counting unit for molecular weight) of CO_2 per square meter of leaf area per second, or μ molm^{-2} s^{-1} (*left*), and reduction in water requirements in grams of water per gram of biomass, or g g-1 (*right*), of seedlings of tropical pioneer species, to exposure to ambient (350 parts per million) and elevated (700 parts per million) CO_2.

Source: Bazzaz (1998). Reprinted with permission from Springer Science and Business Media

Trichospermum) exhibit reductions in photosynthesis, while the fourth (*Senna*) improves. The bottom panel shows that water efficiency improves for all four species.

Figure 5.4 illustrates responses of tropical pioneer species to elevated levels of CO_2 when they are individually grown and when they are grown in a community. Biomass is much higher for each species when they are grown individually, but note that when grown in a community, one species (*Senna*) experiences a decline in biomass with increasing CO_2. Thus, in addition to the uncertainties surrounding how changes in CO_2 and temperature will affect individual plants, there are tremendous uncertainties surrounding how increasing CO_2 and temperature will affect interactions between plants.

Plant architecture also changes in communities. The upper panel of figure 5.5 shows changes in the architecture of pioneer tropical species in the current and in a high CO_2 world when they are grown as individuals, and the lower panel shows what happens for the two cases when these species are grown in a community and are competing with each other. All four species exhibit changes in biomass and architecture, changes that differ between the individual and the community growth cases.

CO_2 enrichment on its own can lead to changes in structure and function. The response of plants as individuals and in competition can differ and can be non-linear. Leaf areas are affected, as are plant architecture and competition for nutrients. There seem to be some improvements for some $c3$ plants, but the effect is less for $c4$ plants. Any enhancement that occurs may not occur to the same degree in competitive situations as it would for plants grown on their own or in monocultures.

OBSERVED IMPACTS OF RECENT CLIMATIC VARIABILITY ON ECOSYSTEMS AND LANDSCAPES

The Third and Fourth Assessment Reports of the Intergovernmental Panel on Climate Change (IPCC) (Gitay et al. 2001; IPCC 2007a) included reviews of current ecosystem conditions to see if there are any changes in those conditions that might be consistent with climate change. One conclusion was that physical and biological systems have been affected already; the effects have been easy to observe because there is a relatively clear relationship between ecosystem changes and increasing temperature. On the other hand, the impacts of changes in observed precipitation have been more difficult to see because we lack data for a long enough period to assess precipitation-related impacts,

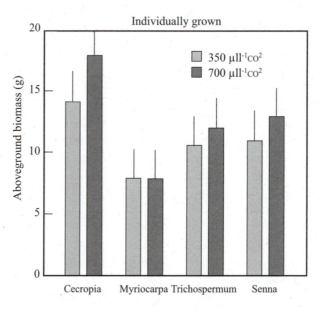

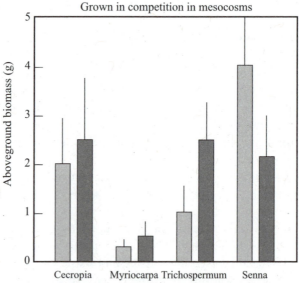

Figure 5.4   Changes in above-ground biomass of seedlings of tropical pioneer species when grown as individuals (*top*) and in competition with other species (*bottom*) after exposure to ambient (350 parts per million) and elevated (700 parts per million) CO_2. *Source:* Bazzaz (1998). Reprinted with permission from Springer Science and Business Media

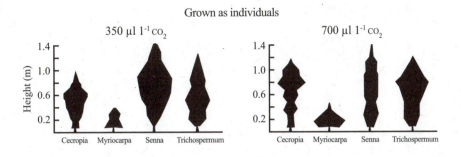

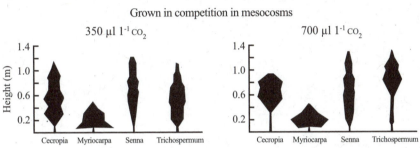

Figure 5.5   Changes in architecture of pioneer tropical species when grown as individuals (*top*) and in competition with other species (*bottom*) after exposure to ambient (350 parts per million) and elevated (700 parts per million) CO_2.
Source: Bazzaz (1998). Reprinted with permission from Springer Science and Business Media

along with the potential impacts of land use changes and pollution (Gitay et al. 2001).

Figure 5.6 shows that most of the observed changes in natural systems have been occurring in the middle and high latitudes, particularly in the northern hemisphere. Smol and Douglas (2007), for example, have concluded that Arctic lake ecosystems have already been dramatically altered by recent warming after having experienced millennia of relative stability. Changes in glaciers and in the tundra environments are consistent with what one would expect to result from a warming. Fewer examples have been identified in the tropics. Is this because we lack observations? Or is the signal in the tropics being confounded by local pollution and land use change? Or are both explanations correct? Observed precipitation trends have varied from place to place: some areas have been getting wetter, while others are drier or have changed very little. Temperature trends are generally easier to see, and figure 5.6 shows that most regions are warming.

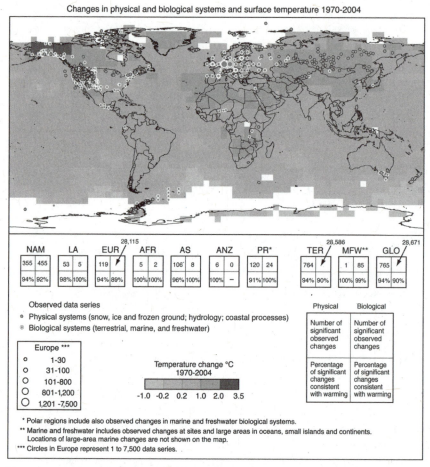

Figure 5.6   Locations of observed changes in natural systems, and trends in surface temperature, 1970–2004. NAM = North America; LA = Latin America; EUR = Europe; AFR = Africa; AS = Asia; ANZ = Australia–New Zealand; PR = polar regions. *Source:* IPCC (2007a). Reprinted with permission of IPCC

Despite the complexities, there does appear to be a general consistency between biological and climate trends. Parmesan and Yohe (2003) have documented such responses for 279 species, including range shifts averaging 6.1 km per decade towards the poles or metres per decade upward in elevation and advancement of spring events by 2.3 days per decade. An example of an impact from a short-term event is provided by McLean et al. (2001) for the effects of the El Niño event of 1997–98 on coral reefs. While warmer water was observed in the Pacific, there were higher temperatures in other places as well. The result was a widespread bleaching of coral. While the cause was a short-term event, observers are concerned that if climate change results in warmer oceans, there could be many more years with extreme conditions and that more coral bleaching will occur.

An example of a longer-term temperature-related impact is the reduction in global sea ice. Between 1979 and 2003 the average Arctic sea ice extent has decreased by about 8 percent, or nearly 1 million km², while summer sea ice extent has decreased by 15 to 20 percent (ACIA 2004). An update of these trends to 2005 is shown in figure 5.7 (IPCC 2007d). Minimum (end of summer) ice extent in the Arctic (top panel) has declined more than 2 million square kilometres in area, or around 20 percent, between 1979 and 2005. The average ice extent (middle panel) declined by around 7 percent. In 2007, minimum ice extent declined by another 1.2 square kilometres, and the Northwest Passage along Canada's coastline was almost completely ice free during August and September 2007 (NSIDC News 2007). In contrast, little change has been observed in the Antarctic (bottom panel). Another phenomenon observed in the Arctic is an increased frequency of landslides as a result of permafrost thaw. A landslide is illustrated in figure 5.8 in a photograph from Tuktoyaktuk, located on the shoreline of the Beaufort Sea. The landslide was likely triggered by a storm surge that occurred many years before the photo was taken. It probably exposed some ground ice, which is common in many permafrost zones. The ice then gradually melted during each succeeding summer and eventually decreased the ground stability enough to cause landslides.

Permafrost thaw is taking place throughout the Arctic, including Canada, Alaska, and Russia. However, this thaw has not resulted exclusively from conduction of heat from the air to the ground. A weather-related trigger, such as a storm surge, forest fire, or river flood, can expose ground ice, which then thaws. If these events occur more frequently because of climate change, landslides could become more frequent in permafrost thaw regions. Changes to ice and permafrost are highly visible now, and this has raised the awareness of northern peoples to the potential long-term implications of climate change (ACIA 2004).

In British Columbia, the expansion of the mountain pine beetle within mature lodgepole pine forests has been linked with recent warming, which has reduced the frequency of the very cold winter days that reduce over-winter survival of beetle larvae. The beetles kill the trees by boring through the bark, cutting off the flow of nutrients and water from the roots. However, this problem is not related purely to climate

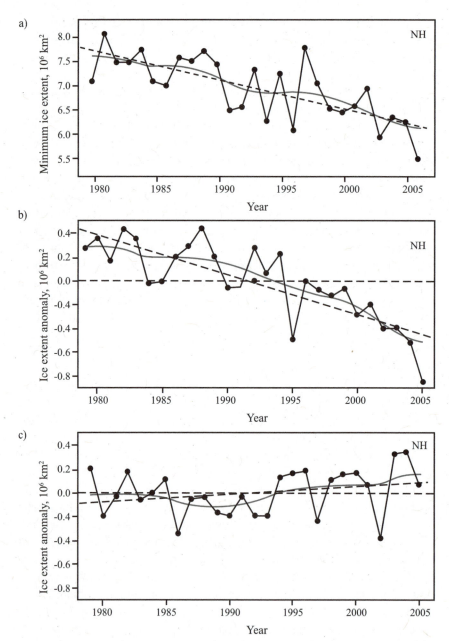

Figure 5.7 Arctic and Antarctic ice trends, 1979–2005: (a) minimum Arctic sea ice extent, (b) Arctic sea ice extent anomaly compared to 1979–2005 mean, (c) Antarctic ice extent anomaly compared to 1979–2005 mean.
Source: Lemke et al. (2007). Reprinted with permission of IPCC

Figure 5.8   Landslides resulting from permafrost thaw near Tuktoyaktuk, Canada.
Source: Aylsworth and Duk-Rodkin (1997). Photo GSC 1996–133B provided by Michel
St-Martin. Natural Resources Canada image produced with permission of Natural
Resources Canada. Her Majesty the Queen in Right of Canada

change, since a climate-related trigger may have been superimposed on
a forestry development decision that perhaps created a new vulnerability on the ground. What do we mean by that?

First, the climate constraints for the mountain pine beetle are cool
summers and winter minimum temperatures below -40°C degrees.
These cold temperatures would normally prevent the beetle from sur-
viving the winter and reproducing. Recent warm winters have not included such cold temperatures, allowing the beetle to expand over an
area exceeding 8 million hectares by 2003 and 14 million hectares by
2008 (http://www.for.gov.bc.ca)(figure 5.9). Why did this happen?

Fire suppression activities have allowed the area of older forests to increase in the British Columbia interior (British Columbia Ministry of Forests and Range 2006), and the older trees are more susceptible to beetle
infestation. The continuation of the fire suppression policy is expected to
lead to a further increase in the average age of pine stands in British Columbia. Species diversity may also be important because it enhances the
resilience of forests against various stresses, including insect attack.

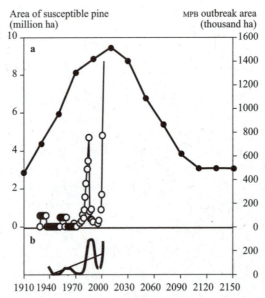

Figure 5.9   Estimated area of pine (*solid circles*) susceptible to mountain pine beetle · outbreaks (*open circles*) in British Columbia (*upper panel*), and ten-year running average mountain pine beetle outbreak area (*lower panel*).
Source: Taylor and Carroll (2004). Reprinted with permission of Canadian Forest Service, Natural Resources Canada © 2003. Her Majesty the Queen in Right of Canada

Natural regeneration after monoculture planting results in mostly mixed forests (British Columbia Ministry of Forests 1992). But observers have raised concerns that natural forests in British Columbia are being replaced by monocultures during post-harvest and post-disturbance tree planting (British Columbia Ministry of Forests and Range 2006). Just when recent winter temperatures have been increasing, there has been a doubling of the amount of land in British Columbia covered by mature lodgepole pine (Taylor and Carroll 2004) as a result of long-term management decisions by government and the forest industry (British Columbia Ministry of Forests and Range 2006). The extensive beetle outbreak that has been ongoing since 1993 thus occurred partly because of an unanticipated warming of winters and drought stress and partly because of the cumulative effect of long-term management decisions. Projected warming is expected to increase the risk of beetle infestation even further (Carroll et al. 2004; Taylor and Carroll 2004).

Beetle-infested trees are now being harvested in an effort to stop the spread of the beetle. What will the post-harvest strategy be? Will potential future warming be considered? Given the conclusion of IPCC Working Group I (Santer et al. 1995; Mitchell et al. 2001; IPCC 2007c) that there is a discernible human influence on climate, the earth of the twenty-first century no longer has a completely natural climate. That does not mean that a particular climate-related event (such as a series of warm winters) would automatically be attributed to anthropogenic climate change. However, it does mean that the assumption of an unchanging climate, even within the next few decades, is no longer appropriate to include in long-term planning. Past climate statistics are no longer an indicator of future climate. As well, it is now known that the link between climate and development decisions can affect the resulting impacts of climatic events and the implementation of adaptation strategies. Tomorrow's series of warm winters may have a different effect on tomorrow's forests, even if the climatic events are similar to those experienced in the last several years (for example, if minimum temperatures remain above the threshold of -40°C for beetle kill).

The process of explicitly putting climate change into ongoing management processes creates an opportunity to try planning in a way that prevents surprises. If adaptation is discussed, then obviously one of the questions will be whether current management practices ought to be continued or perhaps modified in anticipation of future warming. In the case of British Columbia forests, would the monoculture strategy be reconsidered?

POTENTIAL IMPACTS OF CLIMATE CHANGE SCENARIOS

Unlike observed impacts, scenario-based impacts are obtained from results of simulation models that use climate change scenarios as part of their input data. In these types of studies, which necessarily include the uncertainties that are in any biophysical study, the use of climate scenario information in impacts models is always problematic. The differences between scenarios, as well as other factors, affect the projection of impacts. The human element involved in adaptation is going to be very important here: this element will be considered in more detail in chapters 6 and 7.

Gitay et al. (2001) have identified natural systems that are at risk for climate change, including glaciers, coral reefs, forests, polar and alpine ecosystems, prairie wetlands, and some native grasslands. Human systems such as agriculture are also sensitive to climate change, and some of them are vulnerable. Vulnerability in the human context depends not just on exposure but also on capabilities to adapt, which vary between countries and between regions within countries.

Impacts on Crops

Rosenzweig and Hillel (1998) describe a US case study of wheat yields that incorporated both climate change and CO_2 enrichment. Since wheat is a C3 plant, it should benefit from CO_2 enrichment. Figure 5.10 shows a north-south transect in the study, starting in Fargo, North Dakota, and then moving through Nebraska and Texas. A set of arbitrary scenarios was used, rather than GCM simulations, for the purpose of doing a sensitivity study. Arbitrary changes of 1°C or 2°C, for example, were equally imposed on each month's historic temperature record from the station of interest. While such methods are very simple to use, it must be recognized that climate change is probably not going to manifest itself in this way.

The vertical axes in all of the panels of figure 5.10 show percentage changes in the yield of wheat. The white bars (scenario A) show a yield change resulting from equal changes in daily minimum and maximum temperatures. The dark bars (scenario B) are for a case in which the daily minimum temperatures were rising three times faster than the maximum. Why is scenario B of interest? Most of the observed warming that has occurred over the last several decades has been in the form of increasing minimum temperatures (Folland and Karl 2001). One thought is that increases in cloud cover and humidity have affected nighttime conditions and prevented temperatures from dropping as low as they have in the past. If they continue to do so in the future, then it will be important to understand what might happen to crops if the nighttime temperatures warm more than the daytime temperatures. The results indicate that yields are higher in scenario B (the minimum temperature increase is three times that for the maximum) than in scenario A. For loss situations, scenario B losses are not as severe as those of scenario A.

Another example considers the combined effects of climate and of CO_2 enrichment on crop yield for three GCM-based $2xCO_2$ scenarios. Rosenzweig and Hillel (1998) demonstrate that C3 crops, such as wheat, rice, and soybeans, benefit from CO_2 enrichment, while the C4 crop maize benefits only slightly from this CO_2 enrichment. This assessment does not include adaptation, however. The inclusion of adaptations such as changes in planting dates, increased fertilizer applications,

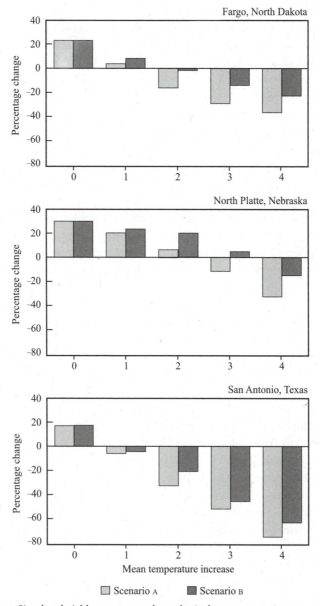

Figure 5.10   Simulated yield responses to hypothetical temperature increase and elevated CO_2 concentration (550 ppm) for several sites in the United States. Scenario A – equal change in minimum and maximum temperature; scenario B – minimum temperature increase is 3x that of the maximum temperature.
Source: Rosenzweig and Hillel (1998). Reprinted with permission of Cynthia Rosenzweig

expanded irrigation, and the development of new crop varieties results in partial amelioration of losses or augmentation of gains. However, the assessment does assume a widespread response, which may not occur in practice, for such responses will be influenced by various economic and institutional factors (such as governance). Even though a technological option or behavioural change may be possible, it will not necessarily be the adaptation that is chosen (see chapter 7).

Different climate scenarios result in different effects, not only on global yields but also on the spatial distribution of these effects. Parry et al. (1999) clarify this lack of consistency in spatial patterns between scenarios. One possible explanation is the difference in precipitation projections among the various GCMs. However, some effects also result from differences in temperature changes in different scenarios. For example, for scenarios of very intense warming in high latitudes, as the crops develop faster, the threshold for benefits is exceeded. As a result, the length of the growing season actually becomes shorter, and less grain is produced.

Impacts on Parks

National parks exist throughout the world, often for the purposes of ecosystem protection. What would the consequences of climate change be for park management?

Scott and Suffling (2000) and Scott et al. (2002) offer a case study for western Canada showing potential changes in ecoclimatic zones. The idea behind an ecoclimatic zone is that a specific ecosystem can be characterized by a particular combination of temperature and precipitation. Classification schemes have been developed and maps constructed based on current climate (for example, see Strahler and Strahler 1997, 184–90). For a particular climate type, such as a grassland ecosystem, the temperature and precipitation boundaries can be established. If the climate change scenario indicates that this set of conditions may be displaced to another location, it implies that the climate that supports that ecosystem is shifting. Thus, in the future an ecosystem from a relic climate would be growing in a new climate. That shift raises questions about adaptation, particularly for authorities with a mandate to manage national parks to preserve ecosystems.

In the example in figure 5.11, Prince Albert National Park in northern Saskatchewan is currently within the boreal ecoclimatic zone. Two climate change scenarios are shown in the lower panels. If the ecoclimatic

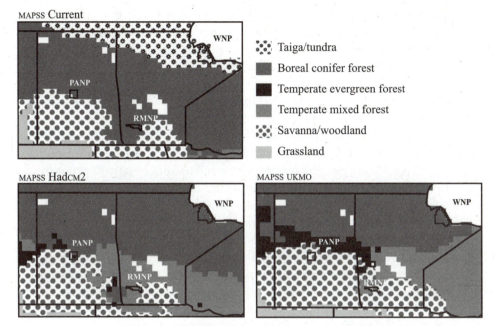

MAPSS Current

WNP

PANP

RMNP

⬚⬚⬚ Taiga/tundra

⬛ Boreal conifer forest

⬛ Temperate evergreen forest

⬛ Temperate mixed forest

⬚⬚⬚ Savanna/woodland

⬚ Grassland

MAPSS HadCM2

WNP

PANP

RMNP

MAPSS UKMO

WNP

PANP

RMNP

Figure 5.11 Potential biome changes in Prince Albert (PANP), Riding Mountain (RMNP), and Wapusk (WNP) National Parks in western Canada. MAPSS is a global vegetation model. UKMO and HadCM2 are GCMs.
Source: Scott, Malcolm, and Lemieux (2002). Reprinted with permission from Daniel Scott

zones shift northward, the park would find itself in a climate zone that ought to support savannah/woodlands. How should park management adapt in this situation? Should it protect boreal and aspen woodlands as a relic, or should it allow the park to adapt and become a grassland park? There are probably ways to maintain the forested landscape, but doing so might involve, for example, an increased effort at fire suppression.

Wapusk National Park in northeast Manitoba faces a different transition. The current climate is classified as taiga/tundra and supports forests located south of the park. In scenarios of climate change, it would shift to one that could support a boreal forest. Should Wapusk National Park managers try to preserve the sub-tundra environments or should they allow the encroachment of trees?

Thus, it can be seen that managing for adaptation or preservation involves choices and trade-offs between objectives, objectives that are likely defined by many groups besides park authorities. Climate change could potentially undermine decades of conservation efforts, and there will be new challenges and perhaps new opportunities for habitat protection and restoration in the future (Scott and Suffling 2000; Suffling 2000; Scott et al. 2002; Lemieux and Scott 2005).

Impacts on Water Resources

Because the hydrologic cycle, including human and ecosystem requirements for water, is sensitive to variations in climate, it is certain to be affected by climate change, which is expected to alter patterns of runoff, evaporation, snowmelt, soil moisture, lake and river levels, and water temperature (including the seasonal formation and melting of ice). These effects will be unique to each region and watershed.

Scenarios of climate change can be tested using a number of water resources tools that are readily available, including hydrologic and water demand models that are designed for local, watershed, or larger scales. Detailed technical reviews of hydrologic applications can be found in Oliver and Oliver (1995), Arnell et al. (2001), and Kundzewicz et al. (2007). Although it is possible for GCMs to provide direct estimates of runoff for each grid cell, hydrologists often use temperature and precipitation outputs from GCMs as direct inputs to hydrologic models calibrated for the watershed of interest. This practice offers a kind of hydrologic downscaling, though the uncertainties associated with applying global-scale climate model simulations still apply.

Figure 5.12 shows one example of a watershed-scale application for the Fraser River in British Columbia (Morrison, Quick, and Foreman 2002). The Fraser River, which is largely influenced by spring snowmelt, is close to the transition between snowmelt-driven and rainfall-driven streamflow regimes. Other snowmelt-driven watersheds that have been assessed include the Columbia River (Payne et al. 2004), the Great Lakes–St Lawrence watershed (Mortsch et al. 2000; Lofgren et al. 2002), the Rhine River (Middelkoop et al. 2001), and the Lule River (Graham et al. 2007). An important concern in such cases is the potential effect of warming on the amount and timing of spring snowmelt and its subsequent effect on the annual streamflow cycle. For the Fraser River, peak streamflow is occurring earlier in the year, as warming progresses with time.

In the Fraser River study, the current observed peak flow occurs around day 160, in mid-May. The thin line in figure 5.12, compared with the base case simulation of the hydrologic model (in this case, the

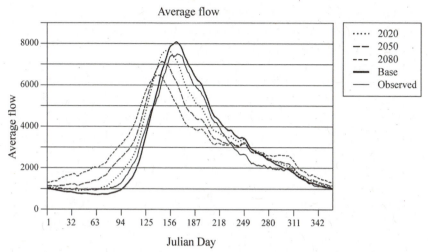

Figure 5.12   Impacts of a climate change scenario on simulated Fraser River streamflow in cubic metres per second or m³/s. "Base" refers to model simulation of observed period of record, and "observed" refers to actual measurements.
Source: Morrison, Quick, and Foreman (2002). Reprinted with permission from Elsevier Limited

UBC Watershed Model), shows how well the model simulates the observed stream flow under the current climate. This provides an indication of the utility of applying this hydrologic model to scenarios of climate change.

There are three different time slices for this scenario: the results for the 2020s are shown as dots; for the 2050s, as long dashes; and for the 2080s, as short dashes. The freshet peak becomes lower and occurs earlier by about four weeks by the 2080s. In all time frames, more water flows through the Fraser River in the winter months, and during the growing season, streamflow is reduced. The annual total volume does not necessarily change, although it does in many cases (Nohara et al. 2006). This freshet shift does, however, have implications for flood control and a number of water uses, including irrigation, fisheries, navigation, and the production of hydroelectricity in the Fraser Basin and in other snowmelt-driven watersheds.

Now taking this example to a larger scale, it is possible to examine runoff calculations directly from the climate models themselves. Arnell (1999a) compares runoff simulations for Europe. There is a difference in the level of detail between exercises at this scale and the application of a basin-scale hydrology model to an individual river. Certain details, such as the influences of landscapes would be difficult to capture, but it can be instructive to see the broad spatial patterns emerging from these simulations. For example, Arnell shows that in scenarios of climate change, colder areas in Russia, Ukraine, and Belarus experience earlier snow melt, so the month of maximum runoff happens sooner. In the Mediterranean, however, the seasonal climate tends to become wetter in the winter and drier in the summer, which makes the resulting scenarios less coherent. In most of these scenarios, there appear to be somewhat later peaks, up to two months later, suggesting that the nature of the wet season or rainy season seems to be shifting. Elsewhere, annual runoff scenarios are generally showing decreases in southern Europe and even in central Europe. There is some disagreement in the 2020s between the results for Norway and Sweden, as well as for Italy, Spain, and the Black Sea region.

An interesting follow-up to this work is an assessment of scenario changes in floods and droughts for Europe (Lehner et al. 2006). Again, two different GCMs were used, but this time as input to an integrated global water model called WaterGAP, which includes a hydrology and water use component. Incorporation of water use information is particularly important for assessments of drought risk, and substantial increases in water use are projected for Eastern Europe. Consistent with the Arnell (1999a) study, drought risk is projected to increase in southern and central Europe, though there is disagreement in results for Italy and the Adriatic and Black Sea regions. Floods are projected to become more frequent in the north in both scenarios (figure 5.13).

Inconsistencies are common in regional-scale scenario comparisons of runoff amounts, owing to differences in precipitation projections, as well as to soil moisture and evaporation sub-model structures noted earlier (chapter 3). Such inconsistencies will continue to confound studies of water-related issues, but at least for those aspects for which temperature is important, consistency across scenarios is more likely, including projections of earlier snowmelt and increased evaporation. A recent comparison of river runoff projections between different AOGCM simulations and different emission scenarios was reported by Arnell (2003). Figure 5.14 illustrates a comparison of consistency in changes in runoff for the A2 emissions scenario (high growth in emissions; see figures 3.20 and 3.23) for eight different AOGCM simulations. During the 2020s, a consistent climate change signal emerges in approximately two-thirds of the world. By the 2080s, this has increased to between 70

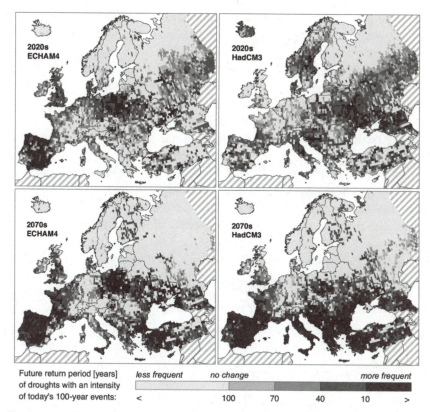

Figure 5.13   Projected changes in recurrence of 100–year droughts in Europe.
Source: Lehner et al. (2006). Reprinted with permission from Bernhard Lehner and
Springer Science and Business Media; graphic courtesy of IPCC

and 90 percent as the projected changes in temperature and precipitation become more pronounced. Areas with consistent increases in runoff include high-latitude North America and Siberia, eastern Africa, and
south and east Asia. Areas with consistent decreases include much of
mid-latitude Europe and North America, northern Africa, and most of
South America. Within this broad consensus, however, are differences
between scenarios in the magnitude and variability of projected changes
in runoff, including drought and flood magnitudes. Arnell (2003) suggests that the main differences between scenarios are largely driven by
the projected patterns of change in precipitation. In addition, differences between individual AOGCMs appear to be greater than differences
between SRES emission scenarios for a given AOGCM.

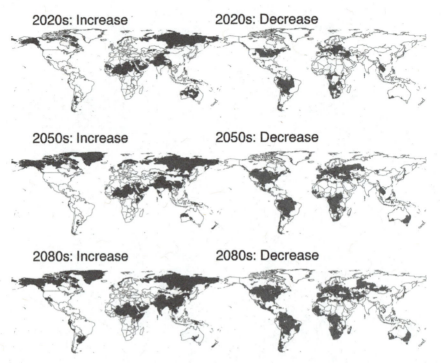

Figure 5.14   Consistency of runoff projections from global climate models from the A2 scenario.
Source: Arnell (2003). Graphic courtesy of Nigel Arnell

Which global-scale scenario is more believable? Finding an answer requires more scenario experiments conducted jointly by climate modelling groups and researchers in hydrology. An example of such an experiment is provided by Nijssen et al. (2001), who compared four GCM-based climate scenarios by applying them as inputs to hydrologic simulations for nine major watersheds around the world, using a hydrology model that was not part of the GCMs themselves (the method was similar to the one used in the Fraser Basin study just described, but it was applied to all nine watersheds). For any individual impact study at the regional-watershed scale, in the face of uncertainties like this, best practice suggests that it is prudent to use more than one scenario, since the population of available plausible scenarios is not known.

An alternative is to combine a number of climate model outputs into an "ensemble" representation of the future. Nohara et al. (2006) constructed a river flow scenario for twenty-four watersheds using an ensemble of nineteen GCM simulations for the SRES AIB scenario (figures 3.20 and 3.23). This approach offers a composite scenario that can illustrate where consensus in scenario projections can be identified. Nohara et al. (2006) produce an overall runoff result that is similar to that reported by Arnell (2003) in terms of consistency of the direction of change for various regions, but they acknowledge that it is difficult to reproduce present river discharges in individual models. They note that the variability in projected changes in runoff is larger than for projected changes in precipitation and evaporation. They conclude that AOGCMs still require improvement in their land surface schemes.

Impacts on Fisheries

Fisheries are expected to be sensitive to climate change, but the relationship is complex, and many other factors can influence the future of fish populations and their distribution. Short-term climatic variability associated with the El-Niño–Southern Oscillation (ENSO) and the Pacific Decadal Oscillation (PDO) has been shown to affect various marine fish populations in the Pacific, including salmon, sardines, and tuna (McLean et al. 2001). ENSO affects currents and associated characteristics of marine conditions, such as sea surface temperature and available nutrients. This complexity has hampered the development of analytical tools similar to crop yield or hydrologic models that could be directly applied to climate change scenarios.

Some applications on small scales offer indicators that may imply a scenario impact on fisheries. An example is the scenario estimate of water temperature for the Fraser River (Morrison, Quick, and Foreman 2002). Water temperature is an important indicator for fish, and each species has its own optimum temperature for various stages of its life cycle. Figure 5.15 shows estimates of scenario changes in water temperatures for two locations in the lower (southern) reaches of the Fraser River. As we move through this climate scenario, through the 2020s, 2050s, and 2080s, the maximum temperature can increase from the base case of 18°C to above 20°C. For salmon, increases in summer freshwater temperatures would increase heat stress, as well as contribute to reduced oxygen levels, which would further hamper migration to spawning areas.

Regarding ocean temperatures, newer versions of atmosphere-ocean global climate models (AOGCMs) provide scenarios that can, in due course, provide some indication of potential changes in marine resources,

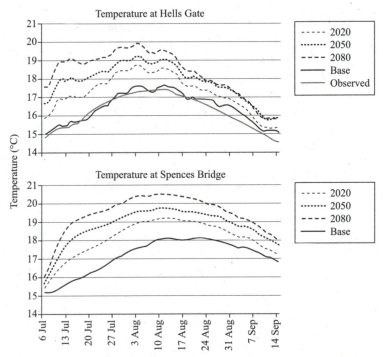

Figure 5.15 Impacts of a climate change scenario on simulated Fraser River temperatures.
Source: Morrison, Quick, and Foreman (2002). Reprinted with permission from Elsevier Limited

although projecting future changes in sea surface temperatures is considerably more difficult than for freshwater bodies (rivers and lakes), since ocean currents may change in the future climate. In the case of cool-water species, such as salmon, warming oceans may force them to shift their migrations routes poleward. In fact, there is some evidence that this is already occurring (ACIA 2004).

Figure 5.16 illustrates how decadal regime shifts in the Pacific Ocean have affected catches of salmon and sardine species. There seems to be some suggestion that when the PDO is in a positive phase, the sardine and salmon catches do better, and when the PDO is in a negative phase, they do less well. The negative phase seems to be correlated with relatively cool conditions, and the positive phase with warm ones. How will longer-term climate change affect these cycles? Will there be any consistency in responses of fish populations that will enable projections of fisheries impacts to be undertaken with high confidence?

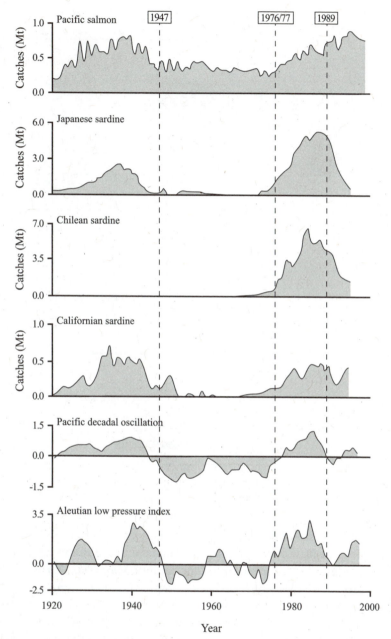

Figure 5.16   Salmon and sardine harvest in the Pacific region (in megatonnes, or Mt) compared with timing of atmospheric cycles.
Source: McLean et al. (2001). Reprinted with permission of IPCC

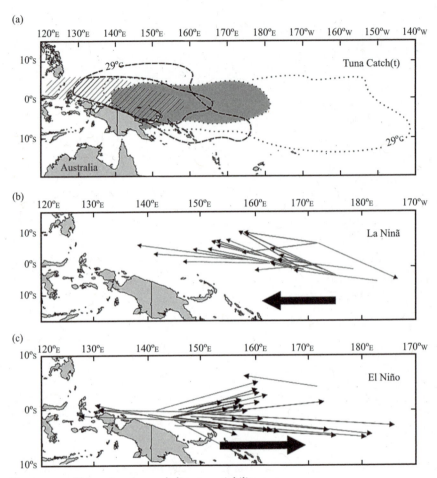

Figure 5.17   Tuna migration and climate variability.
Source: McLean et al. (2001). Reprinted with permission of IPCC

Figure 5.17 illustrates changes in tuna migration during different
phases of El Niño. The major areas of tuna catch are in the western Pacific, including the Philippines, Indonesia, and Malaysia. During the La
Niña years, there is relatively cooler water in the eastern part of the Pacific and warmer water to the west. This difference then appears to lead
to a largely east-west migration of tuna. In an El Niño year, the pattern
is reversed. The warmer water in the eastern part of the Pacific flows
eastward, bringing that warm water towards the coast of Peru and
Ecuador, which leads to an eastward tuna migration. If this relationship
is consistent, one could try to carry it forward into a climate change
scenario. This kind of study would require information about how La

Niña and El Niño would change in such a scenario. Could the El Niño phases become more frequent and the La Niña phases less frequent? Could the El Niño become stronger? There is no strong consensus around this scenario, but suppose it was to occur. A commercial tuna enterprise might have to shift operations, with implications for catch limits in international areas and in coastal areas with state-imposed off-shore limits. How would disputes over quotas be resolved in a warmer world? How should national and international fishing authorities adapt to a change in the El Niño cycle that could result from climate change?

Another aspect of climate change that affects fisheries as well as marine health more generally is the potential acidification of seawater as anthropogenic CO_2 emissions continue to be absorbed by the oceans. What effects would acidification have on marine plants and animals? How would changes in a single species translate into changes throughout the oceans? How would this affect fisheries?

For example, some species of phytoplankton may experience increased rates of photosynthesis due to the increased CO_2 in the water but, based on current literature, it is not possible to draw clear conclusions about the broader effects on marine health and fisheries. Clearly acidification would hamper calcification – the uptake of calcium carbonate for skeletal structures and shells – without which starfish, clams, snails, sea cucumbers, and coral reefs cannot survive, which would have significant impacts on marine health. As a result of these and other growing concerns about the effects of ocean acidification on marine health the German Advisory Council on Global Change (WBGU) has called for increased research efforts in this area (WBGU 2006).

DISCUSSION

The potential effects of future climate changes on ecosystems will occur through the interactions of several types of forcing. They would be driven by changes in temperature, including the length of growing seasons and dates of snowmelt; by changes in precipitation and CO_2 enrichment; extreme event characteristics, such as fire risk; and shorter-term climate cycles, such as ENSO and PDO. The driving forces, however, would not be acting alone. Their effects would be influenced by the human response, or lack of response, to climate change. Observed impacts of recent climate events have occurred when an extreme event or a change in a climate characteristic has been superimposed on landscapes under particular management regimes or on wildlife that are mobile and can shift with the winds and currents.

This chapter has offered a number of cases of potential impacts on climate-sensitive resources. Agriculture is sensitive to shifts in climate, and future climate change may result in decreases in crop yield in many circumstances. In cold regions, however, a crop yield increase could result from a lengthening of the growing season. CO_2 enrichment appears to reduce climate-related losses under certain conditions, especially for the $C3$ plants such as wheat. Plant growth in a high-CO_2 environment can also lead to changes in plant structure and competition for resources, and there may well be winners and losers in this competition. Forests can be affected by changing atmospheric CO_2 concentrations and also by changes in fire and pest risk, both of which are related to climate but also to long-term management strategies (such as fire suppression).

For ecosystems and parks, changes in eco-climates can lead to challenges for park managers, either to preserve a relic or to encourage migration. Human decisions have influenced the outcomes of past events, and prediction of future adaptations and future net impacts will depend on researchers' abilities to predict human behaviour under decision-making environments that are becoming increasingly complex (see chapter 7). Predictions of behaviour will also influence projections of the economic impacts of climate change (see chapter 6).

Water resources are also sensitive to climate, and future climate change will influence the hydrology of rivers and lakes. The Fraser River case, with the projected change in the timing of its peak flow, is representative of many other watersheds that are snowmelt driven. Earlier runoff here and in similar hydrologic regimes elsewhere (such as northern Europe) may force water managers and users into a number of operational adjustments and perhaps into changes in water governance (see chapter 7). For example, given simultaneous impacts on water resources and crops, how should impacts studies of crops incorporate adaptation strategies such as irrigation when the availability of irrigation supplies may also be affected by climate change?

Fisheries can be affected by changes in water temperature, but this is an issue of considerable complexity. The example of ENSO and its effects on fish migration illustrates this influence. Projections of future impacts will depend on projections of changes both in marine currents and climates but also in fisheries management and harvesting.

6

The Economic Aspects of Climate Change

INTRODUCTION

In chapter 5, we addressed a range of potential implications of climate change for climate-sensitive natural resources. The biologist's perspective was important because we need to understand the methodological challenges in determining impacts on agriculture and ecosystems. In this chapter, we shift our focus to the economic aspects of climate change impacts. As was the case in earlier chapters, we are not specialists in this field of study, so we approach this topic from a generalist's perspective. Our purpose here is to try to understand this component of the climate change damage report.

We begin by considering some of the challenges in assessing economic damages from climate change. The next section outlines some of the broad challenges that face economists when considering future climate change scenarios. The following two sections then focus on some basic definitions from the economics literature, including value (market and non-market), welfare, cost, discounting, willingness to pay (WTP), willingness to accept (WTA), purchasing-power parity (PPP), and supply and demand, as well as cost-benefit, Ricardian, and sustainability approaches.

From there, we will discuss several case studies from the literature on sectoral impacts, as well as some examples of what can be called higher-order impacts. For example, after an assessment of specific damages to a cornfield or a coastal zone, what kind of analysis is needed to bring this assessment to a social level? Here we consider insurance, health, and the value of a statistical life, or VOSL, which was a hugely controversial topic when it emerged at the end of the Intergovernmental Panel on Climate Change (IPCC) Second Assessment Report in 1995. Even though that topic was more or less avoided in more recent IPCC Third and Fourth Assessment Reports in 2001 and 2007, respectively, it is still of considerable interest and needs to be better understood.

In order to arrive at a climate change damage report for people in economic terms, their economic status will have to play a role in any related calculations of costs and benefits. Like it or not, governments and industries will make decisions on the basis of whether their policies or strategies will be beneficial from an economic point of view. Even though some things are hard to define economically, such as the value of an ecosystem or the value of a culture, the financial metric will need to be identified and assessed. And in chapter 7, when we consider more of the social aspects of climate change impacts, we move away from the dollar or the Euro as a metric and instead use alternatives to assess these climate change impacts and the many dimensions of adaptation.

CHALLENGES TO ECONOMIC ASSESSMENTS OF CLIMATE CHANGE IMPACTS

As we consider how to define the costs of climate change impacts and of adaptation measures, we must start by determining what difference a scenario of climate change actually makes to a sector or location of interest. For an assessment of a scenario of economic changes that does or does not include climate change, there needs to be a method for measuring the benefits or costs of the way some attribute is changing, whether it is an entire ecosystem, a water supply, or just a single agricultural product.

Economists can compute costs for everything from direct damages from a climatic event to a climate-related policy. Often when economists are computing these costs, they will choose an indicator from the ecosystem or infrastructure of interest and assess that indicator over time. Time becomes particularly important to these economic assessments. Economists will recognize that the values of a particular good will change over time and at different rates, and the values will vary for each region and good. Market forces can also affect the value of a good, sometimes increasing its value even after accounting for inflation (as in the case of land in rapidly growing urban areas). All of this will affect how damage costs and response measures are compared.

Similarly, non-climate forces will affect any comparison between damage costs and the benefits of a specific emissions reduction measure. What is even more problematic in this case is that it is difficult to connect an emissions reduction, which can influence global atmospheric concentrations of CO_2, to a reduction of local flood or drought damage.

How can one determine whether a reduction of 5 or 10 megatonnes (MT) of carbon from an individual country such as Poland or Japan would lead to a particular benefit for a drought-prone country in northern Africa? If it is already very difficult for the physical and biological scientists to establish such a linkage, how will an economist do it?

Another time-related aspect is the rate of climate change itself. Climate change, it is suggested, may happen very quickly in geophysical terms, but relatively slowly in human terms. Climate change is therefore similar to what is known as the creeping environmental problem (see Glantz 2003), which includes examples such as droughts and desertification (see chapter 2). These creeping environmental problems are not like floods, which take place relatively quickly with highly visible short-term effects. As the water rises during the onset of flooding, governments will authorize emergency measures, which will vary according to their capacity to respond (which in turn depends on previous experience, warning systems, levels of planning, and so on). But with a drought or with climate change, early warning signals are not necessarily clearly agreed upon. The signal may be difficult to detect, which makes the rate of change an important factor. As well, the various kinds of observable impacts on ecosystems will happen at different rates. In chapter 5, we saw that some places, particularly in the high latitudes, are already showing observed changes now. Elsewhere, such as in the tropics, it is more difficult to sort out the climate signal from other forces that are affecting the landscape. Differing rates and magnitudes of climate-related signals can also influence people's perceptions of climate change (see chapter 7).

Climate change impacts can happen simultaneously with impacts of other forces of change, such as population growth, technological improvements, and political shifts. There could be cumulative effects resulting from these various forces of change. Could this kind of synergy lead to a cost that is greater than the sum of individual impacts? How does an economist incorporate these synergies? Is it possible to consider the structure of how a particular region's economy works and how all of these direct and indirect impacts may actually happen?

The literature offers a few examples of how such analyses can be done. Climate science has already moved away from the $2xCO_2$ equilibrium scenario towards transient scenarios, beginning in the early 1990s with the arbitrary scenario of a 1 percent CO_2 change per year. The subsequent development of the IS92 and SRES emissions scenarios have resulted in more impacts case studies that are based on either the IS92 or the SRES transient scenarios (see chapters 3 and 10). This means that impacts researchers can now provide economists and social scientists with impacts results in different time series and not just single snapshots of the year that 2xCO$_2$ is reached. This is a small step forward from the earlier impacts research efforts during the 1980s and 1990s, based on the equilibrium scenarios, which made it very difficult for economists to determine climate change costs.

Two interesting elements to consider in conjunction with these other issues are the concepts of a "safe landing" and a "tolerable window." These similar concepts are related to the notion that there is a particular amount of warming that can occur or a particular amount of CO$_2$ that can accumulate in the atmosphere without endangering the earth's eco-systems or its peoples. A CO$_2$ concentration of 370 ppm, which would be a one-third increase in the past century, may be considered to be safe, with perhaps even 400 ppm still being considered safe. Recall that the stated objective of article 2 of the United Nations Framework Convention on Climate Change (UNFCCC) is to avoid dangerous anthropogenic interference, but that objective is not defined in a quantitative manner. What is the threshold then? Is it 450 ppm? Is it 475 ppm? Or should this damage level be defined in terms of temperature? The European Union has recently adopted the position that global warming should be limited to no more than 2°C above pre-industrial times (Commission of the European Communities 2007; Ott et al. 2004).

The issue of what the threshold should be raises an important question about who actually defines such a threshold. The climate scientists provide the climate information, but they do not actually define what level of warming would be considered dangerous: this question is out-side their disciplinary context. Climate science can define temperature changes resulting from an emissions change. Biology and other natural sciences can use this information to assess the implications of climate change for ecosystems, agriculture, and freshwater, but more information is needed about the human dimensions, including the perspective offered by economics.

Economists have a role here because they can define what is potentially economically dangerous. But what indicators should they use? Should they consider a percentage change in gross domestic product (GDP) for a developed country or a developing country? What if these GDP changes differ between countries for the same amount of "global–temperature" change? An ecologist might define "dangerous" by assessing possible extinctions of species. A social scientist might consider implications for community health, community structure, or the stability of particular communities, such as small island states. One might also consider some indicators of sustainability and how climate change may affect a region's ability to attain sustainable development goals (see chapter 11).

TERMINOLOGY AND ANALYTICAL FRAMEWORKS

There are many different branches of economics. In this chapter, we focus primarily on microeconomics because that is where there has been the most research activity related to climate change. Other research contributions have been coming from environmental or ecological economics. In this section, we begin by defining some basic economic terms and then move on to more in-depth discussions of methodological issues in following sections.

Welfare, Value, and Purchasing Power Parity

The IPCC has compiled a glossary of various economic terms that are of interest for both climate change adaptation and mitigation (see Metz et al. 2001). Others who have explored economic aspects of climate change include Pearce et al. (1996), Nordhaus (1998), Jepma and Munasinghe (1998), Mendelsohn and Neumann (1999), Tol (1999, 2002), Tol et al. (2004), Munasinghe and Swart (2005), and Stern et al. (2007). A number of key terms are listed in box 6.1.

First, let us consider the definitions of "welfare" and "value." Welfare is a measure of value and not exclusively of financial costs. Value is determined by the preferences and behaviours of consumers. These things are not clearly physically defined functions, which is why marketing surveys are so important for the business community. These surveys provide some insight into the psychological or sociological aspects of decision making in a quantitative expression of consumer preferences.

Value has several components. Rao (2000) describes direct-use values and indirect-use values for consumptive and non-consumptive uses. For example, ecosystems provide flood control (a direct-use value) and wildlife habitat (an indirect-use value that may be non-consumptive for a bird watcher and consumptive for a hunter). There are also other types of values, such as existence value. For example, knowing that polar bears exist has value to some.

Box 6.1   Basic Economic Terms

Cost. An expense, loss, or sacrifice. In cases of climate change, there are particular costs associated with impacts if there is no adaptation, and there may be residual impacts after adaptation, as well as costs for specific adaptation and mitigation measures.

Cost-benefit analysis (CBA). A process that weighs all favourable and unfavourable effects associated with a policy change. Changes in benefits and costs over time are discounted to the present so that a net present value can be calculated. CBA can be used to rank and compare several possible policy interventions.

Discount rate. The rate per year of decline in the present value of costs and benefits. This rate is different from interest rates established for loans and savings and from inflation rates, which represent increases in costs over time for an unchanging basket of goods. Of relevance to climate change and other public policy concerns is the *social rate of discount,* in which issues of value and equity are considered. This rate establishes how a certain benefit or cost would be valued now if it were to occur some time in the future.

Elasticity of demand. The relationship between changes in the quantity of a good demanded and changes in its price.

Purchasing power parity (PPP). A PPP exchange rate equalizes the purchasing power of different currencies in their home countries for a given basket of goods. This rate differs from currency exchange rates. Application of PPP is controversial because it is hard to find comparable baskets of goods with which to compare purchasing power across countries. PPP estimates tend to lower GDP estimates in industrialized countries and raise them in developing countries.

Ricardian model. A model for estimating the relationship between land prices and variables describing changes in climatic, economic, and soil conditions. The model builds on David Ricardo's theory of comparative advantage, which describes the ability of a particular location to produce a good at a lower cost compared to the cost of producing it at another location.

Supply and demand. The equilibrium market price of a commodity occurs when consumer demand is the same as producer supply. The law of supply states that the higher the price of the product, the more the producer will supply. The law of demand states that the higher the price of the product, the less the consumer will demand. Additional factors can influence these relationships, including technological innovation and trade agreements.

Value. Worth, desirability, or utility based on individual preferences. Different categories of values are associated with environmental assets – values of direct use (consumption), indirect use (functional benefits), and non-use (existence).

Value of a statistical life (VOSL). The attribution of material value to a change in the risk of death, as opposed to the value of human life itself. There are different approaches to estimating VOSL. The preferred approach is based on willingness to pay (WTP) to reduce risks (see willingness to pay, below). Since the VOSL depends on a person's income, VOSL estimates will reflect differences between wealthy and poor communities and countries.

Welfare. A measure of value determined by the preferences and behaviour of consumers.

Willingness to accept (WTA). The willingness of individuals to accept payment to give up a resource or experience some deterioration or damage. WTA can be influenced by behaviour, whereby individuals tend to inflate the amounts they would like to receive or to be averse to risks of losing benefits that already exist or to paying for substitutes that may be difficult to obtain.

Willingness to pay (WTP). The value of an improvement to a person based on what they are willing to pay for it. Unlike WTA, WTP is influenced by the ability to pay, so this can vary considerably between countries or between income groups within countries.

Sources: Pearce et al. (1996), Jepma and Munasinghe (1998), Portney (1998), Mendelsohn and Neumann (1999), Metz et al. (2001), and Munasinghe and Swart (2005)

Another important concept is purchasing power parity (PPP). The world does not use a single currency, and the world is not composed of a single market: different countries have different currencies and different markets. In order to compare what consumers or nation states do, an economist must try to account for the relative value of different currencies for different markets, but this relative value is not defined exclusively by the currency exchange. For example, if one currency falls in relation to another (perhaps because of international trade), this devaluation may not have any immediate effect on the standard of living in that country, including the middle-class. A middle-class person in Bangladesh can be considered to have a relative status similar to a middle-class person in Canada. What a middle class person in Bangladesh can buy locally should therefore be similar, in that context, to what a middle-class person in Canada can purchase and consume. The currencies are different, and the items they buy are different, but a PPP perspective attempts to merge those two societies.

An undercurrent here is related to the barter economy, which exists in many regions amongst advanced industrial economies and indigenous peoples. In this type of economy, people trade things – one good for another – and that trade may not be recorded in national economic statistics. It is difficult for an economist to incorporate such trading into an analysis, because information about it may be anecdotal, or it may be imputed by estimating the average price of the replacement value of a good obtained by traditional harvesting or bartering (Fast and Berkes 1999). If economists leave this type of trading out, however, they risk undervaluing the economies of communities – and perhaps even of entire countries.

Supply and Demand

In general, as the price of a good or service increases, the demand for this good or service will decrease (figure 6.1). And if the price decreases, then the quantity demanded will obviously increase. The intersection of the supply and demand functions represents the market equilibrium, or balance, between the quantity that producers will supply and the price that consumers will pay for a particular good or service.

If there is a change in the climate, however, then the supply and the demand may change. Figure 6.2 illustrates how a supply reduction resulting from adverse climate change would lead to an increase in price. Conversely, a climate change that increased supply would lead to a

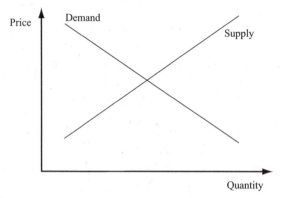

Figure 6.1   Schematic of changes in supply and demand as functions of changes in price and quantity

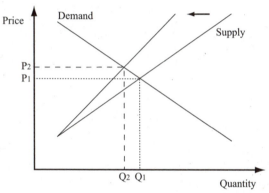

Figure 6.2   Impact of shift in supply resulting from adverse climate change. Adapted from Ausubel (1980)

reduction in price. Climate change may affect the availability of a raw product, such as water, wood, or corn, thereby affecting supply. Changing certain constraints or opportunities may affect demand for these products. For instance, a cool-climate species will not necessarily do well in warmer conditions, but warm-climate species could fare better and expand. Thus, the supply of that species might actually increase, making it cheaper to grow than it was in the former climate regime. For example, if corn displaced spring wheat in a region experiencing climate change, then wheat growers would have to find someplace else to grow their crops. In the meantime, as corn supply increased, corn prices would decrease, assuming there was no change in demand. This scenario would also depend, of course, on the availability of corn or other substitutable products from other competing locations, a possibility that will be discussed later in this chapter.

"Elasticity" is another important term in economics: it denotes the responsiveness of consumer demand to changes in quantity and price. The demand for a particular good is considered to be very elastic if the demand changes very quickly when there is a price change. Demand is considered inelastic if a large change in price does not affect demand to a similar degree. For example, the demand for gasoline is inelastic. Consumers will continue to purchase gasoline despite price increases (within some limits) because they are committed to a particular commuter route or transportation option. If they could change their travel patterns, their demand for gasoline would be more elastic, but many people do not have such flexibility. On the other hand, a high price for gasoline provides an incentive to increase exploration and development of oil resources that may have been too expensive to consider while gasoline prices were lower. There could be increased offshore exploration and remote exploration in places that might not have been explored at a lower price, and if an additional supply became available, it could also affect the price.

Discounting

Economists also have a fairly substantial impact on the climate change debate with their projections or assumptions about how the value of infrastructure or some other good changes over time. This approach is known as "discounting." Nordhaus (2007) describes two discount concepts. With respect to a good or service, discounting means that the price we are willing to pay at a future date is less than we would pay for immediate delivery. However, with respect to the welfare of future generations, discounting means that an action taken today for a future generation is of less value than an action taken for immediate benefit. This is referred to as a rate of social time preference or a "time discount rate." An ethical ideal would be that future generations should be treated equally with present generations, resulting in a time discount rate near zero, but the discount rate for a good would be similar to a rate of return on investment, perhaps 5 percent per year or higher. This means that there can be large differences between these two discount rates (see discussion on ethical concerns later in this chapter).

Discounting is different from tracing the long-term price fluctuations of a commodity like gold or of a currency, both of which can decrease or

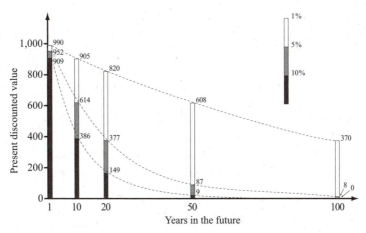

Figure 6.3   Value of US$1,000 worth of damage in the future discounted to the present.
Source: Jepma and Munasinghe (1998). Reprinted with permission of Mohan
Munasinghe and Catrinus Jepma, and Cambridge University Press

increase in relative value according to changing market conditions. Willingness to pay (WTP) can influence the estimates of changing market values, and subsequently, estimates of discount rates (see the next section).

A key consideration for climate change economics is the choice of the
discount rate. For example, figure 6.3 illustrates how the present value
of $1,000 worth of damage would change over time for different rates
of discounting. At a rate of 1 percent per year, an item worth $1,000 to-
day would be worth $370 dollars a hundred years from now. But if a
5 percent rate was used, the value of this item would decline to nearly
zero a hundred years from now. In fact, at this rate, the value is nearly
zero even fifty years from now. As this graph illustrates, there is a huge
difference between a rate of 1 percent and a rate of 5 percent, even after
only ten years. If this graph refers to damage costs associated with future climate change impacts, the choice of discount rate influences the
estimate of the value (cost) of future damages without adaptation, as
well as the savings from damages avoided through planned adaptation.

If we think that the loss from a climate-related event today is worth
$1,000, then that damage value is also being discounted to the future;
that is, today's policy cost is being compared with future discounted damage costs. This comparison tends to tip the balance away from early action on adaptation (and perhaps mitigation as well) and more towards
waiting to see what damages will occur. Even a 1 percent discount rate
makes it difficult to compare the choices "adapt now" or "mitigate now"

with "wait-and-see." Or to put this point another way, at a 1 percent rate, it may be possible to justify a $130 million policy action today in order to avoid $1 billion in damages in 2100, but at a 5 percent rate, only a $35,000 policy measure would be justified (Rao 2000). This conclusion almost guarantees that on an economic basis, the wait-and-see approach would be seen as the preferred option. Obviously, results like this can in turn have a significant influence on the results of cost-benefit analyses of proposed policy measures (see below).

Discounting can also leave out the influence of potential changes in ecosystem services resulting from climate change and the need to account for sustainability requirements of both the market and the non-market aspects of ecosystem services and existence (Rao 2000).

On the other side of this coin, of course, are commentators who would argue that we should not be using discount rates at all when considering responses to climate change. We should be thinking about long-term sustainability, which includes intergenerational equity. In this paradigm, a future generation's requirements would not be discounted against the needs of the current generation, thereby elevating the importance of long-term protection of an asset, whether it was a building or a park. How should economics address these two different paradigms, including potential changes in attitude regarding such values?

The application of discounting in analyses of future costs needs to be considered very carefully. Future generations may value capital, land, and other assets differently than the current generation does. Valuation may also change as development patterns change. Land values often increase as a region's farmland becomes urban land. Other regions that remain rural may not experience such changes. How should these effects be included?

Willingness to Pay and Other Concepts

Economies are complex systems, and it is difficult to track the various indirect relationships within these systems. Besides the concepts noted above, other aspects are worth considering as we try to understand how climate change may affect economies. One question to ponder is, how do our economies and levels of consumption and production affect climate change, which will in turn affect our economies?

First, let us consider the potential for irreversibility. In the case of a rise in sea level affecting a coastline, there may be permanent inundation, which might be considered irreversible. On the other hand, beach nourishment activities and other efforts at coastal reclamation (such as planting various kinds of grasses to attract sand, create artificial sand-dunes, and so on) may offset any notions that coastal inundation is inevitable, except under the most extreme circumstances.

Next, consider the potential for substitutability in the marketplace. A brand of one product can be substituted with another brand of the same product, or presumably a product with similar attributes could be substituted. If salmon declined, tuna might still be available. But can this idea of substitution be applied to, for example, the effects of the loss of a glacier on the quality of life of people who live nearby? Recall the discussion of existence value earlier in this chapter. If a particular glacier melted, could it be replaced by another glacier still existing at another location? Or if all the glaciers were lost, would their replacement by a different ecosystem with habitat for different species of wildlife compensate the marketplace? Could society accept the loss of the glaciers because there would be more alpine forest and meadows where before there was ice? Is that kind of substitution actually possible.

For each trade-off there has to be a determination of what the true balance (or trade-off) actually is between human desires for the environmental services of trees, the existence value of glaciers, and the direct-use value of cars (see the next section). Climate change resulting from GHG emissions is a global-scale human-induced problem, and its effects have many different dimensions and scales. Ultimately, decisions about what to do and what not to do about climate change are going to be based on people's perceptions of what their preferred baskets of goods are, and whether a climate change policy has enough weight in its own right to change development decisions remains to be seen.

If society is to make choices regarding climate change policy and if it wants to apply economics as part of the decision process, the focus will ultimately be on determining the costs and benefits of any proposed action or set of actions. A key consideration in estimates of costs and benefits is willingness to pay (WTP), which is the payment an individual would think acceptable to access something, use something, or protect something. WTP roughly measures the amount of income a person is willing to forego in exchange for an improved state of the world (Fankhauser and Tol 1997). This amount is not necessarily based on ability to pay (ATP). A person may be willing to spend a million dollars to protect local forests from clear-cutting, but that person may not actually have the ability to pay that amount. Similarly, willingness to accept (WTA) represents compensation for a loss, such as the loss of local forests, including aesthetic or commercial losses. This compensation can be estimated for the amount of suffering without monetary compensation or with monetary compensation. The difference is usually that the greater the loss, the higher the compensation required.

WTP and WTA arguments are often viewed as problematic because the valuations that people (the public) ascribe to ecosystems are usually not based on ATP. With the exception of forest and wetland losses, non-market impacts are at best only partially estimated. WTA is often considered to be greater than WTP in cases where there is actually an assumed property right that may become damaged (Tol, Fankhauser, and Pearce 1999). Consistent with this observation is an interesting example related to health issues cited by Frank (2000). In a survey Frank compared individuals' self-reported WTP for a cure for a death-causing disease that they might or might not contract with their self-reported WTA an experimental exposure to the same disease with a similar risk of death. In this example, respondents indicated a WTP of $800 for a cure but a WTA exposure for $100,000, two costs that differ substantially.

WTP and WTA are examples of contingent valuation, in that the values obtained from surveys depend on respondents' knowledge of the asset (such as an ecosystem, a historic site, or a house) to be protected, and the expressed preferences may have little to do with the value of the asset or with the risk to it (Berk and Fovell 1999). Valuing climate change impacts, as well as any related adaptation actions, are very difficult jobs (Munasinghe and Swart 2005). Although it may be possible to describe precautionary or no-regrets actions, given current knowledge about projected climate change, WTP and WTA may be affected by climate-related surprise, because it is hard to define impacts futures well enough to alert people that the future will be different from the past. Since climate change has become visible only during the last quarter century, and notwithstanding the examples of some historic extreme events such as the 1930s Dust Bowl in North America, there is no past human response to a rapidly changing climate from which such WTP and WTA values may be inferred (Berk and Fovell 1999).

The reality of the irreversibility of damages and the potential that substitution may not occur or that people may not be willing or able to afford substitutions, raises the interesting issue of the cost of adaptation and the likelihood that maladaptation will occur despite observed experiences with climate-related events, including extreme events such as storm surges resulting in coastal inundation. As will be discussed in chapter 7, adaptation to an uncertain climate change future will not be

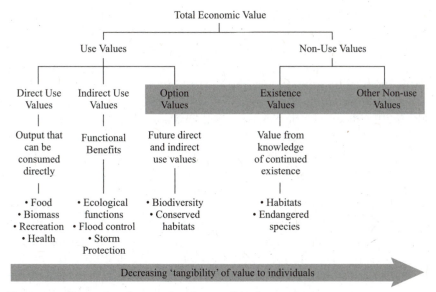

Figure 6.4   Categories of economic values attributed to ecosystems.
Source: Munasinghe (1992) and reprinted in Munasinghe et al. (1996). Reprinted with permission of Mohan Munasinghe and IPCC

easy. How should we determine the costs of adaptation measures if they are implemented outside the normal planning process, with its associated institutional costs?

Market versus Non-market Values

Economics distinguishes between market and non-market values. Some goods and services are difficult to value because they are managed for the general public, rather than for a competitive market that includes ownership of the good or service. Ecosystems are managed for the public good. Economic activities associated with ecosystems do take place, and monetary use values can be associated with them (figure 6.4).

However, there are also non-use values, which may have some intangible attributes. For example, a person may not necessarily visit a wildlife refuge, but, as discussed previously in this chapter, it may still be important to that person that the refuge be protected because of its existence value. There have been estimates of the total economic value of services provided by ecosystems (Costanza et al. 1997) that suggest that these values are substantial, perhaps exceeding current conventional estimates of global GDP. These values include flood control, water quality improvements, food production, genetic resources, cultural opportunities, air quality improvements, and other benefits that may be undervalued by people. Other attributes such as biodiversity, conserved habitat, and the protection of endangered species become less tangible and more difficult to value in monetary terms. The intangible nature of the non-market values of such things as ecosystems and public health makes them difficult to include in cost-benefit analysis (see below).

Fankhauser and Tol (1997) offer a summary of cost assessments of market and non-market impacts of climate change. They have attempted to categorize what the various market and non-market impacts are, impacts such as property loss and ecosystem damage, and to determine what values can be estimated or have already been estimated in the literature. Some updates on these are available in Smith et al. (2001) and Stern (2007).

Some scenario-based case studies and damage cost estimates are available for a few sectors. A number of case studies have focused on agriculture, forestry, water resources, and damages from observed extreme events. If a climate scenario could estimate changes in extreme-event frequency and magnitude (such as changes in hurricanes), it would be possible to estimate a value for damage associated specifically with such changes, under different assumptions of adaptive behaviour (such as scenario changes in insurance coverage; see below).

EXPERIENCES IN DEFINING COSTS

As with most aspects of assessing climate change impacts, many uncertainties are associated with determining costs or benefits of climate change effects, including those accruing from reduced climate-related risks that may occur in some cases, as well as from planned adaptation measures. So far, we have considered supply and demand, discounting, market and non-market values, WTP, WTA, and PPP. In this section, we explore how these concepts are incorporated into different approaches to assessing the costs of projected climate change impacts, or to the "damage report," as well as costs and benefits of various adaptation and mitigation measures.

Cost-Benefit Analysis

Whenever people decide whether the advantages of a particular action are likely to outweigh its drawbacks, they engage in a form of cost-benefit analysis (CBA). Specifically, CBA is an economic tool to aid social decision making, a tool that offers to identify and express in dollar terms all the effects of proposed policies or projects, including the "do nothing" option (Portney 1998). Inputs are measured in terms of opportunity costs – their value in their best alternative use. The process involves comparing the monetary value of initial and ongoing expenses with the expected return.

Constructing plausible measures of the costs and benefits of specific actions is often very difficult. In practice, analysts try to estimate costs and benefits either by using survey methods or by drawing inferences from market behaviour. A CBA attempts to put all relevant costs and benefits on a common temporal footing. A time element is thereby included, necessitating the use of discounting (discussed earlier in this chapter). The selected discount rate is then used to compute all relevant future costs and benefits in present-value terms.

The choice of a discount rate can be very controversial. Government policies or projects typically produce streams of benefits and costs over time, rather than in one-shot increments. Commonly, a substantial portion of the costs are incurred early in the life of a project or policy, while benefits may extend for many years (perhaps beginning only after some delay). Yet, because people prefer a dollar today to a dollar ten years from now, CBA typically discounts future benefits and costs back to present values. However, the costs of a policy change taken today are often far easier to quantify than its future long-term benefits, especially when the policy concerns environmental and health issues (Frank 2000).

Not only are there technical disagreements among economists about the interest rate (or rates) at which these future impacts should be discounted, but there are ethical problems as well (discussed later in this chapter). If the discount rate is relatively high, consider its likely effects on a CBA applied to policies with significant intergenerational effects, such as policies pertaining to the prevention of global climate change or the disposal of high-level radioactive wastes. The short-term costs of policy implementation would likely be assessed to be higher than long-term benefits under such circumstances, thereby leading decision makers to delay implementation (Portney 1998).

During cost-benefit analysis, monetary values may also be assigned to less tangible effects such as the various risks that could contribute to partial or total project failure. This is especially true when governments use the technique, for instance, to decide whether to introduce regulation, build new infrastructure, or change health policy. In the latter case, a value must be put on human life (see the discussion of the value of a statistical life later in this chapter) or the environment (discussed earlier in this chapter), often causing great controversy. The cost-benefit principle says, for example, that we should install a guardrail on a dangerous stretch of mountain road if the dollar cost of doing so is less than the implicit dollar value of the injuries, deaths, and property damage thus prevented (Frank 2000).

In a CBA, climate change adaptation and mitigation responses can be compared in a number of ways. One could add together adaptation costs and residual damage and compare this total with emissions reduction costs, less damages avoided. This calculation would address the question of whether it is of greater benefit to mitigate or to accept the damage and pay to adapt. Which is the more cost-effective solution for climate change?

In a situation like that, there may potentially be winners and losers (Glantz 2003). A farmer in the high latitudes experiencing a lengthening of the growing season may obtain benefits, while a coastal community in a small tropical island state would experience losses from rising sea levels and associated higher storm surges. In a cost-benefit approach, the winners and losers would both count. The winners would be able to keep their winnings even though other people and ecosystems or infrastructures were experiencing losses.

The Ricardian Approach

Mendelsohn and Neumann (1999) organized a study of how the US economy could be affected by climate change. It included a number of case studies of the effects of climate change on water, forests, agriculture, and other climate-sensitive sectors of the economy. The analysis followed what is known as the Ricardian approach (see box 6.1).

According to the Ricardian method, the analysis begins by considering climate change as a change in comparative risk or opportunity. In either case, it is expected that the value of land will change because of changes in risk perception by people, businesses, and governments. Any reaction to a perceived change in risk or opportunity created by climate change should subsequently affect the value (and market price) of land. If the prevailing market view favoured an increase in risk, the value of land would be expected to decline. And if it did, a market-induced adaptation would automatically occur, aside from anything that might come from a climate policy. This Ricardian approach differs very much from one that looks at the physical impacts themselves and uses those as starting points.

As an example, consider the case of a rise in sea level. Rather than computing a potential impact of this change on coastal infrastructure, and regardless of whether this infrastructure was developed with climate change in mind, the Ricardian approach would postulate that if it is known that sea level rise is inevitable, then people, businesses, and governments will react by moving things out of the way, or by not protecting existing structures as they age. Their reaction will then be reflected in the market for land.

Within this scenario, insurance companies may not underwrite development in high-risk zones, thus making the value of land and infrastructure drop, and hindering new development. Once the rise in sea level actually took place, this event and associated higher storm surges would be taking place at a site that no longer had the economic value it had had previously. Therefore, the subsequent damage would be relatively low because of the market's reaction to a perceived change in risk, and not because of a climate change policy (Yohe, Neumann, and Marshall 1999). This damage estimate would be much lower than estimates that assume continued development in the same location.

If climate change results in an increased risk, one might expect a decline in land value (Yohe, Neumann, and Marshall 1999). Similarly, if a climate-related opportunity could be foreseen, such as an expanded growing season in a cold climate region, maybe the land value should be assumed to increase, because more farmers would compete to buy that land for agricultural purposes. In reality, however, business or government responses may not proceed in a simple direct fashion as the change in climate becomes apparent. How would climate change affect the governance of development, such as the zoning of land, or the resolution of conflicts between urban development and the protection of agricultural land reserves? Could local-scale land and resource development policies change in response to climate changes? Would a community's historical and cultural attachment to a particular location drive its preference for re-development in areas that had already experienced a damaging extreme event? Consider, for example, the current debate about the future of post-Katrina New Orleans (Tierney and Guibert 2005; Kunreuther, Daniels, and Kettl 2006). And how would that debate affect land owners, businesses, and communities? These are primarily development questions with implications for the region's ability to adapt, and there are many associated uncertainties.

SUSTAINABILITY APPROACH

In the sustainability approach, the analysis does not trade off benefits and costs, in the belief that if there are losers, then the winners should not accept the benefits. How can a winner take his or her winnings if it means that somebody else has suffered great harm? In this case, there perhaps might be some compensation to offset some or all of the damages. Thus, the sustainability approach is constructed in a different manner from the more traditional cost-benefit approach.

The question of unequal distribution of costs (or losses) and benefits is important because those deciding which economic analysis to accept may need to consider it. It may be easier to just focus on economic efficiency or to assume that everyone should pay the same amount for clean air. However, all people and all countries are not in the same situation, in terms of vulnerability, exposure, GHG emissions history, or wealth.

Some authors have begun to discuss the concept of burden-sharing, which refers to the distribution of the commitments of climate policy targets among nations. "Burden" can be interpreted as referring to the political or economic resistance to reducing GHG emissions or to the potential damages resulting from global warming itself (Aaheim 1999). What is a fair burden for one country may be unfair for another. A country that sees global warming as a serious threat might invest considerably in both GHG mitigation and adaptation measures. Another country that sees advantages in a warmer climate might see that policy measures may cost more than any damages avoided. In other words, what is be considered fair may depend on a country's views of its net costs of policy commitments (benefits from reduced warming minus the costs of policy measures). But as a basis for fair burden-sharing, these net costs may not represent similar burdens for countries with different levels of wealth.

There are other issues to think about when comparing efficiency-based and equity-based approaches. Intergenerational preferences become very important, making it necessary to find a wider definition of the kinds of risk that may be unacceptable. As well, the importance of cultural aspects cannot be ignored in calculating costs. As these models are constructed, could it change how governments and industries and people look at a policy that is designed to deal with future made more uncertain by climate change? How do these models deal with the issue of market and non-market values?

SECTORAL IMPACTS OF CLIMATE CHANGE

We now discuss some of the impacts of climate change on agriculture, water resources, and coastal zones. We also consider some of the disasters resulting from extreme events.

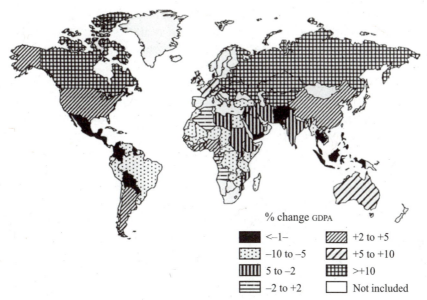

% change GDPA

■	<–1–	▨	+2 to +5
▨	–10 to –5	▨	+5 to +10
▥	5 to –2	▦	>+10
▤	–2 to +2	☐	Not included

Figure 6.5   Impacts of climate change on gross domestic agricultural production.
Source: Fischer et al. (1994). Reprinted with permission from Elsevier Limited

Agriculture

An example of climate change impacts on the agricultural sector is presented in figure 6.5. Typically, a case study of agriculture includes an estimated change in crop yield. This change can be converted to a market value, which can be expressed in monetary terms directly or as a percentage change in some indicator such as GDP.

In this example, changes in the GDP for countries around the world are shown for one of the older climate change scenarios available during the early 1990s, the GISS scenario. Note that different countries experience different directions of change in this scenario, which indicates that it contains both winners and losers. The largest economic losses, resulting from net changes in crop yield, associated changes in prices, and the effects of CO_2 fertilization are estimated for countries in the semi-arid tropics, including the Sahel region of Africa, India, Brazil, other South American countries, and almost all the Central American countries (Fischer et al. 1994). Drought induced by climate change, more than temperature, appears to be the biggest reason for these negative consequences. For the countries that are in colder regions, however, there are projections of benefits caused by a longer growing season.

Since this is an aggregated analysis, changes in Alaska, for example, are seen as exactly the same as changes in the central United States, even though they clearly have different climate constraints. Another "winner" in this simulation is China.

Adams et al. (1999) provide a more detailed regional analysis of US agriculture for hypothetical warming scenarios but not for a GCM or emissions-based scenario (see chapter 3). Results for this analysis indicate that the southeast region of the United States would experience reductions in crop yield, while the northwest region would experience increases. This pattern illustrates the importance of regional differences within countries, differences that can be hidden if analyses are restricted to the national scale.

Gitay et al. (2001) note that other aspects are not well captured in these analyses. Adaptive behaviour is assumed to proceed with nearly perfect foresight by farmers (Schneider, Easterling, and Mearns 2000), and without consideration of potential influences of governance structures, future changes in the availability of irrigation supplies, and emerging trends in population, food demand, and technology. Results are also very sensitive to assumptions about CO_2 fertilization. Darwin and Kennedy (2000) indicate that CO_2 fertilization can potentially result in global yield increases but that the economic value of those increases may not be as high as previously estimated.

Water Resources

Another US case is provided by Hurd et al. (1999), who used the same hypothetical scenarios as Adams et al. (1999) for a study of water demand by various sectors of the US economy. The purpose of this study was to assess welfare impacts of changing availability of water for different uses, including agriculture, manufacturing and industry, thermal electric and hydroelectric production, and other non-consumptive uses (such as navigation, flood control, and recreation).

The analysis used a series of arbitrary cases, ranging from 1.5°C to 5°C warming, combined with precipitation increases of 15 percent or 7 percent or no change in precipitation for four watersheds in the United States. The worst-case scenario for changes in water resources as a result of climate change occurs with a 5°C increase in temperature with no accompanying increase in precipitation. Conversely, the best-case scenario would be a 1.5°C warming in combination with a 15 percent increase in precipitation.

In cases where there is reduced runoff, water prices increase, withdrawals are often, but not always, reduced, and welfare declines. In times of reduced runoff, however, agricultural withdrawals may actually increase in order to meet higher irrigation requirements. Nonconsumptive uses, including hydropower, appear to experience the greatest losses. These results do, however, vary between each watershed. Humid watersheds experience relatively small economic effects of a change in runoff compared with watersheds in arid or semi-arid regions, because water users are less dependent on water services.

This analysis does not include adaptation. Hurd et al. (1999) indicate that institutional arrangements that protect particular water users can potentially result in increased economic losses, and they conclude that institutional adaptation requires further study (see chapter 7). Other cases are summarized in Arnell et al. (2001) and Kundzewicz et al. (2007). There are also many historical case studies of water management for extreme events (e.g., Diaz and Morehouse 2004; Wilhite 2004).

Coastal Zones

A rise in sea level can threaten coastal-zone communities, infrastructures, and ecosystems. A number of impact studies have considered a scenario of a 1 m rise in sea level, and have estimated damage costs, as well as costs of protection. A summary of various case studies is provided in the IPCC Second Assessment Report (Bijlsma et al. 1995). Many of these cases are for small island states and other developing countries. This set of studies predates any Ricardian analyses, so there are no assumptions about market reactions to changes in the perceived risk of coastal flooding. Instead, these estimates stem from scenarios of direct losses of coastline and any structures built within inundated areas.

Many of these studies, including those for developed countries, showed substantial losses. For example, the estimate for the United States was that US$156 billion would be required for protection, while 31,600 km² of land, including 17,000 km² of wetland, would be lost. Some of the small island states would be expected to experience fairly substantial dislocations of people. The same result was determined for countries like Bangladesh, China, and Japan. In terms of the percentage of the GDP, relative impacts on national economies were large only for some of the small island states.

A number of studies of the United States concluded that annual economic losses would be US$5–8 billion. Yohe, Neumann, and Marshall

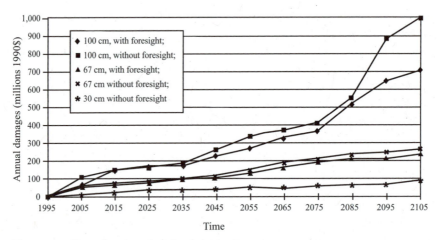

Figure 6.6   Cost of projected sea level rise in the US.
Source: Yohe, Neumann, and Marshall (1999). Reprinted with permission from Gary Yohe and Cambridge University Press

(1999) consider losses based on the likelihood that many vulnerable sites would actually be abandoned, rather than protected. Certain areas would be protected if protection was warranted, but others would be abandoned if protection would be too expensive. Since abandoned properties would be considered as losses, the decision to abandon would affect market values, and there would be uncertainties associated with economic cost estimates of damages resulting from climate change.

The costs of different projected increases in sea level are shown in figure 6.6. This figure illustrates how market-based adaptive behaviour, or "foresight," leads to reduced damages. Note, however, that these estimates do not include the consequences of large numbers of property owners choosing not to abandon property and to actually stay and rebuild after experiencing inundation or a related extreme event. Such circumstances could occur if abandonment was hindered by a lack of alternative sites for relocation, forcing people to remain in vulnerable areas, or if people chose to return, despite the risk, because of important historical, cultural, or personal/familial ties, including a strong sense of attachment to their place of birth.

Disasters from Extreme Events

The human effects of climate change may manifest themselves both through changes in disease rates and through changes in the frequency

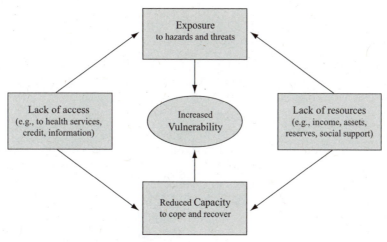

Figure 6.7   Vulnerability to disasters.
Source: McMichael et al. (2001). Reprinted with permission of IPCC

and magnitude of extreme events. Disasters may include damage to human health, as well as damage to infrastructure, which raises some important questions for impacts assessment. As is the case with changes in disease risk, the effects of a particular incident of extreme weather, such as a hurricane, depend very much on the existing coping capacity of the community affected by the event (see chapter 7). What is the state of its emergency preparedness, its civil defence and health services, its enforcement of building codes, and its training of government staff? In other words, how vulnerable is the community or the region to such an event?

Earlier IPCC reports (Tegart, Sheldon, and Griffiths 1990; Watson, Zinyowera, and Moss 1995) did not consider vulnerability in any detail, but more recently, in the IPCC Third and Fourth Assessment Reports (Smit et al. 2001; Schneider et al. 2007), the topic of vulnerability emerges (see chapter 7). Figure 6.7 illustrates the factors that can increase vulnerability for a community or region. Three of the four components relate to the underlying state of development and governance, while the fourth, exposure, includes the weather, or climate statistics. Vulnerability can increase if there is a reduction in capacity to cope and recover from extreme events. A lack of access to services or a lack of access to information can also contribute to this problem. Exposure to hazards and threats because of the physical features of the location of interest can also increase vulnerability. In sum, a lack of resources, income, assets, and social support, combined with potential changes in the frequency and magnitude of the extreme events themselves, can all contribute to an increase in a region's vulnerability to climate change impacts. Note that in this conceptual model, it is possible for vulnerability to change without any change in the climate, which is important when assessing how the costs of climate events have varied in the recent past (for example, consider the case of desertification in the Sahel region of Africa: see chapters 2 and 12).

In chapter 3 we considered how we might identify a climate change signal in the midst of observed variability in climate, and in chapter 5 we assessed whether any changes in ecosystems or landscapes are consistent with projected changes in climate. Here we assess whether there is any climate change signal in observed trends of economic damages related to extreme weather or climate events. When we look at economic indicators, such as trends in annual insured property losses in the United States from weather extremes, no clear trend emerges (Changnon et al. 2000). Individual years have experienced high damages, but they have been separated by years of relative stability. For example, there was a peak in 1992 resulting from Hurricane Andrew. More recently, during 2004, another peak was registered when four hurricanes reached the United States, with additional hurricane damage in 2005. Basically, what Changnon and others have asked is, if we cannot see a clear signal in the climate events themselves, how can we see one in the statistics on damages resulting from extreme atmospheric events? At least in the United States, this trend is not yet apparent, though it continues to be a matter of considerable debate (for additional discussion, see Karl et al. 2008).

There is some evidence, however, that the costs of extreme weather events are increasing worldwide, despite the failure to discern such a trend in the United States. Statistics on extreme-event damage are being compiled by the re-insurance industry (Munich Re 2007), which supports insurance companies around the world. Figure 6.8 shows that there has been a clear increase in the number of weather-related disasters (defined as events with damages exceeding us$billion), which included both uninsured and insured losses. Note, however, that insured losses represent a combination of the effect of weather and what the insurance industry is doing to protect itself and reduce its own exposure by changing its levels of coverage and the rates charged to consumers (including governments). The industry can even choose not to insure certain high-risk areas. The total economic losses, however, will still reflect the fact that some properties and people are in areas of high

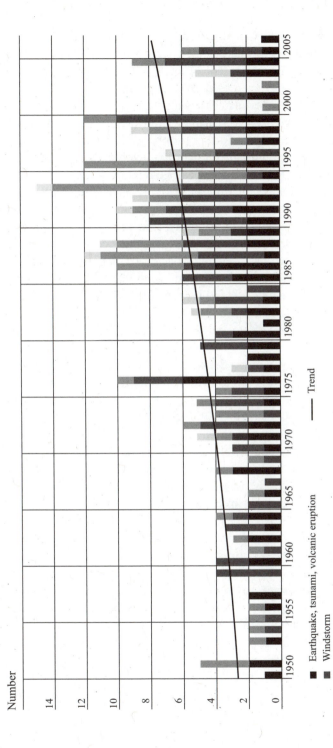

Figure 6.8   Trend in disasters, 1950–2006.
Source: Munich Re (2007). Reprinted with permission of Munich Re Reinsurance Company

exposure and high levels of vulnerability, that people will count on relief from a national government or an international aid agency, and that they will continue to be uninsured. Munich Re (2007) point out that the total economic loss has increased by more than three times between 1980 and 2000. There is evidence that insured and total weather-related losses since 1980 have been increasing at a faster rate than non-weather related losses, GDP, population, and property insurance premiums (Mills 2005). Also, the annual frequency of events exceeding US$1 billion in damages has increased for weather-related disasters but not for geological events such as tsunamis and earthquakes (Munich Re 2007).

What lies behind this trend? Has there really been a change in the meteorological statistics, that could be linked to GHGs? Or are development choices increasing the exposure of property and people to climate, regardless of the climate has changed? Because Changnon et al. (2000) could not really see a rising damage trend in the United States, they concluded that what is being observed is more the outcome of development processes, including land use changes that can affect heat island intensity and runoff from storm events, and less the result of changes in meteorological statistics themselves. For the lower forty-eighth states of the United States, that just may be the case. Or the trend may reflect the net effect of changing weather combined with reactive adaptation measures that are already taking place following extreme events (see chapter 7). Does that explanation also explain the global increase in damages?

Further research is needed in this important area. Why is development creating greater vulnerabilities to extreme weather events while vulnerabilities to earthquakes appear to remain relatively unchanged? How can we determine the relative influences of global climate change and local-scale development over the widely varying worldwide development contexts?

It may be relevant that our current understanding of the potential impacts of climate change on infrastructure is still very limited. Infrastructure typically has a long lifetime, existing structures are aging, and many existing buildings are sited in vulnerable locations. Small increases in the frequency or magnitude of extreme events could bring large increases in damages. However, much of our currently built infrastructure has been designed using climate values (for wind speed, snow load, and so on) calculated from historical data under the assumption that past climate conditions will represent conditions over the lifetime of the structure. Consequently, Auld and MacIver (2004) were able to identify a number of adaptation actions that would be needed to cope with climate change, including updates and revisions for structural codes and standards, enhanced disaster management practices, and closer collaboration with the planning and engineering communities.

HIGHER ORDER IMPACTS

Having considered economic impacts of climate change on renewable resources and property, we now turn to some of the indirect higher-order impacts. We focus here on health impacts, the economic consequences of potential changes in health that could affect the length of human life and the actions of private and public institutions that are charged with health protection and risk management. For example, a basic function of insurance companies is to accept risks, but their acceptance is measured. As risks vary over space and time, insurance companies make adjustments. If climate change leads to detectable changes in the frequency and magnitude of extreme events or of other climate parameters (such as the length of seasons), the industry will adjust. This is an example of what might be called a higher-order impact. It is an indirect effect of climate change requiring consideration of both the direct physical damages from a change in climate and the indirect effects of adjustments to changes in climate-related risk and other threats and opportunities that influence decision makers.

Health

Impacts on human health may come in the form of increased frequencies of outbreaks of disease associated with warm climates and reduced frequencies of outbreaks of disease associated with cold climates, changes in access to food and potable water, as well as effects of climate change on economic development that could influence the availability of public health service. Impacts would be measured in terms of the population at risk or increased mortality, rather than directly in economic terms. As a result, there would need to be additional steps to convert changing mortality rates into economic damages (see the next section).

Of particular concern is the potential for increases in the incidence of malaria. Mosquitoes that carry the malaria virus could spread to higher latitudes as the climate warms. Already, around 40 percent of the world's population, or 3.4 billion people, are at risk for this disease, with about 8 percent of that figure, or 272 million people, being currently infected (McMichael et al. 2001). This means that the population

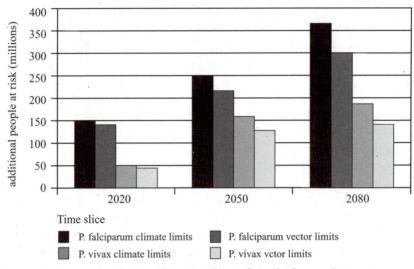

Figure 6.9   Increase in risk (in additional millions of people) from malaria owing to climate change (HadCM3 simulation – IS92a emission scenario) effects on range of *P. falciparum* and *P. vivax* mosquitoes. Climate limits refer to range of climate that could support the mosquito. Vector limits refer to presence of the mosquito.
Source: Martens et al. (1999). Reprinted with permission of Elsevier Limited

at risk is actually ten times the number of people currently infected. It is possible to compute life years lost from premature death for diseases, which for malaria results in 39 million life years being lost.

Other diseases that could potentially expand their ranges because of climate change include schistosomiasis, from the water snail; sleeping sickness, from the tsetse fly; river blindness, from the black fly; and dengue and yellow fever, from mosquitoes. All these diseases depend on an expansion in the range of the insects that are vectors for them. In addition, increases in mortality could result from increasing frequencies of floods and heat waves (Menne and Ebi 2006). Potential health impacts of expanded disease ranges could be affected by any adaptive measures taken by various community and national health systems.

Martens et al. (1999) assessed the potential climate change impacts for malaria. Their analysis was based on a model of the relationship between the life cycle of the mosquito that carries malaria and temperature constraints. Figure 6.9 shows additional people at risk during the twenty-first century. This study also concluded that although the population at risk would increase, the risk of epidemics would actually decline. But as we discussed in chapter 5, changing biology on its own is insufficient for an impact assessment of this kind. Different communities and countries have different capacities to adjust to changing health threats, reflecting variations in institutions, infrastructure (hospitals, the availability of medicines, and technologies), and general health conditions of the population. Should health conditions change, what would be the economic implications?

More recent efforts (Menne and Ebi 2006) have begun to consider new approaches for assessing health impacts and the effectiveness of certain adaptive measures, such as improved early-warning systems, proactive prevention measures, and emergency response plans. A number of research gaps have been identified, including quantification of benefits of climate policies for the health sector.

Value of a Statistical Life

Health care costs continue to present an economic challenge because of many other factors that have little to do with climate, such as increased costs of technologies and treatments. However, another problem may also arive. If climate change leads to changes in disease rates, including mortality rates, then what would be the economic implications of these additional premature deaths before average life expectancy is reached? And this question is not just about the number of years lost because of premature deaths but also about accounting for variations in per capita earnings.

An economic indicator that has been considered in this kind of assessment is the value of a statistical life (VOSL), which represents the lifetime earnings of a person if death occurs at the expected age. VOSL can vary between countries according to the average life expectancy in individual countries, but also according to the average per capita earnings of individual countries. International comparisons of VOSL require consideration of currency exchange rates, so the difference between the currencies in Bangladesh and Germany, for example, would be accounted for in a comparison of VOSL for the two countries. If one were to consider only currency exchange, one would expect a higher VOSL for a German than for a Bangladeshi. However, it is also necessary to account for the fact that all countries still have different income structures. Thus, while a middle-class quality of life in Bangladesh can be attained with a middle-class Bangladeshi income, this income is different from a middle-class German income. The purchasing power parity (PPP) approach introduced earlier in this chapter can be useful in reconciling these differences.

Table 6.1
Mortality Costs under Different Assumed Economic Values of a Statistical Life (VOSL)

Region[a]	Deaths (10^3)	VOSL[b] $(10^6\$)$	Loss $(10^9\$)$	VOSL[c] $(10^6\$)$	Loss (10^9)	VOSL[d] $(10^6\$)$	Loss $(10^9\$)$
EU	9	1.50	13	0.35	3	1.50	13
USA	7	1.50	10	0.35	2	1.50	10
OOECD	8	1.50	12	0.35	3	1.50	12
FSU	8	0.30	2	0.35	3	1.50	12
China	30	0.10	3	0.35	11	1.50	45
ROW	85	0.13	11	0.35	30	1.50	127
World	120	0.35[e]	51[f]	0.35	51[f]	1.50	219[f]

Source: Frankhauser, Tol, and Pearce (1998)
[a] Acronyms stand for, respectively, European Union, United States of America, other member
  countries of the Organization for Economic Cooperation and Development, former Soviet Union,
  China, and rest of the world.
[b] As in original study (Fankhauser 1995).
[c] Global average.
[d] Maximum.
[e] Implied.
[f] Simple sum.

The PPP approach focuses on income levels relative to local populations and not to international standards. Is this a more equitable way to
estimate climate change impacts on VOSL, or is there another metric that
is more appropriate? Recall that article 2 of the United Nations Framework Convention on Climate Change specifies that the objective is to
avoid dangerous anthropogenic interference. How should this be defined
in economic terms? One attempt, reported in the IPCC Second Assessment Report (Pearce et al. 1996) and subsequently by Fankhauser and
Tol (1997), assessed potential changes in the VOSL.

Table 6.1 summarizes different estimates of economic impacts from
increased premature deaths for six large international regions as of the
mid-1990s. The first column shows the total number of deaths expected
from climate change and attributable to projected changes in deaths
caused by such factors as malaria, sea level rise, coastal inundation, and
other disasters. While estimates of premature climate-related deaths are
highly uncertain and highly controversial, let us assume that these figures can represent a starting point for economic analysis. We begin by
considering the estimates of the economic consequences of 120,000 excess deaths per year.

Assuming that US dollars are used as the common currency, such that
all other currencies are converted to American dollars according to

prevailing exchange rates, then for the European Union, the United States, and other members of the Organization of Economic Cooperation and Development (OECD), which includes Canada, Japan, Australia, and other countries, the average VOSL (for the mid-1990s) is US$1.5 million. All these values are based on an average working life of forty years. The values would also represent a proportional weighting of all incomes for various professions, based on available census data. In other regional categories, the average person in the former Soviet Union had an estimated VOSL of US$300,000 and the average person in China had an estimated VOSL of US$100,000. As for the rest of the world, the average person had an estimated VOSL of US$130,000. The weighted global average implied from these figures is US$350,000. The total annual loss in economic output, obtained by multiplying the per capita VOSL by the number of premature deaths, equals US$51 billion.

Now, if we took this global average per capita VOSL of US$350,000 and applied it to all regions of the world, then we would obtain the same total world loss in economic output, but a different regional distribution of these losses. Reduced losses would be estimated for the developed world, and larger losses for China and other developing countries. There would be some problems to consider, however, if VOSL estimation became the accepted method for assessing economic changes to health. For example, because of the higher rates of population growth in developing countries, the VOSL estimates for these countries in future years would be expected to increase more quickly on that basis alone, which is unrelated to economic output.

But suppose we chose a per capita VOSL of $US1.5 million for everybody on earth, which would represent a PPP equivalent to a VOSL for a developed country. And also suppose that the average Bangladeshi was earning as much as the average German (measured in US$). This approach would then result in much higher economic losses coming from the developing countries. Table 6.1 shows a total loss of US$219 billion, compared to the original estimate of US$51 billion. These differences illustrate the sensitivity of the calculation of economic losses to assumptions about the relative values of currencies and the regional economic context.

These VOSL calculation and economic-loss estimation exercises did not include specific adaptation measures. How could adaptation be incorporated into an economic assessment of health impacts? From the examples earlier in this chapter based on the Ricardian approach of market-based adjustments to land values, we might hypothesize that there would be an automatic market reaction to a change in health-related exposure. The market would register how individuals and communities perceived changes in risk and how they worked to increase their protective infrastructures or organize them to avoid or evacuate from the risky areas. If individuals or communities saw a clear signal of a climate-related change in risk or exposure, they would not necessarily wait for agreement on a national or international climate change policy. An assumption of proactive market-driven forces, leading to protection or abandonment of risky areas, could lead to generally lower estimates of damage costs, and in some cases, to net benefits. However, there are other social factors that may not be captured by this analysis (see chapter 7). Additional discussion of recent attempts to incorporate VOSL in costing studies is available in Menne and Ebi (2006).

Total Monetized Damages

Having considered the implications of climate change for individual sectors of the economy, we now come to the compilation of sectoral results to produce national reports of economic consequences. Few examples are provided in the literature, and most of these are for the United States. Fankhauser and Tol (1997) provide a comparison of these US assessments. The national totals are similar, generally around 1–2 percent losses in GDP, but there are substantial differences in the estimates for individual sectors, such as forestry and electricity production. This suggests that there continues to be disagreement on the nature of economic consequences. The disagreement arises from the differences in the climatic and physical impact scenarios of these studies, as well as from the assumptions about costs and market responses. Case studies for other developed countries result in similar percentage GDP losses (Fankhauser and Tol 1997).

Returning to the Mendelsohn and Neumann (1999) study of the United States, they show that when market-based adaptations are assumed to occur in the US context, damages for some sectors are quite small. In the case of agriculture, a 2.5°C warming actually results in a net benefit. This benefit would result from adaptation opportunities assumed to be available in the future economy, including new technologies such as genetically modified organisms, better irrigation delivery, and more effective pesticides, combined with the benefits of longer, warmer growing seasons in cold-climate regions. For timber production, the future economy offers no appreciable advantage over the technology available in the present.

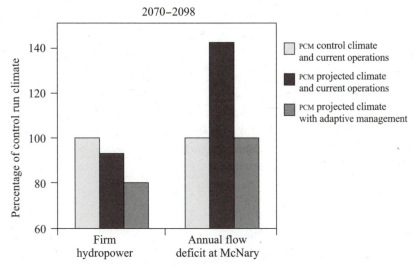

Figure 6.10   Effects of climate change on meeting the trade-off between hydropower production and in-stream fish flows in the Columbia Basin region. PCM is a GCM produced by the National Center for Atmospheric Research (US). "Control climate" refers to current averages. Firm hydropower is electricity provided within contracts of guaranteed delivery from utilities to consumers.
Source: Barnett et al. (2005). Reprinted with permission from *Nature*

Losses continue to be estimated for water resources, primarily because water has to meet a number of objectives. If the hydrologic impacts are projected to include reductions in water supply or changes in timing, then certain objectives may not be reliably achieved. For example, could a utility produce as much hydroelectricity in a future hydrologic regime as it could today? Some case studies suggest that for major hydroelectricity-producing regions, the answer is no: the result could be a huge loss. Another problem will be the requirements to provide water for in-stream needs for fisheries. Balancing hydroelectricity production and in-stream fish flows will be very difficult for many of these watersheds. An example for the Columbia Basin is shown in figure 6.10.

As for the effects on coastal structures, the assumption of Ricardian market impacts results in a diminution of losses to zero. In this narrative, coastal communities could reduce their exposure to avoid sea level rise and storm surges, so that when such events occurred in the future, the land that was at risk would no longer be developed to the same degree. As a result, the total impact of climate change on the US economy would end up being positive: specifically, the Ricardian assumption predicts a

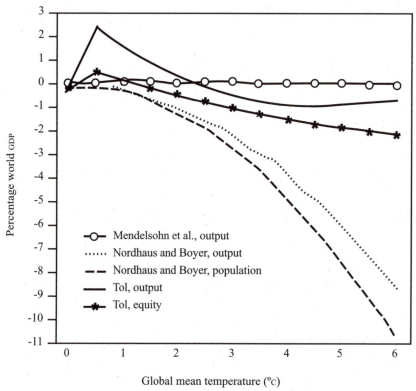

Figure 6.11   Projected global costs of climate change impacts based on results from
Mendelsohn et al. (2000), Nordhaus and Boyer (2000), and Tol (2002). "Output" refers
to weighting by economic output; "population" indicates cost estimates weighted by
population; "equity" accounts for purchasing power parity.
Source: Smith et al. (2001). Reprinted with permission of IPCC

US$36 billion increase in the future economy and a US$8 billion increase
in the current economy, with the same percentage changes in relative
GDP, for a 2.5°C warming scenario.

Figure 6.11 compares the results of several studies of the global economic costs of future climate change. The differences between the loss
estimates are substantial, and for some regions there are projected
losses or gains because of warming. The most pessimistic projection is
by Nordhaus and Boyer (2000), because they include the possibility of
catastrophic effects. Mendelsohn et al. (2000) include optimistic assumptions about adaptation, so that warming results in economic benefits for Russia and China and some reduction in economic outputs in

Latin America and Southeast Asia, with small overall impacts expressed as a percentage of GDP. The Tol (1999) study suggested a loss of 2.7 percent of GDP, assuming world average prices, especially because of what would happen in Africa and Southeast Asia. However, Tol also projected benefits in China, Eastern Europe, and the developed countries. This is a much more optimistic view than the IPCC Second Assessment Report (1995), where losses were expected for all regions.

The divergence in costs seen in figure 6.11 may result from different assumptions about economic damage as a function of global-temperature change. One hypothesis is that there will be a generally linear growth of damages as the climate becomes warmer. Other possibilities are non-linear increases in damage. However, the problem here is to determine where the threshold lies between damage that is modest and not dangerous and damage that is dangerous. For example, Smith et al. (2001) sketch a cubic function with big increases in damages in the 2-3°C range and a hockey stick function with a lengthy period of slow growth in costs, followed by a sudden rapid increase at 5°C warming.

Let us consider further the implications of figure 6.11.The Ricardian model advocated by Mendelsohn conveys a very different narrative of future economic impacts than do the other scenarios. In the Ricardian model, the economic impacts of climate change will be zero, because the market will lead to an automatic response, which will reduce the risk of future damages in excess of current averages. Tol's analyses indicate benefits for a modest 0.5°C or 1°C warming, which change to increasing losses at successive increments of warming. What is labelled here as the equity calculation suggests that this crossover point occurs more quickly than it would if such a weighting was not considered. The rapid increase in losses shown by Nordhaus is in stark contrast to the other two approaches, even at a warming of 2°C. At a warming of 4°C, the difference is even greater. There is no consensus between such different approaches to modelling economic damages, and this graph conveys that message to the negotiators of the climate change convention. Futhermore, these estimates probably still underestimate the true uncertainty, because they exclude certain impacts that are difficult to quantify in monetary terms, as well as the more extreme scenarios of climate change, and because of the sensitivity of projections to the choice of discount rates, future investments in climate change adaptation, and the role of development in reducing or increasing damage costs (Smith et al. 2001; Tol et al. 2004; Stern et al. 2007).

Ethical Concerns Associated with Economic Analyses

Human-induced climate change is a complex problem in which bio-physical and human dimensions interact. The search for answers is fraught with difficulties, not only because of technical challenges but also because of ethical issues associated both with the policy aspects of climate change response and with the way technical information is generated and communicated to decision makers and the public. Economic analysis of climate change is one of these flash points where assumptions about markets and values can influence the estimates of damage costs and of the benefits of policy responses.

Gardiner (2004) identifies some examples from economics that raise ethical concerns. One is the treatment of discounting, discussed earlier in this chapter. The rates employed in various studies vary between 2 and 10 percent for future costs. Gardiner points out that model results can be extremely sensitive to the rate chosen, so that the costs of future climate change damage in present monetary terms appear to be very small, even for projections of increases in extreme events. This has serious consequences for intergenerational ethics, in that the interests of future generations are given relatively lower weighting in favour of short-term concerns.

The recent debate between Nordhaus (2007) and Stern and Taylor (2007) on the role of discounting in the Stern Review (Stern 2007) provides further illustration of the importance of this issue. Nordhaus (2007) asks if particular ethical judgements may be leading to an inappropriate use of relatively low discount rates. Stern and Taylor (2007) respond that both ethics and specific climate change risks provide a logical foundation for choosing low discount rates and that one should not restrict economic analyses to consistency with past market behaviour: "There is no real economic market that reveals our ethical decisions on how we should act together on environmental issues in the very long term" (Stern and Taylor 2007, 204).

Gardiner also identifies a second ethical problem, namely, the inability of economics to adequately capture all the relevant costs and benefits (discussed earlier in this chapter), particularly ecosystem impacts and non-substitutable damages (for example, the visual presence of a mountain glacier). Such analyses also depend on assumptions about future societal changes that could alter fundamental ideas about the production and consumption of goods and services.

Another example worth revisiting is the controversial VOSL calculation, discussed above. The three different approaches in table 6.1

illustrate how assumptions about regional differences in income can affect the calculations of the economic loss associated with premature death. Fankhauser et al. (1998) point out that if the currently observed unequal distribution of incomes between rich and poor countries is maintained in economic analyses, then it will be reflected in the results for a climate change scenario. One alternative is to offer some kind of "equity weighting" that adjusts values for inequalities in income distribution. Another option is to use nationally or even globally averaged per-unit values for income, rather than maintaining regional differentiation.

This kind of analysis could also acknowledge the international differences in health care situations. Instead of assuming that mortality should be directly proportional to population in all regions, estimates should acknowledge that climate change mortality rates are likely to be higher in poorer countries facing increased risk from tropical diseases. The ethical dilemma is that some kinds of health risks, such as a climate-related increase in malaria, may become valued more highly than others (for example, changes in health services related to development). The use of the maximum regional value as the assumed value for all regions (also in table 6.1) may not be equitable either.

DISCUSSION

This chapter has offered a sampling of some basic approaches and assumptions used in economic analyses of the damages from and potential benefits of climate change. We began by assessing some of the challenges to producing economic assessments of climate change impacts and introduced some key economic concepts, including supply and demand functions, PPP, cost-benefit and sustainability analyses, and WTP. We reviewed sectoral and national impacts, including the controversial analysis of changes in the VOSL and its implications. We also considered the Ricardian theory and how it substantially reduces damage projections.

What can we say about the economic implications of climate change impacts and adaptation? First, different approaches lead to different results, whether for sectors or countries. These differences could presumably occur even in predictions about the same physical condition, for example, predictions about how high a sea level rise could be, about how much land would be inundated, what would happen to a tree, or what would happen to a corn crop. Furthermore, even if the scenarios of physical or biological impacts were similar, different results could emerge from the economists, depending on how they chose to model economic impacts, including what assumptions they made not only about market responses but also about adaptation. In chapter 7, we will see that projections of adaptation require assumptions about human behaviour, whether they are assumptions about market behaviour without climate policy or about a specific climate-driven adaptation.

The second point is that assessments of observed damages, such as the analyses by Changnon et al. (2000), as well as by Munich Re (2007), include a consideration of changes in population and property values. Though it is difficult to sort out the drivers in observed damage trends, we can say that some combination of atmospheric and human factors are creating these trends (Mills 2005) and that it will be a challenge to sort out specifically what those factors are. But interestingly enough, the MunichRe analysis shows that weather-related damages have been increasing at a faster rate than earthquake-related damages. Societies appear to have better plans for earthquakes than for extreme weather. Could it be that the weather signal is being affected by a real change in extreme weather frequency, or is there a subtler factor at work?

The third point is that a number of important assumptions influence cost estimates of climate change scenarios. Assumptions about discounting, adaptive behaviour, and the treatment of purchasing power vary between the various case studies. These assumptions contribute to uncertainty in economic assessments that may be comparable to uncertainties in the climate science aspects of climate change.

The intangibles in human behaviour should also be considered, because they may not be consistent with the paradigms of economic rationality. After experiencing four hurricanes during the 2004 hurricane season, a homeowner in Florida might conclude that it is time to move to a less risky location in another part of the country. But others might say that they have lived in Florida for their entire lives and that they intend to come back and rebuild. They like the area, and therefore they will accept a hurricane every now and then. Even in the case of New Orleans, despite the impacts of Hurricane Katrina in 2005, there continues to be strong interest in rebuilding the community in the same location and an expectation that governments will enhance protective infrastructure to make this possible.

Then there are examples from other locations where the residents have no choice but to return to the same high-risk location. Survivors of the 2004 tsunami and coastal inundation in South Asia may find themselves in this situation. That is their world, their marketplace, their context.

Does this mean that on the assumption of economic damages from future extreme events, the $2 million property in the new marketplace would be considered to be worth only, say, $200,000 later and that losses from future storm surges would therefore be reduced? If every actor was prepared to live in a risky area, would they do so only if they paid a reduced cost for the property? Or would market values continue to increase because there would still be aspects of the location that would be attractive to residential or commercial users?

What is an appropriate role for economic information to play in the climate change damage assessments? How should this role be combined with information that comes from ecosystems research, agriculture research, and social studies? What information should economists produce that more equitably represents the potential long-term economic impacts?

PPP is one method economists can use to account for different regional contexts of development and societal circumstance. VOSL is another. Since economic considerations are important for decision making, we cannot avoid the task of converting biophysical considerations into monetary terms for the damage report. This has already influenced the debate over what level of warming may be considered dangerous. We seem to be headed to a consensus that a warming of 2°C is the threshold for a dangerous climate (Ott et al. 2004; Commission of the European Communities 2007), based on economic analyses of climate change impacts and assumed adaptation. This does not include consideration of abrupt, catastrophic, or runaway climate change, which is beginning to be discussed by IPCC and others (see IPCC 2007a). In chapter 7, we consider societal dimensions in more detail and see how adaptation from a social science perspective compares with the economist's assumed market-based behaviour.

7

The Social Aspects of
Climate Change Impacts

INTRODUCTION

In this chapter, we address the social aspects of climate change. We begin by considering some key questions and problems arising out of the social dimensions of climate change, and we try to answer the question, why is all of this important? As was the case in earlier chapters, our approach here is to explore the social sciences from a generalist's perspective. In so doing, we will encounter a new language that describes key processes that may be of interest to us as we attempt to connect global atmospheric and biospheric changes and potential economic implications with human decision making.

It is important to consider the individual, community, or government as a decision maker assessing how to adapt to climate change within a context of other stresses and opportunities. A key part of this approach is the concept of the stakeholder. Stakeholders are increasingly playing greater roles in climate change discussions, from debates about policy to debates about the implications of research. Other important elements to consider are vulnerability, coping strategies, and adaptive capacity (see chapter 4). These human elements help to explain why climate change impacts and adaptive responses will vary by location.

Different countries may be capable of undertaking different adaptive responses, and there are many factors to consider when looking at a country's adaptive capabilities, which can also vary within a country. At both the domestic and the international level, management and governance structures can influence efforts to adapt to climate change in a proactive manner. Management and governance actors operate across different scales, and these various cross-scale interactions can influence the long-term performance of adaptation measures (Adger et al. 2006).

Regional and international differences in adaptation capabilities, as well as the recent increase in weather-related damages from extreme events (see chapter 6), have contributed to an increased effort at including adaptation within climate change policy (Huq and Reid 2004; Huq et al. 2006). Defining adaptation policy targets will continue to be a difficult challenge, however, because of the complex social dimensions of climate-related adaptation and vulnerability prevailing within the unique contexts of social and economic development in different countries. Climate change adaptation efforts will, by necessity, be regionally unique.

THE SOCIAL DIMENSIONS OF CLIMATE CHANGE

Rayner and Malone (1998, 5) ask a series of questions about the social dimensions of climate change. Some of the fundamental ones are

1 How do people decide that climate change is worthy of attention?
2 How do people attribute blame for climate change and choose solutions?
3 How do people choose whom to believe and at what level of risk they should choose to act?
4 What is the relationship between resource management choices in climate change?
5 How are [climate change] policy instruments chosen?

Regarding the first question, one might ask, why should a developing country address climate change when there are other social problems, such as poverty and health, that require urgent attention? A possible response would be that the question should not be framed as an either/or question. While people all have multiple portfolios to deal with, the proponents of climate change policy are not suggesting that climate change should divert attention away from poverty, for example.

Regarding the second question, Rayner and Malone talk about a number of possible factors to blame, including population growth, consumption growth, and economic distortions such as inaccurate prices or inappropriate property rights. Economic distortions arise because there really is no free market operating anywhere in the world, since governments of all types frequently intervene in the marketplace. Subsidies, inflated prices, quotas, or embargoes can all influence the availability of an economic good. Thus, many different factors can be blamed, and some of this blame will influence the energy choices people make, while some of it will influence the way countries develop, which can make them either more or less or exposed to climate change.

The third question can be linked to media coverage of climate change, since this is the main source of information for most of the general public. Recall the discussion in chapter 2 about the notion that balance is bias if it provides unfair weighting to minority points of view (Boykoff and Boykoff 2004). Given the complexity of climate change as a scientific issue with social and political dimensions, how should the media provide coverage?

The other two questions concern the process of decision-making among professionals and governments. Both are influenced by information flow from the breadth of the research community, not just the atmospheric scientists and economists. Climate change poses a challenge to traditional planning, operations, and balancing of management objectives. Changes in climate statistics beyond historical experience mean that available decision models must be applied to new ranges and probabilities of climate-related outcomes, while at the same time, populations, technologies, and economies are also changing. How do we know that these decision models are up to the task? If they're not, how should they be changed?

When considering choices, Rayner and Malone remind us of the importance of property rights in different contexts, institutional and cultural constraints, and the rate of technological change. We also face the difficult challenge of comparing social and equity aspects, such as fairness and values, with economic and technological aspects, such as efficiency. What is fair? What is unfair? It is not easy answer these questions, but by articulating them, we are offered the opportunity to broaden the climate change assessment so that it is no longer exclusively focussed on cloud physics and greenhouse gases, and instead becomes more holistic and multi-dimensional.

BACKGROUND

Let us begin this section by asking the following question: What is a stakeholder? The term "stakeholder" has changed its meaning because of the way people have been applying it. It used to refer simply to the person who held the stakes, and that person had no interest in the outcome. So, for example, say John and George wanted to make a bet, but neither one trusted the other to hold the money while they went through whatever competition they agreed to engage in. They would therefore seek out a neutral party, Ellen, and ask her to hold onto the bets until the contest had been decided, at which time the winner would receive his prize. In this example, Ellen was the neutral stakeholder. Her role was just to hold the money temporarily.

In recent years, however, the term "stakeholder" has taken on a different meaning. The stakeholder is now considered to be an individual, an organization, a community, or a government that is actually not a neutral entity at all but "[a] person or entity holding grants, concessions, or any other type of value that would be affected by a particular action or policy" (McCarthy et al. 2001a, 994). For these entities, the stake is their interest in the outcome; they are not at arm's length, temporarily holding the prize.

In the case of climate change, the stakeholder is considered to have a stake in the proposed policy response and often the research activities as well. The term "stakeholder" can now represent parties or individuals that may be trying to shape the resolution of the issue in question. So, for instance, if we are interested in climate change and water management, the stakeholders we seek to involve in this project will include water boards, municipal water managers, major irrigators, and fisheries managers. We would involve them because perhaps they would have a responsibility to directly manage the resource or operate a facility, maybe even a proprietary responsibility or a governance responsibility. Thus, over time, the definition of a stakeholder has become completely turned around.

The IPCC is building up a glossary of other terms associated with adaptation because of a previous lack of consensus on what some of these terms mean. Adaptation to climate-related phenomena is not a new idea and has been addressed extensively within the literature on natural hazards (see, for example, Burton et al. 1978). On the other hand, the idea has only recently been applied to studies of projected global warming. An increased awareness of the need to incorporate adaptation in climate impact assessments led to the inclusion of the chapter on adaptation by Smit et al. (2001) in the IPCC Third Assessment Report. An emerging concern is that there is a large difference between the research and policy discourses associated with adaptation, on the one hand, and emission reduction or mitigation, on the other. Part of this difference may be caused by the easier quantification of mitigation goals and targets, in contrast to adaptation.

But what exactly does it mean to be more adaptable? Consider some key components of adaptation, and recall from chapter 4 (box 4.1) the term "sensitivity," which denotes the degree to which a system will respond to a change of some kind. Note that a highly sensitive sector will not necessarily also be highly vulnerable. High sensitivity may just be an indicator of reaction time.

Another important term is "adaptability," which is a measure of the degree to which adjustments are possible. A very adaptive system, whether human or natural, can endure considerable changes prior to system failure, and make adjustments very quickly to a change in stress. Other systems that are not as adaptable have a more difficult time making these adjustments. And finally, another important term is "vulnerability," which denotes the extent to which climate change may damage or harm a system. Vulnerability, which will be discussed further in the next section, also depends on both sensitivity and adaptability.

VULNERABILITY

According to Smit and Pilifosova (2003), one way of describing vulnerability is to express it as a function of three attributes of the place or activity of interest:

1 exposure to the weather or climate event,
2 sensitivity to this event, and
3 capacity to adapt.

A community or region could have a high enough adaptive capacity such that it might not necessarily be vulnerable, even though it had a high level of exposure.

For example, in the case of the Dutch coastline, people have been living with exposure to storm surges for hundreds of years. Sophisticated procedures have been created for managing tides and storm surges, including beach nourishment activities and the construction and maintenance of dikes. The Netherlands is therefore considered to have a high adaptive capacity because of its considerable experience with coastal environments and their climate-related sensitivities. A rise in sea level from projected climate change might be presented to the Dutch people as a new risk, and this might present a challenge, but it would not be impossible to overcome though one could imagine that even the Dutch would have difficulty coping with an extreme sea level rise scenario of 5 meters or more in the long-term. However, for a country like Bangladesh, which also has high exposure and sensitivity but which does not have the same capacity to deal with a rise in sea level, this risk presents a big danger. In other words, Bangladesh is likely to be more vulnerable than the Netherlands to future sea level rise, unless it can improve its capacity to adapt or limit human exposure to storm surges. Small island states in the Pacific Ocean are similarly exposed, but the Cook Islands, for example, are currently experimenting with various adaptive measures, including an innovative concrete coastal-protection device that allows for free flow of water underneath and through the barrier (Ingram 2005). Their actions illustrate the region's capacity to adapt, thereby reducing its vulnerability to some degree. Finally, in the case of the US Gulf Coast, the considerable damage recently experienced from hurricanes (including Hurricane Katrina in 2005) tested the limits of the local adaptive capacity. The failure of the protective infrastructure has heightened concerns about the region's level of vulnerability (Tierney and Guibert 2005).

Not only can vulnerability be thought of in terms of the attributes of a place or activity, it can also be thought of in terms of the attributes of the climate-related event that drew attention to the exposure and the sensitivity of particular sites. This makes it more important to define the quantitative nature of climate change impacts, with or without proactive adaptation. The attributes of impacts include

1 their magnitude (e.g., the amount of sea level rise in small island states),
2 their rate and timing (e.g., the rate and timing of impacts on the total and seasonal availability of water supplies), and
3 their likelihood (e.g., the probability that a defined high-temperature threshold will be exceeded in the service area of an electric utility).

Vulnerability can also be defined according to feelings of danger, defined either externally by experts or internally, based on previous direct experience. This can be illustrated in terms of physical vulnerability, such as vulnerability to the bleaching of coral reef systems, or in terms of social vulnerability, such as more people being at risk from malaria. Dessai et al. (2004) conclude that in order to define "dangerous climate change," it is necessary to consider the perceptions of danger that influence the societal view of vulnerability.

ADAPTIVE CAPACITY AND COPING RANGE

The IPCC defines adaptive capacity as the ability of a system to adjust to climate change and variability, including extreme events, so as to moderate potential damages, to take advantage of opportunities, or to cope with consequences (Smit et al. 2001). However, this definition does not explicitly describe the attributes that actually make a particular place highly adaptive or not, and it is important to consider the role of "coping range."

Coping range is the variation in climatic stimuli that a system can absorb without producing significant impacts (Smit et al. 2001). The concept of coping with climate-related variations and extreme events is well known in the natural-hazards literature (see Burton, Kates, and White 1978, 1993). For example, consider a region that is prone to drought, that has had previous extended drought experience, and that has developed its own abilities to cope independently with different levels of soil moisture. For any level of moisture within a particular range, the system can cope without requiring external assistance. If there are brief moments when moisture conditions are below tolerable limits or a defined threshold, then the region may require some outside intervention. If the region began to experience a change in the frequency of conditions, below the threshold such that moisture conditions were below tolerable limits with greater frequency, then this might indicate that climate change was beginning to seriously affect the region. At this point, the region or the community would need to find ways to adjust to these changes and to somehow expand its coping range.

Now what does "changing its coping range" mean in practice? Does it mean that local water managers should divert water from another watershed? Does it mean that local governments should impose conservation requirements or that farmers should change irrigation technologies? A coping capacity may not change in a smooth fashion. Perhaps an extreme event could force a step-like shift in the coping range. Every situation will be regionally unique.

Changes in coping capacity are difficult to represent in graphical form. In the drought example just mentioned, there are more frequent occurrences of drought, but there might also be fewer occurrences of excessive moisture (the opposite condition). It is difficult to capture the impact of changing event frequencies on community and institutional memory. If there were fewer wet events, would the opposite end of the coping range shift away from relatively wet conditions and more towards drier ones? Would vulnerability to wet conditions increase?

Climate change is a creeping problem. One way to monitor its progress is through changes in climate statistics. In a climate change, perhaps there is a change in the mean of a particular climate measure (such as drought frequency or temperature), which in and of itself may not be significant (for a change in mean temperatures, see figure 4.5). However, a change in the mean suggests that there would be more cases within one particular tail of the distribution (such as more cases of severe droughts), if the standard deviation were to remain unchanged. In this new climate regime, a particular coping threshold associated with this parameter would end up being exceeded a lot more often.

Another way to attempt to describe coping range would be to first visualize a stationary climate with only moderate fluctuations and no discernible trend, with the coping range defined as the space between two temperatures, as indicated in the left-hand side of figure 7.1. If temperatures change to new values outside this boundary, a vulnerable situation may occur. In the right-hand side of this figure, the stationary climate shifts to a new climate, but the coping range has not changed, and there are now more cases where the coping threshold is exceeded. How would a community react to that change? The reaction might be to change one of the thresholds to a different value, which in this case would be a higher value. A higher-temperature event would still leave the region vulnerable, but now there has been some level of adaptation (bottom right-hand panel of figure 7.1), on top of the initial coping range.

The time it takes to change a threshold depends on the ability of the region or the community to see a signal of change and to desire to implement the adaptation measure. Seeing the signal is a problem of perception. While statistics may help point out changes in climate, they can sometimes be difficult to see, so that other dimensions need to be brought into the discussion in order to convince stakeholders that behaviour needs to be modified. This problem has led to some recent experiments in the use of visualisation as a means of communicating the potential extent of impacts damage and the nature and effectiveness of potential adaptive responses (Sheppard 2005).

We now turn to the concept of adaptive capacity. What actually influences a region's adaptive capacity? This requires consideration of a range of determinants (Smit et al. 2001). For example, it can be determined by the availability of economic resources, both at the institutional level and at the household level, and it may include international economic support. The availability of technology is also important, though it may not be exclusively associated with an engineered structure, for example, since it could also include warning systems and the delivery of services. Information, skills, and education, along with social infrastructure, including

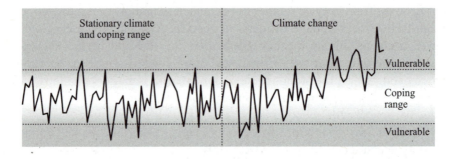

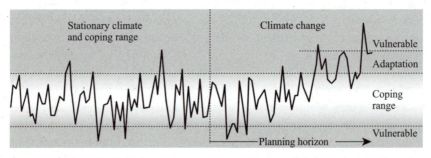

Figure 7.1   Climatic variability and coping range. Upper panel shows increased vulnerability owing to climate change. Effects of adaptation are shown in the lower panel as an increase in coping range.
Source: Lim et al. (2004). Reprinted with permission from Bo Lim, United Nations Development Programme

social and health services, are also important to local adaptive capacity. Institutions are part of this as well, including the legal system, regulations, entitlements, community plans, and resource management committees. Equity should be considered, for example, by asking whether there is an equitable distribution of income, of property rights, and of voting rights. How could all these considerations contribute to a rating of adaptive capacity? To actually weight all these factors and capture them with a number would be very difficult, but it would still be important to attempt to do so when determining what makes a region more or less adaptable. Comparative evaluation of adaptive capacity can identify those areas with relatively low levels of capacity, thereby enabling the targeting of adaptation initiatives (Smit and Wandel 2006).

Another way to think about adaptive capacity is as a measure of a region's or a community's level of awareness, ability, and capability for action (Schröter et al. 2003; Metzger et al. 2006), as illustrated by the Advanced Terrestrial Ecosystem Analysis and Modelling (ATEAM) study

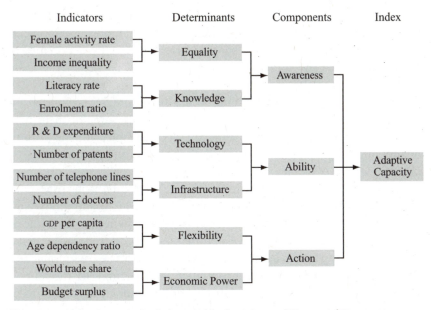

Figure 7.2   Adaptive capacity index used in the Advanced Terrestrial Ecosystem Analysis and Modelling (ATEAM) study.
Source: Schröter et al. (2003); Metzger et al. (2006). Reprinted with permission from Elsevier Limited

(figure 7.2). Awareness is related to education but also to equality, because equality provides equal access to information and to resources. Measures of equality can include indicators such as the Gini coefficient, which is a measure of income distribution. Is the population of a particular country in the same income class, i.e., does the country resemble the ideal communist world? Or is it a society in which a small group owns everything? If one person in a country or region possessed all the income, then the Gini coefficient for that country would be 1. This would represent complete inequality. However, if everyone had the same income, then the Gini coefficient would be 0, representing complete equality. If a country or region has a low Gini coefficient (approaching 0), this means that there is a greater level of equality in income or dispersion of income among the population. In the study by Schröter et al (2003), it is assumed that a higher level of income equality could enable broader societal access to resources needed to adapt to climate change, thereby contributing to a higher adaptive capacity. The World Bank, as part of its consideration of "relative" poverty, identifies the Gini coefficient as the most commonly used measure of inequality within regions and countries (see http://web.worldbank.org, the page entitled PovertyNet).

What about the other indicators? Ability indicators could include technology, infrastructure, patents, investment in research and development, the number of doctors per 1,000 people, and so on. Finally, action indicators could include the state of the national budget, particularly if there was a surplus or a debt.

These various indicators would be applied in an attempt to construct a quantitative measure of adaptive capacity. However, some of them may not be easily related to adaptive capacity. For example, one measure of equality might be the presence or absence of democratic processes in governance. Are democracies more adaptable than other forms of governance? In the climate change context, that's an interesting question. Climate change is a complex global problem with varied and unique implications at national and local levels. Are people living in democracies better able to participate in the decision-making process and thus to make a positive contribution to adaptive capacity? Democracies, with their frequent elections and short-term governance models, may be thought to lack a long-term vision, but is it really true that a democracy cannot make decisions beyond a few years, or the length of time between elections?

While adaptive capacity may be related to awareness and literacy, it is also related to the ability of a country or a region to stay abreast of new developments in research and technology. What is the level of scientific literacy in different countries? There is nothing simple about scientific literacy or its relationship with governance. More generally, we do not want to give the impression that all democracies are more adaptable than dictatorships, since there is no simple relationship between the various indicators of social development and the adaptive capacity of a region: this is part of the problem of defining adaptive capacity. We urgently need many different indicators in order for climate change to move from a problem of natural science to one of social policy.

STUDYING IMPACTS VERSUS STUDYING VULNERABILITIES

In chapter 4 we discussed whether impacts and adaptation studies should be conducted using a top-down or a bottom-up approach. We also considered the issues involved with each approach. Another part of the research question is whether we as researchers should be assessing scenario impacts or whether we should be assessing current vulnerabilities. There are similarities and differences between these assessments, and they may in fact complement each other.

An impacts assessment identifies consequences of an event or a scenario, whereas a vulnerability assessment considers the characteristics of the place or activity that can affect the relationship with climate. The focus is on the processes that shape the consequences of climate variations and change in order to identify the conditions that may amplify or dampen vulnerability to adverse outcomes. Equal attention is given to many drivers of impact or response, including climatic, social, economic, and governance processes, and how these processes contribute to vulnerability and adaptive capacity (Leary et al. 2008a,b). In other words, a vulnerability assessment focuses on the observed behaviour of the system, as well as on the climate context in which the system and its actors function.

However, in each case elements may be missing from the study. How should we address multiple interacting issues in an impact assessment? How can we make a vulnerability assessment of observed events forward-looking? Where is the predictive aspect? Even assuming we could prediction future behaviour or the evolution of future communities, if this prediction was somehow scenario-free, at some point it would become necessary to incorporate scenarios in the assessment. If scenarios were left out, then we would be assuming that the past was indicative of the future, thereby increasing the risk of missing potential surprises. Ultimately, we would need a way to combine these two approaches in order to study the potential effects of climate change on society and possible adaptive responses. Otherwise, important elements would be missing.

In the early 1980s, when impacts studies of climate change were first attempted and published, they tended to be very simple desktop studies. Choose a model, perhaps a crop yield model, insert scenario temperature and precipitation changes, and then observe how the crop model responds. This type of exercise is still useful, but it is no longer sufficient on its own for addressing the human dimensions of climate change impacts and adaptation. We have gone far beyond that now, but how many cases do we have? Have some case studies been able to address both the physical and social aspects of this problem equally well?

DIFFERENTIAL CAPACITIES FOR RESPONSES TO CLIMATE CHANGE

An important element in incorporating social issues into climate change assessments is the heterogeneity of societies around the world. Communities and nations have varying levels of income, social services, educational facilities, and infrastructure. Some nations are struggling with poverty, health concerns, and resource depletion. When climate change is considered in the context of these other problems, it is not surprising that nations will respond in different ways. In this section, we explore some aspects of differential response capacities to climate change.

Climate Change and Human Settlements

Whether it is a small town or a big city, many non-climate factors can affect the exposure or the sensitivity of a community to climate. Population growth, municipal governance, poverty, and technological change may affect how climate change would influence a community. We might ask, for example, whether technological change is affecting a community's vulnerability; whether the society is becoming less vulnerable to climate or whether its vulnerability has changed to a different form. And we might ask whether the sensitivities of the community social systems or health services have changed.

Cities are changing, and large cities are becoming megacities, with populations exceeding ten million people. More than half are in developing countries, including Jakarta, Shanghai, Delhi, Calcutta, Cairo, Sao Paulo, and Mexico City. Regardless of climate change, rapid urban growth affects how a local government manages systems for so many people, even in the developed world. If we are going to assess the impacts of climate change on society and communities, we have to superimpose climate change on the rapid urbanization of our planet.

Technological change must also be considered when assessing the causes of both observed climate-related damages and potential future impacts and adaptive responses. In a commentary entitled *Does Climate Still Matter?* Ausubel (1991) suggested that society is gradually becoming climate-proof. This argument has three components:

1 Improvements to air conditioners, heating systems, water supply systems, and other systems are enabling society to become more adaptable. Why worry about heat waves if air conditioning is readily available? Why worry about drought if our water systems are well-managed?
2 Technology is leading to a decline in our synchronicity with seasonal changes. We are not as attuned to the seasons as we used to be, because we are insulated from weather and climate by the engineered structures around us. So weather and climate play decreasing roles in

our everyday activities. We have artificial snow so that we can ski for longer periods. During summer in the northern hemisphere, we can travel to the southern hemisphere to ski. Ice hockey can be played all year long, even in hot climates, on artificial indoor ice.

3 As succeeding extreme events occur, the impacts of these events gradually decline: this is the "lessening hypothesis." For example, recent droughts in the United States have had fewer economic and societal impacts than the famous Dust Bowl of the 1930s, even though climatically they have been just as severe (Warrick 1980).

There are counter-arguments to the notion that technological change enables society to become climate-proof. For example, societal vulnerability to drought appears to be escalating at a significant rate (Wilhite 2005). Are we really climate-proofing ourselves with all these improvements in technology? Does this increase our adaptive capacity? Or do they actually increase our need to find new, and perhaps more expensive and energy dependent, ways to adapt because society is becoming more sensitive to climate variations? Or as society continues to innovate with new "green technologies," such as the "green roof," can we create a sustainable approach to climate-proofing? The green roof of a building supports live vegetation growing in soil or other growing medium, planted over a waterproof layer. Potential benefits include reducing heat loads on buildings in summer, reducing energy consumption in winter, and providing improvements to air quality (Oberndorfer et al. 2007; Green Roofs for Healthy Cities 2004).

The role of technological change in improving the adaptive capacity of human settlements will likely depend on the context in which it takes place. While there is no defined end point in development, it can nevertheless be seen that different countries are in different stages of economic and technological development. Since technology can change society's relationship with climate, can it also simultaneously change vulnerabilities?

Differential Impacts

How will climate change impacts manifest themselves in different countries? How will different societies cope with climate change as they also continue to cope with development challenges such as poverty, economic instability, low education levels, poor infrastructure, and health and security concerns? Adaptive capacity and climate-proofing should not be seen only through a developed-country lens. The whole question of how a developing country is going to use technology to increase its adaptive capacity and reduce its vulnerability is still very hotly debated. Whose technology? And how does that technology integrate into another climate, into another culture, and into a place with another history? There have been examples illustrating how technology transfers have failed to solve major problems in developing countries, such as inadequate food production, and have instead created new problems, such as water pollution and soil erosion (Pimentel and Pimentel 1990; Kates 2000). The impacts of climate extremes, such as droughts, have not been reduced by new technology, because of the unanticipated effects of other societal decisions, such as changes in land use. Glantz (2003) refers to this problem as the interplay between problem climates and problem societies.

Perceptions of climate change impacts as risky or dangerous vary between countries. Because climate change affects different countries that are at different levels of development, it is important for us to appreciate the differences between developed- and developing-countries' vulnerabilities, between the potential impacts on them, and between their capabilities to adapt.

At the beginning of the twenty-first century, developed countries are generally located in mid-latitudes, while developing countries are located mostly in the tropical latitudes. In general, in the case of projected impacts on the developed countries, there would appear to be some winners and some losers. But it is more difficult to find developing countries that would be winners. All developing regions would be faced with increased heat stress, drought stress, sea level exposure, or pest exposure. There does not seem to be any renewable resource in developing countries that would clearly benefit from climate change. Developing countries are also considered to be more vulnerable than developed countries, which appear to have only modest vulnerabilities, because their economies are richer and their infrastructures are better able to cope. In contrast, developing countries generally suffer from poorer economies, weaker infrastructures, and weaker abilities to cope.

A side effect is that a developed country might look at of differential impacts from a global perspective and see an increase in immigration pressure. The editorial cartoon in figure 7.3 illustrates a possible scenario: environmental refugees are leaving Southeast Asia and trying to find a place with fewer climate-related problems; Australia reacts by erecting a big fence to keep the refugees out. But New Zealand has no fence, so the environmental refugees are all heading there, leading to New Zealand's concerns that the problem is too big for them alone.

Figure 7.3 Cartoon illustrating the potential for environmental refugees coming to Australia and New Zealand.
Source: Tiempo (2001). Reprinted with permission from Tiempo and Lawrence Moore

This hypothetical example serves to illustrate the human face of differential impacts of climate change. Developing countries might experience increased conflicts over resources and increased emigration. Are the refugees economic or environmental and climate change refugees? Either way, as this scenario unfolds, there will be many impacts on people and implications for other kinds of social issues, such as the need for increased foreign aid and peacekeeping efforts. The role of technology transfer is also important in this situation. While developing countries will require more assistance to respond to climate change risks, they are not necessarily able to import a solution from someplace else, for economic, social, and cultural reasons (Kates 2000).

Differential Vulnerabilities and Risks

Suppose that we are assessing future (scenario) climate change impacts for one or more countries and that we want to incorporate the social dimensions of the study areas into our assessment. How should we consider adaptive capacity, exposure, sensitivity, and vulnerability, and what the specific impacts of a scenario might be on natural resources such as water, trees, food, and fish? Is there a way to organize our thoughts around strategies to deal with this complexity?

One approach is to categorize countries or regions according to their prevailing adaptive capacities and potential future impacts. Figure 7.4

Impacts

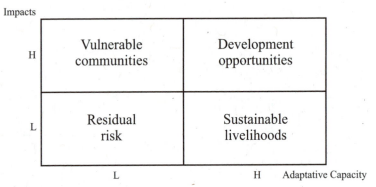

Figure 7.4   Common situations of vulnerability.
Source: Adapted from Tol et al. (2004).

Table 7.1
Examples of Countries within Clusters of Climate Risk

Vulnerable Communities	Residual Risk	Development Opportunities	Sustainable Livelihoods
Colombia	Angola	Brazil	Algeria
India	Iran	China	Bolivia
Mexico	Niger	Egypt	Canada
Sudan	Pakistan	France	Norway
Tanzania	Peru	Indonesia	Russia
Thailand	Romania	Japan	Switzerland
Viet Nam	Spain	United States	Turkey

Source: Adapted from Tol et al. (2004).

illustrates the four categories that emerge from different combinations of these two indicators. It can be argued that this approach is too simplistic, but is there something we can learn from it. In this 2x2 matrix, the best category is one where the expected impacts are low and the adaptive capacity is high. This circumstance is referred to as one of "sustainable livelihoods." Canada could be seen as being in this category, at least in an aggregated sense (table 7.1), although some rural or northern regions might see themselves in another category (for example, see ACIA 2004).

Countries where the impacts and adaptive capacities are low may not experience any severe problems. This circumstance is categorized as one of "residual risk." A number of Mediterranean countries, some Asian countries, and a few African countries provide examples. Another category is comprised of countries that are susceptible to high impact but already have a high adaptive capacity. This circumstance is categorized as one of "development opportunities." If a country in this category uses its available adaptive capacity and modifies its development path, climate-related risks could be reduced. The United States is included in this category, which means that it will experience greater impacts than Canada but will still be able to cope with them because it has a high adaptive capacity. Other examples are Australia, Brazil, China, and some European countries. In the final category there are high impacts but low adaptive capacities. Countries in this category are "vulnerable communities."

We should appreciate that a country-based assessment is an aggregated view of the world, which includes aggregated views of behaviour, economic conditions, exposure, and institutions. At this scale, some intraregional aspects are left out. For example, Alaska's response is mixed in with that of the lower forty-eight states, but its response may not actually be similar to theirs, given the geographical distance between the two areas. Similarly, the higher population and economic power of southern Canada may swamp northern Canada's concerns, creating a generic response that may not actually be representative of responses within this country. We will always have scale and resolution problems, as we saw in the discussion of climate science in chapter 3 when we compared the field of view of a GCM and a regional model. Since similar problems might be encountered in assessments of the social dimensions of climate change, individual regional stakeholders might be concerned that they can not see themselves in such aggregated classifications.

Why pursue this type of classification? Is there any value in splitting the world up into these four categories? One possible incentive is the policy application of such an index. The Kyoto Protocol includes an emissions reduction target but not a vulnerability reduction target because such a target would be difficult to define. A recognized indicator associated with a policy instrument like Kyoto could provide a bench mark for financial incentives and serve as a criterion for investment by donor countries seeking to help developing countries increase their adaptive capacity and reduce their vulnerability. In this way, Kyoto would not act simply as a mitigation instrument but also as an adaptation instrument. (More on the relationship between mitigation and adaptation will be found in chapter 9.)

Identifying with high confidence some highly vulnerable countries in tropical Africa and Latin America would provide a way of measuring the effectiveness of adaptation measures, and it would provide benefits to both the donor and the recipient countries. However, identifying highly vulnerable countries may pose complex problems relating to how the categories are defined. What defines high and low impacts? Where is the boundary between categories? How acceptable would these definitions be to the parties to the Kyoto Protocol?

Table 7.2 offers an example of intraregional variations in impacts and adaptive capacity. Although Canada as a whole may be seen as a part of the sustainable-livelihoods category (table 7.1), a case study from Aklavik, in the Northwest Territories, summarized in table 7.2 illustrates how visions of development futures can influence perceptions of future climate-related risks and opportunities. Gwitch'in and Inuit people populate Aklavik. Aharonian (1994) interviewed a number of people there about what they thought future climate change would mean to them. They had a long list of impacts: greater flooding, muddy roads, outdoor meat storage problems, summer insects, a longer water shipping season, and a shorter winter road season.

Aharonian asked them to look ahead and see these impacts within two different lifestyle visions, or two different development visions. Would their vision of development influence how they would see their future vulnerability to climate change? The left-hand column in the table shows responses within a scenario of continued reliance on subsistence activities: living on the land and harvesting caribou, fish, and berries, supplemented by small amounts of wage activity. In this case, greater flooding would have a negative impact, but the impact of muddy roads would be difficult to determine. On the other hand, building insulation would be more effective in a warmer climate, which would therefore actually provide a benefit. Within this developmental context, there would be a whole range of costs (minus signs), benefits (plus signs), and unknowns (question marks).

Aharonian also asked interviewees to shift their thinking about future lifestyles to a situation in which there was greater reliance on a wage economy, perhaps from employment in the mining industry or from working for the government. In this scenario, they would not spend as much time working on the land, and their wages would be used to purchase food to make up for reduced subsistence harvesting. The result of this change is shown in the right-hand column of table 7.2. Note that the costs, benefits, and unknowns do not apply to exactly the same variables anymore. The respondents simply changed their vision of their development future, but in their view, the new vision changed their relationship with climate and the way climate impacts would affect

Table 7.2
Impacts of Climatic Change on Future Development in Aklavik, Canada

Impact	Continued Reliance on Subsistance Activities	Greater Reliance on Wage Economy and Economic Development
Greater flooding	−	−
Muddy road conditions	?	−
Insulation of buildings	+	+
Easier water delivery	?	+
Less time spent waiting out cold conditions	+	+
Outdoor meat storage	−	−
Uncomfortably hot in summer	−	−
Increased summer insects	−	−
Shorter winter road season	?	?
Longer water shipping season	?	+
Mode of transport	?	?
Infrastructure of camps	−	?
Location of camps	−	?
Changes in wildlife habitat	−	?
Increased sediment load	−	−
Thinner ice	−	−
Greater snowfall	?	−
Variability in timing and consistency of break-up and freeze-up	−	−
Longer ice-free season	?	+
Shoreline erosion and lowland flooding	−	−
Greater variability in decisions/perceptions	−	?

Source: Adapted from Aharonian (1994).

them. Whether they were necessarily thinking about adaptive capacity as such is not clear, but they were nevertheless thinking about their exposure and their vulnerability to climate-related changes.

This case study does not consider whether Aklavik's residents would become more energy efficient, but it does consider how climate change would affect them. While such an analysis does reveal dimensions of the differential-vulnerabilities issue that an aggregated national-level risk index cannot reveal, it does not discount the value of the aggregated index. We will have to find new ways to deal with all the scales of relationships between climate and place (from local to international). Otherwise, we will experience problems in trying to find a climate policy that will do the most good for the most people.

Differential Emissions

Although this chapter focuses on adaptation, in order to appropriately discuss this subject, we must also consider that different countries have different reasons for emitting GHGs. This bring us to an important social aspect of climate change, because it has contributed to defining the Kyoto Protocol around the concept of common but differentiated responsibilities (see chapters 8 and 9).

GHG emissions per capita for developed countries are very high because of lifestyle choices. It is not necessary for developed country inhabitants to consume GHGs at such a rate, but they do so because it is convenient and it creates business or personal opportunities. A very different perspective emerges when we consider GHG emissions for developing countries. Here the per capita rate is low, and furthermore, it is argued, the emissions result from activities undertaken for survival, rather than for lifestyle purposes. Further, if impending climate-related stress induces developing countries to, say, use more concrete for coastal protection, then the associated emissions might be categorized as adaptive emissions. For example, a country like Bangladesh may have to adapt to climate change by increasing, rather than decreasing, its GHG emissions simply in order to protect itself from sea level rise, rather than to encourage economic growth. How would the Kyoto Protocol treat the resulting adaptive emissions? This is an example of a new issue that is emerging from climate policy research, in which the study of linkages between adaptation and mitigation measures can lead to greater understanding of the synergies and conflicts that may occur as a result of their implementation (see chapter 9).

Ultimately, because the stabilization of GHG concentrations will require a much wider range of countries taking on emission targets, it is important to get more countries to commit themselves to clean development (see chapter 9). The atmosphere does not care about the origins of GHG emissions. If a developing country, whether it was Bangladesh or China, eventually committed itself to emissions targets, would an adaptive emission count the same way for a target as a lifestyle emission from a developed country like Canada? Moreover, how likely is it that Bangladesh would agree to such a proposal?

The dilemma posed by adaptive emissions illustrates how difficult it is to address the linkages between mitigation and adaptation. Although they are treated separately in the Kyoto Protocol, it is difficult to completely separate them in practice. Adaptation is a necessary policy instrument for any country and adaptive emissions are a part of it.

Similar linkages can be identified for forestry activities. In this case, consider the relative importance of current and past deforestation. Developed countries are currently concerned about deforestation in developing countries. The Brazilian Amazon rainforest provides the great example. Brazil deforests land at considerable rates for economic growth, but by doing so, it is weakening an important carbon sink (more on sinks in chapter 9), which could have a big impact on climate change. On the other hand, a developing country like Brazil might point out that although there are problems in the Amazon today, we should not forget that in Europe and North America, when settlement and agriculture were expanding in previous decades, deforestation occurred that was never accounted for in the estimates of the available sinks. And under current rules, developed countries with GHG emissions targets, such as Canada, Japan, and Russia, are able to obtain a sink credit for reforestation and, in this way meet their Kyoto target. But in doing so they would simply be taking advantage of the fact that they had cut down trees in the past. If developing countries are to receive incentives for reforestation, they will either need to accept GHG emissions targets or attract funding from developed countries for reforestation projects through one of the Kyoto mechanisms (see chapters 8 and 9). This contrasting situation has understandably prompted some concerns about the political implications of developed countries investing in the reforestation of developing countries.

Equity in Climate Change Response

We have seen that there are substantial differences between developed and developing countries in their per capita GHG emissions, vulnerabilities, adaptive capacities, and potential impacts of climate change. Climate change is a complex global problem. We now have international policy measures in place, and individual states are also responding. We will consider these measures in more detail in chapters 8 and 9, but first it is important to provide some guidance on how an equitable climate policy might be constructed, in order to account for the differential circumstances – impacts, vulnerabilities, and emissions – that currently exist and that may be anticipated over the foreseeable future.

The Kyoto Protocol does not address GHG emissions targets in terms of emissions per capita or emissions per monetary unit of GDP. Only national totals are considered. Adaptation is part of the protocol, but there is no target for adaptation. Since the only indicator of policy success is total national emissions, the perception of what is fair about a climate change instrument will depend very much on how individual countries see themselves measured by this indicator.

Equity, or fairness, has many dimensions. Jepma and Munasinghe (1998) identify four different aspects:

1 Procedural equity. Is the Kyoto process fair? In fact, is the whole United Nations Framework Convention on Climate Change fair? Given nearly twenty years of experience with international climate change negotiations, what elements should be considered for the post-Kyoto process in order to achieve procedural fairness?
2 Equity and economics. Because economics is a key source of information that seems to influence so many people, businesses, and government leaders, the thought process that goes into economics needs to be seen as fair to both developed and developing countries. In chapter 6, we considered the Ricardian model of market-based responses in land values governing adaptive responses and estimates of damage from climatic events. Is the Ricardian idea an equitable one? Does it apply in different regions and in different countries?
3 Intragenerational equity. Within the same generation, is there fairness in climate policy for different regions or countries?
4 Intergenerational equity. Does climate policy treat present and future generations fairly? The role of discounting (see chapter 6) is relevant here. A high discount rate applied to climate change impacts will reduce the value of long-term damages, thereby favouring short-term responses. Would future generations be short-changed in this case?

The main question, though, is perhaps about defining an equitable approach to economic or policy model building. Whose perception of the world should dominate economic thinking? What cultural values should be represented?

Associated with equity concerns are the differences in attitudes about climate change between developed and developing countries. In developed countries, there is some willingness to reduce emissions as long as developing countries also agree. Recall that in the United States shortly after the 1997 Conference of the Parties (COP-3) that produced the Kyoto Protocol, the US Senate voted overwhelmingly to reject it because there were no developing-country GHG emissions targets. And this happened under a presidency that wanted Kyoto to be passed. Developing countries might be willing to reduce their rate of emissions growth, but only under certain conditions. Energy efficiency is good, as long as economic growth is not hindered.

One of the policy concerns raised by developing countries is that GHG emissions reductions on their own do not help them address concerns related to current vulnerabilities and future impacts. These concerns have been most strongly communicated by small island states, which worry about the impacts of rising sea levels on their exposed coastal communities (see chapter 8). As a result, adaptation as a policy measure has gained increased visibility in recent years, and particularly at the last few Conferences of the Parties, especially COP-7, held in Marrakech in 2001.

ADAPTATION

What do we mean by adaptation to climate change? What is the difference between reactive or autonomous adaptation and proactive or planned adaptation? In the first instance, autonomous adaptation is considered to occur as a short-term response to a climatic event. The effectiveness of such a response depends on existing conditions of exposure, vulnerability, and coping capacity. The residual, or net, impacts of the event would be represented by the initial impacts less the effectiveness of autonomous measures (figure 7.5). The net impacts would lead decision makers to initiate policy responses, including planned adaptive measures that could improve adaptive capacity and/or reduce vulnerability and exposure.

When considering what types of adaptive measures may be appropriate, the first question would be about the particular climate-related situation, or, in short, adapt to what? The climate-related stimuli of a particular stress, when combined with relevant non-climate forces, such as the level of development, emergency preparedness, or adaptive capacity, lead to the next elements of this assessment, which are the identification of who the adapters are and how adaptive measures would be implemented. Ideally, there would also be an opportunity to monitor the success of the adaptation measure in order to evaluate its performance.

Who adapts or what adapts depends not only on the characteristics of the systems involved but also on the goals and values of the adaptors. The goal may simply be to manage the risk, to reduce exposure, or to address new opportunities. These different goals may lead to different strategies. Adaptation does not occur in a vacuum. Atmospheric change is only one stress, and it will not be the only thing that people and places adapt to.

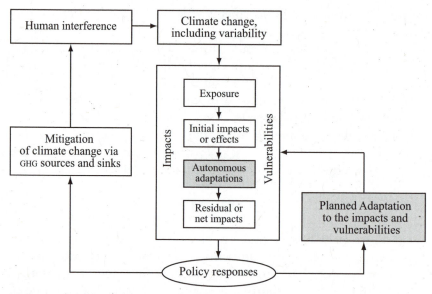

Figure 7.5   Role of adaptation within the climate change issue.
Source: Smit et al. (2001). Reprinted with permission of IPCC

Implementation may involve many technical, institutional, and legal processes. As implementation proceeds, a number of barriers and challenges may need to be overcome. Some of them will be based on perceptions. Others may be institutional, technological, or political. Previous experiences with climate-related stresses offer some learning opportunities. For example, can we assess how well a particular region or business or community overcame such barriers in order to adapt to some stress? Did the adaptive measure it employed actually change the system from its earlier state? Could this be an opportunity to see if the lessening hypothesis, discussed above, is correct, to see if the measure has helped to climate proof the region?

What are the attributes of adaptation? How can adaptive measures be characterized in order to compare their relative effectiveness under various circumstances? Table 7.3 lists some specific attributes and provides some examples for each. "Purposefulness" refers to whether a measure is autonomous and automatic or planned and intentional. Timing may be anticipatory and proactive, or it may be responsive and reactive. There is a range of adaptive functions, including retreating, protecting, preventing, and restoring. The form of adaptive functions can be structural (hard) or non-structural (soft): regulatory measures are an example of the latter.

Table 7.3
Attributes of Adaptation

General Differentiating Concept or Attribute	Examples of Terms Used		
Purposefulness	Autonomous	←→	Planned
	Spontaneous	←→	Purposeful
	Automatic	←→	Intentional
	Natural	←→	Policy
	Passive	←→	Active Strategic
Timing	Anticipatory		Responsive
	Proactive	←→	Reactive
	Ex ante	←→	*Ex post*
Temporal scope	Short-term	←→	Long-term
	Tactical	←→	Strategic
	Instantaneous	←→	Cumulative
	Contingency		
	Routine		
Spatial scope	Localized	←→	Widespread
Function/effects	Retreat – Accommodate – Protect Prevent – Tolerate – Spread – Change – Restore		
Form	Structural – Legal – Institutional – Regulatory – Financial – Technological		
Performance	Cost – Effectiveness – Efficiency – Implementability – Equity		

Source: Smit et al. (2001).

Adaptive measures for climate change are not very different from measures already in use today. Several categories have been identified by Burton, Kates, and White (1978) for climatic extremes and, similarly, by the IPCC for climate change (Smit et al. 2001). They include sharing the loss (insurance, disaster relief), prevention (dykes, zoning), changing use (new tree species, new types of transport), and changing location (relocation of a park or a biosphere reserve). It is also possible to be self-insured and to just bear the loss. Research is, of course, part of adaptation, and so is education and outreach.

Figure 7.6 summarizes the various types of adaptive measures that may become part of a portfolio of responses to climate change. Preventing effects is important because so many different approaches have been

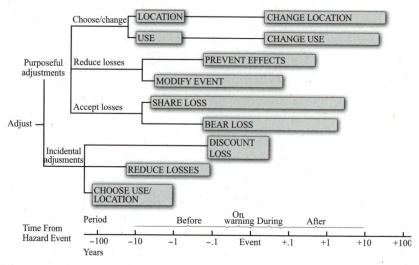

Figure 7.6   A choice tree for adjustment.
Source: Burton, Kates, and White (1993). Reprinted with permission from Ian Burton, and Guilford Press

used to prevent a problem from occurring, ranging from structural, to legislative, to institutional approaches, and so on. Anticipatory responses can include early warning systems, changes in building codes, and changes in the designs of systems and structures. Reactive responses range from the automatic responses of ecosystems to changes in growing-season length, farming practices, and insurance coverage.

The practical aspects of adaptation can facilitate or hinder its effectiveness in current conditions, let alone in future climate conditions. A good example of an anticipatory strategy is an early warning system for droughts (Wilhite 2005). Drought is very difficult to forecast, but it might be possible to provide early warning to a watershed or a farming region that could alert local authorities about an impending water shortage. The warning could then be used to activate emergency conservation measures reducing the consumption of water for irrigation and making sure that domestic uses or fisheries were getting what they needed (figure 7.7).

Changes in building codes are another example of anticipatory adaptation. However, they have been quite problematic even for places that have had experience with a particular problem (Auld and MacIver 2004). Consider a community located in a hurricane zone. Because of previous experience, the community and regional government understand the need

Figure 7.7   Early warning system, Outside Water Use Program, Guelph, Canada.
Photo credit: Reid Kreutzwiser. Photo courtesy of Reid Kreutswizer and Rob de Löe

to maintain a certain standard of building code so that buildings can withstand hurricane force winds, at least up to a certain threshold. Cost will dictate whether it is reasonable to protect against a class 1 or class 2 hurricane, as opposed to a class 4 or class 5. However, there are examples of communities that do not enforce building codes, so that when a hurricane does occur, damages are higher than they should be. This problem occurred in communities in the United States affected by Hurricane Andrew in 1992. It was found that more than 25 percent of the damage could have been prevented if the existing building codes had been enforced (Board on Natural Disasters 1999).

Adaptation to changing health risks, as with the cases noted above, includes familiar measures such as vaccinations, hot-weather response plans, and public reminders about personal behaviour, such as remaining hydrated during hot conditions, using tropical insect repellent, and heeding weather advisories. These measures appear to be self-evident, but circumstances can prevent the implementation of measures that appear to be part of basic common sense.

What kinds of forces, or drivers, influence personal, corporate, and governmental decision making? Drivers can include population and development pressures, regulations from other levels of government, and budgetary restrictions. For example, engineers could create and maintain a water system to deal with any extreme event, but they might be constrained by government budgets or, to give one hypothetical example, because zoning by-laws indicated that water pipes had to be routed in a certain way. However, enabling factors, such as staff or management interest and previous experience with pilot studies, can help make adaptation possible.

Barriers to adaptation can include costs, controls, and lack of acceptance by local practitioners or the public. Other obstacles can arise because of disagreements over who pays for the measure. The availability of conflict resolution methods may therefore become important, but for an uncertain issue like future climate change, the conflict resolution process would need to be complemented by information about future scenarios, and comfortable dialogue structures that allowed all the parties to participate freely.

Because adaptation is a long-term problem, it represents a significant investment. The intellectual effort required to learn about adaptation involves dealing with many complexities, from analysis to implementation. The required resources include land and perhaps water, money, time, and people. Maintenance, technical support, and governance are all necessary elements as well.

NEW ADAPTATION QUESTIONS

As a policy response to climate change, adaptation provides different opportunities, encounters different constraints, and generates dialogues that differ from the highly visible mitigation policy discussions. Adaptation and mitigation are approached in very different ways, perhaps because of the difficulties of defining adaptation targets. With mitigation, parties can set targets and offer specific measures to improve energy efficiency and reduce the carbon intensity of the forms of energy generation employed (see chapters 8 and 9). Adaptation is much harder because it requires acknowledgement of vulnerabilities, and that may be difficult for some nations, communities, and individuals to accept at first. Who wants to be told that they are not allowed to use as much water in their house, or that there is an increased health risk because of more heat waves or more insects? Energy attracts public attention, but health is very personal. What if the ability to adapt depends on what the neighbours are doing? That can also have a big impact on perceptions of whether one can adapt or not.

There are evolving questions about adaptation. Early case study experiences were based on static $2 \times CO_2$ scenarios. Now, case studies offer several time slices of future changes, including combinations of climatic and non-climatic scenarios of change. The whole question of "adapt to what" is no longer as simple as we once thought it was. Many adaptation options may be available, but these various choices will have costs and benefits that will be context-specific, varying with the state of development and ongoing efforts to address current vulnerabilities.

Another emerging probem for adaptation is determining what "dangerous" climate change is. Recall that Article 2 of the UNFCCC states that the ultimate objective is to stabilize greenhouse gas concentrations at a level that would prevent dangerous anthropogenic interference with the atmosphere (see chapter 2). However, this is not simply a question of "gross" biophysical impacts but a question of "net" impacts, one that incorporates the influences of both autonomous and planned adaptation on the initial biophysical concerns. The text of Article 2 acknowledges the role of natural ecosystem adaptation, but not of societal adaptation (Oppenheimer and Petsonk 2005). Could widespread societal adaptation change the threshold temperature (or greenhouse gas concentration) for dangerous interference? If a global-scale warming of 2°C *with* adaptation is considered "safe" (see chapter 6), what level of warming *without* adaptation is safe? How might this threshold be affected by climate adaptation policy or by development policy?

The connections between adaptation and sustainable development are now beginning to be discussed. An initial shopping list is offered in the third and fourth assessments of the Intergovernmental Panel on Climate Change (Smit et al. 2001; Adger et al. 2007) and includes more access to resources, a reduction of poverty, a lowering of inequities, improved education, assurances that responses are comprehensive and integrative and not just technical, and improved institutional capacities. The list poses enormous development challenges, and a climate change policy is unlikely to address them. The UNFCCC and the Kyoto Protocol are not big enough instruments, because climate change policy is not development policy per se. However, is it possible to bring climate change into development policy? Can climate change be made explicit within development policy, and can the two policy communities work together? We discuss these issues further in chapter 11.

Underlying this problem, at least within the impacts-adaptation research community, is the need to find ways to create a more holistic kind of assessment. If the research community has to create the damage report and to describe what the vulnerabilities and adaptation opportunities are, then there must be a different way of doing impacts work. Can we move to a second generation of impact and adaptation assessments, assessments that are more inclusive of socio-economic and cultural perspectives?

One approach would be to increase the intellectual effort applied to understanding vulnerabilities. The history of vulnerability research is rooted in natural hazards research (see Burton, Kates, and White 1978, 1993, for example), which predates work on climate change impacts by ten to twenty years, and ideas about different forms of adjustment (see figure 7.6) have been integrated into the recent dialogue on climate change adaptation (Smit et al. 2001). What else can we gain from natural hazards research that is applicable to a study of future scenarios? How can we apply knowledge of the past to studies of vulnerability to future climate change?

We should explore multiple and interacting stresses, but how should we do that? During the early days of climate change impacts research in the 1980s, it was relatively easy to do limited case studies incorporating the "everything else remains equal" assumption. But recent case studies have acknowledged that climate is not the only element that will change in the future. We do not need to know about population in order to study stream flow. But we know that in a river basin, land use decisions are being made because of development choices, and those decisions have to be incorporated into impact and adaptation studies of future water management. In practice, however, there are few examples in which both climate change scenarios and land use change scenarios have been used to predict future changes in water resources, since it is difficult to predict future changes in land use. In addition, the same effort hasn't been put into constructing local/regional land use change scenarios as has been put into climate change scenarios.

The evaluation of adaptive responses must also be considered, focusing on measures that directly address the underlying causes of vulnerability. Can we improve our understanding of how vulnerabilities have occurred in the recent past? Could this help us to anticipate how vulnerabilities will evolve with future development paths and future responses to climate change (Schneider et al. 2007)?

Stakeholder engagement has become a priority for impacts and adaptation research (see chapter 4), and there appears to have been a lot of improvement in this area. More and more studies have resulted from partnerships between researchers and stakeholders, using the broader definition of "stakeholders" offered earlier in this chapter. Case studies in developing countries are also applying this partnership model within a program called the Assessment of Impacts and Adaptation to Climate Change (AIACC). This program is contributing to the development of a "second generation" of assessment, identifying sources of vulnerability

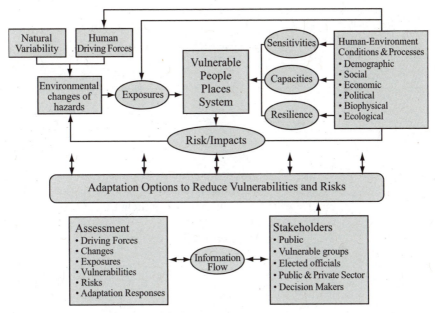

Figure 7.8   Framework for second-generation assessment of climate change impacts and adaptation.
Source: Leary and Beresford (2009). Reprinted with permission from Neil Leary

and risk and evaluating adaptation capabilities and opportunities (Leary and Beresford 2009; Leary et al. 2008a, b).

Figure 7.8 illustrates this more holistic approach, incorporating stakeholder partnerships, vulnerabilities, adaptive capacities, and adaptation options. A range of projects has just been completed in Latin America, Asia, and Africa. The exercise tries to combine impact assessments with increased attention to vulnerabilities, exposures (including the forces that lead to exposures), and the initial conditions that create sensitivities, capacities, and some sense of resilience. These elements are brought together to create a more complete story about what the risks are. Given what is available in the adaptation basket, the study should examine local options and get stakeholders involved in the assessments of what the vulnerabilities and risks are in their region. Thus, there would be a meeting of minds between those doing the research and those providing local information.

A comparison of the so-called vulnerability- and scenario-based approaches was provided in chapter 4. Modern climate change impact studies were originally scenario-based, but the challenge today is to combine

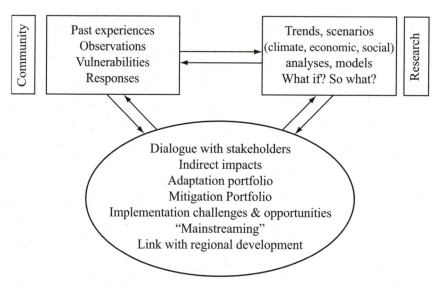

Figure 7.9   Climate change impacts and adaptation research: Partnership in shared learning

both scenario-based and vulnerability-based assessments to create a more holistic study. It is important to point out, however, that these assessments are not as different as they may appear. Both approaches use scenarios. The difference is in the choreography, beginning with the first step in the process. In the scenario approach, the first step in the dance is a "what if" question, which provides a way of initiating a shared learning experience about futures. This is followed by scenario studies assessing the risks and figuring out what kinds of strategies might be available. With the vulnerability approach, the first question, or the first step in the dance, is to focus on current problems, which may be exposures to droughts and floods and severe storms. These current risks would be assessed before subsequently moving into a scenario step.

Figure 7.9 describes how both approaches can be combined with dialogue to create a shared learning experience. This includes the important problem of incorporating climate change adaptation into ongoing management and planning processes, or "mainstreaming." The figure portrays the process as an interactive cycle, rather than as a series of steps.

Adaptation policy analysis requires consideration of the local development context, current policies and management practices, current risks, the adaptation baseline, and proposed policies and measures for improving current adaptation. The design of future alternatives will have to account for future management and environmental trends, future risks, adaptation improvements or innovations, and the evaluation of policy options (Füssel and Klein 2006). These elements underlie what is called an adaptation policy framework (Least Developed Countries Expert Group 2002). Such a framework was developed following a decision at COP-8 in Delhi to provide guidelines for countries seeking to prepare National Adaptation Programs of Action (Lim et al. 2004).

DISCUSSION

This chapter has examined the challenge of adaptation and the social dimensions of climate change. It has also touched on how these elements connect with GHG mitigation, which will be explored further in chapters 8 and 9.

It is also important not to lose the connection between the social aspects of climate change, the biophysical aspects, and the economic aspects, all of which were discussed in chapters 4, 5, and 6. Defining dangerous climate change requires information about biophysical impacts that can clearly describe what a scenario of climate change impacts implies for the basic resources on which countries and peoples depend. However, an impact and adaptation assessment cannot end with biophysical analyses. There has to be a way to account not only for the physical science but also for the economic and social dimensions of climate change. We have to consider the behaviour of people, markets, and governments. We have to consider issues of perception and governance. Because of the social differences between countries, their responses to climate change will be different, depending on their own unique social situations.

If we can not figure out what is dangerous or how much to reduce emissions in order to avoid danger, then what are the GHG targets really based on? The global-scale targets have been defined by a theoretical reduction of a global-temperature increase, assuming temperature as a proxy for damage. Clearly this is not enough. Incorporating vulnerability, adaptation, and development into the dialogue on dangerous climate change and on climate policy would strengthen the linkages between climate change science and policy (see chapter 11). The more we do this, the better we can engage all countries and make it more likely that they will be part of the climate policy process.

8

Mitigation Responses to Climate Change: Overview of the Process

INTRODUCTION

Overall, the narrative that we have described in previous chapters has the following highlights:

- GHG emissions have increased primarily because of fossil fuel burning and land use change.
- Temperatures have increased, but not in a linear trend, meaning that there is still a mixture of natural and anthropogenic forces influencing climate patterns.
- Uncertainty continues to influence what atmospheric scientists can say about future climate change, especially regarding regional changes in precipitation.
- Uncertainties are associated with projections of GHG emissions, since they depend on future changes in development and associated economic and political activities.
- Impacts on ecosystems are expected, and some may already be observed, particularly in the Arctic.
- Some plants will benefit from elevated CO_2 concentrations, while others will not.
- Costs attributable to weather events have increased, but governments and industries are making development choices that may be creating new vulnerabilities to weather and climate.

The last point has attracted considerable attention because of the economic implications of attributing recent trends to a particular cause or set of causes. Recent work has suggested that, at least in the United States, we are not seeing a clear, direct, straight-line increase in costs associated with climate change. Individual years with extreme events have exhibited huge increases in costs. On the other hand, the re-insurance industry has indicated a growth in the number of billion-dollar events and in insured and uninsured losses around the world, suggesting that both development choices and climate change are contributing to this growth in costs. Is vulnerability changing? Is it changing even in areas that are supposedly highly developed? And if so, how?

Some indirect social side effects could occur if vulnerable populations found that climate change pushed them beyond their capacities to cope with various other problems (for example, resource depletion and increased disease rates). Could we see a growing wave of environmental refugees? How significant this problem would become would depend very much on a country's ability to adapt, which would be based on its vulnerability and its capacity to adapt. We have already discussed adaptation challenges and options in chapters 4 to 7, and we'll revisit this topic again in chapter 11 when we examine linkages between climate change and sustainability.

We now consider mitigation responses and associated policy instruments. The international response has centred on the United Nations Framework Convention on Climate Change (UNFCCC) and the Kyoto Protocol. In this chapter, we look at the policy language in these two documents, so we now have to step away somewhat from the perspective of science and economics and put on our policy hat. And like most of our discussions, this policy discussion will be from a generalist's perspective.

We recognize the importance of understanding policy and policy documents and using science information to solve policy problems. The Intergovernmental Panel on Climate Change (IPCC) has played a very important role in this approach. It was designed as a mechanism for bridging science and policy without actually becoming policy-prescriptive. While the IPCC provides a worthwhile vehicle for allowing scientists to get involved (Shaw 2005), the translation of science into a policy document, such as the Kyoto Protocol, is a much more difficult problem. Some of the policy-oriented concepts that we will consider include "additionality," "leakage," and the instruments that are part of Kyoto, including emissions trading (ET), markets, and carbon sinks.

In chapter 9, we dive deeply into the subjects of carbon sinks, joint implementation (JI), clean development mechanisms (CDMs), and ET. These concepts are supposed to provide Kyoto with the means to be equitable, regardless of whether a country's economy is rich or poor. Now that Russia has ratified Kyoto, enabling it to come into force on 16 February

2005, we are entering into unknown policy territory, moving from abstract ideas to the challenges of implementation.

BACKGROUND

Within the UNFCCC and the Kyoto framework countries are grouped into annexes, and each one has a different set of rules, purposes, and roles to play in the attempt to control GHG emissions and reduce vulnerabilities. The UNFCCC groups forty developed countries, along with the EU, into the Annex I category, which consists of the countries that have established emissions baselines. This list is similar to, but not the same as, the list of countries grouped into Kyoto's Annex B category. The thirty-eight countries in the Annex B grouping consist of countries that have assigned emissions reduction targets.

The Annex II countries of the UNFCCC, on the other hand, form a subset of developed countries that provide financial support for either the bilateral development mechanisms or the multi-lateral development mechanisms of Kyoto. Canada is part of Annex I and also part of Annex II. Russia, on the other hand, is not part of Annex II, but it is part of Annex I.

Kyoto's Annex A contains a list of GHG gases and sources, including CO_2, CH_4, N_2O, and various CFCs. The non-Annex countries are the countries, including China, India, and Brazil, that have ratified Kyoto but that are not on one of the other lists and do not have emissions reduction targets. However, by ratifying, they gain access to Kyoto instruments, and they also accept rules and responsibilities of their own. A very interesting part of the policy debate concerns the role of these non-Annex countries. Kyoto critics often claim that non-Annex countries are not part of the mitigation effort at all; in other words, they do not count somehow. That statement is untrue, but it is clear that at some point some of these non-Annex countries will have to consider a formal emissions reduction target (see chapter 11).

Some key items within the protocol document are important to understand. The first is the Quantified Emission Limitation or Reduction Commitment (QELRC) or Obligation (QELRO), which refers to the targets that are listed in Kyoto for the Annex B countries. If Annex B countries are to be able to claim emission credits that count towards meeting these targets, they will have to prove that a specific climate change investment made the claim possible. One of the tests for this is "additionality."

Additionality is the notion that a particular action undertaken using a Kyoto instrument is an addition to what would otherwise have occurred (Metz et al. 2001). For example, a development agreement between Bangladesh and Canada could oblige Canada to pay to have a highly efficient district energy system built in Dhaka, for which, in return, Canada would receive an emissions credit. The two parties would have to prove that this system would not have been built without the Kyoto instrument in place. If the system was part of an ongoing Bangladeshi economic-development plan, such that the Bangladeshi government accepted Canada's money to build the energy system but then used its own money on something else, the new system might not be considered "additional," and it would not therefore qualify Canada for receiving a GHG credit. One can imagine how hard it would be to prove additionality, but regardless of the difficulty, the purpose of this provision is to make climate change policy an explicit part of what countries do, rather than a source of income for general revenues.

Kyoto was developed with a particular objective in mind, that is, that there should be an explicit development path that reduces emissions or that slows the rate of growth of emissions beyond what would have happened without Kyoto. Thus, countries need to establish baseline emissions estimates and projections of future emissions and to provide them to the Secretariat of the Framework Convention. Once they have done this, they can then show how their emissions reduction activities will achieve a saving below this initially forecasted emissions growth, and they can show that the difference should be credited to the donor country. Basically, once a country has established a baseline, it should be able to prove additionality.

Another important term, "differentiation," from Article 3.1 of the UNFCCC refers to the idea that every country will have an individual target. For example, Canada, Europe, and Australia have different targets, and for good reasons. The Kyoto targets resulted from negotiation rather than scientific analysis, making them somewhat arbitrary. However, it is also important to consider that individual countries are at different stages of economic development, they have different dependencies on fossil fuels, and they face different challenges related to their unique geographic circumstances (transport distances, climate, and so on). Kyoto mechanisms are described as flexible, meaning that there is no single prescribed way for countries to achieve their targets and that each country should be able to find its own way to do so.

The UNFCCC also specifies that developing countries do not have targets because the Annex I countries should be leaders in the mitigation effort (UNFCCC Article 4.2). That does not mean that China will never have an emissions target, but it does mean that Canada, say, has to first demonstrate that it is trying to reduce its emissions, since developed countries caused the problem in the first place. Since global society endorsed this principle as an equitable foundation for climate change policy, having already ratified the UNFCCC, then Annex I countries have to be the first to reduce emissions.

Not only must Annex II countries provide funds to meet the costs of these emissions reduction instruments; they must also assist in meeting the costs of adaptation (UNFCCC, Article 4.4). It is very difficult to determine how much Kyoto money should go to adaptation and how one could measure the success of an adaptation investment. The Kyoto Protocol does not have vulnerability reduction targets, only GHG emissions reduction targets. However, there is language in the policy to suggest that Annex II countries have to provide some funds for adaptation and also for technology transfer (UNFCCC, Article 4.5) and that developing countries' actions depend on the actions of developed countries (UNFCCC, Article 4.7).

There are also concerns that policy responses or development actions could lead to GHG "emissions leakage." That is, an emissions reduction might be offset by an emissions increase elsewhere. For example, a country could achieve a reduction in its emissions simply by outsourcing or contracting out "dirty industries" to another country. It could be argued that this has been happening all along, with the kinds of trading patterns that have emerged in recent years. Developed countries' economies have become based around service industries, while the economies of developing countries are now based around the production of goods using the dirty industries that operated decades ago in developed countries. Does that mean that some countries have become cleaner because they have become smarter and more efficient? Or have they just contracted out the dirty production? In GHG accounting, how does this kind of leakage become included in a way that all parties will feel is fair?

Use of the Kyoto Protocol mechanisms must supplement domestic actions. "Supplementarity" is the notion that a country cannot depend completely on a Kyoto mechanism such as ET or CDMs. A developed country has to achieve some emissions reductions through domestic actions, for example, in the form of a regulation on the auto industry or a domestic carbon tax, since no carbon tax is included in Kyoto. However, supplementarity does not appear to have precise limits. Can a

Table 8.1
Greenhouse Gases in the Kyoto Protocol and Their Global Warming Potentials (GWP) Relative to Carbon Dioxide for 20- and 100-Year Horizons

Greenhouse Gas	GWP: 20-year	GWP: 100-year
Carbon dioxide (CO_2)	1	1
Methane (CH_4)	72	25
Nitrous oxide (N_2O)	289	298
Chlorofluorocarbons (CFCs)	5,310 to 11,000	4,750 to 14,400
Hydrochlorofluourocarbons (HCFCs)	273 to 5,490	77 to 2,310
Hydrofluorocarbons (HFCs)	437 to 12,000	124 to 14,800
Perfluorocarbons (PFCs)	5,210 to 8,630	7,390 to 17,200
Sulphur hexafluoride (SF_6)	16,300	22,800

Source: Forster et al. (2007).

country really offer emissions reductions based entirely on trading or an another Kyoto instrument? If there really is a limit, say 50 percent, then a country can use Kyoto reductions for only 50 percent, and the other 50 percent has to come from some domestic action.

In chapter 3, we discussed the different levels of radiative forcing that characterize various GHGs. These different levels have attracted attention within the policy community, resulting in the concept of global warming potential (GWP). This concept recognizes that not all GHGs affect climate in the same way. CO_2 has lower radiative forcing per unit than other GHGs, such as CH_4 and CFCs, and if we are really going to solve climate change, we can not focus just on CO_2.

So, can Kyoto be used to provide incentives for countries to manage all their GHG emissions, and not just CO_2? And again, in order to be scientifically accurate, it is important to account for the different radiative forcings of each gas. GWP is supposed to be a measure that allows countries to present their plan for dealing with the totality of their emissions. For example, it would allow countries to get more credit for CH_4 emissions reductions than CO_2 emissions reductions, because CH_4 has a more powerful radiative effect than CO_2. But not only do these gases have different radiative effects, they also have different lifetimes in the atmosphere, as well as different sources of emission. And so the question is, can GWP be used as an index for policy purposes instead of simply using the CO_2 rise and fall as a barometer?

The Annex A list of gases includes all the GHGs that could be part of the calculation of GWP. Table 8.1 shows that if CO_2 is given the value of 1

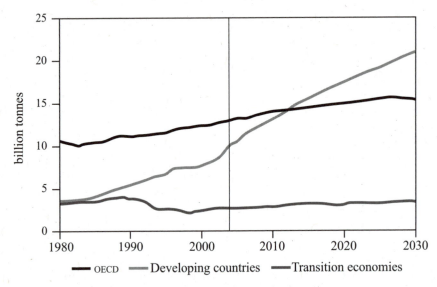

Note: Excludes emissions from international marine bunkers.
© OECD/IEA 2008

Figure 8.1   Energy-related CO$_2$ emissions trends, 1980–2004, and projections, 2004–30.
Source: IEA (2006, figure 2.9). Reprinted with permission from IEA

and the other gases are compared to it, the GWP of CH$_4$ would be 72 times more powerful within a twenty-year time horizon and 25 times more powerful over the long term, while N$_2$O and the fluorocarbons would be 300 times and thousands of times more powerful, respectively.

EMISSION TRENDS, SCENARIOS, AND STABILISATION

GHG emissions have been increasing largely because energy consumption has been increasing. Total CO$_2$ emissions for 2004 were around 26 Gt per year for energy-related activities (IEA 2006), with an additional 8 Gt per year attributable to deforestation. When CH$_4$ and other GHGs are added, total CO$_2$ equivalent emissions for 2004 were estimated to be 49 Gt per year (IPCC 2007b). Of the energy-related emissions, the percentage that is caused by the industrialized countries is getting smaller (figure 8.1). This trend is expected to continue in the short term, so by the 2010s, the emissions of the industrial countries and the developing countries would be close to equal.

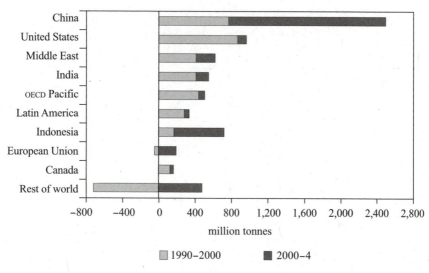

Figure 8.2   Trends in energy-related CO_2 emissions by region.
Source: IEA (2006, figure 2.7). Reprinted with permission from IEA

In China and other Asian developing countries, emissions are increasing much more rapidly than in Latin America and the developed countries. The "rest of world," including the "economies in transition" (the former Soviet Union and Eastern Europe), shows a decline in the 1990s, followed by recent increases (figure 8.2). In the long term, different development paths can lead to very different GHG emissions paths. A number of studies have produced GHG emissions scenarios on the basis of different scenarios of economic and population growth, land use change, and technology transfer. Among these are the SRES scenarios referred to earlier, in chapters 2, 3, and 6.

What were the underlying assumptions that went into these different SRES paths? Figure 8.3 illustrates trajectories of various indicators within each of the main SRES storylines (see also figure 3.19 and 3.20 and the accompanying text). Recall that each of these six groups of scenarios represents several individual scenarios. The A1 scenario family develops into three groups, A1FI, A1B, and A1T, which describe alternative directions for technological change. These three groups, along with B1, and B2, are represented by illustrative, or "marker" scenarios (Nakicenovic and Swart 2000). Also recall that the A scenarios represent economic imperatives, while the B scenarios promote environment as a

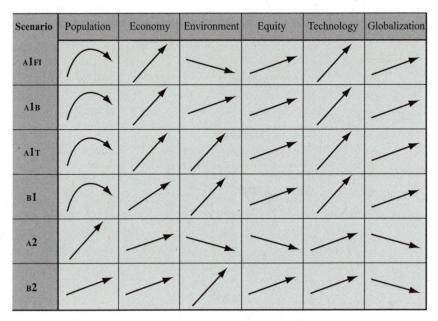

Figure 8.3   Directions of different indicators within each scenario of SRES. See
figures 3.19 and 3.20 for information on SRES storylines.
Source: IPCC (2001d, figure TS.1). Reprinted with permission from IPCC

high priority. In addition, the A1 and B1 families are globally oriented,
whereas the A2 and B2 families are regionally oriented (figure 3.19). The
global imperatives, A1 and B1, assume a population peak and then a decline, while A2 and B2, the regional imperatives, assume a continuous
increase through the twenty-first century. In all cases, there is economic
growth, but countries that are pushing the economic imperative have a
more rapid rate of increase than those that are pushing a different imperative.

As already discussed in chapter 3, environmental indicators do exhibit divergence in these narratives. The A2 scenario and the A1FI fossil
fuel scenario represent the worst cases for environmental trends. However, the scenarios in the A1 family, including the balance scenarios
(A1B) and the clean-technology scenarios (A1T), suggest environmental
improvements. The same is true of both the B1 and the B2 families. This
suggests that, with the exception of the A2 scenario, equity will improve
over time in all cases. As well, technology will improve in the global
cases, but not as much in the regional cases. Globalization advances in
the global cases, whereas the international movement of goods and

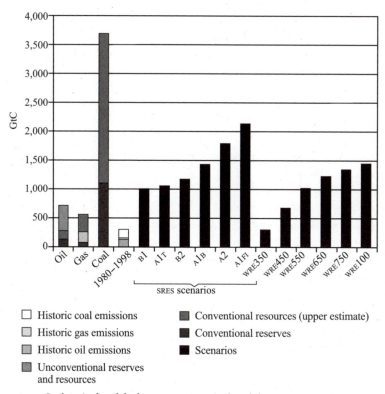

Figure 8.4   Carbon in fossil fuel reserves compared with historic emissions and scenarios. WRE profiles from Wigley et al. (1996).
Source: IPCC (2001c, figure SPM-2). Reprinted with permission from IPCC

people declines in the regional cases. As we have illustrated, different assumptions were used to construct the different SRES emissions scenarios, and these scenarios have subsequently become the basis for recent climate change simulations and impact studies.

Figure 8.4 shows that projected carbon emissions could have a range anywhere between a cumulative total of 1,000 and 2,100 Gt of carbon by 2100. The lowest emissions are predicted for the B1 case and the A1 technology case, whereas the highest emissions are predicted for the A2 case and the A1FI case. These scenarios all contain much higher emissions than has been observed during the previous 120 years. Note that there is still a very large reserve of coal available for future energy use. There could potentially be 3,700 Gt of carbon available for consumption, which is far more than the carbon that would be available from oil and natural gas.

Figure 8.4 also includes an older set of scenarios labelled WRE. The WRE scenarios are named after the first initials of the last names of the authors of a study (Wigley, Richels, and Edmonds 1996), whose computations focused on estimating stabilization scenarios. The issue of stabilization is very important here from a policy perspective, specifically relating to Article 2 of the UNFCCC (see chapter 2). Stabilization of GHG concentrations means that these concentrations would be managed to remain at a particular level, thereby preventing further increases. The choice of the stabilization level would be determined by the associated increase in global temperature. Even though it is difficult to define a dangerous amount of global-temperature increase and consequently, a dangerous GHG concentration, it is instructive to know how much fossil fuel emissions would result in a particular GHG concentration. If we wanted to stabilize according to the WRE 550 ppm scenario, global carbon consumption should not exceed 1,000 Gt over the twenty-first century. The only SRES narratives that predict stabilization at 550 ppm are the B1 case and A1T case.

According to the WRE assessment, if global development happened to follow one of these two particular development paths, only a modest climate policy would be needed to achieve a stabilization of 550 ppm. But, if development followed the SRES A1FI path, there would need to be an emissions reduction of 50 percent to achieve 550 ppm stabilization. Finally, if 550 ppm was considered dangerous, and 450 ppm was to become the goal, emission reductions would still be required in even the most optimistic SRES cases. Note that this has not yet accounted for the possibility of large scale changes in the capacity of carbon sinks.

As with the intercomparisons of the different SRES trajectories, when the various WRE stabilization paths are compared, they all suggest that future changes would be non-linear. With SRES, some scenarios would exhibit a deceleration in the growth of GHG emissions, while others would exhibit a shift from increasing to decreasing emissions (figure 8.5). Stabilization would require that emissions diverge from the given development path over several decades.

In the high-emissions SRES cases, such as A1FI, a large emissions reduction would have to occur more quickly for 450 ppm or even 550 ppm to be an achievable stabilization goal within this century. In the B1, B2, and A1T worlds, a policy of modest emissions reduction could be effective. In the B1 world, GHG emissions would peak at about 10 or 11 Gt of carbon and then fall back to around 8 Gt to reach 550 ppm. However, if we were in the A1FI world, in order to achieve stabilization at 550 ppm, there would need to be an emissions reduction

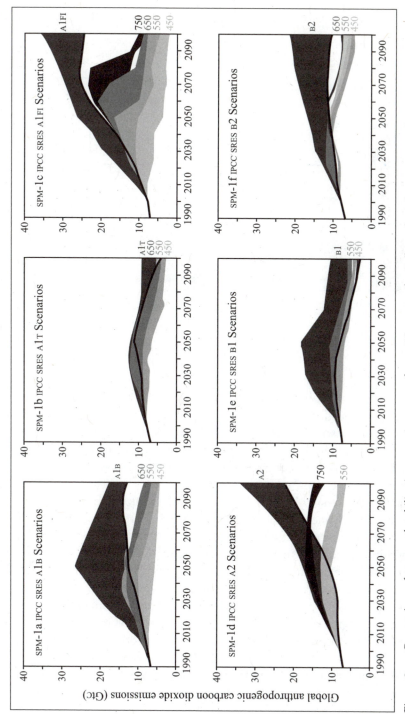

Figure 8.5 Comparison of SRES and stabilization scenarios. SPM refers to "Summary for Policymakers."
Source: IPCC (2001c, figure SPM-1). Reprinted with permission of IPCC

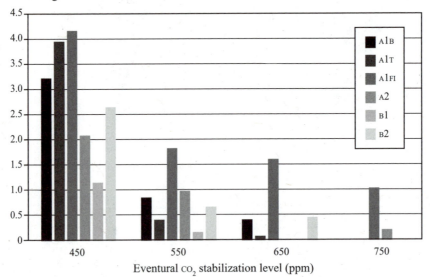

Figure 8.6   Costs of stabilization for SRES scenarios.
Source: IPCC (2001a, figure 7.4). Reprinted with permission of IPCC

from 20 Gt to 10 Gt by the 2030s. In other words, a 50 percent reduction would be needed almost immediately in order for that to be possible. This comparison exercise does not specify how stabilization is to be achieved, but rather, it merely illustrates the nature of the challenge to do so. A climate policy required in the AIFI world would likely be very different from one required in the BI world.

What would actually be required to achieve stabilization in these various cases? How much would it cost? Figure 8.6 provides estimates of potential reductions in average global GDP for different levels of stabilization within each of the SRES worlds. For example, if 550 ppm was the stabilization target, and we were in the AIFI world, we would expect to see a GDP reduction around 1.75 percent. But if we were in the BI world, the economy would experience only modest effects. Recall that in economic analyses (see chapter 6), assumptions are needed regarding future changes in behaviour, technology, governance, and other factors. Again, in these cases the cost estimates depend on the economists' assumptions about the impacts of an energy strategy associated with climate change. Now suppose that 550 ppm was perceived as an inadequate stabilization

Emissions, concentrations, and temperature changes corresponding
to different stabilization levels for CO_2 concentrations

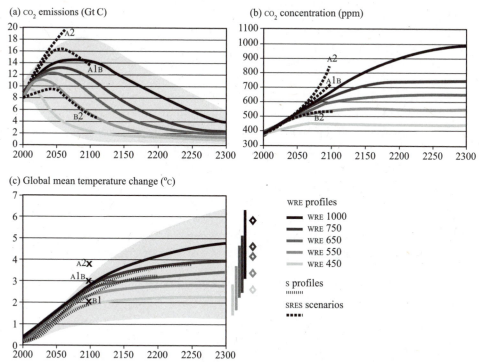

Figure 8.7   Stabilization at 450–550 ppm slows the rate of warming. See figure 8.4
for WRE stabilization profiles, and figures 8.3 and 8.4 for SRES profiles. The S profiles
refer to an alternative set of stabilization profiles provided by IPCC.
Source: IPCC (2001a, figure 6.1). Reprinted with permission of IPCC.

goal and that 450 ppm was chosen as a more appropriate stabilization
target. This would result in larger policy costs for either the Kyoto instruments in general or the Kyoto instruments plus whatever domestic emissions reductions would be required. These costs would be larger for all
SRES situations.

What would global temperature change look like in these stabilization scenarios? In the best case, which is B1, it is estimated that they
would result in a warming of about 2°C by 2100, followed by little additional forcing (figure 8.7). In other words, the anthropogenic GHG effect would be 2°C, and that effect would be superimposed on prevailing
natural climatic variability. Recall that the SRES narratives do not include a specific policy on climate change. The stabilization scenarios

represent different emission paths but do not suggest how they should be achieved. If the best-case situation among this set of calculations is 2°c of warming, which suggests that we are already committed to 2°c of warming, does this mean that even the best case is dangerous? The IPCC's *Third Assessment Report*'s conclusions about reasons for concern (IPCC 2001b) suggest that 2°c of warming may not be dangerous for the world's economy as a whole but that it may be dangerous for some regional economies and for all ecosystems.

If 2°c of warming was to become recognized as the limit for avoiding dangerous interference, what should the stabilization target be? This would depend on the climate's sensitivity to elevated CO_2 concentrations; in other words, it would depend on how much warming would occur for a given increase in CO_2 (see chapter 3). Because of this uncertainty, climate scientists express their estimates of stabilization targets in probabilistic terms. An example is provided by Hare and Meinshausen (2004), who suggest that the target CO_2 concentration should be 440 ppm, since at this level there is a 66 percent chance of limiting global mean temperature increases below 2°c. At higher concentrations, this probability decreases.

This exercise of linking SRES storylines and stabilization scenarios represents an opportunity to connect climate change to the larger challenges of sustainable development. If policy measures can encourage a broader development effort that takes global economies through a low emission path, then climate policy would be a lot easier to formulate. We will discuss more on the linkages between climate change and sustainable development in chapter 11.

THE UNITED NATIONS FRAMEWORK CONVENTION ON CLIMATE CHANGE AND THE KYOTO PROTOCOL: THE NEGOTIATION PROCESS

Before we address the specific measures that are part of the Kyoto Protocol, let us explore the negotiation process surrounding emission reduction targets that has emerged since 1992, because it says something about how different countries feel about emissions reduction and about how they are incorporating it into their domestic and foreign policies. Previously, in chapter 2, we explored the timeline of climate policy development. The key events were the 1992 signing of the UNFCCC and its subsequent ratification in 1994, followed by the signing of the Kyoto

Protocol in 1997 and its subsequent ratification in 2005. Here we discuss some of the key events in the negotiation process.

When the UNFCCC was ratified, an annual series of Conferences of the Parties (COPs) was initiated. All countries that have ratified the UNFCCC, regardless of their position on the Kyoto Protocol, have standing at the COPs. Each COP has provided a forum for policy dialogue and a congress for policy decisions. The best examples are the signing of the Kyoto Protocol at COP-3 in 1997 and the Bali Action Plan at COP-13 in 2007. The latter lays out the post-2012 process for global action on adaptation and emissions reductions, including mitigation actions by developing country parties (UNFCCC 2007a). The COPs, as well as the recently initiated Meetings of the Parties of the Kyoto Protocol (MOPs) have also attracted many non-government actors who have organized side events on scientific and policy matters.

The Negotiation of Emission Reduction Targets

Climate policy negotiations have led to the formation of various alliances, or blocks, of countries promoting common positions on emissions targets, rules for implementing measures, and specific texts in the relevant documents. These blocks have evolved over time as the negotiation process advances through various phases.

During the pre-Kyoto period up to December 1997, the European Union (EU), Economies in Transition states (EIT – the former republics of the Soviet Union), the G77 group of developing countries, and the Alliance of Small Island States (AOSIS) all shared a common position. There was also a group of developed countries initially known by the acronym JUSCANZ and later JUSSCANNZ (Japan, the United States, Switzerland, Canada, Australia, Norway, and New Zealand) that were looking for a compromise position on emissions targets.

The group that advocated large emissions reductions was AOSIS. The states in AOSIS had banded together because they shared a similar vulnerability to a rise in sea levels. AOSIS wanted to see an emissions reduction for all countries of 20 percent below 1990 levels by 2005. The EIT bloc had no particular view about targets, but they did want flexible mechanisms. The EU was interested in a 15 percent reduction by 2010, and they were advocating what was called the "bubble" concept. That is, that the EU would act as a bubble, and each individual country would have its own domestic target so that collectively the EU would provide the 15 percent reduction (Grubb, Vrolijk, and Brack 1999; Oberthür and Ott 1999). For example, Portugal would have a different target from Greece, Germany, and so on.

The G77, which includes China and over 130 other members, wanted to see commitments from developed countries first, though it was not clear that all the G77 countries felt that way. Some of them were rapidly growing developing countries, such as South Korea, and they were thinking they might be interested in targets if incentives, such as selling credits, were provided. In other words, some countries were considering accepting targets if they could partipate in an emissions trading market or another mechanism, since countries needed to have targets to be able to sell credits. All countries could participate in at least some of these mechanisms, but a country could not buy and sell credits unless the country made a commitment to a target.

In between the strong position of the EU and the much weaker position of the EIT states of Eastern Europe, the JUSSCANNZ bloc promoted various emissions targets. Initially Japan wanted a 5 percent reduction, while the United States wanted stabilization at 1990 levels. Canada changed its target during COP-3 in response to a change in the US target to 7 percent (Bruce and Russell 2004). JUSSCANNZ countries were interested in having flexible mechanisms and ensuring that different countries had different targets. Differentiation was an important issue for Canada at the time.

Post-COP 3, negotiations became more complex. Countries formed new groupings as each one began articulating the different position it wanted (Yamin and Depledge 2004). Kyoto identified particular roles and commitments of the Annex I and Annex II countries. However, these countries were not negotiating as a group, whereas AOSIS still was. There were also several former Asian members of the Soviet Union countries with access to oil resources that identified a common negotiating position, so they became a small group of their own. There was also another mixture of countries called the Environmental Integrity Group (Mexico, Republic of Korea, Switzerland), as well as other groups, including countries from the Organization of Petroleum Exporting Countries OPEC. The EU continued to negotiate as a bubble, and the G77 did so as well. The Umbrella Group evolved from the former JUSSCANNZ to also include Russia, Iceland, and Ukraine, and it continued to look for a compromise between the stronger positions advocated by the EU and AOSIS and more modest targets considered by other countries. For a complete list of groupings of negotiating parties to reader is referred to the UNFCCC website (http//www.unfccc.int).

The COPs of 1998–2004

Following COP-3, discussion focused on technical aspects of the Kyoto mechanisms. At COP-4, in 1998, questions related to emissions trading, compliance, and the adequacy of commitments were discussed. Argentina, the host country that year, became the first developing country to accept a voluntary emissions target. Only three small island countries had ratified Kyoto at that time. There was also the Buenos Aires Plan of Action, which called for providing support for the various Kyoto instruments, as well as technical studies. These were implemented in COP-6.5 (also known as COP-6, Part II) in 2000. This was the second COP-6 event, which was held after the first COP-6 event ended in disarray.

There had to be two meetings that year because the first COP-6 had ended without agreement on the next steps. Indeed, it was feared that the whole process was going to collapse, but it was revived through the efforts of a diplomat from the Netherlands who brought the focus onto implementation of Buenos Aires Plan of Action (IISD 2000, 2001; President of COP-6, no date). One of the outcomes was the establishment of the Special Climate Change Fund for Adaptation, to be funded from a 2 percent share of clean development mechanism (CDM) proceeds, thereby creating an adaptation investment. There was an agreement on supplementarity that was a compromise position that ensured that developed countries would not rely entirely on Kyoto mechanisms to reach their emissions targets. However, there was no agreement on an amount, that is, on how much of Canada's or France's emissions reduction target could be achieved through the Kyoto instruments and how much through domestic actions?

Another outcome was that nuclear power could not become part of a JI or a CDM activity. In other words, a country could not use Kyoto to buy a nuclear plant and place it in another country. Also, Kyoto could not be used to divert money from ongoing development assistance programs. So if Germany had been donating funds for development in Southeast Asia, for example, it could not take 30 percent of that donation and place the funds in a CDM investment.

Adaptation mechanisms became a central focus at COP-7 in Marrakech. In effect, this was a revival of interest in article 4.9 of the UN-FCCC, which specifically called for the establishment of adaptation mechanisms. The Marrakech Plan established three funds for adaptation, expanding from the earlier levy on the CDM to create the Lesser Developed Countries Fund, the Special Climate Change Fund, and the

Adaptation Fund (Huq 2002). These will be supported by the UN Global Environmental Facility (GEF), which supports many programs besides climate change. As of 2007, these funding mechanisms had not been completely worked out. At the 2007 MOP-3, held in Bali in parallel with COP-13, a mechanism was put in place to support adaptation projects funded through the Adaptation Fund by creating an Adaptation Fund Board to manage funds obtained from certified emission reductions issued by the CDM Executive Board (UNFCCC 2007b).

COP-8 in Delhi and COP-9 in Milan raised the profile of sustainable development within the climate change discourse. The one hundredth country ratified Kyoto in January 2003, and Canada also ratified Kyoto in 2003. However, at this point still only 44 percent of Annex I emissions were accounted for, because Russia had not ratified yet, and this was slowing down the process for bringing Kyoto into force. By 2004, Russia was making its ratification intentions known, and it finally ratified Kyoto in the fall of 2004. On 16 February 2005, Kyoto came into force with 126 countries having ratified the agreement. The United States continues to remain on the outside of this agreement. However, with Russian ratification, COP-10 participants turned their attention to the initial start-up of the CDM because this "bank" could now start to make investments. And of course, one of the big concerns was the level of investment from Annex B countries. Considerable attention was also paid to emissions trading rules and permit allocations, as well as to sinks allocations.

INTRODUCTION TO THE KYOTO INSTRUMENTS

Having discussed the negotiation process leading up to and following the ratification of the UNFCCC and the Kyoto Protocol, we now turn our attention to the instruments themselves. Although the UNFCCC introduced possible mechanisms for emissions reduction and stabilization, it did not offer any specifics. Instead, the Kyoto Protocol includes specific language on several instruments and supporting infrastructures that are designed to encourage cleaner development.

Overview of the Kyoto Instruments

Yamin and Depledge (2004) provide an extensive discussion of the Kyoto instruments. Our discussion here and in chapter 9 offers an introduction to these measures.

Here are some starting points:

- Articles 3.3 and 3.4 – Carbon Sinks. The text describes the requirement for verifiable changes in carbon stocks since 1990, which is the same base year as for GHG emission targets. There are three categories of sinks activities: afforestation (planting trees in previously non-forested areas), reforestation, and deforestation.
- Article 6 – Joint Implementation (JI). A credit is given to an annex I country for emissions reduction achieved through individual projects in other countries. This is a bilateral mechanism.
- Article 12 – the Clean Development Mechanism (CDM). A CDM is described as something like a bank or a portfolio. For example, Canada can invest in a CDM project and receive a certain share of the carbon savings of the entire portfolio. This is supposed to be specifically about financial assistance to the non-Annex I parties. In other words, it is not the Eastern Europeans who are supposed to benefit from this. They will benefit from JI. This money is supposed to go to countries in the developing world, such as China, India, and Saharan Africa, but not to Ukraine or Bulgaria.
- Article 12.8 – Adaptation. Part of the CDM investment is supposed to contribute to the costs of adaptation. However, at this time only a small percentage is to be applied to adaptation, which is a concern for developing countries because they see significant vulnerability to current extreme events, such as floods, food shortages, and disease outbreaks. Investments solely in GHG emissions reduction do not address these immediate vulnerability problems. On the other hand, one might ask whether a climate change mechanism is appropriate for solving current vulnerability problems. Should that solution not come from a sustainable-development mechanism or other forms of development assistance? Why climate change?
- Article 17 – Emissions Trading. All parties that have accepted emissions targets may participate in trading. A developing country, such as China, can not be a trader, but a lot of money could conceivably be made by selling credits, which could provide an incentive for China and other developing countries to accept an emissions target. What target would be appropriate? Would China's target resemble Canada's target of reductions below 1990 levels? This would be highly unlikely. It could accept a reduction in its rate of emissions growth, rather than a reduction below 1990 levels. But, how could this be equitably determined? It would have to be compared to a baseline, so

what baseline of growth would be assumed for China or other developing countries? What would be an appropriate reduction in that rate of growth? What would be the best accounting practice to use for verification for China, India, Korea, or Brazil? The text of article 17 is quite specific – to be a trader, the country (Party) has to accept a target, and the COPs have to define the rules and the guidelines, including verification and reporting of any changes in GHG emissions.

The Kyoto Protocol also identifies supporting mechanisms. It is important to keep in mind that a global agreement like this requires infrastructure that supports the whole negotiation process. Some of this infrastructure is discussed in specific articles of the protocol. For instance, research is mentioned in a number of articles, including research to support studies of carbon sinks (Articles 2 and 3) and to update GWPs (Article 5). Article 9 talks about supporting assessments, including the IPCC, and Article 10 talks about broader education and public awareness. Article 7 addresses the need for all countries to produce up-to-date GHG inventories as part of determining the baseline emissions trajectory without a climate policy. Article 3.14 establishes funding for technology transfers. As well, Article 15, which is linked back to the original Framework Convention, establishes two supporting subsidiary bodies that are negotiating the rules behind the scenes: the Subsidiary Body for Scientific & Technological Advice (SBSTA) and the Subsidiary Body for Implementation (SBI).

Returning to Article 5 for a moment, GWP has been updated as part of the IPCC review process. The radiative forcing for CH_4 from the Second Assessment Report was updated for the Third Assessment Report. The IPCC actually changed the relative weighting from 21 to 23 (Ramaswamy et al. 2001), which could lead to greater attention being focused on CH_4 compared with N_2O and other minor GHGs.

Supporting Infrastructure

The COP apparatus that led to the signing of Kyoto at COP-3 includes institutions that enable participating countries to work cooperatively on the technical issues associated with climate policy measures and to vote on resolutions and agreements. The IPCC is one of these institutions, and its role is to provide ongoing scientific advice.

In addition, there are the two other bodies just mentioned: the Subsidiary Body for Scientific and Technological Advice and the Subsidiary

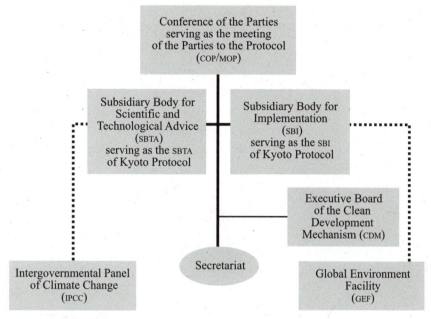

Figure 8.8   The institutions of the Kyoto Protocol.
Source: Oberthür and Ott (1999). Reprinted with permission from Hermann Ott, and Springer Science and Business Media

Body for Implementation. The SBSTA receives information from the IPCC and advises on how this information can be applied to the various technical mechanisms. The SBI focuses more on implementation itself, as a policy advisory group, and it is linked with the Global Environmental Facility (GEF), which the UN established in part to provide funds for research, as well as to provide funds that would go into these mechanisms (figure 8.8).

Figure 8.8 shows how the Executive Board of the CDM relates to the COP and supporting bodies. This multilateral bank was set up to provide funding for projects in developing countries that were meant to reduce the rate of growth in emissions. Once the Kyoto Protocol was ratified, the annual COP meetings shifted to being Meetings of the Parties (MOPS). This shift signified the transition from negotiation and discussions about the design of the instruments to their implementation.

Before examining the Kyoto instruments in detail, in chapter 9, we first consider how a particular country could take advantage of all of these mechanisms. Figure 8.9 illustrates their application. Suppose Party A is an Annex B country, such as Canada, France, Japan, or the

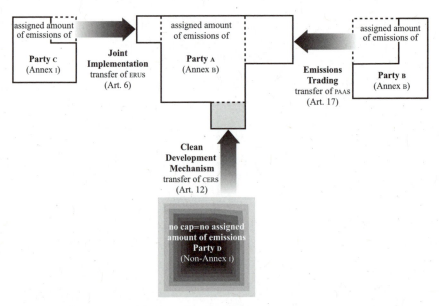

Figure 8.9   Application of the Kyoto mechanisms.
Source: Oberthür and Ott (1999). Reprinted with permission from Hermann Ott, and Springer Science and Business Media

United States (assuming it has ratified the protocol, which it has not done as of 2008). Party A initially has an assigned amount of emissions, which is denoted by the square that is bounded partly by dashed lines on the left, right, and bottom. This square represents the country's assigned GHG emissions amount, which is the net of its 1990 emissions minus (or plus in some cases, such as Iceland) its targeted reductions (or increases). In Canada's case, with a 1990 baseline of 240 Mt of carbon and a targeted reduction of 6 percent, how could it take advantage of these various instruments in order to help reach its target?

It could enter into a JI arrangement with an Annex I country (generally one of the Eastern European countries or former Soviet Republics), shown as Party C. As the donor, Party A would receive what is called an Emissions Reduction Unit (ERU), which is indicated in Article 6 of the Kyoto Protocol. Whatever emissions reduction is created by this particular JI activity would then be subtracted from what Party C is allowed to emit and would be transferred over to Party A. This transfer is represented by the additional space on the upper left-hand side of the square.

Party A could also enter into an emissions trading arrangement with an Annex B country, labelled in figure 8.9 as Party B. In that arrangement,

Party A would buy carbon from Party B in a transaction within the trading market. A Partial Allocated Amount (PAA), which would be part of the total assigned amount that a country is permitted to trade, would be transferred from Party A to Party B. The accounting used to determine a PAA would be different from what is used to establish what an ERU is. For a PAA a paper transaction would be taken into account, rather than the monitoring of an individual facility.

In the case of a JI arrangement, Party A would buy and pay for a physical structure itself and establish it in Party C. Thus, a technical exercise would determine whether the district heating plant, say, or the local afforestation project or another eligible activity would produce fewer emissions (or a stronger sink) than would have been produced under baseline development conditions. Would the new structure or project make a difference to the amount of emissions that Party C would actually emit?

The CDM activity is illustrated in figure 8.9 as an arrangement with another country, called Party D. In this case, according to the current CDM rules, Party D is a non-Annex I developing country and cannot be an Eastern European Annex B country. Recall that the difference between the non-Annex I country and any of these other parties is that the non-Annex I country has no emissions target, or in the Kyoto language, no assigned amount of emissions, whereas all the other countries do have targets. Any country that has ratified Kyoto, whether it has a target or not, can be involved, but only the ones without a target, the developing countries, can be recipients of CDM projects. Party A receives a Certified Emission Reduction (CER) credit under a CDM activity. This hypothetical example illustrates how Party A is now capable of actually emitting more than its assigned amount because of these three transactions.

In another hypothetical illustration, this one for the United States, Grubb, Vrolijk, and Brack (1999) sketch how the various mechanisms might be used to augment domestic action in order to achieve the 2010 target. In their example, the assumed trend for GHG emissions to 2010 results in emissions being around 25 percent above the base year and around 31 percent above its target, which is similar to Canada's situation. As discussed earlier in this chapter, this is referred to as the Quantified Emission Limitation or Reduction Commitment (QELRC). A possible portfolio of instruments would be applied along with a relatively small proportion of the emissions reduction achieved through domestic action. In this example, trading provides the greatest reductions. Why could it provide this much?

This example assumes that there is no cap on how much of a developed country's target should be met by instruments and that there is no minimum amount that should be met by a domestic action. That it would be possible for a developed country to just buy its way out of its commitment is, of course, a huge bone of contention among many parties, certainly among developing countries. Canada, for example, could comply with Kyoto simply through accounting provisions that would allow it to take credit for forest-based carbon sinks and through fulfilling the remaining emissions reduction requirement through emissions trading (Smith and Victor 2004). But unless a cap is imposed by the parties, it will continue to be possible for developed countries to meet all their Kyoto obligations through the use of instruments.

SUMMARY

In this chapter, we introduced a number of policy concepts associated with the UNFCCC and the Kyoto Protocol. We also described the negotiations that led to the signing of the UNFCCC and Kyoto and the negotiation of emissions reduction targets. We also took an introductory look at the instruments of the Kyoto Protocol:

- carbon sinks (articles 3.3, 3.4),
- Joint Implementation (article 6),
- the Clean Development Mechanism (article 12),
- adaptation (article 12.8), and
- emissions trading (article 17).

Most of these mechanisms are designed to support GHG emissions reduction and are therefore influencing the negotiation of emissions reduction targets. We will take a more in-depth look at each of these instruments in the next chapter.

9

Mitigation Responses to Climate Change: Trading and Investment Mechanisms

INTRODUCTION

Chapter 8 introduced the various mechanisms of the Kyoto Protocol. In this chapter, we look at them in more detail. In addition, we shall also explore carbon sequestration (or carbon sinks) as a measure for reducing GHG emissions that may attract interest within the Kyoto mechanisms. Even though there has been a tremendous amount of negotiation activity specifically around credits sinks for carbon, the application of those credits as a policy tool will take place through one of the trading and investment mechanisms, because of the financial incentives involved. Here we discuss some of the challenges of monitoring carbon sinks and the other Kyoto instruments, including concerns about carbon accounting.

We also address some issues arising with the implementation of climate change policies, the role of technology, and the linkages between mitigation and adaptation. As we have seen, climate change policies will not affect developed and developing countries in the same way, and different considerations need to be taken into account for each group when establishing emissions targets and adaptation targets. We conclude by considering whether climate change policies, like the Kyoto Protocol, can actually succeed in reducing the effects of climate change.

CARBON SINKS

Kyoto carbon sinks involve removal of CO_2 through a specific human management activity. Recall that in our review of the carbon cycle (chapter 3), important natural sinks were identified in terrestrial and ocean reservoirs. For the purposes of the Kyoto Protocol, the sinks being considered are specific human actions to manage carbon, which pose an important technical challenge. What can a person do on a plot of land or an ocean site to affect the amount of carbon that is absorbed or sequestered there? In order for the land or ocean site to qualify as a sink for Kyoto, the individual or the state has to demonstrate that a human activity changed the sink strength of a particular piece of farmland, forest land, or ocean reservoir.

The Kyoto Protocol addresses the question of sinks in several articles. Article 3.3 describes activities that would qualify for credit. "Afforestation" refers to trees planted on land that has not previously been forested for a period of at least fifty years, nor converted to a non-forest use such as agriculture (UNFCCC 2001, 2005). "Reforestation" refers to the planting of trees on land that was previously forested. For example, suppose that some forest land was cleared for farming several years ago and that the farm was later abandoned. If trees were then planted on this land, the planting would be considered to be reforestation. If the site in question was a natural, semi-arid grassland, on the other hand, and a decision was made to plant trees on that site, then that would qualify as afforestation. Both these activities would increase the sink strength of the land in question. But deforestation, the removal of trees from a site, would result in a deduction from the total sink capacity of that site.

What is the base year for land use change that can be considered by the protocol? Article 3.4 identifies other human activities that can affect sources and sinks. Article 3.7 explains that areas currently showing a net terrestrial loss of GHGs but which were a net source in 1990 can use 1990 levels as a reference. In other words, forested, agricultural, or other lands that were net emitters of carbon in 1990 would be seen as lands that could be managed for carbon sequestration, and the effects of management activities could be accounted for. Conversely, if a country could show that its forest and agricultural lands were already carbon sinks in 1990, it might be more difficult to clearly account for the effects of sequestration activities. A different reference year would need to be identified.

What are the available options for sink enhancement? One is agroforestry. Tree plantations with relatively short harvest cycles would be established, for example hybrid poplar (*Populus* spp.) plantations. They are often mentioned as potential carbon sinks because the annual growth of poplar requires approximately double the carbon that can be fixed by non-tree crops. The Climate Trust of Oregon and the Tree Canada Foundation are financially supporting the use of poplar plantations

Figure 9.1 Cartoon illustrating concerns about carbon sinks.
Source: Change (1999). Reprinted with permission from Martin Middelburg, RIVM

for sequestration projects (Stanton et al. 2002). However, concerns arise because the trees in these plantations may be different from those in the natural forest environment. Should hybrid poplars be planted in a place that used to be coniferous? And how does that affect the attainment of other management objectives for that piece of land, such as biodiversity, wildlife protection, watershed management, soil erosion reduction, and so on? To manage that land specifically as a carbon sink is different from managing it for other purposes.

There are also various CH_4 options. It may be possible to reduce emissions from mines or to reduce leaks from energy systems. There could also be CH_4 capture from landfills or reductions in CH_4 emissions through changes in cultivation practices. These are ways of reducing emissions from areas that could have been big sources.

Concerns have been raised that sinks could just provide a convenient excuse for high rates of energy consumption to continue. Figure 9.1 satirizes the idea that lifestyle emissions could continue at the current pace as long as trees are planted somewhere else. Perhaps sinks have the potential to absorb a considerable amount of carbon emissions, or maybe

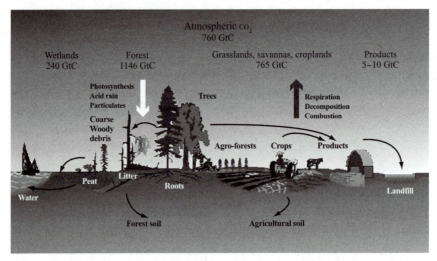

Figure 9.2 Carbon stocks associated with terrestrial ecosystems and human activities.
Source: Kauppi et al. (2001). Reprinted with permission of IPCC

even almost all of it. But, what would it take to actually achieve that? And if the sinks instrument could actually solve global warming by it-self, what would that mean for other development objectives?

Carbon Sinks and the Carbon Cycle

Before we proceed any further, let us return to our earlier discussion in chapter 3 of the carbon cycle. This will help us to understand some of the technical challenges of managing land as carbon sinks.

Figure 9.2 shows the current atmospheric reservoir of CO_2 – 760 Gt of carbon. Grasslands, savannahs, and croplands store a similar amount. Forest sinks store more, and wetlands store less, about 240 Gt. Manufactured products, such as food, wood furniture, and buildings contain a very small reservoir of carbon.

Defining the magnitude of these natural sinks is important because it provides context for assessing the significance of human activities. The natural ocean sink is enormous – 38,000 Gt of carbon are in this reser-voir. The biosphere sink contains around 2,000 Gt. The annual global fluxes in a balanced carbon budget should include some transfer or flux of carbon, around 60 Gt per year, between the land base and the atmo-sphere and back. There would also be a transfer around 90 Gt between the ocean and the atmosphere.

As discussed in chapter 3, as long as those fluxes remain relatively constant, the concentration in the atmosphere should not increase. However, we know that since the Industrial Revolution, atmospheric concentrations of CO_2 have increased by more than 30 percent, which means that those fluxes have obviously been changed by human activity. Carbon emissions during the 1990s were estimated to be around 6.4 Gt of carbon per year (table 3.1) from energy consumption and production, plus an additional 1.6 Gt from land use change, including tropical deforestation. This total of 8.0 Gt was higher than the rate of 6.8 Gt per year estimated for the 1980s. While this was partially offset during the 1990s by an increase in the land sink of around 0.9 Gt per year and the ocean sink around 0.4 Gt per year, there was no change in the rate of atmospheric accumulation between the two periods. However, during 2000–5, continued increases in emissions led to increased accumulation of carbon in the atmosphere, while the terrestrial and ocean sinks have not kept pace (IPCC 2007d). Could this be a sign that available sinks are reaching their limit?

Currently, estimated gross primary production (see chapter 5) is 120 Gt of carbon per year, with about half coming from net primary production. These are much larger quantities than the above estimates of anthropogenic inputs of carbon. After accounting for decomposition and disturbance, only 1 Gt per year is stored within the global biome. All these estimates are highly uncertain, however, and future rates of photosynthesis and storage may not be sustained if carbon emissions rates continue to increase (Watson et al. 2000b). Furthermore the offset is not happening at the same rate every year, because natural forces are influencing how much carbon is actually getting into the atmosphere. In some years, atmospheric concentrations can increase relatively quickly because of major atmospheric events, such as El Niño (Prentice 2001).

Several important factors can affect terrestrial fluxes. First, CO_2 can act as a fertilizer providing plants with the ability to gain more biomass, so that their rate of growth is enhanced, but in that case the ecosystem composition is also altered. In chapter 5, we saw that plants experience benefits as a result of the addition of carbon, but only to a certain threshold of concentration. This qualification is important for thinking about a sink policy.

Second, as a side effect of climate change, warmer temperatures can change the strength of terrestrial sinks. As warming occurs, species currently adapted to cold temperatures will see their ranges contract, while warm-temperature species will expand to higher latitudes and higher altitudes. The expected change in precipitation will also influence terrestrial sinks, but the net effect will depend on overall changes in growing conditions. Land use and land management decisions will also have an impact. These various drivers are likely to affect future spatial and temporal patterns of vegetation growth, and where the plants grow will influence their effectiveness as carbon sinks (Marland et al. 2003).

Challenges with Carbon Accounting

For carbon sequestration to become an effective policy tool, it needs to be supported by an accounting system that enables parties to clearly quantify any changes in the sink value of a site. This means that a carbon baseline needs to be established for any site being managed for sequestration. Establishing this baseline would require a clear narrative about the non-intervention, or business-as-usual, case (however that case may be defined for the appropriate local context), which would be used to establish the expected land use patterns and estimates of sinks and sources under those conditions. (This was the focus of the special IPCC report *Land Use, Land Use Change, and Forestry* (LULUCF: Watson et al. 2000b).) Whatever that baseline is, the next step will be to assess the effects of any changes in emissions on carbon concentrations using carbon budget models. Those models will have both a land component and an ocean component.

Now let us consider the current state of the terrestrial sink. If deforestation is a source of 1.6 Gt of carbon per year and if net terrestrial uptake is around 0.7 Gt per year (Watson et al. 2000b), then the current strength of the terrestrial sink is around 2.3 Gt per year. If terrestrial sinks are to become a Kyoto instrument, then any new set of initiatives will have to be compared against this number, which, as we have seen, has recently increased for reasons unrelated to a specific policy on climate change (see chapter 8).

The LULUCF report includes estimates of global carbon stocks for each of the major biomes (table 9.1), estimates that take into account the area of each biome. Note the stock split between the vegetation component of the biome and the soil component. For example, tropical forests hold nearly half the carbon stock in the vegetation, and so the big concern with tropical deforestation (burning and logging) is that it is a large source of carbon being emitted to the atmosphere. Tropical forest soils do not contain much carbon, however, so what trees can be replanted to sequester carbon in those areas? In a boreal forest environment, this risk

Table 9.1
Global Carbon Stocks for Major Biomes

Biome	Area (10⁹ ha)	Global Carbon Stocks (Gt c)		
		Vegetation	Soil	Total
Tropical forests	1.76	212	216	428
Temperate forests	1.04	59	100	159
Boreal forests	1.37	88	471	559
Tropical savannas	2.25	66	264	330
Termperate grasslands	1.25	9	295	304
Deserts and semideserts	4.55	8	191	199
Tundra	0.95	6	121	127
Wetlands	0.35	15	225	240
Croplands	1.60	3	128	131
Total	15.12	466	2,011	2,477

Source: Watson et al. (2000a)
Note: There is considerable uncertainty in the numbers given because of ambiguity of definitions of biomes, but the table still provides an overview of the magnitude of carbon stocks in terrestrial systems.

may be smaller, since the amount of carbon in the soil is five to six times as much as the amount of carbon in vegetation. Even grasslands have a relatively high amount of soil carbon. In semi-arid and arid regions, almost all the carbon is in the soil. What is the potential for successfully sequestering carbon in arid regions, where much of the carbon stocks are already in the soil and not in the vegetation?

There are various other sinks besides the forested ones, and not all of them are equally feasible prospects. These other sinks include large-scale ocean storage, and the geological storage, and suppression of forest disturbances. In terms of their feasibility, some are not very attractive. However, besides the forestry options (afforestation, reforestation) there are some agricultural options, particularly the practice of "no till" farming. Using no-till, instead of turning the ground over before seeding, the farmer forces the seed into the ground. That keeps some of the CH_4 in the ground, rather than allowing it to escape into the atmosphere. More carbon could also be sequestered in agricultural products, as well.

There is evidence that, at least in Canada, farmers are moving towards no till practices already. Figure 9.3 shows that the amount of agricultural land in Canada storing carbon has tripled since 1990 because no till is becoming more widespread. The projection is that this trend

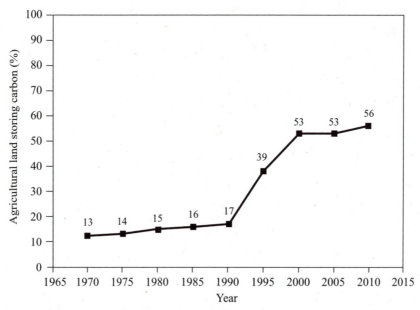

Figure 9.3   Percentage of agricultural land in Canada storing carbon.
Source: Smith, Desjardins, and Pattey (2000). Reprinted with permission from Raymond Desjardins

will continue to the point that Canadian agricultural soils will actually become a carbon sink. Does this mean that it will be easier or more difficult for Canadian agriculture to claim no till activities as eligible for Kyoto carbon credits?

The partitioning of carbon between vegetation and soil is part of the calculation required for accounting for natural and anthropogenic changes in carbon sinks. Two different accounting schemes have been assessed in the LULUCF report: a land-based scheme and an activity-based scheme. Accounting is generally based on sampling a part of the complete inventory, rather than on detailed counts of every single item. This is done to increase the efficiency and reduce the costs of the accounting procedure. In the case of carbon accounting, the question of sampling is important because it can influence the determination of the strength of a carbon sink and its ultimate value for the country's carbon inventory report (and therefore whether the country can reach its Kyoto target).

In land-based accounting, all changes in carbon stock on afforested, reforested, and deforested lands are counted, beginning with the start of the 2008–12 commitment period specified by the Kyoto Protocol (in other words, 1 January 2008). For example, in this case, decaying slash from a

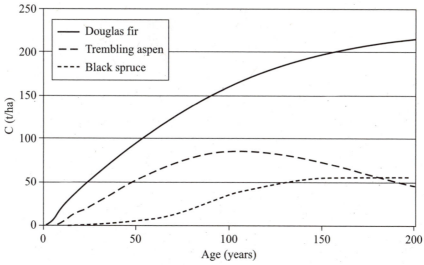

Figure 9.4 Biomass accumulation for three tree species in Canada.
Source: Graphic courtesy of Brian Simpson and Werner Kurz

harvest followed by reforestation would be counted as a negative carbon stock change (in other words, a carbon source). In activity-based accounting, only changes in carbon stock directly resulting from afforestation, reforestation, or deforestation activities is counted. In this case, decaying slash from a harvest that is followed by reforestation would not be counted (Watson et al. 2000b, section 3.3.2). As a result, it has been determined that these two accounting systems could lead to different results. For example, estimates of afforestation and reforestation for the boreal region using land-based accounting suggested that the boreal region would be a carbon source during 2008–12. But in the activity-based accounting, the boreal region became a carbon sink (Watson et al. 2000b). At COP-7, in Marrakech, the decision was made to select activity-based accounting for all human-induced activities, such as afforestation, reforestation, cropland management, and grazing-land management, in all regions (UNFCCC 2001).

An accounting challenge specific to forestry is the changing rate of carbon accumulation as a tree ages, which will vary by species. Figure 9.4 illustrates this variation for three species in Canada, Douglas fir, trembling aspen and black spruce. The Douglas fir accumulates carbon at a faster rate than the other two trees, and continues to accumulate carbon beyond 150 years of age. Trembling aspen's accumulation peaks at around 100 years and declines thereafter as the tree decays. Black spruce accumulates carbon relatively slowly, but does not decay even at

200 years of age (Simpson and Kurz, personal communication, 2007). These results suggest that for maximum carbon accumulation, assuming reforestation with the same species immediately following harvest, aspen should be harvested around 60–80 years of age, black spruce around 120 years, and Douglas fir around 80–100 years. But how would this affect the attainment of other forest management (e.g., timber supply) or land management (e.g., habitat protection) objectives? How would this affect the design of fire and pest management strategies? How would this affect the nature of sequestration agreements? Would the agreements be of different lengths, varying by species? Would this affect their relative trading values on a carbon market? And how would these differences affect national GHG reporting to determine compliance with Kyoto targets?

Although forest management will be important for carbon sequestration worldwide, each region will face its own unique management challenges. Kauppi et al. (2001) describe the importance of fire management for the United States, Canada, Australia, and even the EU countries. For Japan, fire is a less significant issue, since pest management and fertilization would be more valuable for improving carbon sequestration. Other strategies include restoration of degraded lands and forest protection, including taking forests out of commercial production.

The potential for forest management to improve carbon sequestration is substantial in some countries. In fact, the magnitude of carbon sequestration in Canada and Australia could potentially exceed these countries' total carbon emissions (Kauppi et al. 2001). It is important to note, however, that these estimates do not necessarily reflect the sinks entitlements that have been negotiated within Kyoto. In addition, pest and fire disturbances in Canada, and in eastern Russia, have led to declines in carbon stocks within the boreal forests in these regions, thereby changing these regions from sinks to sources, while stocks elsewhere, such as in the United States and Europe, are increasing (Goodale et al. 2002). What are the implications of these trends for the potential application of forest sequestration within the Kyoto Protocol?

Developed and developing countries have different perspectives on historic land use change. The choice of 1990 as a baseline means that pre-1990 deforestation in developed countries does not count as contributing to emissions, but it does create additional opportunities for reforestation. Since 1990, while tropical (mostly developing) countries have exhibited substantial rates of deforestation, mid-latitude (mostly developed) countries have seen an increase in forested land at the expense of grass and cropland (Kauppi et al. 2001).

The challenge for developed countries will be to demonstrate that a reforestation project would be additional to ongoing trends that are likely taking place for reasons other than climate change policy. For developing countries, it may be easier to prove additionality for reforestation projects. However, current deforestation rates represent the reality of current development pressures, which may be a deterrent to accepting GHG emissions reduction targets.

Carbon Sinks as a Policy Mechanism

Carbon sequestration from forests, especially in tropical regions, has considerable potential and can be designed to create synergies with adaptation and sustainable development (IPCC 2007b). Carbon emissions resulting from deforestation, however, are difficult to monitor precisely. We have also seen that there are different definitions and different accounting approaches for quantifying the magnitude of carbon sequestration, which can lead to very different estimates of changes in stocks. This is why a common method had to be negotiated and agreed upon within the Kyoto framework. However, this is not the only concern with utilizing sinks as policy mechanisms. There are also concerns related to defining baselines and determining additionality. How can we determine that a particular reforestation activity is being carried out specifically to meet a climate change objective? And how can leakage be accounted for? In other words, if a forest was planted in one country but that same country purchased ownership of a dirty industry in another country, how should the combination of these two activities be accounted for in its national emissions report? Furthermore, that activity could lead to the displacement of another activity, particularly if it resulted in reduced access to food, land, or other resources.

Finally, there is the important problem that carbon sequestration as a management objective could be competing with other objectives. Marland et al. (2003) discuss the potential for the sinks mechanism to actually conflict with the goal of GHG emissions reduction. From a climate science perspective, it is important to acknowledge the role of afforestation and reforestation in changing the albedo. If forest lands expanded in high-latitude regions, the albedo would be reduced, resulting in increased absorption of solar radiation, which could offset cooling from the increased forest sink. On the other hand, in tropical forests, reforestation is seen as a benefit, because it would enhance transpiration, adding to the cooling effects of the increased forest sink. Uncertainties remain as to how these issues could be accounted for in climate change policy.

JOINT IMPLEMENTATION

In chapter 8 we briefly introduced joint implementation (JI) as a bilateral arrangement in which a developed country pays for an emissions reduction activity in a developing country to slow its rate of emissions growth. Given this arrangement, how does a developing country actually incorporate this new activity into its long-term climate change plans? One of the problems for a developing country is the question of baseline or reference emissions scenarios. How does the JI activity affect a country's emissions baseline (Swisher 1997)? In the near future, if a developing country wants to take on a target so that it can become an emissions trader, what does the importing of JI projects do to the calculation of that target? This question pertains to both new infrastructure and to carbon sinks. Many of the pilot (pre-ratification) JI projects were sinks projects, which can also affect the emissions baseline computed by a developing country.

All JI projects face potential implementation barriers. Can a developing country be a good host? Can it control costs? Are there sufficient local trained personnel? What about the monitoring and verification of a particular project? Will it be accepted locally? All these questions introduce uncertainties into the implementation and measured success of JI activities.

The progress of JI activities has been tracked by the Joint Implementation (JIN) Foundation, which publishes a newsletter called the *Joint Implementation Quarterly*. In 2002, it listed 186 pilot (pre-ratification) projects, including 6 projects in the EIT countries (of the former Soviet Union), in which there was an agreed anticipatory emissions reduction transfer (JIN Foundation 2002). These six projects were referred to as Anticipatory Article 6 JI projects and included municipal co-generation projects, a hydropower project in Romania, and a wind power project in Poland.

The other pilot projects were referred to as Activities Implemented Jointly (AIJ), because they were not yet official JI projects. Many of the pilot projects were in Eastern Europe, but there were also a few in Africa, Asia, and Central America, especially Costa Rica. The United States had been one of the major investors in AIJ projects. Even though the US government announced that it would not ratify Kyoto, it continued to show interest in the JI instrument and was investing in a wide range of projects in countries around the world, including projects focusing on fuel switching, energy efficiency, fugitive-gas capture, and renewable energy, as well as sinks, afforestation, reforestation, forest preservation, and agriculture. As can be seen, sinks were very much a part of JI projects.

How would the ratification of Kyoto affect the JI instrument? First, there would be a focus on the EIT countries, as specified in Article 6. All other countries would be funded through the CDM. In the long term, with the emerging reality of meeting emission targets, there could be increased investment as the international carbon market developed. Attention might also shift to other or additional Kyoto instruments. For example, in 2004/5, Austria received new proposals for twenty-one JI projects and forty-six CDM projects, with particular interest in CDM coming from India (JIN Foundation 2005).

THE CLEAN DEVELOPMENT MECHANISM

Article 12 of the Kyoto Protocol established the Clean Development Mechanism (CDM). In principle, this mechanism enables activities similar to JI to occur with non-Annex I countries. Its stated purpose is to help developing countries achieve sustainable development, and at the same time, to assist Annex I countries in achieving their emissions reduction targets through the generation of Certified Emission Reduction (CER) credits.

Article 12 also established three bodies to oversee the CDM: the representatives of the COP, an executive board established by the COP, and independent auditors to verify project activities. Article 12.6 states that the CDM is to assist in arranging funding of certified project activities. However, the Kyoto Protocol provided almost no guidance on what exactly the CDM would do or how it would operate. Instead, the structure and authority of supervisory bodies and the CDM were left for future negotiation (post-1997).

While JI and CDM offer investment incentives, they do not actually involve the same process. Besides the differences in host countries for projects (EIT now being the focus of JI), CDM differs from JI in two ways (Grubb, Vrolijk, and Brack 1999). First, in contrast to the bilateral nature of JI, there is multilateral control over the process in CDM activities. Second, CDM includes investment in adaptation. Grubb, Vrolijk, and Brack (1999) describe CDM as the "Kyoto surprise" (101) because of its potential to create multilateral portfolios of projects with both public- and private-sector investment, but also because JI had initially been seen as primarily an instrument for short-term projects (the so-called low-hanging fruit) and for sinks activities that could take land away from agriculture and create dependencies on food imports. The creation of CDM as an instrument specifically for investment in developing countries (including technology transfer) helped to overcome developing-country resistance to JI, thereby leading to developing-country support for Kyoto as a whole.

Project types large enough to be economically viable include landfill gas capture, methane reductions in the oil and gas industry, renewable electricity generation, afforestation, and reforestation. Initially, landfill gas projects appeared to be the activity of choice among CDM proposals (Pearson 2005). Recent trends (up to May 2006) suggest increased interest in projects related to electricity production and the reduction of nitrous oxide (N_2O) and trifluoromethane (HFC-23), a CFC substitute that is also a powerful greenhouse gas (figure 9.5). One unanticipated result has been that the CDM has created a financial incentive for proposing HFC-23 reduction projects, which often have little tangible benefits for local sustainable development, low potential for technology transfer, and are likely to be concentrated in only a few countries (Ellis et al. 2007). This incentive can, in a perverse way, lead to increased production of HFC-23 refrigerant in advance of the CDM proposal because proponents can earn almost twice as much from CDM credits as they can from selling refrigerant gases (Wara, 2007). A more hopeful sign is that energy efficiency projects and renewable energy projects are estimated to have significant potential, and the upward trend is encouraging, but they make up only a minority of carbon credits. The limited number of energy-related projects to date suggests that they face barriers to implementation. Pearson expresses concerns that, rather than promoting sustainable development, the CDM is merely a vehicle for low-cost emissions reductions that are not connected with long-term development goals. It has also been difficult for CDM proposals to prove additionality under current rules (JIN Foundation 2005). Munasinghe and Swart (2005) suggest that the Least Developed Countries Fund was created because of the belief that the poorest countries were least likely to benefit from the CDM (see chapter 11).

EMISSIONS TRADING

Several different types of trades are possible in an emissions trading system. The first type is a Credit Trade, whereby a source can use credits generated by having some other source reduce its emissions below a

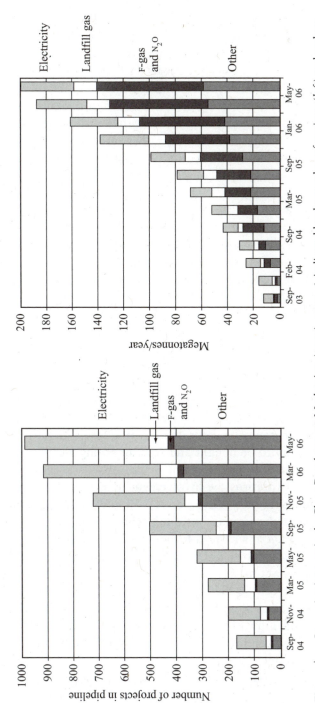

Figure 9.5   Increasing interest in the Clean Development Mechanism (CDM), 2003–6, indicated by the number of projects (*left*) and carbon credits in megatonnes/year (*right*). "F-gas" refers to fluorine gas reduction projects (chlorofluorocarbons–CFC and CFC substitutes). *Source:* Ellis and Karousakis (2006). Graphics courtesy of Jane Ellis. Reprinted with permission of IEA. © OECD/IEA, figure 2.7, 80, and figure 2.9, 82

predicted baseline: this, of course, requires knowledge of the predicted baseline. A particular savings that has been generated by one country could be sold as a credit to another country. The country purchasing this credit could then use it to help meet its emissions reduction target.

There are two other models for trading: the Cap and Emission Allowance and Cap and Carbon Coupon Trading. The difference between these two types and the Credit Trade is that they include an emissions cap. Because governments define the caps, there are limits on how much carbon can actually enter into a trading system. This restricts the amount of carbon that can be bought and sold, which can potentially have a huge impact on the price of carbon. A higher price for carbon would ultimately attract more potential sellers to the market, which could mean that more JI and CDM projects could be undertaken.

Victor (2001) describes a problem with the caps. As mentioned previously, caps on the quantity of credits could lead to higher prices, which would then increase a country's interest in becoming a seller rather than a buyer of carbon credits. As a contrasting analogy, consider the 2004–5 labour dispute within the National Hockey League, in which the team owners sought to impose a cap on the negotiation of player's salaries by placing a cap on total team salaries. The players were against this move because it would have restricted their ability to negotiate. Since the cap in this situation would have restricted the amount of money that was spent and not the number of players, it was actually the opposite of a cap on carbon trading, which restricts the amount of carbon but not the amount of money that may be spent on acquiring credits. If carbon is to become a commodity to be bought and sold, imposing a cap on a trading market will serve to force prices up.

Another problem concerns the involvement of sequestration projects in a carbon-trading market (Victor 2001). Should these sequestration projects be discounted, since land uses may change? As is the case with other commodities, there will need to be a date of delivery (or vintage) for the sequestered carbon (i.e., the carbon credit). Sinks projects may have dates in the distant future, and the viability of a sink will change as trees grow, so what will be the date of delivery for the carbon credit? Also, can CH_4 be traded or only CO_2? And what about credit for early action before ratification of Kyoto, such as pilot trades in Canada? Now that Kyoto has been ratified, would these trades gain credit during the 2008–12 commitment period?

The considerable variability of energy prices in the past creates another uncertainty. Oil prices, for example, have fluctuated between

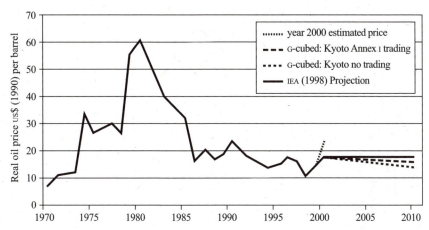

Figure 9.6   Real oil prices and the effects of Kyoto implementation. "G-cubed" refers to a global energy model developed to test the effects of emission trading.
Source: Barker et al. (2001, figure 9.1). Reprinted with permission of IPCC

US$8 and US$100 per barrel since 1970, without the imposition of a specific global-scale energy tax or other measure related to a policy on climate change. How would Kyoto measures affect energy prices? Figure 9.6, which was produced in 2001 (Barker et al. 2001), suggests that trading would not affect oil prices in a significant manner and would perhaps result only in a modest decline. However, the modelling that produced the prices in the figure did not capture the post-2001 increase to above US$90 to US$100 per barrel, so there are still uncertainties associated with such estimates including possible effects of future price and availability on emissions trajectories and investment decision. The rapid increase in oil prices since 2001 reflects the growing insensitivity of oil demand to price. This is because of the increasing share of demand for transportation, which is price-inelastic (see chapter 6), combined with government subsidies that reduce price impacts on consumers (IEA 2006).

Leaving aside the uncertainties for a moment, figure 9.7 shows that trading could reduce the costs of implementing Kyoto, compared with what the projected costs would be without trading. Note that this figure illustrates that trading would actually partially offset the reduction in the rate of GDP growth estimated for Kyoto without trading. According to the model used to produce these estimates, there could be savings in all the developed countries, including the United States, with the use of carbon credit trading.

Percentage of GDP loss in the year 2010

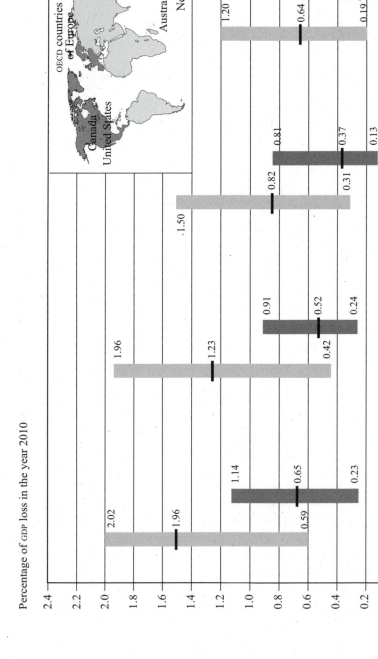

Figure 9.7 Cost of implementing Kyoto without (*left bars*) and with (*right bars*) emissions trading. Maximum, mean, and minimum cost projections from global energy models are indicated for each Annex II region or country.
Source: IPCC (2001a). Reprinted with permission of IPCC

Despite the optimism expressed in figure 9.7, Victor's (2001) argument is that if the market turns carbon into a new asset, countries will want to protect it from being devalued. This goal relates to the choice of base year in several ways:

- 1990 was the base year for most Annex I countries;
- some countries were permitted to choose different years; and
- in post-2012, additional countries entering the market with targets may also request base years that best suit their circumstances.

A carbon seller (such as an EIT country) will not want to see the price go down, which means that it may withhold carbon from the market on some occasions. It may be that one of those sellers would support a cap, but only as long as it got its desired portion of the cap. There could be arguments between countries about dividing up the total within the cap, in order to figure out how much of that cap would go to each country. The imposition of a cap would mean that the carbon market would not be a completely free market and that it would not function in the way it should.

Challenges with "Hot Air"

The important role of the designated base year in calculating emissions credits creates an additional mitigation dilemma. This dilemma is specific to the international effort to bring the Eastern European countries into annex I so that they will accept targets during the first phase of Kyoto. This is called the "hot-air" problem. The simplest definition is that if a country had lower emissions now than it had in 1990, lower not because of climate policy but for other reasons (such as the economic collapse in Russia), this country would find itself with a surplus of credits to sell. Thus, with the creation of carbon as a commodity comes the potential for a huge windfall of billions of dollars for Russia, Ukraine, and other EIT states.

Now, consider the effects of caps on trading. If there were no caps, countries with hot-air credits could flood the market with them and reduce the incentive for other countries to reduce their emissions. A large quantity of credits could be bought at a relatively low price per unit, which would put the sellers at a disadvantage. Prospects of low trading prices were partly responsible for the delay in Russia's decision to finally ratify Kyoto. The Russian energy ministries were actually in favour of

Figure 9.8   Cartoon illustrating the role of new technology influencing household energy use.
Source: Change (2002). Reprinted with permission from Martin Middelburg, RIVM

ratification because they saw how much money could be made (Kokorin 2003). They also saw the advantage of Joint Implementation in providing investment to modernize the country's industry and support economic growth (JIN Foundation 2004). Ultimately, however, Russia's ratification in 2004 required a tie-in with other international trading concerns beyond climate policy.

In any event, it remains to be seen how significant a problem hot-air trading will become. Recent increases in emissions in EIT countries are reducing the gap between current and 1990 base year emissions.

NEW TECHNOLOGY

An important consideration in future climate policy is the role of new technology. There are, of course, many futurists who try to predict how technology will evolve. For example, figure 9.8 shows a cartoonist's rendition of how several forms of energy might be combined to provide electricity through a common power grid to the end user, a person using a vacuum cleaner. The grid is no longer strictly driven by fossil energy; it is also driven by solar power, wind power, and energy from recycled materials and biomass.

Moomaw et al. (2001) compiled an inventory of the potentials of various technologies for saving energy, as well as their probabilities of implementation and costs. This has been recently updated by Barker et al. (2007).

Improvements in residential buildings are projected in developed countries by 2030, including reduction in carbon-based electricity and fuel demand through increased use of photovoltaics, co-generation, passive solar, and heat pumps, as well as fuel switching from coal to natural gas. This is projected to be up to 3.4 Gt per year CO_2 equivalent. A similar reduction is projected for developing countries (Barker et al. 2007). Projected efficiency improvements for appliances (such as refrigerators) could lead to a big reduction in energy costs because of reduced demand. Efficiency improvements are also projected for transportation, though at a relatively high cost. Potential increases in efficiency by 2020 are also indicated for many countries, including developing countries, but the probability of their implementation appears to be low. More recently, however, we have seen the emergence of hybrid vehicles, such as the Toyota Prius, as commercially viable transportation alternatives. Perhaps there can now be increased optimism regarding energy savings in transportation.

Moomaw et al. (2001) also project modest improvements for manufacturing, such as blended cements, N_2O reduction by the chemical industry, and CFC substitutes. However, some of these improvements are available only at high cost. Overall, the implementation and costs with manufacturing technologies are a mixed bag.

Energy savings are projected for agriculture, especially through soil carbon sequestration and changing tillage practices. Projected emissions reductions by 2030 at a global rate scale are similar to those projected for buildings, but in this case most of the reductions are projected to come from developing countries (Barker et al. 2007). It is not clear how likely these reductions are to be adopted worldwide, so they are given a middle ranking in terms of probability and potential of implementation. CH_4 reduction options are also not rated very highly for potential or probability of implementation and costs are high. CH_4 capture from landfills has relatively high potential, with a high probability of adoption, at least in developed countries (Moomaw et al. 2001).

Fuel switching, such as substituting nuclear energy for fossil fuels, is also a highly rated option (Moomaw et al. 2001). Nuclear power, which accounted for 16 percent of total electricity supply in 2005, is projected to have an 18 percent share by 2030 if carbon prices increase (IPCC 2007b). In the near term, switching from coal to gas should continue as it is already commercially available (IPCC 2007b). A relatively new technology called Carbon Capture and Storage, which is the underground storage of CO_2 removed from natural gas, is projected to become commercialized before 2030 for biomass, coal-fired electricity generating facilities, and industrial processes, as well as for gas (IPCC 2007b).

Another interesting question is whether it is possible or feasible for wind to substitute for coal and gas. The probability of substitution by the 2020s is predicted to be very high (Moomaw et al. 2001). Renewable energy, including wind, solar, biofuels, and hydroelectricity, which accounted for 18 percent of electricity supply in 2005, is projected to have a 30 to 35 percent share by 2030 if carbon prices increase (IPCC 2007b). Switching from fossil fuels to hydro, wind power, and bioenergy could provide global emission reduction of around 3 Gt CO_2 equivalent per year by 2030, while geothermal and solar (including photovoltaics) could provide a further reduction of 0.7 Gt CO_2 equivalent per year (Sims et al. 2007). There is concern that additional large hydro facilities may create local flooding and environmental problems and displace populations (Sims et al. 2007). Perhaps it might be possible to improve the efficiency of existing hydro sites as a complement to developing new sites.

To summarize, technology appears to offer many opportunities, but with mixed potential for success. In a recent update, Barker et al (2007) conclude that the total range of potential GHG mitigation is 13 to 26 Gt of CO_2-equivalent (incorporating all GHGs) at a cost of less than US\$50 per ton of CO_2-equivalent (or US\$185 per ton of carbon). Other non-technology options at this price, including incentives for more afforestation and reforestation, as well as fuel switching, could provide additional savings. The new technologies could become part of domestic climate policies, as well as being used in transactions within Kyoto mechanisms at the international scale. More detailed information on technologies is available from the IPCC 4th Assessment Report, Working Group III (IPCC 2007b). For purposes of comparison, it is useful to point out that prices in the EU Emissions Trading System during 2005–6 varied between US\$6 and US\$40 per ton of CO_2. This is only slightly below the price range indicated for these emission reductions, which are consistent with stabilization at around 550 ppm CO_2 equivalent (Barker et al. 2007).

CONTRACTION AND CONVERGENCE

An area of interest in Kyoto-related discussions concerning mitigation is the notion of targets for per capita emissions. As of 2007, the Kyoto Protocol has no global targets for per capita carbon emissions; existing targets are just for particular countries, specifically, developed countries. There is no policy measure that addresses the atmosphere as a whole,

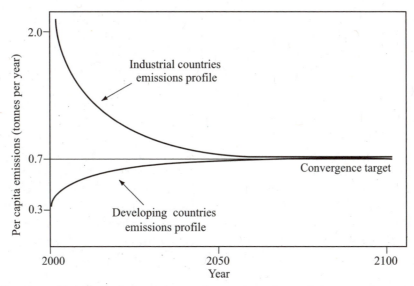

Figure 9.9   Trajectories for convergence of per capita carbon emissions.
Source: Shukla (1999). Reprinted with permission of P.R. Shukla, and Earthscan

since existing instruments are all based on only a part of the world's emissions. Outside the Kyoto process, particularly in developing countries, a number of authors have written about the desire to create a more equitable approach for "sharing" the atmosphere based on establishing that all countries are entitled to the same per capita consumption of energy and materials and are therefore also entitled to equal per capita GHG emissions rights. This approach is known as "contraction and convergence," an idea initiated by the Global Commons Institute during the 1990s (see http://www.gci.org.uk/).

Shukla (1999) illustrates two ways in which this kind of per capita convergence could occur. Under the conventional convergence concept developed and developing countries would converge around 0.7 tonnes of carbon emissions per person per year around 2050 (figure 9.9). In an alternative model, just and equitable convergence, developed countries would rapidly reduce their emissions to a level that would actually be less than developing-country per capita emissions by 2030. In this way, developing countries would be permitted additional emissions growth before coming back down to the target, and the developed countries would have to emit below the convergence target before being allowed to increase later on.

More detailed discussion on various forms of contraction and convergence is available in Global Commons Institute (2008).

Recall that developing countries have not yet been willing to accept an emissions target. However, this could change (see chapter 11). How will this idea of contraction and convergence influence the newly ratified Kyoto Protocol, and any new agreement to replace Kyoto post–2012?

ADAPTATION AND MITIGATION LINKAGES

Throughout our discussion of adaptation in chapter 7, we occasionally dipped our toes into the shallow end of the mitigation pool. Similarly, throughout our discussion of mitigation in chapter 8 and in this chapter, we also included some aspects of adaptation. We did so because there are linkages between climate change adaptation and efforts to mitigate GHG emissions (Klein et al. 2007). For example, in chapter 7 we discussed the concept of adaptive emissions, as well as the notion of differential emissions and different adaptive capacities for different circumstances of development.

We now offer a framework that might be useful in categorizing linkages between adaptation and mitigation. Consider a 2x2 matrix in which the vertical axis represents adaptation (figure 9.10). Recall that the purpose of adaptation is to reduce exposures and vulnerability, so if we move from bottom to top on the vertical scale, we are doing better at adaptation and are reducing vulnerability. The horizontal axis represents mitigation: GHG emissions are reduced as we move from left to right.

The worst-case situation is a combination of low adaptation and low mitigation. In such a situation everything might be completely development-driven and there might be no consideration for climate change issues or environmental issues in general. Rapid deforestation for land use change (perhaps for agriculture or mining) would be an example. The lower left-hand corner of the figure shows this situation; here, both adaptation and mitigation are negative.

The lower right-hand corner represents a case where a mitigation strategy dominates adaptation strategies, without considering whether or not exposure has changed. An example of this situation could occur if an energy source switched from fossil fuels to an expanded large hydroelectric development. This would be rated as a negative on the adaptation scale but as a positive on the mitigation scale. Although it might be desirable to substitute hydro for coal, hydro depends on water, and water is very sensitive to shifts in climate. If climate change affected rainfall patterns, evaporation patterns, snow packs, and glaciers, a new vulnerability could possibly be created as a result of this measure.

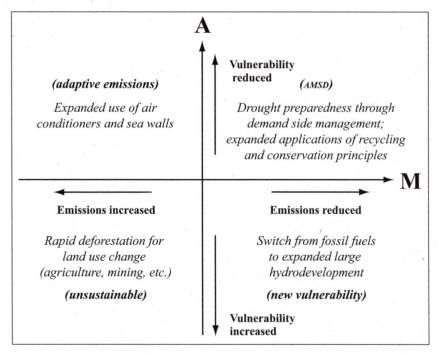

A

(adaptive emissions)

Vulnerability reduced *(AMSD)*

Expanded use of air conditioners and sea walls

Drought preparedness through demand side management; expanded applications of recycling and conservation principles

M

Emissions increased

Emissions reduced

Rapid deforestation for land use change (agriculture, mining, etc.)

Switch from fossil fuels to expanded large hydrodevelopment

(unsustainable)

(new vulnerability)

Vulnerability increased

Figure 9.10   Linkages between adaptation (A) and mitigation (M)

On the upper left-hand side of the figure, which represents high adaptation but increased GHG emissions, consider a situation where sea walls are constructed in order to protect an exposed coastline. Obviously this is a way of protecting a region from sea level rise and reducing vulnerability, which makes this action an adaptation measure. However, the amount of concrete required to build the sea walls would be enormous. Because concrete production requires a lot of fossil fuels, in order for the region to adapt, it would have to increase its emissions. This is a great example of the adaptive emissions problem. Imagine that the Maldives had to build a sea wall in order to protect its islands from sea level rise. Now imagine a climate change policy that would penalize the Maldives if that government agreed to an emissions target but then could not meet the target because of increased emissions from the building of this sea wall. How would Kyoto address this problem?

Finally, the upper right-hand corner represents the ideal kind of option that meets both the adaptation and the mitigation goal and that links with sustainable development (or AMSD). The example offered here is drought preparedness through demand-side management. In other words, potential water issues are managed, but not through supply-side measures. The approach would focus on water conservation measures through low-flow technologies for delivering water to crops, through high-efficiency plumbing, or through other similar measures. These measures are not energy intensive and may actually be energy savers. As a result, fewer materials are consumed, and vulnerability to drought is reduced. If this kind of strategy could be identified for other problems, the situation would be ideal.

These linkages have both policy and research implications. One thought is that some developmental paths could lead to unusual kinds of exposures that are referred to as syndromes of global change and that would quickly lead to deterioration. In these syndromes, one action can lead to a chain reaction of degradations (Moldan and Billharz 1997). An example was provided by agricultural policy in the former Soviet Union when the expansion of irrigated cotton in a semi-arid region eventually led to the retreat of the Aral Sea (Glantz 1999).

Another example took place in the Sahel region of Africa. As was noted in chapter 2, this semi-arid region includes many countries where nomadic goat herding has been part of traditional culture. During the 1960s and 1970s, rainfall in the region declined for a lengthy stretch of time. Desertification followed, along with food shortages and displacements of people. Were these impacts a result of the decline in rainfall, or did they occur because of a lack of control over the nomadic herds, the weak structures of government, or the fact that many of the countries in the region had just become independent and had little experience in governing? As discussed in chapter 2, it is generally agreed that bad management was a more important factor than climatic variability in drought and food problems in the Sahel region (Glantz 1976; Garcia 1981; Slater and Levin 1981).

As noted previously, one of the central differences between adaptation and mitigation measures is the way targets are defined. The Kyoto Protocol has carbon reduction targets, but there are no targets for impact or vulnerability reduction. Another difference is that impacts and vulnerabilities tend to be public-domain problems rather than individual-consumption problems. For example, part of the challenge to protect small island states from sea level rise is a problem not about what one person does but about whether the government is prepared to either build the sea walls, support beach nourishment activities, or find some high ground that people can evacuate to. If they cannot do so, then their state is in danger. Small island states have been extremely vocal about wanting GHG emissions reduced as quickly as possible, because they do not see a stabilization scenario that would work for them, at least not the way such a scenario is currently defined. This is another reason for making adaptation targets public.

Two other possible adaptation targets could be one associated with food availability and one related to water stress reduction. For example, an adaptation target could be to increase per capita food supply in poor countries. There would be serious impacts if climate change reduced the total amount of food available per person below what it would have been without climate change. An adaptation goal could be to cut this loss in half. But is that a reasonable adaptation target? And how can Kyoto achieve these types of goals?

CLIMATE CHANGE POLICY CHALLENGES AND DILEMMAS

Can we somehow control GHG concentrations in the atmosphere? Thinking about this problem is similar to thinking about controlling a very large body of water, such as the Great Lakes in Canada, where structures such as dams and locks are used to control lake levels. This type of control occurs at many other water bodies, with varying degrees of effectiveness. It is possible that controlling water levels creates a dependency on stable water levels, to the point that the moment levels fluctuate by even a small amount outside their control range, there are significant impacts for shippers, hydroelectric producers, or people who live near coastlines. Is society prepared to exert this kind of control on the global concentration of a constituent of the atmosphere? Also, is it plausible given natural variations in carbon fluxes from land and ocean and changes in the effectiveness of sinks?

Governance mandates cover many different aspects of human existence. Climate policy actions represent only a small part of the portfolio. As climate policy continues to evolve, new situations may be encountered that would lead to conflicts between policy goals. Gupta and Tol (2003) provide a list of climate change policy dilemmas that they anticipate will emerge in the coming years. Table 9.2 describes several dilemmas that may be encountered by developed countries. They can relate specifically to climate change, as well as broader concerns of globalization, creating situations of "double exposure" (Leichenko and O'Brien 2008). The first is the dilemma of timing, that is, of whether it would be better to act now or act later. Kyoto does not offer credit for

Table 9.2
Climate Change Policy Dilemmas: Developed Countries

Dilemma	Description	Relation to Climate Change
Timing	Action now or later	Early ET vs R&D and regime building
Industrial transformation	Don't sacrifice growth	Adopt new technology and stay competitive
Wealth I	Spend without waste	Phase out the old without losing capital
Wealth II	Assist without compensating	Don't be penalized for going first
Privatization	Can the private sector solve public problems?	Who's responsible? Can old polluter take this on?
Ecospace	Human rights or property rights?	Basis for allocation of environmental space
Negotiation	Don't commit too much	International leadership vs domestic interests

Source: Adapted from Gupta and Tol (2003).

early action, although a few authors have proposed this idea. Early participants in pilot trades of carbon credits are trading for the learning experience, but it would be nice to know that these activities would count during the 2008–12 commitment period. There are incentives to act early because in doing so, countries carry out important research and development. This regime building, as Gupta and Tol (2003) call it, also creates additional support for policy measures. But maybe it is better to wait longer and let others take the early risks of investing in unknown and unproven mechanisms.

The second dilemma relates to industrial transformation and to the unknown economic costs of climate policy. Countries would prefer to avoid climate policy if it meant sacrificing economic growth. A climate change policy must therefore enable countries to stay competitive, and new technology could help them to achieve this goal.

There are two dilemmas related to wealth, as well. The first one is called spending without waste. Is it possible to phase out old technology and old capital without losing too much money? A manufacturing facility may have been built with a planned lifetime of fifty years, but if after twenty years it is seen as a major point source of carbon emissions, what happens to the investment? How can the facility be phased out without losing the capital investment? The second wealth dilemma, assisting without compensating, is related to the dilemma of timing: Early actors receiving political support from governments do not want to be

Table 9.3
Climate Change Policy Dilemmas: Developing Countries

Dilemma	Description
Development	Modernize without westernizing
Poverty I	Survival without squandering resources
Poverty II	Borrow (beg) without mortgaging the future
Privatization	Empower the private sector to solve public problems
Environmental space	Environment or economy?
Economic	Short-term business interests vs long-term economic interests

Source: Adapted from Gupta and Tol (2003).

penalized financially for being the first to undertake policy actions that may be expensive for them to carry out but in later years may become less costly as the action becomes more popular.

Other dilemmas for developed countries include the privatization dilemma, the ecospace dilemma, and the negotiation dilemma. The privatization dilemma asks whether the private sector can solve public problems and whether the responsibility can be shared between the private and public sectors. The ecospace dilemma asks about the relative importance of property rights and human rights. Finally, the negotiation dilemma considers the question of balance between international and domestic interests.

Gupta and Tol (2003) also explore climate change policy dilemmas in developing countries (table 9.3). The development dilemma asks how a developing country can modernize without Westernizing, that is, without losing its traditional culture. Indigenous peoples also face this challenge. Climate change becomes one of many factors that may push peoples and countries towards a particular development path, influencing land use, resource harvesting, transportation, and lifestyle. The development path can lead to serious questions about cultural protection, which is not addressed by the Kyoto Protocol. Kyoto says nothing about it because in the Kyoto world, carbon is everything. And maybe cultural issues are better addressed in other kinds of conventions, such as conventions concerning the globalization of trade, for instance. But it still remains difficult to separate these various policy concerns. Perhaps climate change problems can be addressed through trade, but how does that affect other political goals of the developing countries?

Developing countries must also confront poverty dilemmas. How can developing countries survive without squandering resources? How can

Figure 9.11 Cartoons on emissions credits.
Sources: left panel, Change (1998), reprinted with permission from Martin Middelburg, RIVM; *right panel*, published 12 December 1997 in the *Vançouver Sun*, reprinted with permission from Roy Peterson Ink Inc.

they borrow without mortgaging the future? Both these questions are really very difficult to answer. Some developing countries have huge debts already because they have been importing high-value products while selling commodities at low prices. How can they enter into a climate change agreement that threatens their ability to solve poverty issues? Why should they care about climate change or the environment when they have such low levels of income?

In 1997, concerns were raised at COP-3 regarding the potential economic consequences of the Kyoto Protocol itself. The resulting variation in the commitments of different countries led to some media commentary on emissions credits. In figure 9.11 the cartoon on the left, which is from the Netherlands, reads, "The real question is, have you bought your emissions rights yet?" The cartoon on the right, which is from Canada, shows a person with the same problem as his Dutch colleague, but he is considering emigration to Australia, Norway, or Iceland. What is so special about those three countries? In the initial set of targets outlined in Kyoto, although they were to slow their rate of emissions growth, they were nevertheless given targets that allowed an increase in GHG emissions above 1990 levels.

These cartoons do not address the issue that developing countries do not have emissions targets. How will it be determined when they should acquire them? Although it may be unfair to expect that climate policy will, on its own, solve major development challenges, the UNFCCC and the Kyoto Protocol do offer new mechanisms that could work in tandem with development policies. We will return to this topic and discuss the linkages between climate change policy and sustainable development policy in chapter 11.

CAN KYOTO SUCCEED?

A big issue for debate is whether the Kyoto Protocol will help us, as humans, mitigate the global damage we have caused through anthropogenic GHG emissions. Ratification of Kyoto has changed the dynamics of international climate negotiations between countries, as well as domestic actions within countries. ET, JI, CDM, and sinks have changed from being theoretical constructs to real mechanisms with financial obligations and technical rules attached to them. This has also led to the emergence of private initiatives to offer carbon offsets to consumers (for example, airline passengers) in which a transaction fee paid to the carbon offset company is invested in an activity that reduces emissions (or strengthens sinks) equivalent to the emission associated with the consumer's purchase. Now all eyes are focused on global GHG concentrations, which are used as the main indicators of success or failure. Kyoto is not designed to reverse increasing GHG trends by 2012. It is only a relatively small mechanism with modest targets as a first step. However, can Kyoto show any reduction in the rate of growth of emissions and concentrations? Regardless of any reporting from individual countries, in the end it is the global GHG concentration that will be the primary barometer to watch.

Individual country reports will be difficult to interpret because economic-development decisions may possibly alter the GHG inventory without actually increasing energy efficiency or reducing global emissions. Besides the problems of proving additionality and supplementarity, there may also be many incidents of leakage. For example, if China bought a Canadian mining company, China could import energy or mineral resources from its new subsidiary as a way to meet its future growth. Canada's emissions would increase in its mining sector to meet China's needs, while China's mining-related emissions would not. China might then claim that its GHG emissions per unit of GDP were showing a reduction, thereby representing a reduction from a baseline scenario of emissions growth parallel to anticipated economic growth.

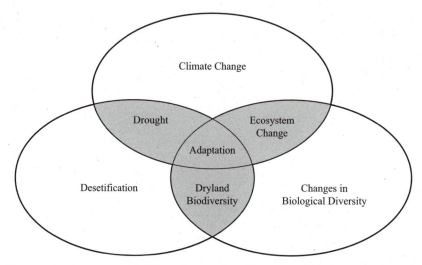

Figure 9.12   Intersection of climate change, desertification, and biodiversity, adapted from Least Developed Countries Expert Group (2002).

If leakage prevention is enforced, how would this type of transaction be accounted for? Would China be forced to adjust its baseline emissions path because of this outsourcing of mining? How would China's actions affect Canada's record for meeting its Kyoto target? Should Canada obtain a credit for the export of clean minerals that displaces a high-emissions activity in China? A similar argument was raised by Canada when seeking credits for so-called clean-energy exports (Smith and Victor 2004). In this case, Canada sought credits for sales of natural gas to the United States to offset increased domestic use of coal. Canada's emissions would increase while the United States would experience a reduction in emissions. So far, however, clean-energy credits have not been allowed in this case.

The effect of Kyoto on other environmental policy objectives is also worth watching. One example is the relationship between the Kyoto Protocol and the Conventions on Biodiversity and Desertification (figure 9.12). The Convention on Biological Diversity, for example, is meant to protect species diversity and prevent species extinction. At the same time, Article 2 of the Framework Convention on Climate Change identifies one of the reasons for avoiding dangerous anthropogenic interference as enabling ecosystems to maintain themselves. Thus, it is ironic that a Kyoto instrument specifically designed to promote a particular action on land, such as carbon sequestration, may also lead to a change in ecosystems. As a result, carbon sinks incentives could hamper the achievement of objectives of the Convention on Biodiversity (SCBD 2003). How can this contradiction be addressed? Is the primary objective to find ways of reducing the throughput of the carbon into the atmosphere, or does that objective have to be balanced with other environmental objectives from other agreements?

This leads to the bigger question of how societies and governments will react to Kyoto now that it is real instead of only theoretical. Will they pay greater attention to it? Will disagreements result in legal actions such as lawsuits? If so, who would be sued and who would arbitrate the case? Perhaps one of the greatest benefits of the ratification of the Kyoto Protocol is that we are now provided with an opportunity to observe the performance of the Kyoto mechanisms. As of 16 February 2005, the "Kyoto 101" class is in session. Now it's a matter of waiting to see what the Kyoto Protocol can and cannot accomplish by 2012.

DISCUSSION

This chapter, along with chapter 8, has reviewed the emissions reduction instruments within the Kyoto Protocol, as well as the challenges and opportunities posed by the worldwide effort to control GHG emissions. One theme that has emerged is that it is important to consider the context of current and future development paths when assessing options for GHG mitigation. There can be conflicts with development that can make it more difficult to achieve mitigation targets. We have also seen examples of climate-related development choices creating new vulnerabilities. On the other hand, it may be possible to find solutions that meet both climate change and sustainable-development goals. But finding these solutions will not be easy. If it was, they would already have been found. Figure 9.13 illustrates the continued increase in global emissions, at a faster pace than population growth and despite reductions in energy and emissions intensities (IPCC 2007b). Note that intensity indicators describe efficiency. For example, emission intensity refers to the amount of emissions per unit of GDP. This is determined from carbon intensity, which indicates the amount of carbon per unit of energy supply, and energy intensity, which is the amount of energy use per unit of GDP. Some have suggested that emission intensity reduction targets be used for policy purposes instead of emission reduction targets. Figure 9.13 shows that it is possible to achieve reductions in intensity yet still observe increases in emissions. During 1970–2004, the effect on global emissions of decreased

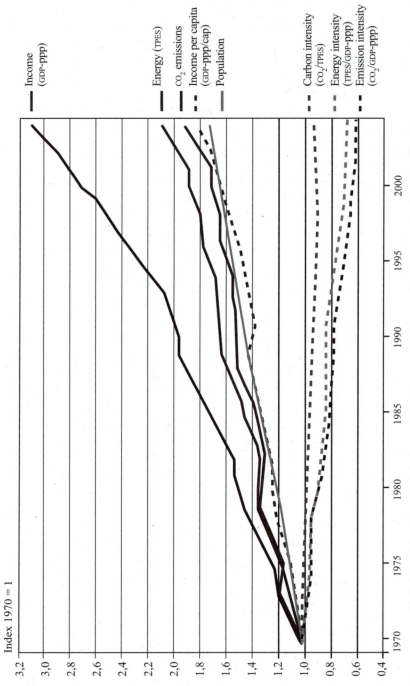

Index 1970 = 1

Income (GDP-ppp)

Energy (TPES)
CO_2 emissions
Income per capita (GDP-ppp/cap)
Population

Carbon intensity (CO_2/TPES)
Energy intensity (TPES/GDP-ppp)
Emission intensity (CO_2/GDP-ppp)

Figure 9.13   Global trends in per capita income, energy use, CO_2 emissions, and indicators of carbon, energy, and emission intensities, compared to 1970. GDP is gross domestic product; PPP is purchasing power parity; TPES is total primary energy supply.
Source: IPCC (2007b). Reprinted with permission of IPCC

emission intensity was much smaller than the combined effect of growth in income, population, and energy use. The atmosphere cares about total emissions, not about emission intensities alone. Nevertheless, within the global trend illustrated in figure 9.13, each country will have to face its own unique challenges, and they will not be solved by science and technology alone. As we consider problems of such complexity, we will see that new approaches are needed to study such problems and to connect these research efforts to decision makers that are charged with addressing these problems on society's behalf.

Our story is now moving to a very important phase. This one concerns the need to find new ways to share learning experiences between researchers from different backgrounds, and to share these experiences with decision makers. It will be argued as well that this collaborative approach can provide a way to link the climate change issue with the broader challenge of improving the future development prospects for our world.

10

Integrated Assessments of Climate Change

INTRODUCTION

In this chapter, we turn our attention to a family of research methods known as integrated assessment methods. This topic is different from other topics discussed in this book because it focuses more on a method than on a specific aspect of the climate change issue. Integrated assessments have helped to define and even redefine the climate change issue, bringing it closer to some of the broader issues of global change and sustainability.

This chapter includes discussions of both modelling and participatory approaches. We will illustrate how integrated assessment models, or IAMS, are constructed and applied by exploring three different models. Participatory integrated assessment, or PIA, involves the incorporation of dialogue exercises as a key component of the assessment. It is also possible for a PIA to utilize various analytical tools and models, including IAMS. We will consider this issue as well.

THE INTEGRATED ASSESSMENT TOOL KIT

We begin by considering the reasons for organizing and carrying out an integrated assessment of climate change. Why pursue this kind of exercise in order to understand either the impacts-adaptation or the emissions-mitigation aspects of climate change? And indeed, why has this kind of approach become of interest for broader global change issues?

First of all, there are many issues besides climate change, including desertification, biodiversity, trade, poverty, development, security, and health issues, that pose problems of great complexity. These concerns extend beyond the ability of a single discipline to address, so the integration of different approaches to problem solving becomes necessary. We know that the various forcing factors interact with each other. Not only have the scales of problems increased from local to international and from short-term to long-term, but the intensity, in terms of economic and human costs has also increased. This lends some urgency to the search for new tools.

Commentators also recognize that these various problems can behave in non-linear ways. It seems that we are constantly being surprised by global changes, and so we have much to learn by going through a more integrative learning process that can help us to anticipate some of these potential surprises. Are there any tools or methods available that make it possible to explore complex problems, such as human-induced climate change? Yes, there are, and these are collectively known as integrated assessment tools. Proponents suggest that if these tools can provide new insights into complex issues, then perhaps they can help to improve decision making (Janssen 1998).

Please note that we are not saying that these tools are crystal balls or truth machines. The tool builders themselves are also cautious about what can be achieved by using these tools. What is important is whether these tools can contribute to an improved discourse on complex problems that would ultimately lead to an improved capability to plan for and respond to such challenges. Let us now take a look at the tool kit by beginning with a basic definition of integrated assessment (IA). Rotmans (1998) describes IA as an interdisciplinary process of combining, interpreting, and communicating knowledge in order to better understand complex phenomena. He does not restrict his definition to a particular kind of tool but instead includes both computer models and participatory approaches in his definition. The point of using a tool is that it has to have added value compared to what would be determined from a single discipline like engineering, atmospheric science, or economics.

Rotmans goes on to discuss how IA is supposed to be designed to help in decision making. It is not a curiosity-driven kind of activity, as basic science is. This means that IA does not exist simply to advance understanding for its own sake. A mission orientation or perhaps a policy requirement motivates much of this kind of work. Moreover, a considerable amount of previous knowledge also has to be available before an IA can be undertaken. As well, issues of scale become important. One of the advantages of IA, though, is that there is an opportunity to focus on indirect effects of stresses and response measures. A very important goal of IA is to help frame the issue and its boundaries. The assessment could address policy strategies, risks, or ways to communicate complex issues in more direct and simple visual methods.

Rotmans splits the various approaches into two large groups. The first group of approaches is comprised of the analytical, quantitative tools, including IAM, scenario exercises, and risk analyses. They offer a quantitative assessment of the effects of complex problems and policy responses to such problems. A concern here is that one can construct a model and that it can produce numbers to many decimal places, but uncertainty surrounds how much trust can be placed in the accuracy of the model results. As a result, what level of confidence can be ascribed to these models? Rotmans describes this as a situation of false precision. How readily can a modeller or model user trace the pathways from initial inputs through to a result?

The other family of approaches is comprised of the participatory methods. Participatory integrated assessment can include dialogue exercises, policy exercises, and mutual learning, which can be combined with model simulations (Rotmans 1998; Hisschemöller, Tol, and Vellinga 2001). This approach brings groups of people together for a series of exercises that create narratives and stories, which may lead to consensus on how a complex problem or solution should be described. Is this consensus real? Or is this what Rotmans calls negotiated nonsense? And how do we trace or measure the quality of that kind of dialogue? This will depend on who is in the room, what background knowledge they have, and whether the science that has been introduced to them has made a difference in what they have said. If new information did not make a difference, such that the participants offered only a predetermined point of view, would the exercise have failed to stimulate any learning?

Different sets of skills are required for IAM and PIA. Both approaches will be affected by the uneven state of background knowledge and the differences in problem perception. Furthermore, how processes and systems are represented in models will also depend on the perception of the modeller. The modeller may include personal values or perceptions when constructing models that include human behaviour, such as goals, trade-offs, and market responses. The question is, how does one negotiate through them?

INTEGRATED ASSESSMENT MODELS (IAM)

Several different types of models have been developed since the 1970s when the first global-scale system dynamics models were developed for the "limits to growth" study (Meadows et al. 1972). *The Limits to Growth* attracted both praise, for its innovative use of computer-based modelling to describe global interdependence, and criticism, for its extrapolation of exponential growth rates (Edwards 1996; AtKisson 1999; Toth 2003). Some observers thought this approach was quite imaginative, while others angrily denounced it as being unrealistic. Even after three decades, perceptions of that experience can still raise emotions. Economists, in particular, criticized the notion of the study that zero growth was necessary to avoid environmental and societal collapse. Nevertheless, this pioneering study became an international bestseller that inspired others to pursue integrated modelling as an approach to addressing problems of great complexity.

Janssen (1998) describes four types of integrated assessment models:

- System dynamics models. These models describe interacting feedback loops, stocks, and flows.
- Optimization models. These models select the best goal or decision within constraints, or they optimize key policy variables, given certain policy goals.
- Simulation models. These models provide a deterministic prediction of system behaviour, as well as stochastic predictions using probability distributions.
- Complex adaptive systems models. These models incorporate agents of change that are used to understand system behaviour.

Each of these types of models can bring together scientific knowledge from various disciplines into a single model, but they each do so with a different purpose. The way a modeller or a modelling group constructs equations and linkages between equations differs between the model types. Models can be designed to describe cause-effect relationships or to explore cross-linkages and interactions between issues. They can also bring various aspects of a complex issue, such as climate change, together in a single large modelling box. Not all models are focused on the same goal. Some models are focused on economics, whereas some have biosphere components. Many models have both. A very difficult balancing act is required to keep the models simple but to also address the complexities of the issues.

Another IA modelling challenge is to balance aggregation and realism. A global model may not be able to represent small regions in detail, and qualitative information may be difficult to incorporate into global

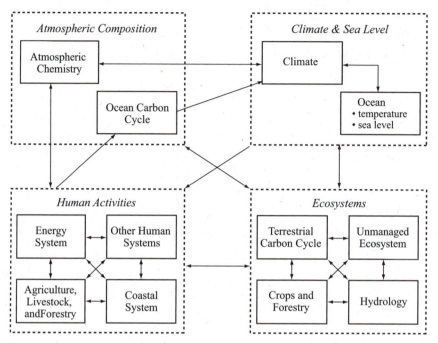

Figure 10.1   General structure of integrated assessment models of climate change.
Source: Weyant et al. (1996). Reprinted with permission of IPCC

models. However, participatory processes must confront this challenge as well, since it is difficult to measure the value of qualitative discourse. Finally, there is the treatment of uncertainty. As with climate model outputs (see chapter 3), with IAM outputs it is difficult to know the population of all possible outcomes. As well, model errors for simulations of past conditions do not necessarily tell us what errors to expect in projections of future conditions.

A number of IAMs of global climate change have a three- or four-box structure (figure 10.1). Each box represents a large module with several specialized models in each. In this example, in the upper left-hand corner there is an atmospheric-composition module that includes an atmospheric-chemistry model and an ocean carbon cycle model. Emissions information, which comes from the human activities module, and information about the feedbacks, which comes from other components, are both required as input into the atmospheric composition module. Since changes in emissions lead to changes in atmospheric chemistry, this, in turn leads to changes in the climate model within the climate and sea level module.

Considering these two modules together, and independently of the other modules, one might think one was looking at a GCM. Note, however, that this would not be a complete version of a GCM, but rather a simplified version, which would draw on the structure of GCMs, as well as on the results of GCM simulations. IAMs of global climate change require more breadth in the inputs than GCMs do, and they therefore include more modules. Individual modules have to be simpler representations of more complex models so that IAMs can function within existing computer resources.

The module on the lower right-hand side of figure 10.1 is the ecosystems module. This example includes models of the carbon cycle, unmanaged ecosystems, hydrology, crops, and forestry. The final module, on the lower left-hand side of the figure, is the human-activities module. It focuses on energy, industry, and transportation, but also on the commercial aspects of livestock, forestry, and agriculture.

This basic structure suggests that IAMs have been oriented more towards assessments of GHG emissions trajectories and their direct impacts. Many of these models have either not explicitly included adaptation, or the modeller has induced the adaptation (Toth et al. 2001). In other words, the modellers make an assumption about behaviour, perhaps through some change in the supply-demand curve for agricultural products, for example, and include this in the model.

Cultural Theory

Some models also incorporate different perspectives on human behaviour and the robustness or fragility of nature within a model. These perspectives are part of cultural theory. We are not necessarily advocating the view that cultural theory provides the best approach for incorporating the complexity of natural and human systems into a model. However, we do feel that it is important to understand how some modelling groups are trying to incorporate these perspectives, because it is recognized that there is no single way to look at a complex system like the earth-atmosphere system. As well, cultural theory allows us to step away from automatically using statistics to deal with uncertainty.

Cultural theory provides a way of describing a cultural perspective on how nature is constructed or perceived: a cultural perspective is a combination of social relations and cultural bias (Janssen 1998). Change in nature occurs when an event occurs that comes as a surprise to the preconceived notion that an individual or society may have about whether

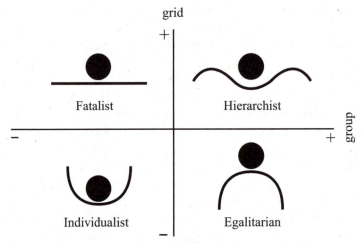

Figure 10.2 Cultural perspectives used in integrated assessment models.
Source: Janssen (1998). Reprinted with permission from Marco Janssen

nature is really robust or fragile when experiencing stress caused by natural or human forces.

Figure 10.2 illustrates four main groups of cultural perspectives. The vertical axis, labelled "grid," represents the influence of external forces. The horizontal axis, labelled "group," indicates the strength of internal constraints or rules. The four categories that emerge from this combination of internal and external forcing can be used to generate model assumptions that would be internally consistent with a particular view of the world. Such world views can provide only a partial representation of reality and so may be considered to be caricatures of aspects of reality (Gunderson and Holling 2001).

In this figure, the fatalist and hierarchist categories represent worlds in which external forces, opinions, and stresses are very important and strongly influence society's vision of how the world works. External forces matter less in the individualist and egalitarian world. The individualist view also does not care much about internal forces. Since the fatalist view sees no internal control, only external control, nothing can be done on this view to improve or change the system. A ball on a flat plane that can be rolled, pushed, or blown anywhere illustrates this view. The egalitarian view is more influenced by internal forces and not by any external stress or forces, making this view very much dependent on consensus between group members. Without consensus, the system can easily change in one direction or another. On the hierarchist view

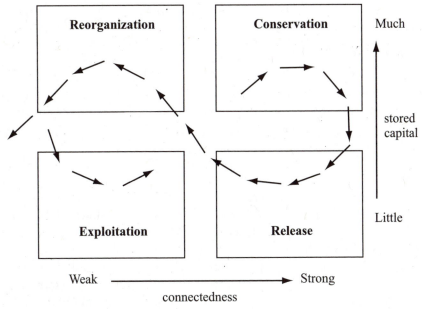

Figure 10.3   Model of adaptive cycle.
Source: Janssen (1998). Reprinted with permission from Marco Janssen

the system can be controlled in various phases. The system is not quite as deeply embedded as in the individualist's world, and it could move from one state to another if there was enough force for it to do so.

Complex Adaptive Systems

Another idea that is attracting attention in the modelling field, and perhaps elsewhere, is the notion of complex adaptive systems. On this view, a system is seen as evolving through a four-phase adaptive cycle, which has recently been given the name "panarchy." Panarchy represents a structure in which natural systems are linked together in adaptive cycles. Gunderson and Holling (2001) describe panarchy as a way of understanding transformations in human and natural systems. The evolutionary path of an adaptive cycle begins with a conservation phase, where energy and materials accumulate to a fairly high level and a system with very strong connectedness is established (figure 10.3). At some point after that, the accumulated energy is released, and the system moves into a reorganization phase, which could lead to exploitation and a new version of the system or to something else altogether.

Gunderson and Holling (2001) have proposed that panarchy can provide a theory of adaptive change integrating various drivers of change across different scales of space and time. They note that the impacts of global climate change on regional ecosystems and local human health provide examples of cross-scale influences. Part of the cause of local climate-related problems of today may be located in another part of the world, and the problems may be emerging from many decades of slow changes to the atmosphere and ecosystems.

Examples of IAMs

One of the first IAMs to be developed for assessing climate change was IMAGE; the acronym stands for "Integrated Model to Assess the Greenhouse Effect." Figure 10.4 illustrates the framework for version two of this model (Alcamo 1994); its structure is very similar to what was described earlier in this chapter. The energy/industry system module simulates GHG emissions from energy production and industry. The terrestrial ecosystem module assesses changes in land use and agriculture. Outputs from this module include changes in food production, land use, and carbon emissions from terrestrial sources. The atmosphere ocean system uses emissions data to assess changes in atmospheric concentrations of GHGs, sea level rise, and changed climate. The emissions module itself directly produces GHG emissions outputs, and there is an opportunity to use that output to formulate emissions reduction policy as well.

These outputs eventually feed into the terrestrial environment system module for agriculture, land use, vegetation, and carbon. This module produces simulations of agricultural impacts, new land use patterns, and potential implications for ecosystems. After several iterations, a change in land use could feed back to the emissions model.

When it was first developed, IMAGE had quite an impact on the communication of climate change and created substantial visibility for this type of analysis (see Weyant 1996). Other researchers from the same institution in the Netherlands that had created IMAGE subsequently created the TARGETS model (Tool to Assess Regional and Global Environmental and health Targets for Sustainability.) TARGETS is different from IMAGE, in part because it uses cultural theory to create agents of change within the model. In the TARGETS model (Rotmans and de Vries 1997), cultural theory is applied in order to assess different scenarios of external forces superimposed on assumptions of how a system would respond to such forces. Function lines, or curves, such as supply and demand curves, would look different depending on which target worlds or "utopias" are chosen.

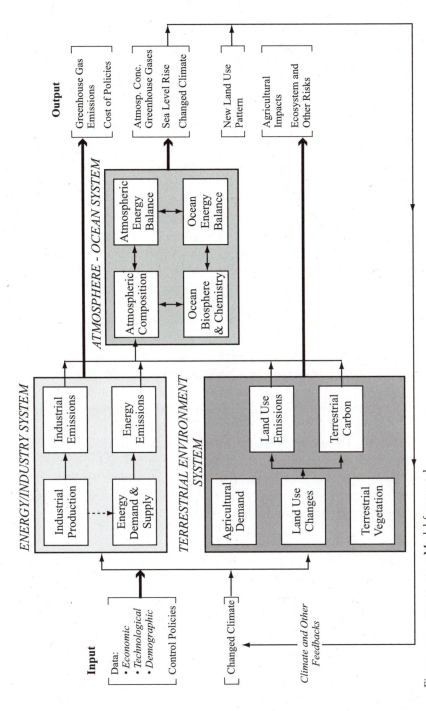

Figure 10.4   IMAGE 2.0 – Model framework.
Source: Alcamo (1994). Reprinted with permission from Joe Alcamo, and Springer Science and Business Media

In the case of how nature responds to stress, the egalitarian view would see nature as fragile, the hierarchist would see it as tolerant within limits, and the individualist would see it as robust and able to handle almost anything. TARGETS also makes assumptions about human behaviour, specifically about whether people choose prevention or adaptation as their mantra for response and whether they are risk-adverse, risk-accepting, or risk-seeking.

The point of this discussion is to provide some background on what modellers have assumed about various functions as they simulate climate impacts. The application of cultural theory offers a sensitivity test for the model, which is a way for the modeller to step back from a personal bias in modelling, although modellers may personally identify with one of the utopias. However, one should be careful about interpreting such results. In a global model, how can one assume that human behaviour within a particular utopia would be similar in every region of the world from Sweden to Pakistan to the Seychelles?

CASE STUDIES OF IAM SIMULATIONS

In this section, we consider three IAM-based case studies of climate change. The first one, which was just described briefly, is TARGETS. This model has been used to assess a wide range of questions. We focus on the specific example of the application of cultural theory to simulations of the effects of climate change on global water issues. The second example is ICAM (the Integrated Climate Assessment Model), and in this case, it provides an assessment of a carbon tax policy. In the last example, using AIM (the Asia Integrated Model), we look at both the impacts of Kyoto instruments on GHG emissions in Asia and the implications for global water issues.

TARGETS

TARGETS was completed in 1997 by a team in the Netherlands led by Rotmans and de Vries (1997). The model team attempted to use cultural theory as a way of incorporating different resource management styles into a study of global water resources. Table 10.1 shows the assumptions used within three different utopias (hierarchist, egalitarian, and individualist) for a number of response variables. In other words, through cultural theory, the modelling group assumed different management styles for water savings, water-saving technology, and the relative use of different

Table 10.1
Water Management Indicators in the TARGETS Model

Variable or Management Parameter	Hierarchist	Egalitarian	Individualist
Water pricing	Increasing charges	Water taxing	Market pricing
Development of water-saving technology	No strong technological push	Strong push for small-scale technology	Stimulation of new technology if water becomes scarce
Relative use of different water sources	No change	Decreased use of groundwater	Increased desalination
Price elasticities of water demand	Medium	Low	High
Glacier melting parameter	Medium	High	Low
Rate of technology diffusion	Low	High	Medium

Source: Adapted from Rotmans and de Vries (1997).

water sources. The assumptions they made were supposed to be consistent with particular views of the universe. Water pricing, for example, was represented in different ways, which affected the mathematics that described functions and relationships within the model. Note the specific assumptions that were made within each utopia for parameters such as the price elasticity of the demand for water, the sensitivities of the natural environment (glaciers and ice sheets) to climate change (glacier melting), and the rate of technology diffusion.

In this example, each utopia is represented by a particular management style, a view of the sensitivity or vulnerability of the natural environment, and a perception of human behaviour. In the egalitarian world view glacier melting will be particularly fast per degree of warming, in the individualist world view it will be very low, and in the hierarchist world view, it will be somewhere in between. These predictions derive from a perception of nature. The varying assumptions about the rate of technology diffusion represent different perceptions of human behaviour. All of these perceptions are modelled into the cultural universe in the water model.

What was the result of the TARGETS simulation? The individualist utopia visualized a six-fold increase in global water supply during the twenty-first century, the egalitarian utopia saw little change, and the hierarchist utopia saw a tripling of supply. These differences are explained by the varying levels of economic activity and population growth, the varying assumptions about water use efficiency improvements, and the changes in economic subsidies and taxes that were incorporated into the model. The model also made other predictions. The egalitarian utopia was assumed to have lower irrigation requirements, and consequently a lower food supply, so there was little growth in irrigation. As well, the individualist utopia assumed increased efficiency in industrial water use (Rotmans and de Vries 1997).

No probability estimate was offered for each of these utopias of future water supply conditions, and therefore no statement was made as to which vision would be more likely to occur. This exercise served to offer insights that might not otherwise be considered in a non-integrative approach. It also exposed the sensitivity of models to assumptions, and the powerful influence of modeller bias on the results.

ICAM

The ICAM example provides an assessment of the economic effects of a carbon tax policy on various world regions (Morgan and Dowlatabadi 1996). The modellers altered the assumptions in the model as a sensitivity test, in order to create what were described as alternative model structures.

Five different model choices were presented. Discounting could be applied at the same level globally, or it could be based on a regional per capita growth rate. Technological change could occur autonomously, or it could be induced by a carbon tax. In other words, the tax policy could be directed at encouraging new technologies. Aerosol effects on climate could be included or excluded. Adaptation could occur after detection of a climate change impact, or adaptation could not occur and the impact would be permanent. Finally, oil and gas reserves could be exhausted by 2050, or new reserves could be discovered.

These five choices lead to many possible model combinations, and six of these were assessed. The results were expressed for different world regions as probabilities that the carbon tax policy would have a positive net present value. In other words, the results were presented in terms of whether the carbon tax policy would benefit the countries' economies.

The results showed that in all six cases, China exhibited the lowest probability of benefiting from a carbon tax policy. OECD countries and Latin American countries tended to have the highest probabilities of benefit. The model combination with the highest probabilities of benefit was the one that assumed regional discounting, carbon-tax-induced technological change, no aerosol effects, no adaptation, and no new oil and gas reserves. The lowest probabilities of benefit were obtained for the model that included regional discounting, carbon-tax-induced technological change, aerosol effects, successful adaptation, and the discovery of new oil and gas reserves.

What has been learned from this sensitivity test? Morgan and Dowlatabadi (1996) explain that the important finding is the change in value from case to case, not the absolute probability for any particular case and region. Also, it is important to note that regardless of what structural assumptions were made in the model, interregional differences remained in the various model runs, such as differences between China and the OECD.

AIM

The third example, AIM (the Asia Integrated Model), is, despite its name, a global model. The model construction was coordinated and led by a group in Japan, in cooperation with other groups throughout Asia (Kainuma, Matsuoka, and Morita 2003). One part of AIM is a GHG emissions linkage model. Socioeconomic scenarios, including GDP, population, and lifestyle, provide input to a complex emissions model, which includes submodels of energy efficiency, technological change, and consumption. These submodels are linked with an energy-economic model and a land-equilibrium model, which includes submodels on cropland and forests. All these models and submodels contribute to estimates of future GHG emissions, which subsequently provide information for a climate model and an impact model.

One output of the emissions linkage model is a series of estimates for changes in GDP required to achieve Kyoto emissions reduction targets, with and without emissions trading. This exercise is similar to the one illustrated above for ICAM, though it is for a different policy measure. Table 10.2 shows results for different trading scenarios that include, or do not include, participation of the United States in a global trading market. The "boycott" scenarios assume that there would be a boycott of goods exported to non-ratifying countries. The "technology" scenario assumes price incentives to induce technological change. The "combination" scenarios include both of the above. Most of the projected GDP changes are negative, indicating losses, though there are benefits in some cases. The former Soviet Union countries benefit from emissions trading, and China benefits if trading is combined with the

Table 10.2
Impacts of Kyoto Instruments on GDP, Percentage Change in 2010

	Japan	USA	EU	FSU	China
ET–yes; USA–no	−0.06	0.00	−0.08	0.92	−0.03
ET–yes; USA–yes	−0.14	−0.33	−0.19	3.50	−0.09
ET–no; USA–no (boycott)	−0.47	−0.92	−0.45	−0.16	−0.17
ET–no; USA–yes (technology)	0.27	0.06	0.35	−0.31	−0.05
ET & CDM–yes; USA–yes	0.00	−0.20	−0.09	1.44	0.51

Source: Adapted from Kainuma et al. (2003).
ET = emissions trading.
CDM = clean development mechanism.
FSU = former Soviet Union.

CDM. Generally speaking, losses are higher (or benefits are lower) without the United States ratifying Kyoto.

Another major component of AIM is its impact model framework, which includes water resources. The water demand module estimates current and future water demands for different economic and population growth scenarios, including changes in agriculture and domestic and industrial withdrawals. Water supply is obtained from a runoff model for three different GCM-based scenarios. The values for water demand and supply are totalled up for large basins.

The results show that water supply will vary with each climate scenario. This is not new. What is new, however, is the calculation by an IAM of demand-supply ratios for particular watersheds. Figure 10.5 shows annual changes in demand-supply ratios for the Ganges and Mekong River Basins for three GCM-based scenarios. For the Ganges, the ratio will not change very much in two of the scenarios because the projected increases in runoff will be matched by increased demand resulting from population growth and economic development. A third scenario, based on the Japanese GCM, has higher ratios, which indicates greater water stress. For the Mekong, ratios increase in all cases, but the ratios themselves are still relatively small.

PARTICIPATORY INTEGRATED ASSESSMENTS

As a complement or alternative to IAMs, the participatory integrated assessment (PIA) approach is a framework that utilizes dialogue as a research tool. This is not talk simply for outreach or even simply for one-way teaching, but instead it is for two-way or multi-voice teaching. A

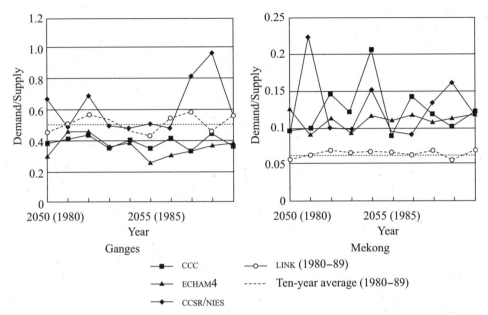

Figure 10.5   Changes in supply/demand ratio for water, 2050–59, compared to 1980–89, for the Ganges and Mekong River basins. LINK refers to the observed global climate data set provided by the LINK program in the UK. CCSR/NIES refers to the GCM produced in Japan. CCC is an earlier version of the GCM produced by the Canadian Centre for Climate Modelling and Analysis. ECHAM4 is a GCM produced in Germany. Each GCM was run using an emission scenario of 1 percent increase per year.
Source: Harasawa et al. (2003). Reprinted with permission from Springer Science and Business Media

PIA can create a shared learning experience for scientists, business inter-ests, community representatives, aboriginal peoples, resource managers, governments, or any stakeholder with knowledge to share and a reason to be part of the process.

Recall that in chapter 7, we offered a non-traditional definition of "stakeholder". We were not talking about disinterested parties who simply hold the stakes but rather about people who do have a stake in the outcome. In a PIA, individuals agree to participate in a process that lets them use dialogue to approach a complex problem. There may be issues that must be overcome when people are brought together who may have completely opposite points of view on an issue. Confronta-tions or contradictory information may also need reconciliation. The dialogue is intended to find a way to navigate through these problems without taking on the atmosphere of a judicial inquiry or some other form of legal proceeding. It is meant to create an environment that is, it is to be hoped, at another level and that keeps politics out. Again, the task is difficult to attempt, but interest in this tool is growing. One example of that interest is the creation of the Integrated Assessment Society (TIAS), which promotes scholarship in PIA, as well as in model development and application (see the TIAS website at http://www.tias-web.info/).

PIA has evolved from a number of different pedigrees. For example, participatory action research (PAR) is a well-known approach that social scientists have used in studies of the traditional practices and environmental knowledge of aboriginal communities (see, for example, Johnson 1992). The researcher moves into the community and lives there for a long period, and through informal dialogue and interviews obtains information that could not be obtained from a telephone-based survey.

Dialogue can be supported or facilitated by outputs of models (Tansey et al. 2002). The reverse can also be true. Perhaps dialogue can support model building through the process of participatory modelling, including, for example, mediated modelling (van den Belt 2004). Still, the success of a PIA depends on who is in the room. The researcher has to convince people to participate, and perhaps to participate for a prolonged period, not simply during a two-hour meeting in a hotel. The researcher may ask the participants to come back several times over the course of six or twelve months. An example is provided by a study from the Netherlands called the COOL project (Climate Options for the Long Term). COOL focused on Dutch national policy for reducing emissions (van de Kerkhof 2004) and extended over several years.

Participatory processes are important in integrated assessments because they can help to frame problems. In its simplest terms, an assessment of a complex problem like climate change may involve researchers, including natural and social scientists, and stakeholders, including practitioners such as resource managers and planners, community representatives, and governments (figure 10.6). The scientists discuss what is possible and what is plausible. The stakeholders discuss concerns about their industry or their community, and their main concern is about determining a desirable outcome. If the "integrator" can bring together the suppliers of the science information with those who are demanding a particular kind of information, then between the two groups it may be possible to obtain what Rotmans (1998) calls an "integrative narrative." This narrative would help to define the problem, leading to a consensus-building process and, ultimately, to a set of decisions that could then be

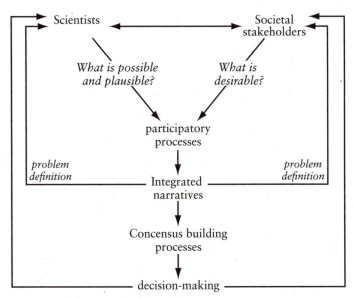

Figure 10.6   Cyclical framework of mutual learning.
Source: adapted from Rotmans and van Asselt (1996)

revisited in a second increment. This fits into the bigger picture by giving both sets of participants a sense of ownership in the process.

Part of what distinguishes PIA from IAM is the application of dialogue techniques. Dürrenberger et al. (1997) categorize various dialogue techniques according to two criteria: (1) embeddedness which is the level reached by the process of decision making, ranging from low (information gathering) to medium (advice) to high (the decision itself); and (2) the level of conflict, which ranges from absent to latent to acute.

In a situation with acute conflict and high embeddedness, the technique most likely to be used is mediation. In a research situation, with low to medium embeddedness, there are other options, such as focus groups, planning cells, and consensus conferences. Climate change research, dialogue, or negotiation can include situations that cover much of this range of embeddedness and conflict, but the choice of a dialogue exercise really depends on what the objective is.

Figure 10.7 shows a range of dialogue exercises mapped according to the objectives that they are designed to address. The vertical axis represents a scale of agreement among dialogue participants, ranging from consensus to a diversity of opinion. Policy exercises and focus groups,

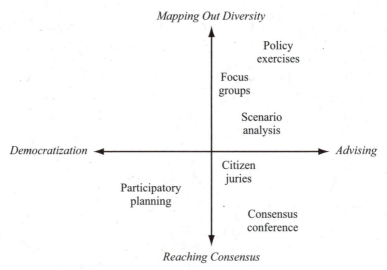

Figure 10.7   What dialogue exercises can do?
Source: van Asselt and Rijkens-Klomp (2002). Reprinted with permission from Elsevier Limited

which are rated towards the diversity end of the scale, are designed to bring out the range of positions, rather than to force a consensus. In other words, the task here is not to reach agreement but rather to find out what all the positions really are. The horizontal axis measures whether the exercise is meant to broaden (i.e., democratize) participation in a policy process or only to offer advice. The choice of which exercise is worth pursuing depends on which of these combinations of objectives are to be undertaken.

Returning to the example of the COOL project, van de Kerkhof (2004) explored a number of dialogue exercises and attempted to measure how well they worked, and in particular, what the quality of learning was for each kind of exercise. She used several indicators, including distance and involvement. For distance the question was, does the approach enable participants to distance themselves from short-term concerns and focus on wider, long-term issues? For example, suppose we want to discuss climate change with a manager of a business or a manager of a reservoir. They have their own particular planning horizons. Can the exercise enable them to think outside a two-year or five-year view, to think in terms of thirty to fifty years in the future?

Involvement measured whether there was successful transfer of information to the dialogue participants from the scientists or the technical staff who were providing the background information. In other words, did the technical or background materials teach new concepts or impart new knowledge to the participants? Also, was there a balance between distance and involvement?

Other indicators of learning were the encouragement of debate and argument, the use of the scientific knowledge that was being offered, homogeneity or heterogeneity in the makeup of the group and in the sources of information, and commitment, trust, fairness, and transparency in the dialogue process. As with the IAM, it would be difficult to define a base case against which the performance of a dialogue exercise within a PIA can be measured.

Stakeholder Commitment

Success in a PIA, or in any dialogue process, for that matter, will ultimately depend on convincing stakeholders to agree to remain committed to the process. In that respect, it is probably more difficult to organize and sustain dialogue within a PIA than it is for a modelling group to construct an IAM, because response rates can be influenced by many external factors, such as participants' commitments to their jobs and families. How can the PIA maintain a high level of interest so that there will be a high rate of participation? Rotmans and van Asselt (1996) suggest that it is important to provide a sense of ownership in an exercise in shared learning.

My own experience has suggested several ways to attract participants. They are not mutually exclusive but should be reinforcing. Speaking metaphorically, the first is with beer – with an offer of a relaxed approach, rather than a situation where there may be a high level of emotion or conflict. The second is with chicken soup – with comfort and problem solving. A third is with chocolate – with a reward after accomplishing a difficult task.

These three metaphors are meant to suggest that a way to get people who are very busy in their own jobs to take a day out and come to a dialogue exercise is to convince them that there is something in it for them. They may not obtain their reward immediately, since the exercise can be lengthy, but if it will be addressing a problem they are interested in and if it will involve an explicit search for solutions, they see might that as another reason to come.

An additional metaphor to consider is symbolised by caribou (or another native wildlife species), representing respect for local knowledge and experience. The caribou represents respect for the knowledge of Aboriginal people in the Arctic, people who are very proud of the state of the caribou herds. If the herds are in good health, they reflect the Arctic communities' abilities as stewards to manage them well. They reflect their local knowledge, and so to talk about local foods (or country foods) generally is to indicate a respect for local knowledge, whatever it happens to be.

Obtaining stakeholder commitment to a PIA process is important for its success, and building relationships of trust is an inherent part of this. However, the incorporation of stakeholder input into an IA process may be jeopardised if participants feel that they are not making a contribution or that their knowledge is not adequately interpreted or represented (Kloprogge and van der Sluijs 2006).

Organizing Integrated Assessments of Climate Change Impacts

An early attempt at an integrated assessment of climate change impacts was the Mackenzie Basin Impact Study (see below). Figure 10.8 is based on that experience and is meant to provide a more general framework for outlining the various steps. Much of this framework may be seen as providing a common-sense approach to building a collaborative team that can incorporate both scenario exercises and dialogue with stakeholders.

The first step is for the core proponents to prepare a first-draft definition of the study area and problems of interest. The next step is to establish a preliminary plan for integration, which can include both modelling and participatory approaches. With this first iteration in hand, it is then time to start looking at expanding the core group of people and to establish working committees, integration sub-committees, and communications mechanisms. Once this structure is in place, two paths of knowledge integration should be initiated. One is the horizontal-integration path. The objective is to get the different disciplines working together on scenario construction and on identifying sectoral studies. The other path, vertical integration, involves establishing the linkage between the researchers and the decision makers. The consultations that are required for this objective can lead to a revision of the initial framing of the problem. Eventually, the reporting of this exercise emerges from this process.

Many tools are available to be incorporated into integrated assessments of impacts and adaptation. Current practice includes the application of analogue and model-based scenarios, decision support models,

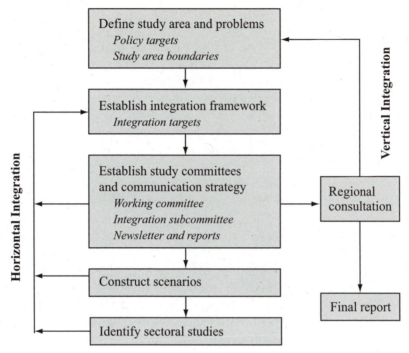

Figure 10.8   Approach for organizing an integrated assessment of climate change.
Source: Cohen (1996)

economic models, and expert judgement. There are also examples of incorporating local knowledge, sometimes referred to as a traditional-knowledge assessment or a folk assessment. The global-scale IAM exercises were initiated primarily to assess GHG emissions reduction options (see Bruce, Lee, and Haites 1996), but more of these exercises are now being applied to impacts. Finally, it is important to appreciate the opportunity for integration to be based not on the analytical tool but on the place, theme, or policy instrument itself.

A recent innovation involves combining scenarios of climate change and development in order to assess future impacts within alternative development paths. This approach was tried in a case study organized through the UK Climate Impacts Programme (UKCIP). UKCIP has supported regional-scale integrated impact and adaptation assessments, incorporating stakeholder involvement in study design, the design of analytical tools, site selection, and scenario construction. The case study focused on flooding, agriculture, and water resources in two regions within the United Kingdom (Holman, Rounsevell et al. 2005;

Holman, Nicholls et al. 2005). This study, known as Reg1s, constructed two development scenarios, one of which involved a "sustainable" future, indicative of the growing desire by researchers and governments to better define what it means to develop in a sustainable manner. It also recognized that climate change and sustainable development need to be more explicitly linked in analysis, as well as in policy (see chapter 11).

What constitutes a good integrative assessment? Morgan and Dowlatabadi (1996) list a number of "unofficial commandments" for producing a high-quality integrated assessment:

- Characterization and analysis of uncertainty should be a central focus.
- The approach should be iterative. The focus of attention should be permitted to shift over time, depending on what has been learned and which parts of the problem are found to be critical for answering the questions being asked.
- The parts of the problem about which we have little knowledge must not be ignored. When formal models are not possible, we can use "order-of magnitude" analysis, "bounding" analysis, and expert judgment.
- The treatment of values should be explicit and parametric (where possible), so that many different actors can make use of results from the same assessment.
- Climate impacts should be placed in the context of other natural and human background stochastic variations and secular trends.
- A set of coordinated analyses that span the problem, and not a single model, should be used. As well, different analytical strategies may be needed.
- There should be multiple assessments, with different formulations, where needed, since no single project will get everything right.

CASE STUDIES OF PIAS

We now turn our attention to two examples of impact and adaptation studies in Canada that were carried out using participatory processes. The first one is a project from the early 1990s in northwest Canada called the Mackenzie Basin Impacts Study, or MBIS. The second one is focused on water management in the Okanagan region of British Columbia. Both studies were developed as collaborative efforts between researchers and stakeholders, and they employed GCM-based scenarios, sectoral models, integrated assessment models, and various approaches for creating dialogue for shared learning.

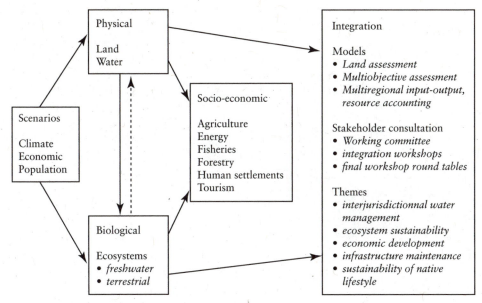

Figure 10.9   Mackenzie Basin Impact Study (MBIS) framework.
Source: Cohen (1997b)

The Mackenzie Basin Impacts Study (MBIS)

The Mackenzie Basin watershed, one of the largest watersheds in North America, is located in northwest Canada. Because the downstream portion of the basin experiences a sub-Arctic climate, potential impacts on permafrost and ecosystems and consequent effects on Northern peoples are of particular interest.

In 1990, I initiated the Mackenzie Basin Impacts Study (MBIS) as a collaborative, integrative activity. I wanted to bring together as many interests as possible from different disciplines and communities to try to address impacts problems. The study was organized as a series of individual assessments that were connected with each other by using common scenarios. Some study components also utilized outputs from other components. Figure 10.9 shows the overall framework for the MBIS.

The scenarios provided information that could be used by physical, biological, and socio-economic studies, including studies of agriculture, forestry, and tourism. For example, could agriculture in cold margins benefit from warming? What were the implications of changing ice and permafrost for energy exploration? How would Aboriginal communities be affected by impacts on ecosystems? Information from the sectoral

Figure 10.10   Round table discussion on sustainability of ecosystems, MBIS Final Workshop, 5–8 May 1996, Yellowknife, Canada. *Photo credit:* Isobel Hartley. *Source:* Cohen (1997a)

components was fed into a series of integration exercises, some of which were model-based. There were also theme-oriented round tables and an ongoing consultation process carried out through a working committee composed of research and stakeholder representatives (figure 10.10).

Stakeholder roles in the MBIS were fairly wide-ranging. Stakeholders were involved in the study committee as advisors and proposal reviewers, and as persons assisting with the outreach. Some of them were research participants, subjects of interviews, and panellists in round tables. They participated in the study from an early stage, not just at the end. It was hoped that if stakeholders were brought in early on and if they were offered key roles in advising, problem framing, and dialogue, they would feel a sense of ownership in the results, thereby raising the visibility of the study among decision makers in the region and elsewhere, and perhaps leading to some stakeholders acting as extension agents for climate change within their regions and networks.

The impacts story that was generated by the MBIS included now-familiar concerns about permafrost thaw and landslides, forest fires, changes in wildlife, and the drying of wetland areas, particularly in northern Alberta. The future of northern communities depended on choices regarding economic development, governance, and lifestyles. Improved opportunities for agriculture, particularly wheat, might benefit the region, but it was not known how those opportunities would affect traditional food harvesting, particularly for caribou, an important source for the sub-Arctic food supply. What would be the cultural implications of such a change? The magnitude and severity of climate change impacts would depend not only on climate change itself but also on how well prepared the region would be. The MBIS was clearly successful at raising awareness in the region, and this led to some important follow-up activities, including regional assessments throughout the Arctic and the creation of the Northern Climate Exchange at Yukon College.

This team-building process seemed to work most of the time (Cohen 1997b). Personal contact was very important, which posed a challenge given the long distances between participants and regional interests in the sub-Arctic and given the fact that electronic communication was not yet universally available in the region. The dialogue process itself was tested on several occasions. Sometimes, dialogue participants would want to introduce other topics, often without advance notice. Since the climate change stage can be used to promote other causes, it is important to be prepared for this problem.

Okanagan Water Resources

The Okanagan region of British Columbia is a rapidly growing agricultural area with a semi-arid climate. The population has nearly tripled since the 1970s, and agriculture has evolved from mostly pasture and livestock agriculture to intensive horticulture, including the culture of fruits and vineyards. The Okanagan Water Resources Study was more narrowly focused than the MBIS, but there was still a wide range of stakeholder interests, including the interests of stakeholders in government, agriculture, fisheries, advocacy groups, and academia.

The scenario of interest was one of the changing amount and timing of the water supply, coupled with potential increases in water demand owing to a longer and warmer growing season, increased evaporation loss, and a growing population. The climate scenarios were used as inputs to models of hydrology, crop water demand, and residential demand. The results showed that the risk of drought would increase for all scenarios of warming. An example is shown in figure 10.11, which illustrates that as this scenario develops over the course of the twenty-first century, the number of high-risk years with low supply and high demand changes from a one-in-thirty-year frequency to one in three.

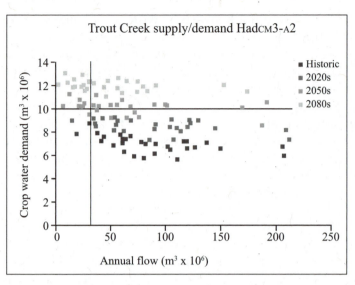

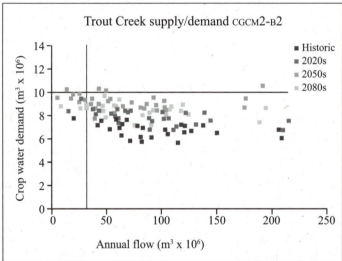

Figure 10.11   Trout Creek water supply/demand scenarios. High-risk cases occur when demand exceeds 10 million m³ (maximum observed demand) and supply is less than 30 million m³ (below the drought threshold defined by the local water management committee).
Source: Neilson et al. (2004), in Cohen, Neilsen, and Welbourn (2004)

The question was, how could the dialogue be broadened beyond hydrology and crop water needs, so that we could consider water management options that were within the local development context? And how could this exercise encourage local interests to talk about planned adaptation? The dialogue has evolved through several stages, each one accompanied by technical information provided by the study team. In the first stage a series of focus groups generated lists of different kinds of measures, such as building dams and buying out water licenses. The measures were listed according to local preferences, but participants were also asked to indicate the implications of their choices, such as high costs or reduced flexibility in system management.

The scenario work was accompanied by an examination of the history of local institutions adapting to water stresses (Shepherd et al. 2006), a review of the costs of measures oriented to supply and demand, and a series of brainstorming workshops designed to address the social aspects of implementing adaptation measures. It is important that there was no attempt in the dialogue to rank options. Participants were asked to identify barriers and opportunities for implementation of various measures as part of a portfolio of measures for the Okanagan.

The discussion centred on the social, legal, and political dimensions of the problem, not on engineering. It was assumed that there were no significant technical barriers to building a pipe or drilling a well. What we wanted to know was what local interests thought about the acceptability of an adaptation measure, so there were different dialogues at the community and basin scales. The latter dialogue was more strategic. It was about creating a sense of belonging to the basin and the roles that regional agencies would play in implementing the possible adaptation measures (Cohen, Neilsen, and Welbourn 2004).

The most recent phase of this study built on the existing collaborative effort in order to try something new. Local water practitioners were invited to assist the study team in constructing a system model for the Okanagan. The model uses system dynamics software, and in the collaborative approach, known as "meditative modelling," practitioners are consulted at various stages of the model construction process. Results of this process have led to a broader understanding of the implications of climate, population, and housing scenarios for the region's water balance (Langsdale et al. 2007; Cohen and Neale 2006). Without proactive adaptation to climate change, demand would exceed supply by the 2020s during relatively dry years, and by the 2050s during "average" years. A wide range of adaptation options can be assessed by the model, and certain combinations may be quite effective at maintaining a satisfactory water balance that incorporates the needs of all water users, but additional research is needed to address uncertainties associated with land use change, groundwater, and the role of governance.

In the Okanagan study, the roles of stakeholders have gone beyond the MBIS experience. The wider range of dialogue exercises employed in the Okanagan case was part of a multi-step process to move the dialogue closer to a shared-learning partnership. The group-assisted model-building activity represents a significant commitment on the part of local practitioners to bring their knowledge to the table and to see it expressed in a new way. If they have a stake in the construction of the model, then one hopes that they and their peers in the community will become interested in using it as a decision-support tool and seeing what insights can be gained. This relatively young field of endeavour is bringing in stakeholders or local knowledge holders to help build models. We have come a long way from using stakeholders simply as recipients of outreach and are now getting them to develop and construct models.

MODELLING VERSUS PARTICIPATORY PROCESSES

Complex problems such as global climate change can be assessed through a four-step process: problem identification, analysis of options, identification of strategies, and communication of results. At each level, it is necessary to ask what the role of participation is and what the role of modelling is. Although one may be prepared to use both sets of techniques or only one specific approach, there is no recipe for deciding which approach is better.

Part of the challenge, and also the opportunity, of combining modelling and participatory approaches is tracking the flow of information on climate change, including climate science, impacts, adaptation, and mitigation. In chapter 7, we considered the role of shared learning in linking research-based and community-based knowledge (see figure 7.10). Shared learning exercises offer exchanges of information between actors from varied backgrounds and experiences. Climate science information becomes transformed, or translated, into indicators that are directly relevant to decision makers and their supporting professional/technical staff, i.e., to practitioners. This translation requires the use of various kinds of tools that serve as filters, as is illustrated in figure 10.12.

Some of these tools may be able to apply climate information directly, while others may be able to do so only indirectly. For more complex

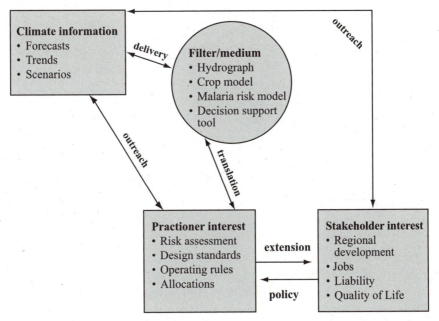

Figure 10.12   Information flow linking climate science, practitioners, and stakeholders

tools, including decision-support tools, as outlined for the Okanagan case, information from many sources might be necessary. The process can become quite complex to manage, but the results can extend beyond research alone. The experience can lead to increased awareness among practitioners and, through them, among decision makers and the public. One may consider this process to be analogous to the creation of "extension agents" for promoting community-based responses to climate change, building on the twin foundations of research and local knowledge.

When climate change impacts research began in the 1980s, a very simple desktop study would apply a scenario to a tool, such as a corn yield model, for a particular station, while everything else was assumed to remain equal (EERE). These simple studies could not address non-climate aspects, such as the behaviour of farmers and markets, institutions, or governance. They were an example of a single-sector study at a local site, using one of the older $2xCO_2$ equilibrium scenarios from the first-generation GCMs. In terms of temporal or spatial integration, they were at the low end of the integration scale (figure 10.13).

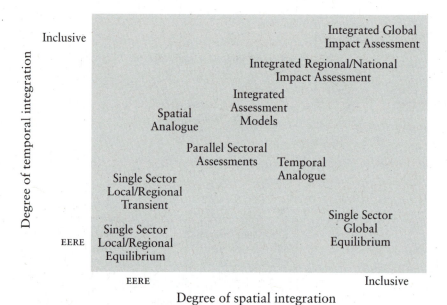

Figure 10.13 Hierarchy of climatic impact assessment frameworks.
Source: adapted from Cohen (1996)

As impacts researchers expanded their efforts to consider transient scenarios from newer GCMs, to be carried out over a larger area with the consideration of the human dimensions of corn production and distribution, these exercises had more integration potential, either temporally (using time series instead of snapshots) or spatially. Besides GCMs, there have been analogue studies based on warm climates of the past or of another location, which are called temporal and spatial analogues, respectively (see chapter 3). Parallel sectoral assessments are collaborative efforts that can include a number of components but that may not be linked by any formal integrated modelling or dialogue process. Studies of food, water, and forests, for example, may be carried out with the same climate change scenarios, but they are not necessarily cross-linked to each other in an integrative way.

The most inclusive exercise would work with a combination of global-scale integrated assessment models and participatory processes carried out in a coordinated fashion worldwide. This exercise has not yet been done, although a number of global-scale IAMs have been used to simulate impacts, as well as GHG emissions scenarios at regional and global-scales. We are also beginning to see regional-scale exercises that include both modelling and dialogue.

FUTURE CHALLENGES AND OPPORTUNITIES

IAMs and PIAs offer complementary sets of methods and tools for exploring global climate change. There are two aspects to this. First, there are the indirect linkages within various aspects of the climate change issue, such as atmosphere, ecosystems, and GHG emissions. Second, there are the links between climate change and broader societal concerns, such as sustainable development (see chapter 11). These are promising approaches that can lead to creative interdisciplinary thinking about complex problems, of which climate change is but one example.

In comparing the IAM and PIA examples, several challenges emerge that need to be addressed before these approaches will be used more widely, and perhaps more readily, by researchers and stakeholders. Global-scale IAMs are often criticized for being too aggregated and coarse in their field of view, with the result that important regional details can be missed. How can they be downscaled? While a regional PIA continues to make assumptions about external forcing that can affect regional economic and decision-making contexts, a global model will probably miss trade-offs between individual stakeholders and actors. Some global models have assumed extrapolation of relationships from particular countries where the modellers are located. In fact, AIM was initiated because it was recognized in Asia that existing European- or American-built IAMs might not capture Asian economic realities and landscape relationships (Kainuma, Matsuoka, and Morita 2003). Does this then mean that an African version of AIM is needed?

Dialogue-based approaches also create challenges, particularly in the assessment of their effectiveness, such as measuring the quality of dialogue. The van de Kerkhof (2004) study offers considerable detail on various tests that were used to measure the quality of dialogue in the COOL Project in the Netherlands. Was distance achieved? Was involvement achieved? Was learning achieved? Why did certain approaches to dialogue work for some stakeholder groups and not for others?

The role of scenarios continues to evolve. The TARGETS utopias, derived from cultural theory, differ markedly from the SRES family of GHG emissions scenarios. How do they compare in terms of underlying assumptions about economic development, population growth, and so on? Should SRES or something like it be the standard for scenarios? Should there even be a standard?

Models do not draw the same amount of their information from every source but draw more heavily from some disciplines than from others.

There may be some anchoring of the choice of sources of information, as well as some anchoring of the expected model results, since some fields of study offer more quantitative information, while others provide more qualitative narratives. How can participatory approaches best be applied as a complement to modelling? Are group-based modelling approaches the way to proceed? Where does integrated assessment of climate change go from here? What are the next steps? Indeed, there are many questions to consider.

Certainly, for the models there is likely to be continued interest in assessments of policy instruments, such as emissions trading, including aspects of timing and location of their application. Does it matter when an instrument is brought into the process? Does it matter where it is implemented? And how well are these instruments functioning during the Kyoto commitment period of 2008–12? IAMS are also likely to be used for testing policy options post-2012, otherwise known as the post-Kyoto period.

For PIA the challenge is to continue to find opportunities for active involvement in climate change research beyond simply being part of the outreach. Concerns about potential disempowerment need to be addressed, so that stakeholders feel that they have been able to contribute to the IA process, that their participation made a difference (Yohe et al. 2007). As well, it is necessary to see whether or not this can help to link global climate change to regional sustainable development (see chapter 11). Dialogue processes with models, and even without models, can help build this bridge.

Growing interest in the behaviour of complex systems, including adaptive systems, will attract more efforts directed towards both IAMS and PIAS. Adaptation-mitigation linkages need more study. Social learning emerging from these assessments could support decision making and consensus building and facilitate the mainstreaming of climate change response measures into the regional-development context.

DISCUSSION

This chapter has provided an overview of model-based and participatory approaches to the integrated assessment of climate change. Several IAM and PIA case studies were used to illustrate how such exercises could provide unique insights into various aspects of climate change.

In the above examples, IAM sensitivities were made visible by altering the assumptions of various model parameters. The example for water from the AIM illustrates differences between climate change scenarios. Some results were affected by model modifications or by the climate scenario that was chosen, but others were not. Although this might suggest a higher confidence in some results and a lower confidence in others, it also means that considerable uncertainties are associated with such models. Nevertheless, IAM simulations can offer some unique opportunities for assessing climate change in a way that smaller sectoral models may miss.

The two PIA experiences illustrate how dialogue is being used as part of the integration process, complementing what can be achieved through models. Although there are reasons for optimism about what PIA can achieve, a note of caution is warranted. The experience to date has been that there are no guarantees that dialogue alone will link local issues and global climate change. Some stakeholders may not participate, and while some dialogue events may promote debate, participants may not actually be learning anything new.

The conclusion that I have come to from this experience is that we need to find ways to support dialogue with a variety of other mechanisms that are not specifically research-oriented. Study-sponsored events, regional professional gatherings, and links with ongoing government planning exercises can be helpful. Local professionals can become partners like the well-known "extension agents" that have bridged the gap between research and practice, particularly in agriculture and urban and regional planning. In the Okanagan case, one regional district was updating its water resources management plan, and our team agreed to provide some study results. The plan that was subsequently produced by the district agency explicitly included consideration of climate change scenarios (Summit Environmental Consultants Ltd 2004). After the release of Cohen and Neale (2006), a regional water strategy was proposed for the entire Okanagan watershed that would include explicit consideration of climate change (Okanagan Water Stewardship Council 2008).

At this point it is obvious that further linkages between analyses of adaptation and mitigation need to be established. Both modelling approaches and participatory approaches can help in this process. As well, both kinds of approaches can help to bridge the gap between climate change issues and other global change issues, including sustainable development. More on this topic is discussed in the following chapter.

11

Context: Climate Change and Other Global Environmental Problems

INTRODUCTION

One of the important themes about human-induced climate change in this book is that research, dialogue, and policy should consider the larger context of other challenges that face our world. It was no accident that the United Nations Framework Convention on Climate Change (UNFCCC) was signed at the 1992 Earth Summit, an event that was organized to address several major global challenges. Desertification, biodiversity, climate change, and sustainable development are all connected (see figure 9.12). Research and action in one of these areas are affected by, and can influence, the others.

Since 1992, progress on these various challenges has been difficult to assess. The terms describing them have become part of common language, and the characteristics of the problems have been articulated, but consensus on appropriate policy responses continues to be elusive. Climate change has been described as both a challenge and an opportunity for sustainable development. Wilbanks (2003) describes how climate change can be seen as a threat to sustainable development, particularly if it proceeds at a faster pace than global rates of adaptation. On the other hand, despite this threat, the climate change dialogue has triggered broader international discourse on resource allocations to meet sustainable development needs.

In this chapter, we explore some of the linkages between climate change and sustainable development. Can policy measures addressing these two concerns mutually reinforce each other? Or, do they affect each other in ways that create new problems?

DEFINING DANGEROUS CLIMATE CHANGE

We begin by revisiting article 2 of the UNFCCC, which deals with the prevention of dangerous anthropogenic interference with the atmosphere (see chapters 2, 4, and 7). The whole process behind the UNFCCC and the Kyoto Protocol, as well as the various efforts at research and dialogue, have been based on first trying to determine what dangerous is and then figuring out how to avoid it.

Figure 11.1 illustrates some reasons for concern about projected climate change impacts. This figure was one of the key results of the *Third Assessment Report of the Intergovernmental Panel on Climate Change* (IPCC). The report avoided specifying a warming threshold for "dangerous," since value judgements are associated with specifying such a threshold and science on its own is therefore unlikely to be the final arbiter defining dangerous warming. Instead, several other issues were taken into consideration and combined with the results from the SRES projections to produce categories of risks. We look first at the warming predictions and then at the risks that emerged.

Figure 11.1 contains several important messages. The left-hand panel shows temperature changes for the various SRES and the 1S92A emissions scenarios. Recall from chapters 2 and 3 that the 1S92A scenario is the old 1992 business-as-usual case, which was part of the 1S92 emissions scenarios. In this figure, the range of warming projected for these scenarios would be between one and a half and six degrees by 2100. The SRES scenarios shown in this figure are marker scenarios, which means that they represent groups or families of similar storylines. The trends shown in the figure represent the average warming for each family of scenarios. Within each family, of course, there are variations in warming trends. The grey shading thus represents the broader warming range outside the individual paths indicated on this graph.

The SRES narratives were used as inputs for a range of climate model simulations (see chapter 3), which resulted in a wide range of global temperature outcomes that differ from straight extrapolations of historic trends in GHG emissions and global temperature. Temperature predictions were useful, but they were only part of the story: the question of what level of warming was actually dangerous remained unanswered. There needed to be some expression of critical thresholds for the various parameters that would indicate a substantial change in condition or state. A group of IPCC authors created a set of barometers

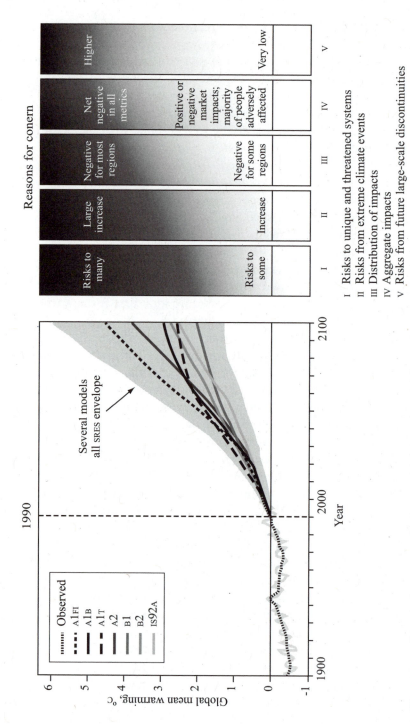

Figure 11.1   Reasons for concern about projected climate change impacts.
Source: IPCC (2001b). Reprinted with permission of IPCC.

and, from the literature, identified different levels of risks or levels of impacts. They are illustrated in the right-hand panel of figure 11.1.

The first barometer indicated risks to unique and threatened systems, which were ecosystems such as alpine tundra, coastal mangroves, and boreal forests. This indicator represented a discourse about environmental vulnerabilities. A yellow alert (light grey in the black and white version shown here) was assigned to the beginning of a temperature change, indicating that some ecosystems would experience new climate-related risks even at small changes in temperature. This yellow (light grey) alert extended to a warming of around 1.5°C, at which point the indicator became red (dark grey), signifying risks to many ecosystems. The second barometer, which indicated risks from extreme climate events, was just slightly different from the first one. The threshold for a large increase in risk was set around 2°C.

The other three barometers were more difficult because of the complexity of the issues that had to be considered. The indicator labelled "distribution of impacts" was meant to show that initially some sectors and regions might benefit from the first increment of warming, while others might experience damage or loss. At what point in the warming path would everybody lose? As a social concern, this is very problematic, because in the initial stages of warming, the negative effects on some regions may be quite substantial compared to those on other regions. For example, citizens of a semi-arid tropical country or a small island state may object to the idea that a cold region such as Canada would benefit from the first 0.5°C or 1°C of global-scale warming, even though the sea level would be rising up to their doorsteps. How could a cold region enjoy increased wheat yields if small island states would be worried about the survival of their communities in the face of sea level rise and storm surge? This indicator suggests that impacts become negative for most regions at a point where damages and losses are felt in cold regions as well, and this threshold was defined as being between 2°C and 3°C. A similar compromise was generated for the fourth indicator, on aggregate impacts, which was an expression of economic gains and losses.

The fifth category, risks from future large-scale discontinuities, represented the low probability but high-risk scenario illustrated in the movie The Day after Tomorrow. This is the risk of a shutdown of the thermohaline circulation in the North Atlantic Ocean, resulting from freshwater inputs from ice melting in the Arctic and Greenland lowering the salinity of the ocean in the North Atlantic. Although it is likely that there will be some impact on North Atlantic circulation, IPCC (2007c) has concluded that a shutdown is very unlikely. Other possible extreme risks include the failure of the Asian monsoon. For this category, a higher risk is indicated occurring only at a warming of about 5°C. Following the publication of this figure (IPCC 2001b), a discourse on dangerous climate change has emerged, and there has been a somewhat informal consensus that a warming above 2°C would be dangerous (Hare and Meinshausen 2004; Ott et al. 2004).

LINKING CLIMATE CHANGE AND SUSTAINABLE DEVELOPMENT

Climate change and sustainable development create complex issues that draw on scholarship and dialogue from diverse communities. Both issues have become visible to the public, although they are poorly defined and poorly understood. It might be assumed that sustainability is a good goal to achieve or that climate change is a big problem that can hamper efforts at achieving sustainability, but the two discourses about these two problems have evolved in quite different ways. It has been difficult to bring the two together for the purposes of policy-making and problem solving. The two issues do have common elements, and the IPCC has recently recognized the need for articulating how climate change and sustainable development should be linked. However, there is still a long way to go before science policy advice will emerge that can address both challenges in a holistic way.

The Evolution of the Climate Change Discourse

The climate change discourse has evolved from several distinct research efforts that are roughly divided in a manner similar to the division of the IPCC Working Groups (figure 11.2). The root, or pedigree, of climate science (Working Group I), impacts and adaptation studies (Working Group II), and energy and GHG emissions studies (Working Group III) can be traced to research activities that coalesced around these themes during the 1970s and 1980s. The research effort did not appear to include any clearly recognizable set of sustainability or development research specialists or practitioners.

The climate science discourse evolved from atmospheric and carbon cycle modelling and oceanography to the development of the first-generation general circulation models (GCMs) in the early 1980s. They were followed by more advanced global climate models, as well as

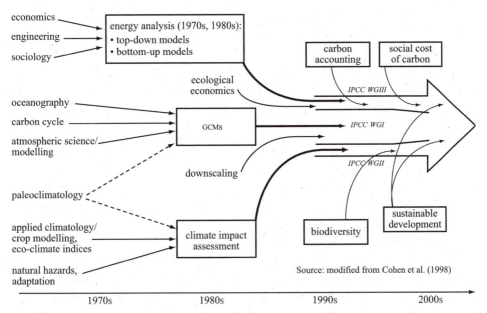

Figure 11.2   Evolution of climate change discourse, 1970 to present.
Source: Updated from Cohen et al. (1998)

downscaling from the global to a regional scale. This change contributed to the body of knowledge being generated within Working Group I. Initially, this topic dominated the *First Assessment Report* (Houghton, Jenkins, and Ephraums 1990), which is why the horizontal bar on the right-hand side of figure 11.2 is drawn more broadly than the ones representing the other two working groups.

The discourse of Working Group II (on impacts and adaptation) originated largely from the rather fragmented field of climate impact assessment, which drew its information and its tools from natural-hazards studies, applied climatology, crop modelling, ecoclimatic indicators, and paleoclimatology. Working Group III, which focused on GHG mitigation, brought in knowledge from the energy-modelling efforts that were taking place in the 1970s and 1980s, including efforts in economics and engineering, some sociological perspectives on the diffusion of energy technologies, and more recently, some information from ecological economics.

As the IPCC process advanced through second and third assessments, more attention was given to the impacts and adaptation issues and the mitigation issues, as shown by the widening of two of the bars in the arrow in figure 11.2, so that all three become more equal in width.

The Evolution of the Sustainable Development Discourse

The Stockholm Conference on Environment and Development, held in 1972, helped launch a generation of research and activism, ultimately leading to international action. Sustainable development as a concept can be traced back to Brown (1981), who wrote about the idea of a sustainable society. This became the theme of the World Commission on Environment and Development (WCED), led by Prime Minister Brundtland of Norway, which became known as the Brundtland Commission (WCED 1987).

Sustainable development was defined as "development that meets the needs of the present without compromising the ability of future generations to meet their own needs" (WCED 1987, cited in McCarthy et al. 2001a, 994). This represents a call for intergenerational equity. Although it has been difficult to define this idea in practical terms, the WCED indicated that it involved three pillars: economic, environmental, and social. Development was meant to provide economic prosperity, preserve ecological integrity, and ensure equitable access to resources, the latter being a measure of social justice.

The sustainability dialogue evolved from a number of threads. Robinson (2004) outlines the history. One thread was the long-standing desire for the preservation of nature, which was challenged by the idea of using technology to ameliorate environmental degradation. In other words, a choice was to be made between conservation through a technical fix and lifestyle adjustment through value change. Figure 11.3 illustrates how, ultimately, the ideas of preservation, conservation, and responding to various environmental challenges, as well as concerns of developing countries, coalesced around the ideas of limits to growth (see chapter 10) and sustainable development. Developing countries have long been concerned about the unequal distribution of income whereby a small percentage of the world's population controls such a large amount of the world's income. This creates disparities in decision making and access to resources, and it forces people to do environmentally damaging things with their land that perhaps they would not want to do. Sustainable development would avoid producing the stresses (or forces) that bring about such environmental damages.

The key argument supporting the need for a broader definition of development as sustainable has been that social, economic, and environmental concerns need to be integrated. Environmental problems should not be the sole focus but must become connected with such issues as

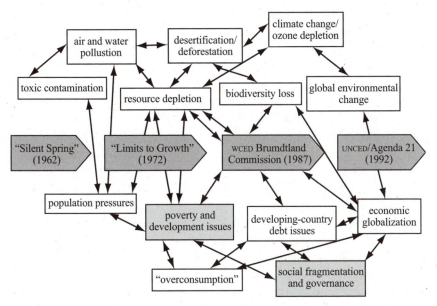

Figure 11.3   Evolution of sustainable development discourse. WCED is the World
Commission on Environment and Development, led by Prime Minister Brundtland of
Norway. UNCED is the United Nations Conference on Environment and Development,
also known as the Earth Summit, which took place in Rio de Janeiro.
Source: Robinson and Herbert (2001). Reprinted with permission of John Robinson and
Deborah Herbert

poverty, trade, culture, investment, and jobs. Robinson and Herbert
(2001) point out that this connection would offer a new way to concep-
tualize response options and that it would organize our thinking about
future worlds and future possibilities.

Planning for sustainable development has, however, become a very
complex problem. The lack of consensus on what this concept actually
means has led to the view that it can be what anybody wants it to be. In
other words, "sustainable" can be attached to "development" without
any real change in the process of planning and practice (Magalhaes
1998). This is a direct challenge to the idea that there are limits to
growth. One way to confront such limits has been to focus on technical
fixes that can enable economies to grow in a clean manner (consider the
Kyoto measure CDM). Rather than forcing us to accept the old idea that
GHG emissions increases are an inevitable part of economic growth,
technology should make it possible for us to decouple energy demand
and/or GHG emissions from increases in gross domestic product. But as

Robinson (2004, 379) points out, "deferring the arrival of limits does not make these limits non-existent."

Consequences of the Separation of the Climate Change and Sustainable Development Discourses

We can see differences in the origins of the climate change and sustainable development discourses when we compare the two. Climate change was initially perceived as a science problem defined by government and academic scientists who then convinced a few other people in governments, who convinced more people, until the belief that it was a problem subsequently mushroomed from there. The idea of sustainable development, however, originated from people who were largely in nongovernment, academic, and community-based organizations and who were recognizing problems and articulating those problems through public communications, such as Rachel Carson's *Silent Spring*.

It is actually quite remarkable that the message about potential warming of the global climate could be presented, and taken seriously, when the first global climate model projections for increased concentrations of CO_2 were published in the 1960s (see chapter 2). At this time temperatures had declined since the 1940s, and the opinions of climatologists regarding future climate trends were divided (National Defense University 1978; Glantz, Robinson, and Krenz 1985). The message must have been difficult to deliver, and yet within just a few years, before the warming trends of the 1980s and 1990s were observed, a global movement emerged that ultimately led to the UNFCCC (see chapter 2). Does that mean the climate models really got it right? Or are we still experiencing something else?

A comparison of the climate change and sustainable development discourses reveals some significant differences in their origins, evolution, and how they are perceived. First, the research efforts that led to their public visibility were quite different. Climate change research efforts were, and still are to some extent, dominated by natural scientists. Economics is important in research on GHG mitigation, and it could play a greater role in impacts and adaptation issues. Social science research concerning impacts and adaptation is also expanding (see chapters 4 and 7). On the other hand, the sustainable development literature is largely an effort from the social sciences, and a lot of it is not very well developed.

Climate change was initially defined as an emissions reduction problem. Science identified the link between GHG emissions and future changes in climate, but it has been more difficult to identify the potential impacts and vulnerabilities. The original Kyoto Protocol document has much more language and policy measures on mitigation than on adaptation, and it has been only recently, particularly since the Marrakech Agreement at COP-7, that specific measures to support adaptation have been identified for financial support (see Yohe et al. 2007; see also chapters 8 and 9).

Sustainable development was defined as a problem through a number of different kinds of interests, and it was easy to attract a lot of support for policy actions that had tended to be rather vaguely defined. The Millennium Development Goals or MDGs (United Nations 2004) have identified some specific actions on, for example, poverty reduction and improvement of water supplies that in principle are easy to agree with and support. The 2002 World Summit on Sustainable Development adopted the Johannesburg Declaration, which included a call for improved efficiency in the use of resources and for a reduction in degradation and waste. Within national programs, GHG emissions reduction is specifically identified as a sustainable development measure that also addresses climate change (UNFCCC 2004). However, GHG mitigation has been seen as a threat to the fossil fuel industry, so any policy instrument designed specifically to reduce fossil fuel production and consumption has faced resistance by businesses and governments that depended on those fuels for their economic survival and growth.

The long separation of the climate change and sustainable development discourses has led to three problems. First, the two communities have been looking at the future very differently, and because both had to do research based on scenarios of the future, how those scenarios were constructed made a difference to their views of the future. Initially, the climate change scenarios that the IPCC developed in 1992 (the IS92 series) were quite narrowly defined as extrapolations or changes in certain economic and energy growth indicators. On the other hand, the narratives used for constructing development scenarios included narratives about international relationships and technological development (Gallopin et al. 1997; Robinson and Herbert 2001). More recently, the IPCC created a different set of storylines for their emissions scenarios, the SRES scenarios (see chapters 2, 3, and 8).

Second, because climate change was so focussed on mitigation, even as adaptation became more visible as a policy measure, climate change and sustainable development were seen as separate endeavours. That meant that there was institutional separation within governments, with different departments focussed on different aspects of climate change policy. Energy and ecosystem issues were not addressed in an integrative manner, which led to a narrowing of the debate about climate change responses.

Third, the separation affected the relationship between science and policy. Climate change was seen not as part of the bigger development problem but as something narrower, and since climate policy was defined mostly with respect to GHG emissions, it left out other concerns (Cohen et al. 1998). Meanwhile, sustainable development programs have communicated concerns about climate change responses being focussed on GHG emissions. For example, the Millennium Development Goals (United Nations 2004) identified specific targets, such as poverty and hunger reduction, reversal of deforestation, and improvement in water supplies, that are very similar to the goals of improving adaptive capacity and reducing vulnerability to climate change. However, the language of the MDGs does not link these goals to climate change. In other words, both communities continue to communicate climate change largely as posing a GHG emissions mitigation challenge, without expressing the adaptation challenges that are common to both (Yohe et al. 2007).

This does not mean that the linkage between development and climate change adaptation remains unrecognized within the development community. Climate change is identified as a serious risk to poverty reduction in developing countries, particularly because these countries have a limited capacity to cope with climate variability and extremes. The World Bank (2003) indicated that adaptation measures will need to be integrated into strategies of poverty reduction to ensure sustainable development and that doing so will require improved governance, mainstreaming of climate change measures into poverty reduction strategies and strategies for sustainable development, and the integration of climate change impacts information into national economic projections.

EFFORTS TO LINK CLIMATE CHANGE AND SUSTAINABLE DEVELOPMENT

There are two-way linkages between climate change and sustainable development. Any policy that is developed for either of the two issues could affect the other issue (figure 11.4). Sustainable development policies can influence climate change through alternative development paths, sectoral policies, institutional changes, and technological changes. What happens with sustainable development could very easily affect

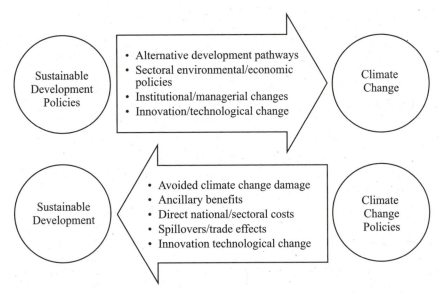

Figure 11.4   Two-way linkages between sustainable development and climate change responses.
Source: Swart, Robinson, and Cohen (2003)

emissions paths, land-use choices, and development choices. A specific climate change policy emerging from a Kyoto instrument, including emissions trading and joint implementation, would have implications for development. If the Kyoto instruments were successful at reducing GHG emissions, climate change damage could be avoided.

If there was a successful adaptation program, which might not have occurred without a climate change policy, climate change damage could be avoided again. There could be indirect benefits, and there could also be indirect costs. Climate change adaptation policy could become expensive. Some adaptation strategies, such as large-scale irrigation and hydroelectric development, would benefit large groups and national interests but might harm local, indigenous, and poor populations (Kates et al. 2001; Huq et al. 2003). There could be direct national and sectoral costs, as well as trade effects. And like any sustainable development policy, this could spur on innovation and technological change. Two different sets of policies and two different sets of policy discourses are emerging with the potential to affect each other.

Recognition of the need to improve the communication and research linkages between the climate change and sustainable development efforts led the IPCC to address these linkages in a conceptual way in the

Third Assessment Report (Banuri et al. 2001) and to construct the SRES GHG emissions scenarios according to development narratives, rather than basing them on the extrapolation of past economic and emissions trends, which was done with the IS92 scenarios. This effort broadened to include a wider range of literature in the *Fourth Assessment Report* (Yohe et al. 2007; Sathaye et al. 2007).

Meanwhile, the Millennium Ecosystem Assessment (MEA) has constructed another set of global-development scenarios: Global Orchestration, Order from Strength, Adapting Mosaic, and TechnoGarden (MEA 2005). In some ways, these are similar to the SRES storylines. Global Orchestration and TechnoGarden include high levels of international cooperation similar to the SRES A1 and B1 scenarios, respectively. The Order from Strength and Adapting Mosaic storylines focus on regional-scale actions similar to SRES A2 and B2, respectively. Both sets of scenarios incorporate a range of driving forces, including population, the economy, technology, energy, and land use change.

An important difference between the SRES and the MEA stories is that for the first time an explicit assumption about climate policy is incorporated into one of the MEA scenarios. The TechnoGarden scenario includes stabilization of GHG concentrations at the CO_2 equivalent of 550 ppm (table 11.1). Resulting climate change is indicated to be +1.9°C by 2100. This amount of warming is the lowest of the four MEA scenarios. The SRES B1 case has similar CO_2 concentrations, but without an explicit climate policy. The projected warming is also similar. The warmest scenarios are Global Orchestration and SRES A1FI, with warming by 2100 of 3.5°C and 4.8°C, respectively. A1FI assumes a global population of 11.3 billion by 2050 and 12–15 billion by 2100. None of the MEA scenarios exceed a population of 10.5 billion by 2100.

Another difference is that the MEA series distinguishes between outcomes for industrial and for developing countries in each scenario. The scenarios include indicators of provisioning services (for example, food and water), of regulating services (for example, climate regulation and disease control), and of cultural services (for example, cultural diversity and knowledge systems). The worst-case scenario is Order from Strength, in which developing countries are predicted to experience degradation of all services, while industrial countries would see most of their provisioning services remain unchanged and other services degrade.

The MEA (2005) has assessed the effectiveness of a wide range of policy responses that have been implemented to achieve various policy goals. The main areas of interest are biodiversity conservation, food,

Table 11.1
Comparison of SRES and MEA Temperature Scenarios

	SRES–A1	SRES–A2	SRES–B1	SRES–B2	MEA Global Orchestration	MEA Order from Strength	MEA Adapting Mosaic	MEA Techno-Garden
Population in 2050 (billions)	8.7	11.3	8.6–8.7	9.3	8.1	9.6	9.5	8.8
Climate policy	No	No	No	No	No	No	No	Stabilize at 550ppm
Warming (°C) by 2100	2.6 (A1T) to 4.5 (A1FI)	3.8	2.0	2.7	3.5	3.3	2.8	1.9

Source: Adapted from Nakicenovic and Swart (2000), Cubasch et al. (2001), and MEA (2005).

fresh water, forest products, nutrient cycling, flood and storm regulation, disease regulation, cultural services, climate change, and integrated responses. The specific climate change measures are the UNFCCC and the Kyoto Protocol (institutional), GHG emissions reduction (technological), land use and land cover change, market mechanisms, and adaptation. All these measures are seen as promising, such that they are likely to succeed or there are ways of making them more effective. However, the UNFCCC and the Kyoto Protocol are also rated as problematic because their emissions reduction targets may not be met.

The MEA's rating of integrated responses is also promising, and indeed, the sub-national and local approaches are rated as effective. Examples include sustainable-forest management, integrated coastal-zone management, and integrated river basin management. Some concerns have been raised regarding the lack of implementation capacity in some countries.

It is important to note that these measures can also be part of climate change adaptation policy, and there may be opportunities for shared investments in these measures. It is not clear, however, whether there has been a real integration of climate change adaptation and sustainable-development efforts. The Millennium Development Goals (United Nations 2004) include ensuring environmental sustainability, such as through the reversal of deforestation and through improving water supplies. Unfortunately, since 1990 progress has been slow or insignificant in many developing regions, particularly in sub-Saharan Africa and Oceania.

How has the IPCC brought sustainable development issues into the climate change process? Figure 11.5 illustrates how climate policy should

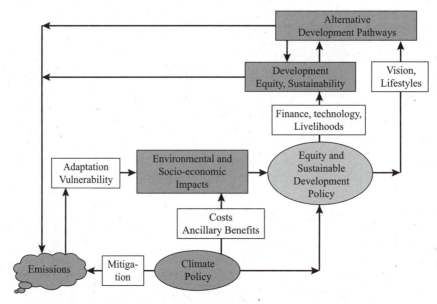

Figure 11.5   Linking climate policy and development policy.
Source: Banuri et al. (2001). Reprinted with permission of IPCC

become part of development policy. The promotion of alternative development pathways is linked directly to GHG emissions. Adaptation would influence how emissions would lead to impacts, but it is mitigation that directly emanates from climate policy. More recently, the IPCC has offered expanded assessments of linkages between climate change and sustainable development, from both the adaptation and the mitigation perspectives, including consideration of new analyses of the social cost of carbon, which offers an indicator of overall global damage cost due to climate change per unit of carbon emission (Sathaye et al. 2007; Yohe et al. 2007).

THE EMERGENCE OF A SOUTH-NORTH DIALOGUE

Climate change has often been characterized as being solely a challenge of GHG mitigation. Most national economies have been closely linked with their GHG emissions, because high levels of GDP and economic growth have historically been accompanied by high per capita GHG emissions (figure 11.6; also see figure 9.13). Recognition of this fact led to the Kyoto Protocol identifying emissions targets only for developed countries. Of course, this did not mean that the purpose of these targets

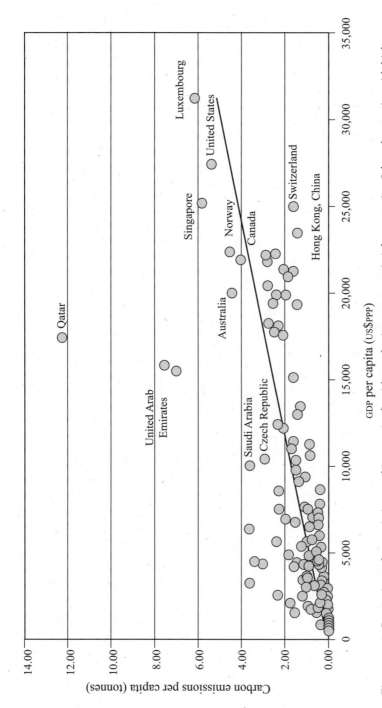

Figure 11.6 Per capita carbon emissions and income (us$, with purchasing power parity) for countries. Selected countries with high income and/or high per capita carbon emissions are named.
Source: Banuri et al. (2001). Reprinted with permission of IPCC

was to reduce economic growth. The goal was to encourage cleaner development paths that "de-link" GHG emissions and economic growth, at least to some degree. The question is, how could this be achieved in developed and developing countries, given their unique circumstances of resource availability and human capacity for both mitigation and adaptation? And, since it is clear that no climate policy could succeed without all countries participating in efforts to create cleaner development paths, how could such policies be equitably created so that no country felt that it was being unfairly burdened? In other words, how should climate policy evolve post-Kyoto?

One recent example of a new dialogue on climate policy is a "south-north" dialogue organized by the Wuppertal Institute in Germany (Ott et al. 2004). If economic growth is still coupled with emissions growth, then how can an equitable approach to mitigation be defined? How can the dialogue on emissions reduction move beyond this notion that the world can be split into the two camps of developed and developing countries? Developing countries are contributing to increases in GHG concentrations, and the atmosphere does not care where the emissions come from. While developing-country emissions are part of the problem, at the moment these countries do not have emissions targets. So, how are they to play a part in the solution? As well, no distinction is made between larger industrializing developing countries, such as China and India, and poor agrarian countries in sub-Saharan Africa. How can the climate policy dialogue move to another stage where we no longer see the developing world as one giant block?

In this dialogue (Ott et al. 2004), the idea is to find consensus on differentiated mitigation commitments for developing countries. Developed countries would still continue to financially support this effort. By taking on such targets, however, developing countries may actually start to do things to influence their own development paths, and so climate policy would contribute to sustainability for these countries. The second part of this solution is to find ways to incorporate adaptation as well, because there are no adaptation targets in any climate change instrument. Is there a way to create an appropriate sharing of the burden to address the needs of vulnerable countries?

In chapter 9, we introduced the idea of contraction and convergence, which says that every country should have the same per capita GHG emissions rate. This would mean that China, India, and other developing countries would be entitled to increases in per capita emissions, while developed countries, including Canada, would have to reduce their per capita rates. Ultimately, all per capita emissions rates would converge around a mid-point (Jepma and Munasinghe 1998; Shukla 1999; Global Commons Institute 2008). But what should this convergence point be? Should it be based on a GHG stabilization level, and if so, how should this be determined?"

This new south-north dialogue represents an alternative to a forced contraction and convergence. Rather than treating all developing countries as forming one big undifferentiated group, this idea urges us not to put China, Bangladesh, and Mali in the same category, since there ought to be opportunities for these countries to engage differently. If they accepted emissions reductions targets, developing countries would then be considered as Annex I countries under the UNFCCC and so would become eligible to participate in emissions trading while still receiving investments through the CDM.

Four broad themes have been proposed for an equitable approach to climate policy (Ott et al. 2004):

1 Differential capabilities in accepting emissions targets. Certain developing countries would accept emissions targets, but those targets might not necessarily look like Canada's target or Great Britain's target. Nevertheless, they would still be targets.
2 Differential impacts and differential adaptive capabilities. Impacts and capabilities need to be recognized and addressed, with support offered to improve adaptive capacity.
3 Different capacities to engage in an equitable climate policy at the political level within developing countries.
4 Intra-national equity and recognition of differential capabilities within countries. For example, within Canada, there is a big difference between how the Arctic and the Great Lakes become involved in climate policy. Similarly in Brazil, there are differences between the regions in the northeast and in the south.

Ott et al. (2004) proposed grouping the developing countries into four categories (table 11.2). Each group is distinguished by their emissions rates and economic status. Note how they compare with Annex II countries. The fifteen Newly Industrial Countries (NIC) have higher emissions per unit GDP than the Annex II countries. They also tend to have higher per capita emissions rates but lower incomes and lower total emissions. Their incomes are higher than those of the EIT countries. These indicators suggest that the NICs have relatively dirty economies,

Table 11.2
Criteria for Differentiating Groups of Countries for Emissions Targets

Countries	Annex II (25[a])	NICS (15)	RIDCS (37)	Other DCs (39)	LDCS (49)
CO₂/GDP (tonnes CO₂/ million US$)	210–706 (EIT = 385 – 1,768)	48–2,325	109–867	86–1,833	17–1,015
GHG/capita (tons CO₂)	7.1–24.9 (EIT = 4.4–14.0)	4.5–67.9	1.3–19.8	1.0–11.5	0.2–5.7
GDP/capita (USD PPP)	16,530–53,410 (27,526) (EIT = 7,011)	1,700– 23,700 (10,701)	3,740–20,330 (5,025)	860–8,900 (2,602)	450–5,650 (1,205)
Emissions in 2000 (Mt CO₂)	13,622 (EIT = 3,829)	1,714	8,695	4,095	945

Source: Adapted from Ott et al. (2004).
[a] This number does not include the 15 EIT countries: EIT = economies in transition (former Soviet Union and Eastern Europe).
Note: The four groups are newly industrialized countries (NIC; e.g., Israel, South Korea, Saudi Arabia), rapidly industrializing developing countries (RIDC; e.g., Brazil, China, Mexico), other developing countries (ODC; e.g., Egypt, India, Paraguay), and least developed countries (LDC; e.g., Bangladesh, Mali, Samoa). Number of countries in each group indicated in parentheses.

which means that it takes a lot of CO_2 to earn a dollar. Why? Is it because of inefficient technologies? Or, is it because the commodities they produce are not worth very much compared to the high-end service activities that are produced by developed countries? The other categories exhibit progressively smaller emissions rates and economic activity. The least-developed country (LDC) category includes some Sahel countries that emit less than one tonne of GHGs per person.

The proposal for differentiated commitments calls for the NICs to accept absolute reduction targets through domestic mitigation efforts. NICs would help fund their own mitigation efforts, and additional funding would be provided by Annex II countries. The next category, the rapidly industrializing developing countries (RIDCs), would also have domestic targets if, in addition to providing some of their own funding and technology, the Annex II countries provided considerable financial support using the CDM. Recall that the Annex I group includes the EIT countries from Eastern Europe, whereas Annex II does not. The other two groups of countries, the other developing countries (other DCs) and the LDCs, would not be obligated to accept an emissions target and would receive support payments from Annex II to support clean development.

Now, how did this dialogue address adaptation? It was proposed that adaptation would be funded by the Annex I countries. Capacity building would be needed for specific sectors, but there would also have to be more education. The current funding rules at the UN Global Environmental Facility (GEF) would need to be modified to remove the constraint that adaptation projects had to demonstrate global benefits. Like the rules designed for emissions reduction activities, the current GEF rules focus on global benefits of projects. This focus can be appropriate for emissions reduction, since if there is a reduction of a tonne of carbon anywhere, it is easy to show a connection to global GHG concentrations, radiative forcing, and resulting climate change. For example, in Costa Rica, the reduction of a tonne of carbon through a particular activity would have a global benefit. However, if a different activity could reduce vulnerability in Costa Rica, then it would have a local benefit, rather than a global one. But if the rule said that Costa Rica had to show that this vulnerability-reduction project had benefits at a higher scale, there would be a big concern that there would be no incentive to fund an adaptation activity. Dialogue is continuing on this point (Huq 2002; Huq and Reid 2004).

Risk transfer mechanisms, including insurance, could also play a part in adaptation. Could they become part of international climate policy? One proposal is to create burden sharing through public-private partnerships. Could a mixture of governments and private insurance companies combine to help support risk reduction in developing countries? Could that be supported within a Kyoto framework? And could the availability of insurance be used as an incentive to reduce vulnerability? Hamilton (2004) cites examples of a catastrophe insurance fund that could serve as an incentive for local governments to enforce building codes more rigorously than they presently do or to take other prescribed loss reduction measures in order to be eligible for coverage. Such a fund would reduce weather-related damages incurred during floods and other extreme events.

SUSTAINABLE DEVELOPMENT POLICY AS PART OF CLIMATE POLICY

Ratification of the Kyoto Protocol has led to implementation of its mechanisms, including the CDM. This offers an early opportunity to assess their effectiveness in meeting both climate policy and sustainable development policy goals. There are some preliminary indications that

CDM projects in developing countries are leading to reductions in GHG emissions, but they are not contributing to poverty reduction or employment generation, two key indicators of sustainable development (Michaelowa and Michaelowa 2007; Sutter and Parreño 2007).

What policy actions should be taken in order to improve the performance of climate policy measures in achieving sustainable development goals? One proposal for incorporating sustainable development policy within the UNFCCC is for developing countries to commit themselves to implementing and accelerating national sustainable development plans (Winkler et al. 2004). Developing countries would quantify the effects of such plans on GHG emissions, in order to determine which plans create synergies between development and climate change, and which cause conflicts. In a manner similar to the south-north idea described above, these measures could become mandatory for middle-income developing countries (Bodansky, Chou, and Jorge-Tresolini 2004). Funding could be through existing UNFCCC and Kyoto programs, including CDMs and the GEF. A key issue here would be the designation of countries for mandatory participation and the nature of the review process for monitoring compliance. As well, this proposal does not suggest any emissions targets for developing countries.

CLIMATE POLICY AND SUSTAINABLE DEVELOPMENT

In their landmark publication, *Human Choices & Climate Change*, Rayner and Malone (1998) offered a number of suggestions addressing the human dimensions of climate change. Many of them can be applied to the challenge of linking climate change and sustainable development. The first suggestion is that climate change should be viewed holistically and not simply as a problem of emissions reduction. This suggestion is relevant not only for those interested in climate policy, but also for those who seek to represent climate change within the development context, for a particular community or for the world as a whole. The MEA and MDG efforts illustrate how climate change is being considered as a development challenge. The search is still on, however, for practical approaches to implement measures that address both emissions and vulnerabilities. There are technical challenges in doing this, but if there are shortcomings, it won't be for lack of trying.

A second idea is about the importance of institutional limits, namely, the ability of different countries in different regions to address climate change from a governance perspective. What is a good governance model for preparing a jurisdiction for an externally driven global problem that affects each place differently? It is not enough just to regulate the local smoke stack.

A number of other drivers will have greater direct impacts on populations than climate change alone. We can not assume that in the future everything else will remain equal and only climate will change. Planning is an important component of governance, and there are many examples of community and national development plans, but there will be limits to them, and we have to anticipate those limits.

Rayner and Malone (1998) also point out that the research effort needs to avoid being bounded by disciplinary constraints. We should not put all our analytical eggs in one basket. It is to be hoped that many different disciplines will contribute to finding an answer. There may be policy models that work well in theory, but practical applications will depend on convincing a broad array of practitioners and community leaders to buy in (see chapter 12). In the "real world," decision makers are faced with immediate concerns related to economic development, health, resource management, and community safety. How can climate change concerns be incorporated into this kind of decision-making environment? The term mainstreaming is now being used to describe the act of bringing into focus an issue that may have been previously perceived as out of range or irrelevant by decision makers and the public at large (for example, Huq et al. 2003). Can climate change be mainstreamed into current debates about transit, health systems, navigation, and so on? Can we take regional and local approaches to an issue that is global in scale?

Vulnerability reduction is an important goal, but actions are difficult to define. If it was easy, it would have been done long ago. There are many reasons why it is so difficult. Local-scale vulnerability reduction, the promotion of resilience, and building adaptive capacity are far away from the realms of climate models. And yet, the climate change issue, which was initially expressed through climate model simulations and biophysical-impact models, has contributed to a new research effort on climate change scenarios that has generated new insights about potential future surprises. These insights have injected new energy into a debate about global development futures by reminding everyone that we should not be complacent about the future somehow taking care of itself.

But if current policy on climate change is seen as problematic (MEA 2005), what then is the way forward? The IPCC (Banuri et al. 2001;

Sathaye et al. 2007) has indicated that for Kyoto mechanisms to work, there need to be supportive policy decisions by national governments directed at capacity building, institutional development, and mainstreaming climate change into domestic planning processes, and at approving and monitoring emissions reduction projects. The perception of Kyoto-related decisions will be influenced by attitudes about climate-related vulnerabilities, uncertainties, and risks.

This is an international problem. It will be individual countries that respond, and they will need institutional capabilities if their response is to be efficient, reliable, and affordable. Increasing the capacity of governments to manage the processes of climate change project approval, project monitoring, and GHG emissions reporting will be crucial in enabling countries to be able to participate in Kyoto mechanisms such as the CDM and JI. Participation in ET and other mechanisms will require national governments to organize reporting and verification activities that will include the private sector and community interests.

The role of communication is also very important for both climate policy and sustainable development policy. Governments may be able to propose policy changes, but the ability to carry these changes out will depend on public acceptance. Moser (2004) identifies five connections between communication and social change:

1 problem detection and identification,
2 communication to educate the public,
3 problem framing,
4 communication from the public to governments, and
5 identifying accessible solutions.

Problem framing, for example, is important because it puts climate change into a broader context as something more than just simply a science problem. If climate change is presented as an issue of sustainability, rather than just an issue of science, this characterization will influence who feels addressed, what counts as convincing evidence, and how the problem evolves as a policy matter.

Where is this debate going? Clearly there are two-way linkages between climate and sustainability issues that depend on underlying development paths, yet development choices are being made without thinking about sustainability or climate change. How can climate change policy be mainstreamed into the places where people live while somehow remaining consistent with development goals, preferably sustainable development goals? Where are new technologies going to fit into this? Clearly opportunities are emerging. Hybrid cars, green roofs, and other emerging technologies appear to be promising. How can such technologies become incorporated into developing countries?

And, what about vulnerability reduction and adaptation? What does the hazards community have to offer? We have had considerable experience with hazards in different contexts, and yet for some reason, there are still problems with weather-related extreme events, even in developed countries with high adaptive capacity. Mileti (1999) points out that our society still assumes that technology and management can control nature and protect people. There are of course various ways to protect people, including soft approaches such as land use zoning to keep high-density residential developments or expensive industrial developments out of vulnerable areas, but there are driving forces that lead people and businesses to locate in areas vulnerable to weather-related events. They do so because governments provide structures and facilities that are designed to offer protection.

Wilbanks (2003) identifies how increased awareness of climate change at the local level can induce cities to explore local adaptation strategies and at the same time raise their voices in support of global GHG mitigation efforts through the International Cities for Climate Protection Programme. This suggests that place-based analyses can identify connections between sustainable development and climate change impacts, which could influence attempts to mainstream climate change adaptation into development plans, particularly in developing countries. It would then be possible to build on this and create a learning opportunity that includes mitigation as well. Bizikova et al. (2007) describe opportunities for local-scale case studies that link adaptation-mitigation-sustainable development, or AMSD, which could address the kinds of problems described earlier, in figure 9.10.

The climate change challenge involes a lot more than climate. It is a hybrid: an interdisciplinary science challenge and a science-policy bridge-building challenge. It clearly needs a broader definition and a broader research effort than it has had, especially regarding human dimensions. That does not mean that all the biophysical aspects of climate change are known. Scientific uncertainties continue to affect the confidence of scientists in reaching conclusions about various aspects of climate trends, climate futures, and impacts futures.

DISCUSSION

Climate change and climate change policy will have an impact on how countries choose alternative development paths. Development policy will affect the production and consumption of energy and materials and the patterns of movement of goods and people. These patterns will in turn influence future global GHG emissions, local vulnerabilities, and the capacities of developed and developing countries to adapt. But how would climate change affect development paths? This is an interdisciplinary research challenge. There are a number of options, including integrated assessments using both models and participatory approaches. Now that Kyoto is ratified, the future of climate change and sustainable development policy will depend on advances in technology, learning more about science, finding better ways to link climate change to the development process, and making the dialogue better, richer, and more meaningful to governments and the people they serve. These tasks will require a sustained investment in shared learning experiences between researchers and communities of all kinds.

12

Conclusion

With this chapter, we now reach the conclusion of our tour through the many dimensions of human-induced climate change. This is a complex story of biophysical systems being affected by human activities and creating a phenomenon that is commonly known as global warming. As we have seen, the global-warming story is being weaved from a combination of theories, observations, scenarios, and arguments, many of which remain contentious. Despite the uncertainties, however, there is consensus on some key aspects.

First, the chemistry of the atmosphere is being altered by human activities. There is no doubt that atmospheric concentrations of CO_2, CH_4, and other GHGs are rapidly increasing because of emissions from fossil fuel burning and land use changes. Second, this change in atmospheric chemistry is leading to an increase in the trapping of long-wave radiation by the earth's atmosphere. This change in radiative forcing of around 2 to 3 w/m^2 appears to be relatively small, less than 0.25 percent of the radiative power of the sun, but this additional radiative energy is accumulating.

Third, observed climate patterns show a warming trend that started at the end of the nineteenth century and is continuing into the twenty-first century. This trend is not linear; it is a real warming and not an artifact of station movements or contamination of observations from local-scale urban heat islands. Evidence to support this observed warming trend has come from observations of Arctic snow cover and sea ice trends, mountain glacier retreats, and the changing phenology of plants and wildlife.

Fourth, the frequency of high-cost weather-related extreme events has been increasing, while the frequency of high-cost earthquakes has not. Although it is not yet clear whether there has been any significant change in extreme weather frequencies that could account for this increase in costs, this trend has drawn attention to the way communities and countries are developing and whether their development paths are leading to unanticipated vulnerabilities.

Fifth, there is scientific consensus on some of the scenarios of biophysical impacts. Examples include impacts on permafrost, mountain glaciers and vegetation, cold region (middle-to high-latitude) agriculture, and coastal zones threatened with sea level rise. There is less certainty regarding other biophysical concerns such as wildlife, biodiversity, and human health.

Uncertainties continue to influence research and policy on a range of questions about climate science, scenario impacts, and adaptation and mitigation. These questions include such diverse problems as cloud processes in climate models, costs of impacts without and with adaptation, and market responses to Kyoto-based and domestic mitigation initiatives. There is also the central question of defining dangerous anthropogenic interference with the climate system, a question that has led to a growing debate regarding a threshold of 2°C as the safe limit of warming. And there continue to be arguments advanced by climate change skeptics who claim that increases in GHG concentrations will have little or no impact on climate or society and that a more significant concern is the potential economic effect of climate change policy measures.

The transformation of global warming from an issue of science to a matter of policy has taken place over a remarkably brief period. My own participation in climate change research began twenty-five years ago, and at that time global warming was not yet on the international political map, but its visibility as an important concern for society was on the verge of increasing dramatically. The first World Climate Conference in 1979 highlighted the impacts of climatic events during the 1970s, particularly the drought in the Sahel and the ENSO effects in Peru. The literature on natural hazards had been bolstered by the publication in 1978 of the Burton, Kates, and White book *The Environment as Hazard*. The emergence of global warming as a societal concern was evident in Kellogg and Schware's (1981) publication, *Climate Change and Society – Consequences of Increasing Atmospheric Carbon Dioxide*, which illustrated the linkages between climate-related ecological impacts and societal structures. They also identified the importance of human perceptions of impacts, and how they would influence the public demand for mitigation and adaptation responses. Climate impact assessment emerged as a field of study with the publication in 1985 of

Climate Impact Assessment, by Kates, Ausubel, and Berberian. This book included chapters on climate sensitivity, biophysical impacts, historical cases, economics, social analysis, perception, and integrated assessment.

Meanwhile, the first GCM simulations of increased CO_2 atmospheres were being published. They provided an opportunity to apply research tools from natural hazards and climate impact assessment to the emerging field of global-warming research. The first case studies based on the first-generation climate model simulations of a doubling of carbon dioxide concentrations, or $2xCO_2$ scenarios, were being published during the 1980s, including a paper I wrote on Great Lakes impacts (Cohen 1986). These scenario studies attracted a great deal of public attention and contributed to the growing effort to craft an international policy on climate change, to be known eventually as the United Nations Framework Convention on Climate Change, which was signed in 1992.

If we consider the pedigree of climate change research at the beginning of the twenty-first century, we can trace its origins to a diverse array of disciplines and interdisciplinary studies. Atmospheric science, oceanography, and studies of the carbon cycle have been the foundation of modern research efforts on climate models, climate trends, and attempts to detect the fingerprint of human interference with the climate system. Studies in natural hazards and applied climatology led to a framework that enabled specialists in fisheries, forestry, health, and other fields to engage in a wider range of studies in which climate change scenarios were applied to various impacts concerns. Energy analyses, which underlie the various GHG emission scenarios, drew on studies of the technical and social aspects of energy production and demand emerging from engineering, economics, and sociology.

Twenty-five years ago, society was on the verge of receiving messages from researchers about natural hazards and the need to prepare for them, about climatic variability and its environmental and societal effects, and about the prospects of global warming from increasing atmospheric concentrations of GHGs. But there were other voices expressing concern that advice and warnings about climate impacts might not be heard. The well-known climatologist Ken Hare raised concerns about the widespread indifference among economists and policy-makers, despite the best efforts of natural scientists: "We [natural scientists] desire to export our convictions, but the buyers are reluctant" (1981, 14). He suggested two possible reasons for this indifference:

1 Climate impacts are often buffered by trade and relief efforts, so identifying the role of climate (e.g., in the food system) is hindered by
  non-linearities and time lags in response.
2 In developing countries, technological, social, and political changes
  have fundamentally altered climate-society relationships and perceptions of risk.

An example was desertification in the Sahel. Slater and Levin (1981)
and Garcia (1981) suggested that desertification and the associated
food supply shortages were more likely the result of bad land management than climatic variability, even though it was known that rainfall in
that region was well below average at that time. In their view, a more
important factor was the change by local herders from a nomadic lifestyle to the development of permanent communities, following the introduction of deep-tube well technology. Instead of adjusting to
seasonal rainfall patterns and water availability, herders kept their livestock near these wells, which eventually led to overgrazing, reduced
vegetation cover, and ultimately a widespread loss of livestock. The
point raised by investigators was that human activity on the ground,
rather than any shift in climate, created this desertification problem.
This example was believed to show how a new technology that offered
to improve conditions for livestock herders became a liability instead.
Garcia (1981) titled his work *Nature Pleads Not Guilty*. Years later,
Michael Glantz (1994) published a book with similar conclusions, entitled *Drought Follows the Plow*.

Meanwhile, others were saying that climate itself was becoming less
important because of changing technologies and lifestyles. A study of
the US Midwest suggested that the impacts of succeeding drought events
would gradually decline because of improved planning and early warning systems. This was known as the "lessening hypothesis" (Warrick
1980). For example, droughts in the United States in the 1970s had less
significant economic and societal impacts than the famous Dust Bowl of
the 1930s, even though they were just as severe climatically. A decade
later, in a commentary entitled *Does Climate Still Matter?*, Ausubel
(1991) suggested that society was gradually becoming climate-proof because of improvements in technology such as heating and air conditioning systems, and irrigation and because of travel opportunities. These
improvements were leading to improved adaptability and a decline in
synchronicity, the natural enforcement of seasonal activities (such as in
agriculture or outdoor recreation).

Twenty-five years later, does Ken Hare's argument still hold? Are the buyers still reluctant? Indeed, is society really becoming climate-proof? How do we sort out the arguments that, say, on the one hand, we are creating new vulnerabilities on the ground, yet on the other hand, we are becoming climate-proof? And, how do we sort this out in a futures-context? We are familiar with arguments about uncertainties in climate models and climate science. But it may be that what we have are clear indications of uncertainties in our understanding of relationships between climate and society, past, and present. If that is the case, what do we need to do in order to improve our understanding of the societal implications of future climate change scenarios?

Clearly, global warming challenges us to be forward-looking and to be extremely cautious about relying on past and present events as analogues of the future. Michael Glantz's *Forecasting by Analogy* (1988) details how analogues may be useful but warns that we could easily fall into the trap of using inappropriate analogies in attempting to assess the implications of a warmer future climate, a climate that is expected to be very different from the climate of the past and present. In a chapter of Glantz's book, Jamieson (1988) pointed out that analogies may fail because of significant differences in technology, differences in political and social organizations, and differences in available information. Even though scenarios carry with them uncertainties about climate and societal futures, scenario-based studies have been and will continue to be a necessary part of the research and dialogue effort to bring the climate change issue closer to the context of decision makers.

In the last quarter century, various research efforts have increased. Climate science research has expanded. Impacts and adaptation studies are now being carried out differently, with greater attention to local interests and local knowledge. Scenarios of future GHG emissions are also being constructed differently, and the literature on mitigation is growing. More and more, climate change studies and assessments are becoming collaborative efforts between disciplines, researchers, and stakeholders (including public- and private-sector resource managers, planners, and community groups). Indeed, as global warming continues to attract attention, it will in due course become best practice to use participatory approaches for climate change adaptation and mitigation research, or at least for consultation and outreach and perhaps for problem framing and expert judgment. But we are not there yet. And in any event, we need to go farther.

Recent extreme events like the 2003 heat wave in France and the ongoing mountain pine beetle epidemic in British Columbia and the

Yukon (an epidemic that now threatens Alberta) are telling us that developed countries with so-called high adaptive capacities are still being surprised by the climate. Munich Re Reinsurance (2007; see also figure 6.8) has shown how the costs of weather-related disasters have been increasing worldwide. The United Nations Development Programme (UNDP 2004) reports that annual natural disaster losses have increased from US$75 billion in the 1960s to US$660 billion in the 1990s (cited in Wilhite 2005). Wilhite's recent book *Drought and Water Crises* concludes that today's droughts are creating greater losses and conflicts than those of several decades ago. Is this really consistent with a lessening hypothesis?

We are now confronted by a new debate – a debate about why the results of climate change impacts, adaptation, and mitigation research are encountering barriers to being "mainstreamed," that is, being applied by governments, communities, and the private sector in an explicit manner within normal planning and management practice. These barriers are also hindering progress on adapting to current climate variability, as well as climate change. Burton and May (2004) have described the adaptation deficit as the gap between the sustainable use of resources and present practice and have argued that climate change will lead to an increased future adaptation deficit. It has also been reported that GHG emissions have been increasing in most developed countries since the 1992 signing of the UNFCCC (MEA 2005; IEA 2006; IPCC 2007b). Economic growth is not being decoupled from GHG emissions growth, at least not yet.

Climate science is promising further advances in climate modelling, particularly in downscaling to regional scales. So as climate models improve, how should we prepare ourselves to generate new opportunities to translate climate futures into damage reports and evaluations of adaptation options? And how should dialogue on mitigation options overcome some of the mistrust that has built up between advocates and opponents of GHG controls, so that a higher level of competence is achieved among the various actors in the dialogue (van de Kerkhof 2004)? One option would be to take what Michael Glantz calls a climate affairs approach. Glantz (2003) proposed that such an approach would look at climate within its human context. Climate affairs would "merge science, impacts, policy, law, economics, and ethics" (xiii). This approach would be needed in order to distinguish those elements that can be legitimately linked to the physical aspects of climate from those that can be linked to societal changes. Glantz concludes by calling for a greater focus on climate-society linkages and on how societal development choices are changing these linkages. Climate change will occur over a moving societal target, with its ever-changing paths of development, so recognizing these linkages is important.

One way to offer a climate affairs perspective is to create participatory processes that are two-way mutual-learning exercises, rather than one-way exercises in consultation and outreach. An example is the study of water management and climate change in the Okanagan region described in chapter 10 (Cohen, Neilsen, and Welbourn 2004; Cohen and Neale 2006). This study evolved over several phases, beginning with scenario studies of water supply and demand and assessments of historical adaptation experiences, leading to group-based model building in partnership with local experts and decision makers. Scenario information was used as input for water management plans (Summit Environmental Consultants Ltd 2004; Okanagan Water Stewardship Council 2008).

The most recent phase of this study included dialogue on design and implementation of adaptation measures, which was facilitated by construction of the group-based model of the Okanagan water system. This model was constructed using dialogue and linkage with previous studies and existing decision support tools (Cohen and Neale 2006; Langsdale et al. 2007). The system model would show the effectiveness of adaptation choices within future scenarios of changing water demand and supply. This would not be a forecast of adaptation performance but a learning opportunity that could help in the mainstreaming of climate change into the regional planning and development context. And it would be the context of the stakeholders as adaptors, not the context of the research team, that would shape the final product.

A general model for a partnership in shared learning about climate change was shown in figure 7.10. The partnership can be initiated either by researchers or community interests. In other words, the choice of originator should not matter. Rather than the initiators distinguishing between top-down and bottom-up approaches – the labels are ambiguous – the choreography of this learning experiment may be determined by whether the initial concern is related to the nature of the biophysical stress itself or socio-economic concerns about climate-related events or policy options.

But, how can research opportunities like this be sustained over the long term? How can we in Canada, and elsewhere, find investors, or indeed, find careers that make it possible to keep such activities going? In agriculture, there has long been a tradition of extension agents acting as a bridge between research and practice. Where are the climate change extension agents? Could this model provide the answer to the adaptation (or mitigation) deficit? Who should support them – federal governments, regional governments, international agencies, or non-government entities? And do we know enough to provide a "best practice" guide for climate change extension work that could be applicable to the regional context in an appropriate manner?

Although it is easy to be pessimistic about future prospects for global-warming research and policy, there are in fact reasons for optimism. Many interesting research efforts are under way around the world, either through international organizations like the United Nations or through bilateral arrangements between developed and developing countries. Many countries maintain domestic research efforts as well, and communications technologies (particularly the Internet) are making these readily accessible to anyone with a personal computer. But just as the Internet can be used for spreading accurate information, it can also, and just as frequently, be used for spreading inaccurate information. The use of the Internet to disseminate information also necessarily excludes those people who do not have access or cannot get access to it.

The sustainability of future learning about climate change will depend on maintaining an open attitude about knowledge that comes from unfamiliar sources. Climate models and integrated assessment models are examples of unfamiliar sources. Dialogue is often seen as a tool of outreach, but dialogue can also be a source of new knowledge, both across disciplines and across cultures. Climate change is the type of mega-problem that cries out for both interdisciplinary and intercultural learning.

In conclusion, we'd like to make three recommendations regarding future directions of climate change research:

1 Learn from the past, but focus on the future. This means that scenarios need to be included in an explicit manner in research and dialogue.
2 Develop partnerships and investments in shared learning, and openly disseminate that learning to the public.
3 Create extension agents for climate change adaptation and mitigation as part of the legacy of shared learning experiences.

An ample literature shows that the communities of academia, government, and non-government bodies have given us an established history of climate change research. Their work was not just produced after the

United Nations Framework Convention on Climate Change was signed. We need to remember this history, and we need to use it to build a climate change community that can offer intellectual growth and improve the quality of its discourse with policy-makers and the public. We need to take advantage of tools that encourage interdisciplinary research and communication and shared learning experiences with practitioners and decision makers. Our hope is that governments, communities, researchers, and individuals with an interest in climate change can continue to forge a research and policy effort that is forward-looking and that is sustained by long-term financial, institutional, and intellectual investments.

Bibliography

Aaheim, H.A. 1999. The appropriateness of economic approaches to the analysis of burden sharing. In *Fair weather? Equity concerns in climate change*, ed. F.L. Toth. London: Earthscan.

Aarhenius, S. 1896. On the influence of carbonic acid in the air upon the temperature of the ground. *Philosophical Magazine*, Series 5, 41(251):237–76.

ACIA (Arctic Climate Impact Assessment). 2004. *Impacts of a warming Arctic.* Cambridge: Cambridge University Press.

Adams, R.M., B.A. McCarl, K. Segerson, C. Rosenzweig, K.J. Bryant, B.L. Dixon, R. Conner, R.E. Evenson, and D. Ojima. 1999. Economic effects of climate change on US agriculture. In *The impact of climate change on the United States economy*, ed. R. Mendelsohn and J.E. Neumann. Cambridge: Cambridge University Press.

Adger, W.N., S. Agrawala, M.Q. Mirza, C. Conde, K. O'Brien, J. Pulhin, R. Pulwarty, B. Smit, and K. Takahashi. 2007. Assessment of adaptation practices, options, constraints, and capacity. In *Climate change 2007: Impacts, adaptation and vulnerability. Contribution of Working Group II to the fourth assessment report of the Intergovernmental Panel on Climate Change*, ed. M.L. Parry, O.F. Canziani, J.P. Palutikof, P.J. van der Linden, and C.E. Hanson. Cambridge : Cambridge University Press, 717–43.

Adger, W.N., K. Brown, and E.L. Tompkins. 2006. The political economy of cross-scale networks in resource co-management. *Ecology and Society* 10 (2): article 9 (online).

Agrawala, S. 1998a. Context and early origins of the Intergovernmental Panel on Climate Change. *Climatic Change* 39:605–20.

– 1998b. Structural and process history of the Intergovernmental Panel on Climate Change. *Climatic Change* 39:621–42.

Aharonian, D. 1994. Land use and climate change: An assessment of climate-society interactions in Aklavik, NWT. In *Mackenzie Basin impact study interim report*, no. 2, ed. S.J. Cohen. North York, ON: Environment Canada.

Ahmad, Q.K., R. A. Warrick, T.E. Downing, S. Nishioka, K.S. Parikh, C. Parmesan, S.H. Schneider, F. Toth, and G. Yohe. 2001. Methods and tools. Chap. 2 in *Climate change 2001: Impacts, adaptation, and vulnerability. Contribution of Working Group II to the third assessment report of the Intergovernmental Panel on Climate Change*, ed. J.J. McCarthy, O.F. Cnaziani, N.A. Leary, D.J. Dokken, and K.S. White. Cambridge: Cambridge University Press, 105–44.

Ainsworth, E.A. and S.P. Long. 2005. What have we learned from 15 years of free-air CO_2 enrichment (FACE)? A meta-analytic review of the responses of photosynthesis, canopy properties and plant production to rising CO_2. *New Phytologist*, 165:351–72.

Albritton, D.L., L.G. Meira Filho, U. Cubasch, X. Dai, Y. Ding, D.J. Griggs, B. Hewitson, J.T. Houghton, I. Isaksen, T. Karl, M. McFarland, V.P. Meleshko, J.F.B. Mitchell, M. Noguer, B.S. Nyenzi, M. Oppenheimer, J.E. Penner, S. Pollonais, T. Stocker, and K.E. Trenberth. 2001. Technical summary. In *Climate change 2001: The scientific basis. Contribution of Working Group I to the third assessment report of the Intergovernmental Panel on Climate Change*, ed. J.T. Houghton, Y. Ding, D.J. Griggs, M. Noguer, P.J. van der Linden, X. Dai, K. Maskell, and C.A. Johnson. Cambridge: Cambridge University Press, 21–83.

Alcamo, J., ed. 1994. *Image 2.0: Integrated modeling of global climate change*. Dordrecht: Kluwer.

Arnell, N. 1999a. Climate change and global water resources. *Global Environmental Change* 9:s31–s49.

– 1999b. The effect of climate change on hydrological regimes in Europe: A continental perspective. *Global Environmental Change* 9:5–23.

– 2003. Effects of IPCC SRES emissions scenarios on river runoff: a global perspective. *Hydrology and Earth System Sciences* 7: 619–41.

– 2004. Climate change and global water resources: SRES emissions and socio-economic scenarios. *Global Environmental Change* 14 (1): 31–52.

Arnell, N., C. Liu, R. Compagnucci, L. da Cunha, K. Hanaki, C. Howe, G. Mailu, I. Shiklomanov, and E. Stakhiv. 2001. Hydrology and water resources. Chap. 4 in *Climate change 2001: Impacts, adaptation, and vulnerability. Contribution of Working Group II to the third assessment report of the Intergovernmental Panel on Climate Change*, ed. J.J. McCarthy, O.F. Canziani, N.A. Leary, D.J. Dokken, and K.S. White. Cambridge: Cambridge University Press, 191–234.

Atkisson, A. 1999. *Believing Cassandra: An optimist looks at a pessimist's world*. White River Junction, VT: Chelsea Green Publishing.

Auld, H., and D. MacIver. 2004. Cities and communities: The changing climate and increasing vulnerability of infrastructure. In *Climate change: Building the adaptive capacity*, ed. A. Fenech, D. MacIver, H. Auld, R. Bing Rong, and Y. Yin. Toronto: Meteorological Service of Canada, Environment Canada.

Ausubel, J. 1990. Economics in the air: An introduction to economic issues of the atmosphere and climate. In *Climatic constraints and human activities: Task force on the nature of climate and society research, February 4–6, 1980*, ed. J. Ausubel and A.K. Biswas. Oxford: Pergamon Press.

– 1991. Does climate still matter? *Nature* 350:649–52.

Aylsworth, J., and A. Duk-Rodkin. 1997. "Landslides and permafrost in the Mackenzie Valley." In *Mackenzie Basin Impact Study (MBIS) final report*, ed. S.J. Cohen. Toronto: Environment Canada.

Bach, W., J. Pankrath, and J. Williams, eds. 1980. *Interactions of energy and climate*. Dordrecht: D. Reidel.

Baede, A.P.M., E. Ahlonsou, Y. Ding, and D. Schimel. 2001. The climate system: An overview. Chap. 1 in *Climate change 2001: The scientific basis. Contribution of Working Group 1 to the third assessment report of the Intergovernmental Panel on Climate Change*, ed. J.T. Houghton, Y. Ding, D.J. Griggs, M. Noguer, P.J. van der Linden, X. Dai, K. Maskell, and C.A. Johnson. Cambridge: Cambridge University Press, 85–98.

Banuri, T., J. Weyant, G. Akumu, A. Najam, L. Pinguelli Rosa, S. Rayner, W. Sachs, R. Sharmi, and G. Yohe, 2001. Setting the stage: Climate change and sustainable development. Chap. 1 in *Climate change 2001: Mitigation. Contribution of Working Group III to the third assessment report of the Intergovernmental Panel on Climate Change*, ed. B. Metz, O. Davidson, R. Swart, and J. Pan. Cambridge: Cambridge University Press, 73–114.

Barker, T., I. Bashmakov, A. Alharthi, M. Amann, L. Cifuentes, J. Drexhage, M. Duan, O. Edenhofer, B. Flannery, M. Grubb, M. Hoogwijk, F. I. Ibitoye, C.J. Jepma, W.A. Pizer, K. Yamaji, 2007: Mitigation from a cross-sectoral perspective. In *Climate change 2007: Mitigation. Contribution of Working Group III to the fourth assessment report of the Intergovernmental Panel on Climate Change*, ed. B. Metz, O.R. Davidson, P.R. Bosch, R. Dave, L.A. Meyer. Cambridge: Cambridge University Press, 619–90.

Barker, T., L. Srivastava, M. Al-Moneef, L. Bernstein, P. Criqui, D. Davis, S. Lennon, J. Li, J. Torres Martinez, and S. Mori. 2001. Sector costs and ancillary benefits of mitigation. Chap. 9 in *Climate change 2001: Mitigation. Contribution of Working Group III to the third assessment report of the*

Intergovernmental Panel on Climate Change, ed. B. Metz, O. Davidson, R. Swart, and J. Pan. Cambridge: Cambridge University Press, 561–99.

Barnett, T.P., J.C. Adam, and D.P. Lettenmaier. 2005. Potential impacts of a warming climate on water availability in snow-dominated regions. *Nature* 438: 303–9.

Barry, R.G., and R.J. Chorley. 1982. Atmosphere, Weather and Climate, 4th ed. London: Methuen.

Bauer, E., M. Claussen, and V. Brovkin. 2003. Assessing climate forcings of the earth system for the past millennium. *Geophysical Research Letters* 30 (6): doi: 10.1029/2002GL016639.

Bazzaz, F.A. 1998. Tropical forests in a future climate: Changes in biological diversity and impact on the global carbon cycle. *Climatic Change* 39:317–36.

– 1990. The response of natural ecosystems to the rising global CO2 levels. *Annual Review of Ecology and Systematics* 21: 167–96.

Berk, R.A., and R.G. Fovell. 1999. Public perceptions of climate change: a "willingness to pay" assessment. *Climatic Change* 41: 413–46.

Bijlsma, L. 1995. Coastal zones and small islands. Chap. 9 in *Climate change 1995: Impacts, adaptations, and mitigation of climate change. Contribution of Working Group II to the second assessment report of the Intergovernmental Panel on Climate Change*, ed. R.T. Watson, M.C. Zinyowera, and R.H. Moss. Cambridge: Cambridge University Press.

Bizikova, L., J. Robinson, and S. Cohen, eds. 2007. Integrating climate change actions into local development. *Climate Policy, Special Issue* 7 (4): 267–376.

Board on Natural Disasters. 1999. Mitigation emerges as a major strategy for reducing losses caused by natural disasters. *Science* 284: 1943–47.

Bodansky, D., S. Chou, and C. Jorge-Tresolini, eds. 2004. *International climate efforts beyond 2012: A survey of approaches*. Arlington, VA: Pew Center on Global Climate Change.

Bonan, G. 2002. *Ecological Climatology: Concepts and Applications*. Cambridge: Cambridge University Press.

Boykoff, M.T., and J.M. Boykoff. 2004. Balance as bias: Global warming and the US prestige press. *Global Environmental Change* 14:125–36.

Bretherton, F.P., K.Bryan, and J.D. Woods. 1990. Time-dependent greenhouse-gas-induced climate change. In *Climate Change, the IPCC Scientific Assessment. Report prepared for IPCC by Working Group I*, ed. J.T. Houghton, G.J. Jenkins, and J.J. Ephraums. Cambridge: Cambridge University Press, 173–94.

Briffa, K.R., T.J. Osborn, F.H. Schweingruber, I.C. Harris, P.D. Jones, S.G. Shiyatov, and E.A. Vaganov. 2001. Low-frequency temperature variations from a northern tree-ring density network. *Journal of Geophysical Research* 106: 2929–41.

British Columbia Ministry of Forests. 1992. *British Columbia's forests: Monocultures or mixed forests?* Victoria: Silviculture Interpretations Working Group, Ministry of Forests, Government of British Columbia.

British Columbia Ministry of Forests and Range. 2006. The state of British Columbia's forests, 2006. Victoria: Government of British Columbia.

Brown, L. 1981. *Building a Sustainable Society.* Washington, DC: Worldwatch Institute.

Bruce, J.P., H. Lee, and E.F. Haites, eds. 1996. *Climate change 1995: Economic and social dimensions of climate change. Contribution of Working Group III to the second assessment report of the Intergovernmental Panel on Climate Change.* Cambridge: Cambridge University Press.

Bruce, J.P., and D. Russell. 2004. A Canadian policy chronicle. In *Hard choices: Climate change in Canada,* ed. H. Coward and A.J. Weaver. Waterloo: Wilfrid Laurier University Press.

Brückner, E. 1915. The settlement of the United States as controlled by climate and climate oscillations. In *Memorial volume of the transatlantic excursion of 1912 of the American Geophysical Society,* 125–39. Cited in S. Weart, *The discovery of global warming,* Cambridge: Harvard University Press 2004. Available online at http://www.aip.org/history/climate/.

Budyko, M.I. 1982. *The earth's climate: Past and future.* Vol. 29, International Geophysics Series. New York: Academic Press.

Burton, I., R.W. Kates, and G.F. White. 1978. *The environment as hazard.* New York: Oxford University Press.

– 1993. *The environment as hazard.* 2d ed. New York: The Guilford Press.

Burton, I., and E. May. 2004. The adaptation deficit in water resources management. *IDS Bulletin* 35(3):31–7.

Callendar, G.S. 1938. The artificial production of carbon dioxide and its influence on climate. *Quarterly Journal of the Royal Meteorological Society* 66:395–400. Cited in S. Weart, *The discovery of global warming* (Cambridge: Harvard University Press 2004). Available online at http://www.aip.org/history/climate/.

Carroll, A.L., S.W. Taylor, J. Régnière, and L. Safranyik. 2004. Effects of climate change on range expansion by the mountain pine beetle in British Columbia. In *Mountain pine beetle symposium: Challenges and solutions, October 30–31, 2003, Kelowna,* ed. T.L. Shore, J.E. Brooks, and J.E. Stone. Victoria: Natural Resources Canada, Canadian Forest Service, Pacific Forestry Centre, Information Report BC-X-399.

Carter, T.R., M. Hulme, J.E. Crossley, S. Malyshev, M.G. New, M.E. Schlesinger, and H. Tuomenvirta. 2000. *Climate change in the 21st century: Interim characterizations based on the new IPCC emissions scenarios.* Helsinki: Finnish Environment Institute.

Chamberlin, T.C. 1897. A group of hypotheses bearing on climatic changes. *Journal of Geology* 5:653–83. Cited in S. Weart, *The discovery of global warming* (Cambridge: Harvard University Press 2004). Available online at http://www.aip.org/history/climate/.

Change. 1998. *Newsletter from the Netherlands Global Change Program*, issue 47. Available online at http://www.nop.nl.

– 1999. *Newsletter from the Netherlands Global Change Program*, issue TBD. Available online at http://www.nop.nl.

– 2002. *Newsletter from the Netherlands Global Change Program*, issue 61. Available online at www.nop.nl.

Changnon, S., R.A. Pielke Jr, D. Changnon, R.T. Sylves, and P. Pulwarty. 2000. Human factors explain the increased losses from weather and climate extremes. *Bulletin of the American Meteorological Society* 81(3):437–42.

Christy, J.R., R.W. Spencer, and W.D. Braswell. 2000. MSU tropospheric temperatures: Dataset construction and radiosonde comparisons. *Journal of Atmospheric and Oceanic Technology* 17:1153–70.

Christy, L.C., C.E. Di Leva, J.M. Lindsay, and P.T. Takoukam. 2007. Forest law and sustainable development: Addressing contemporary challenges through legal reform. Washington: The World Bank.

Clark, W.C. 1982. *Carbon dioxide review*. New York: Oxford University Press.

Cohen, S.J. 1986. Impacts of CO_2-induced climatic change on water resources in the Great Lakes basin. *Climatic Change* 8(2):135–53.

– 1996. Integrated regional assessment of global climate change: Lessons from the Mackenzie Basin Impact Study (MBIS). *Global and Planetary Change* 11:179–85.

– ed. 1997a. *Mackenzie Basin Impact Study (MBIS) final report*. Toronto: Environment Canada.

– 1997b. Scientist-stakeholder collaboration in integrated assessment of climate change: Lessons from a case study of northwest Canada. *Environmental Modeling and Assessment* 2:281–93.

Cohen, S.J., D. Demeritt, J. Robinson, and D. Rothman. 1998. Climate change and sustainable development: Towards dialogue. *Global Environmental Change* 8(4):341–71.

Cohen, S., and T. Neale, eds. 2006. *Participatory integrated assessment of climate change and water management in the Okanagan Basin, British Columbia*. Final report, Project A846, submitted to Climate Change Action Fund, Natural Resources Canada, Ottawa.

Cohen, S.J., D. Neilsen, and R. Welbourn, eds. 2004. *Expanding the dialogue on climate change and water management in the Okanagan Basin, British*

Columbia. Final report, Project A463/433, submitted to Climate Change Action Fund, Natural Resources Canada, Ottawa.

Commission of the European Communities. 2007. Communication from the Commission to the Council, the European Parliament, the European Economic and Social Committee and the Committee of the Regions: Limiting Global Climate Change to 2 degrees Celsius (dated 10 January 2007: Brussels).

Corbett, J.B., and J.L. Durfee. 2004. Testing public (un)certainty of science: Media representations of global warming. *Science Communication* 26(2):129–51.

Costanza, R., R. d'Arge, R. de Groot, S. Farber, M. Grasso, B. Hannon, K. Limburg, S. Naeem, R.V. O'Neill, J. Paruelo, R.G. Raskin, P. Sutton, and M. van den Belt. 1997. The value of the world's ecosystem services and natural capital. *Nature* 387:253–60.

Covey, C., K.M. Achutarao, P.J. Gleckler, T.J. Phillips, K.E. Taylor, and M.F. Wehner. 2004. Coupled ocean-atmosphere climate simulations compared with simulations using prescribed sea surface temperature: Effect of a "perfect ocean." *Global and Planetary Change* 41: 1–14.

Coward, H., and A.J. Weaver, eds. 2004. *Hard choices: Climate change in Canada*. Waterloo: Wilfrid Laurier University Press.

Crowley, T.J. 2000. Causes of climate change over the past 1000 years. *Science* 289: 270–7.

Crowley, T.J., and T. Lowery. 2000. How warm was the Medieval Warm Period? *Ambio*, 29, 51–4.

Cubasch, U., G.A. Meehl, G.J. Boer, R.J. Stouffer, M. Dix, A. Noda, C.A. Senior, S. Raper, and K.S. Yap. 2001. Projections of future climate change. Chap. 9 in *Climate change 2001: The scientific basis. Contribution of Working Group 1 to the third assessment report of the Intergovernmental Panel on Climate Change*, ed. J.T. Houghton, Y. Ding, D.J. Griggs, M. Noguer, P.J. van der Linden, X. Dai, K. Maskell, and C.A. Johnson. Cambridge: Cambridge University Press.

Darwin, R., and D. Kennedy. 2000. Economic effects of CO_2 fertilization of crops: Transforming changes in yield into changes in supply. *Environmental Modeling & Assessment* 5(3):157–68.

de Löe, R. 2003. Email communication to author, 7 April.

Denman, K.L., G. Brasseur, A. Chidthaisong, P. Ciais, P.M. Cox, R.E. Dickinson, D. Hauglustaine, C. Heinze, E. Holland, D. Jacob, U. Lohmann, S Ramachandran, P.L. da Silva Dias, S.C. Wofsy, and X. Zhang. 2007. Couplings between Changes in the Climate System and Biogeochemistry. In

Climate Change 2007: The Physical Science Basis. Contribution of Working Group 1 to the fourth assessment report of the Intergovernmental Panel on Climate Change, ed. S. Solomon, D. Qin, M. Manning, Z. Chen, M. Marquis, K.B. Averyt, M. Tignor, and H.L. Miller. Cambridge: Cambridge University Press, 499–587.

Dessai, S., W.N. Adger, M. Hulme, J. Turnpenny, J. Köhler, and R. Warren. 2004. Defining and experiencing dangerous climate change. *Climatic Change* 64:11–25.

Dessai, S., and M. Hulme. 2003. *Does climate policy need probabilities?* Tyndall Centre for Climate Change Research, Working Paper 34, University of East Anglia, Norwich.

– 2004. Does climate adaptation policy need probabilities. *Climate Policy,* 4:107–28.

Diaz, H.F., and B.J. Morehouse, eds. 2003. *Climate and water: Transboundary challenges in the Americas.* Dordrecht: Kluwer Academic Publishers.

Dürrenberger, D., J. Behringer, U. Dahinden, A. Gerger, B. Kasemir, C. Querol, R. Schüle, D. Tabara, F. Toth, M. van Asselt, D. Vassilarou, N. Willi, and C. Jaeger. 1997. Focus groups in integrated assessments: A manual for a participatory tool. ULYSSES Working Paper, WP-97-2, Darmstadt University of Technology, Darmstadt.

Edwards, P. 1996. Models in the policy arena. In *Elements of change,* ed. J. Katzenberger and S.J. Hassol. Aspen, CO: Aspen Global Change Institute.

Ellis, J., and K. Karousakis. 2006. The developing CDM market: May 2006 Update. OECD/IEA Annex I Expert Group, Paris.

Ellis, J., H. Winkler, J. Corfee-Morlot, and F. Gagnon-Lebrun. 2007. CDM: Taking stock and looking forward. *Energy Policy* 35, 15–28.

Esper, J., E.R. Cook, and F.H. Schweingruber. 2002. Low-frequency signals in long tree-line chronologies for reconstructing past temperature variability. *Science* 295, 2250–53.

Fankhauser, S. 1995. *Valuing climate change. The economics of the greenhouse.* London: Earthscan.

Fankhauser, S., and R.S.J. Tol. 1997. The social costs of climate change: The IPCC second assessment report and beyond. *Mitigation and Adaptation Strategies for Global Change* 1:385–403.

Fankhauser, S., R.S.J. Tol, and D.W. Pearce. 1998. Extensions and alternatives to climate change impact valuation: On the critique of IPCC Working Group III's impact estimates. *Environment and Development Economics* 3: 59–81.

Farhar-Pilgrim, B. 1985. Social analysis. In *Climate impact assessment: Studies of the interaction of climate and society,* SCOPE 27, ed. R. Kates, J.H. Ausubel, and M. Berberian. Chichester, West Sussex: John Wiley & Sons.

Fast, H., and F. Berkes. 1999. Climate change, northern subsistence, and land-based economics. In *Securing northern futures*, ed. D. Wall, M.M.R. Freeman, P.A. McCormick, M. Payne, E.E. Wein, and R.W. Wein. Edmonton: Canadian Circumpolar Institute Press.

Fischer, G., K. Frohberg, M.L. Parry, and C. Rosenzweig. 1994. Climate change and world food supply, demand and trade: Who benefits, who loses? *Global Environmental Change* 4(1):7–23.

Fleagle, R., and J. Businger. 1963. An introduction to atmospheric physics. New York: Academic Press.

Folland, C.K., T.R. Karl, J.R. Christy, R.A. Clarke, G.V. Gruza, J. Jouzel, M.E. Mann, J. Oerlemans, M.J. Salinger, and S.-W. Wang. 2001. Observed climate variability and change. Chap. 2 in *Climate change 2001: The scientific basis. Contribution of Working Group 1 to the third assessment report of the Intergovernmental Panel on Climate Change*, ed. J.T. Houghton, Y. Ding, D.J. Griggs, M. Noguer, P.J. van der Linden, X. Dai, K. Maskell, and C.A. Johnson. Cambridge: Cambridge University Press, 99–181.

Forster, P., V. Ramaswamy, P. Artaxo, T. Berntsen, R. Betts, D.W. Fahey, J. Haywood, J. Lean, D.C. Lowe, G. Myhre, J. Nganga, R. Prinn, G. Raga, M. Schulz, and R. Van Dorland, 2007. Changes in atmospheric constituents and in radiative forcing. In *Climate change 2007: The physical science basis. Contribution of Working Group 1 to the fourth assessment report of the Intergovernmental Panel on Climate Change*, ed. S. Solomon, D. Qin, M. Manning, Z. Chen, M. Marquis, K.B. Averyt, M. Tignor, and H.L. Miller. Cambridge: Cambridge University Press, 129–234.

Frank, R.H. 2000. Why is cost-benefit analysis so controversial?" *Journal of Legal Studies* 29 (2): 913–30.

Füssel, H.-M., and R.J.T. Klein. 2006. Climate change vulnerability assessments: An evolution of conceptual thinking. *Climatic Change* 75, 301–29.

Gallopin, G., A. Hammond, P. Raskin, and R. Swart. 1997. *Branch points: Global scenarios and human choice*. Stockholm: Stockholm Environment Institute.

Garcia, R. 1981. *Drought and Man*. Vol. 1 of *Nature pleads not guilty*. Oxford: Pergamon Press.

Gardiner, S.M. 2004. Ethics and global climate change. *Ethics* 114:555–600.

Gates, W.L., J. Boyle, C. Covey, C. Dease, C. Doutriaux, R. Drach, M. Fiorino, P. Gleckler, J. Hnilo, S. Marlais, T. Phillips, G. Potter, B.D. Santer, K.R. Sperber, K. Taylor, and D. Williams. 1999. An overview of the results of the Atmospheric Model Intercomparison Project (AMIP I). *Bulletin of the American Meteorological Society* 80:29–55.

Geer, I.W., ed. 1996. *Glossary of weather and climate with related oceanic and hydrologic terms.* Boston: American Meteorological Society.

Gelbspan, R. 1997. *The heat is on.* Reading, MA: Perseus Books.

Gerber, S., F. Joos, P. Brügger, T.F. Stocker, M.E. Mann, S. Sitch, and M. Scholze. 2003. Constraining temperature variations over the last millennium by comparing simulated and observed atmospheric CO_2. *Climate Dynamics* 20:281–99.

Giorgi, F., and B. Hewitson. 2001. Regional climate information: Evaluation and projections. Chap. 10 in *Climate change 2001: The scientific basis. Contribution of Working Group I to the third assessment report of the Intergovernmental Panel on Climate Change,* ed. J.T. Houghton, Y. Ding, D.J. Griggs, M. Noguer, P.J. van der Linden, X. Dai, K. Maskell, and C.A. Johnson. Cambridge: Cambridge University Press.

Gitay, H., S. Brown, W. Easterling, B. Jallow, J. Antle, M. Apps, R. Beamish, T. Chapin, W. Cramer, J. Frangi, J. Laine, L. Erda, J. Magnuson, I. Noble, J. Price, T. Prowse, T. Root, E. Schulze, O. Sirotenko, B. Sohngen, and J. Soussana. 2001. Ecosystems and their goods and services. Chap. 5 in *Climate change 2001: Impacts, adaptation, and vulnerability. Contribution of Working Group II to the third assessment report of the Intergovernmental Panel on Climate Change,* ed. J.J. McCarthy, O.F. Canziani, N.A. Leary, D.J. Dokken, and K.S. White. Cambridge: Cambridge University Press, 235–342.

Glantz, M.H. 1976. Nine fallacies of natural disaster: The case of the Sahel. In *Politics of natural disaster: The case of the Sahel drought,* ed. M.H. Glantz. New York: Praeger.

– 1994. *Drought follows the plow: Cultivating marginal areas.* Cambridge: Cambridge University Press.

– 1996. *Currents of change: El Niño's impact on climate and society.* Cambridge: Cambridge University Press.

– 2003. *Climate affairs: A primer.* Washington, DC: Island Press.

Glantz, M.H., ed. 1988. *Societal responses to regional climate change: Forecasting by analogy.* Boulder, CO: Westview Press.

– 1999. *Creeping environmental problems and sustainable development in the Aral Sea Basin.* Cambridge: Cambridge University Press.

Glantz, M., R. Katz, and M. Krenz (eds.) 1987. *The societal impacts associated with the 1982–83 worldwide climate anomalies.* Boulder, CO: United Nations Environment Programme, and National Center for Atmospheric Research.

Glantz, M.H., J. Robinson, and M.E. Krenz. 1985. Recent assessments. In *Climate impact assessment: Studies of the interaction of climate and society,* SCOPE 27, ed. R. Kates, J.H. Ausubel, and M. Berberian. Chichester, West Sussex: John Wiley & Sons.

Global Commons Institute. 2008. Carbon Countdown: The Campaign for Contraction & Convergence®. The Global Commons Institute, London, 35 p.

Goodale, C.L., M.J. Apps, R.A. Birdsey, C.B. Field, L.S. Heath, R.A. Houghton, J.C. Jenkins, G.H. Kohlmaier, W. Kurz, S. Liu, G.-J. Nabuurs, S. Nilsson, and A.Z. Shvidenko. 2002. Forest carbon sinks in the northern hemisphere. *Ecological Applications* 12:891–9.

Graham, L.P., J. Andreasson, and B. Carlsson. 2007. Assessing climate change impacts on hydrology from an ensemble of regional climate models, model scales and linking methods – a case study of the Lule River basin. *Climatic Change* 81:293–307.

Green Roofs for Healthy Cities. 2004. *Green Roof Infrastructure Monitor.* Toronto: The Cardinal Group Inc., on behalf of Green Roofs for Healthy Cities – North America Inc. Available online at http://www.greenroofs.org.

Griffin, J.M., ed. 2003. *Global climate change: The science, economics, and politics.* Cheltenham, England: Edward Elgar.

Grubb, M., C. Vrolijk, and D. Brack. 1999. *The Kyoto Protocol: A guide and assessment.* London: The Royal Institute of International Affairs.

Gunderson, L.H., and C.S. Holling. 2001. *Panarchy: Understanding transformation in human and natural systems.* Washington, DC: Island Press.

Gupta, J., and R.S.J. Tol. 2003. Why reduce greenhouse gas emissions? Reasons, issue-linkages, and dilemmas. In *Issues in international climate policy: Theory and policy,* ed. E.C. van Ierland, J. Gupta, and M.T.J. Kok. Cheltenham, England: Edward Elgar Publishing.

Hamilton, K. 2004. Insurance and financial sector support for adaptation. *IDS Bulletin* 35(3):55–61.

Hansen, J., I. Fung, A. Lacis, D. Rind, S. Lebedeff, R. Ruedy, G. Russell, and P. Stone. 1988. Global climate changes as forecast by the Goddard Institute for Space Sciences three-dimensional model. *Journal of Geophysical Research* 93:9341–64. Cited in F.P. Bretherton, K. Bryan, and J.D. Woods, Time-dependent greenhouse-gas-induced climate change. Chap 6. in *Climate change: The IPCC scientific assessment. Report prepared for IPCC by Working Group 1,* ed. J.T. Houghton, B.A. Callander, and S.K. Varney (Cambridge: Cambridge University Press 1990).

Harasawa, H., Y. Matsuoka, K. Takahashi, Y. Hijioka, Y. Shimada, Y. Munesue, and M. Lal. 2003. Potential impacts of global climate change. In *Climate policy assessment: Asia-Pacific integrated modeling,* ed. M. Kainuma, Y. Matsuoka, and T. Morita. Tokyo: Springer-Verlag.

Hare, B., and M. Meinshausen. 2004. *How much warming are we committed to and how much can be avoided?* PIK Report No. 93. Potsdam: Potsdam Institute for Climate Impacts Research.

Hare, F.K. 1981. Climate impact on food supplies: Can it be identified? In *Climate's impact on food supplies: Strategies and technologies for climate-defensive food production*, edited by L.E. Slater and S.K. Levin. AAAS Selected Symposium 62, American Association for the Advancement of Science. Boulder, CO: Westview Press.

Harries, J E. 1996. The greenhouse earth – A view from space. *Quarterly Journal of the Royal Meteorological Society* 122: 799–818.

Hecht, A.D., and D. Tirpak. 1995. Framework agreement on climate change: A scientific and political history. *Climatic Change* 29:371–402.

Hegerl, G.C., F. W. Zwiers, P. Braconnot, N.P. Gillett, Y. Luo, J.A. Marengo Orsini, N. Nicholls, J.E. Penner, and P.A. Stott, 2007: Understanding and attributing climate change. In *Climate change 2007: The physical science basis. Contribution of Working Group 1 to the fourth assessment report of the Intergovernmental Panel on Climate Change*, ed. S. Solomon, D. Qin, M. Manning, Z. Chen, M. Marquis, K.B. Averyt, M. Tignor, and H.L. Miller. Cambridge: Cambridge University Press, 663–745.

Henderson-Sellers, A. 1996. Soil moisture simulation: Achievements of the RICE and PILPS intercomparison workshop and future directions. *Global Planetary Change* 13:99–115.

Hisschemöller, M., R.S.J. Tol, and P. Vellinga. 2001. The relevance of participatory approaches in integrated environmental assessment. *Integrated Assessment* 2:57–72.

Holling, C.S. 1986. The resilience of terrestrial ecosystems: Local surprise and global change. Chap. 10 in *Sustainable development of the biosphere*, ed. W.C. Clark and R.E. Munn. Cambridge: Cambridge University Press.

Holman, I.P., R.J. Nicholls, P.M. Berry, P.A. Harrison, E. Audsley, S. Shackley, and M.D.A. Rounsevell. 2005. A regional multi-sectoral and integrated assessment of the impacts of climate and socio-economic change in the UK. Part II: Results. *Climatic Change* 71:43–73.

Holman, I.P., M.D.A. Rounsevell, S. Shackley, P.A. Harrison, R.J. Nicholls, P.M. Berry, and E. Audsley. 2005. A regional multi-sectoral and integrated assessment of the impacts of climate and socio-economic change in the UK. Part I: Methodology. *Climatic Change* 71:9–41.

Houghton, J.T. 2004. *Global warming: The complete briefing*. 3d ed. Cambridge: Cambridge University Press.

Houghton, J.T., B.A. Callander, and S.K. Varney, eds. 1992. *Climate change 1992: The supplementary report to the IPCC scientific assessment*. Cambridge: Cambridge University Press.

Houghton, J.T., G.J. Jenkins, and J.J. Ephraums, eds. 1990. *Climate change: The IPCC scientific assessment. Report prepared for the IPCC by Working Group 1*. Cambridge: Cambridge University Press.

Huq, S. 2002. The Bonn-Marrakech agreements on funding. *Climate Policy* 2:243–6.

Huq, S., A. Rahman, M. Konate, Y. Sokona, and H. Reid. 2003. *Mainstreaming adaptation to climate change in least developed countries (LDCs)*. London: International Institute for Environment & Development.

Huq, S., and H. Reid. 2004. Mainstreaming adaptation in development. *IDS Bulletin*, 35(3):15–21.

Huq, S., H. Reid, and L.A. Murray. 2006. Climate change and development links. Gatekeeper Series 123, International Institute for Environment and Development, London.

Hurd, B., J.M. Callaway, J.B. Smith, and P. Kirshen. 1999. Economic effects of climate change on US water resources. In *The impact of climate change on the United States economy*, ed. R. Mendelsohn and J.E. Neumann. Cambridge: Cambridge University Press.

Idso, S.B. 1980. The climatological significance of a doubling of Earth's atmospheric carbon dioxide concentration. *Science* 207:1462–3.

– 1981. Carbon dioxide: An alternative view. *New Scientist* 92:444.

Ingram, I. 2005. An adaptation strategy in the Cook Islands. Tiempo Climate Newswatch, 8 January 2006; available at http://www.tiempocyberclimate.org/newswatch/index.htm.

IEA (International Energy Agency). 1998. *World Energy Outlook 1998 Edition*. Paris: IEA and Organization of Economic Cooperation and Development.

– 2006. *World Energy Outlook 2006*. Paris: IEA and Organization of Economic Cooperation and Development.

IISD (International Institute for Sustainable Development). 2000. Summary of the Sixth Conference of the Parties to the Framework Convention on Climate Change, 13–25 November 2000. Earth Negotiations Bulletin 12 (163). Winnipeg: International Institute for Sustainable Development.

– 2001. Summary of the Resumed Sixth Session of the Conference of the Parties to the Framework Convention on Climate Change, 16–27 July 2001. Earth Negotiations Bulletin 12 (176). Winnipeg: International Institute for Sustainable Development.

Institute for the Study of Society and the Environment, National Center for Atmospheric Research (Boulder CO, USA). http://www.isse.ucar.edu.

IPCC (Intergovernmental Panel on Climate Change). 2001a. *Climate change 2001: Synthesis report. A contribution of Working Groups I, II, and III to the third assessment report of the Intergovernmental Panel on Climate Change*. Cambridge: Cambridge University Press.

– 2001b. Summary for policymakers. In *Climate change 2001: Impacts, adaptation, and vulnerability. A report of Working Group II of the Intergovernmental Panel on Climate Change*, ed. J.J. McCarthy, O.F.

Canziani, N.A. Leary, D.J. Dokken, and K.S. White. Cambridge: Cambridge University Press.

– 2001c. Summary for policymakers. In *Climate change 2001: Mitigation. A report of Working Group III of the Intergovernmental Panel on Climate Change*, ed. B. Metz, O. Davidson, R. Swart, and J. Pan. Cambridge: Cambridge University Press.

– 2001d. Technical summary. In *Climate change 2001: Mitigation. A report of Working Group III of the Intergovernmental Panel on Climate Change*, ed. B. Metz, O. Davidson, R. Swart, and J. Pan. Cambridge: Cambridge University Press.

– 2007a. Climate change 2007: Impacts, adaptation and vulnerability. Summary for policymakers. Geneva: IPCC.

– 2007b. Climate change 2007: Mitigation of climate change. Summary for policymakers. Geneva: IPCC.

– 2007c. Climate change 2007: The physical science basis. Summary for policymakers. Geneva: IPCC.

– 2007d. Climate change 2007: The physical science basis. Technical summary.

– 2007e. Climate change 2007: Synthesis report. Geneva: IPCC.

Jäger, J., and T. O'Riordan. 1996. *The history of climate change science and politics*. In *Politics of climate change: A European perspective*, ed. T. O'Riordan and J. Jäger. London: Routledge.

Jamieson, D. 1988. Grappling for a glimpse of the future. In *Societal responses to regional climatic change: Forecasting by analogy*, ed. M.H. Glantz. Boulder, CO: Westview Press.

Janssen, M. 1998. *Modelling global change*. Cheltenham, England: Edward Elgar Publishing.

Jepma, C.J., and M. Munasinghe. 1998. *Climate change policy: Facts, issues, and analyses*. Cambridge: Cambridge University Press.

JIN Foundation (Joint Implementation Foundation). 2002. Planned and ongoing Art.6 JI projects, and planned and ongoing AIJ pilot projects. *Joint Implementation Quarterly: Magazine on the Kyoto Mechanisms* 8(4):14. Available online at http://www.jiqweb.org.

– 2004. Russia needs Kyoto to "buy" its sustainable economic growth. Interview with I. Bashmakov. *Joint Implementation Quarterly: Magazine on the Kyoto Mechanisms* 10(2):2–3. Available online at http://www.jiqweb.org.

– 2005. Austrian JI/CDM tender programme well underway. Interview with N. Müllebner. *Joint Implementation Quarterly: Magazine on the Kyoto Mechanisms* 11(1):3–4. Available online at http://www.jiqweb.org.

Johnson, M., ed. 1992. *Lore: Capturing traditional environmental knowledge*. Ottawa: Dene Cultural Institute and the International Development Research Centre.

Jones, P.D., K.R. Briffa, T.P. Barnett, and S.F.B. Tett. 1998. High-resolution palaeoclimatic records for the last millennium: Integration, interpretation, and comparison with General Circulation Model control run temperatures. *Holocene* 8:455–71.

Jones, P.D., and M.E. Mann. 2004. Climate over past millennia. *Reviews of Geophysics* 42, RG2002, doi.10.1029/2003RG000143.

Kainuma, M., Y. Matsuoka, and T. Morita, eds. 2003. *Climate policy assessment: Asia-Pacific integrated modeling.* Tokyo: Springer-Verlag.

Kainuma, M., Y. Matsuoka, T. Moria, T. Masui, and K. Takahashi. 2003. Cost analysis of mitigation policies. In *Climate policy assessment: Asia-Pacific integrated modeling,* ed. M. Kainuma, Y. Matsuoka, and T. Morita. Tokyo: Springer-Verlag.

Karl, T.R., G.A. Meehl, C.D. Miller, S.J. Hassol, A.M. Waple, and W.L. Murray, eds. 2008. *Weather and climate extremes in a changing climate. U.S. climate change science program synthesis and assessment product 3.3.* Washington. U.S. Climate Change Science Program. 162 p.

Kates, R.W. 2000: Cautionary tales: Adaptation and the global poor: *Climatic Change* 45: 5–17.

Kates, R., J.H. Ausubel, and M. Berberian, eds. 1985. *Climate impact assessment: Studies of the interaction of climate and society,* SCOPE 27. Chichester, West Sussex: John Wiley & Sons.

Kates, R.W., W.C. Clark, R. Corell, J.M. Hall, C.C. Jaeger, I. Lowe, J.J. McCarthy, H.J. Schellnhuber, B. Bolin, N.M. Dickson, S. Faucheux, G.C. Gallopin, A. Grübler, B. Huntley, J. Jäger, N.S. Jodha, R.E. Kasperson, A. Mabogunje, P. Matson, H. Mooney, B. Moore III, T. O'Riordan, and U. Svedin. 2001. Sustainability science. *Science* 292(5517):641–2.

Kauppi, P., R. Sedjo, M. Apps, C. Cerri, T. Fujimori, H. Janzen. O. Krankina, W. Makundi, G. Marland, O. Masera, G-J. Nabuurs, W. Razali, and N.H. Ravindranath. 2001. Technological and economic potential of options to enhance, maintain, and manage biological carbon reservoirs and geo-engineering. Chap. 4 in *Climate change 2001: Mitigation. Contribution of Working Group III to the third assessment report of the Intergovernmental Panel on Climate Change,* ed. B. Metz, O. Davidson, R. Swart, and J. Pan. Cambridge: Cambridge University Press.

Keeling, C.D. 1960. "The concentration and isotopic abundances of carbon dioxide in the atmosphere." *Science* 286:1531–3. Cited in S. Weart, *The discovery of global warming* (Cambridge: Harvard University Press 2004). Available online at http://www.aip.org/history/climate/.

Kellogg, W.W. 1987. "Human impact on climate: The evolution of an awareness." *Climatic Change* 10:113–36. Reprinted in *Societal responses to regional climate change: Forecasting by analogy*, ed. M.H. Glantz (Boulder, CO: Westview Press 1988).

Kellogg, W.W., and R. Schware. 1981. *Climate change and society: Consequences of increasing atmospheric carbon dioxide*. Boulder, CO: Westview.

Kelly, P.M., and W.N. Adger. 2000. Theory and practice in assessing vulnerability to climate change and facilitating adaptation. *Climatic Change* 47:325–52.

Kiehl, J.T., and K.E. Trenberth. 1997. Earth's annual global mean energy budget. *Bulletin of the American Meteorological Society* 78:197–208.

Kimball, J.W. 2005. *Kimball's biology pages*. An online biology textbook. Available online at http://users.rcn.com/jkimball.ma.ultranet/BiologyPages/.

Kirschbaum, M.U.F., P. Bullock, J.R. Evans, K. Goulding, P.G. Jarvis, I.R. Noble, M. Rounsevell, and T.D. Sharkey. 1995. Ecophysiological, ecological and soil processes in terrestrial ecosystems: A primer on general concepts and relationships. In *Climate change 1995 – impacts, adaptations and mitigation of climatic change: scientific-Technical analyses*, ed. R.T. Watson, M.C. Zinyowera, and R.H. Moss. Cambridge: Cambridge University Press.

Klein, R.J.T., S. Huq, F. Denton, T.E. Downing, R.G. Richels, J.B. Robinson, and F.L. Toth, 2007: Inter-relationships between adaptation and mitigation. *Climate change 2007: Impacts, adaptation and vulnerability. Contribution of Working Group II to the fourth assessment report of the Intergovernmental Panel on Climate Change*, ed. M.L. Parry, O.F. Canziani, J.P. Palutikof, P.J. van der Linden and C.E. Hanson. Cambridge: Cambridge University Press, 745–77.

Kloprogge, P., and J.P. van der Sluijs. 2006. The inclusion of stakeholder knowledge and perspectives in integrated assessment of climate change. *Climate Change* 75:359–89.

Kokorin, A. 2003. What the Kyoto Protocol means for Russians. *Change* 64:1–5.

Kundzewicz, Z.W., L.J. Mata, N.W. Arnell, P. Döll, P. Kabat, B. Jiménez, K.A. Miller, T. Oki, Z. Sen, and I.A. Shiklomanov. 2007. Freshwater resources and their management. In *Climate change 2007: Impacts, adaptation and vulnerability. Contribution of working group II to the fourth assessment report of the intergovernmental panel on climate change*, ed. M.L. Parry, O.F. Canziani, J.P. Palutikof, P.J. van der Linden and C.E. Hanson. Cambridge: Cambridge University Press, 173–210.

Kunreuther, H., R. Daniels, and D. Kettl. 2006. *On risk and disaster: Lessons from Hurricane Katrina*. Philadelphia: University of Pennsylvania Press.

Lacis, A., J. Hansen, P. Lee, T. Mitchell, and S. Lebedeff. 1981. Greenhouse effect of trace gases, 1970–1980. *Geophysical Research Letters* 8:1035–8.

Lamb, H.H. 1982. *Climate, history, and the modern world*. 2d ed. London: Methuen.

Langsdale, S., A. Beall, J. Carmichael, S. Cohen, and C. Forster. 2007. An exploration of water resources futures under climate change using system dynamics modeling. *The Integrated Assessment Journal* 7:51–79.

Leary, N., J. Adejuwon, V. Barros, I. Burton, J. Kulkarni, and R. Lasco, eds. 2008. *Climate Change and Adaptation*. London: Earthscan.

Leary, N., and S. Beresford. 2009. Vulnerablility of people, places and systems to environmental change. In *Integrated regional assessment of global climate change*, ed. G. Knight and J. Jäger. Cambridge: Cambridge University Press. In press.

Leary, N., C. Conde, J. Kulkarni, A. Nyong, and J. Pulhin, eds. 2008. *Climate Change and Vulnerability*. London: Earthscan.

Least Developed Countries Expert Group. 2002. *Annotated guidelines for the preparation of national adaptation programmes of action*. Bonn: United Nations Framework Convention on Climate Change Secretariat.

Leggett, J., W.J. Pepper, and R.J. Swart. 1992. Emissions scenarios for the IPCC: An update. Chap. A3 in *Climate change 1992: The supplementary report to the IPCC scientific assessment. Report prepared for IPCC by Working Group I*, ed. J.T. Houghton, B.A. Callander, and S.K. Varney. Cambridge: Cambridge University Press.

Lehner, B., P. Döll, J. Alcamo, T. Henrichs, and F. Kaspar. 2006. Estimating the impact of global change on flood and drought risks in Europe: A continental integrated analysis. *Climatic Change* 75:273–99.

Leichenko, R.M., and K.L. O'Brien. 2008. *Environmental change and globalization: Double exposures*. Oxford: Oxford University Press.

Lemieux, C.J., and D.J. Scott. 2005. Climate change, biodiversity conservation and protected area planning in Canada. *The Canadian Geographer* 49:384–99.

Lim, B., E. Spanger-Siegfried, I. Burton, E. Malone, and S. Huq. 2004. *Adaptation policy frameworks for climate change: Developing strategies policies and measures*. United Nations Development Programme. Cambridge: Cambridge University Press.

Lindzen, R.S., A.Y. Hou, and B.F. Farrell. 1982. The role of convective model choice in calculating the climate impact of doubling CO_2. *Journal of Atmospheric Science* 9:1189–1205.

Lofgren, B., A. Clites, R. Assel, A. Eberhardt, and C. Luukkonen. 2002. Evaluation of potential impacts on Great Lakes water resources based on climate scenarios of two GCMs. *Journal of Great Lakes Research* 28:537–54.

Long, S.P., E.A. Ainsworth, A.D.B. Leakey, J. Nosberger, and D.R. Ort. 2006. Food for thought: Lower expected crop yield stimulation with rising CO_2 concentrations. *Science* 312:1918–21.

Machta, L. 1971. The role of the oceans and the biosphere in the carbon dioxide cycle. Nobel Symposium 20, 16–20 August, Gothenberg, Sweden. Cited in SMIC (Study of Man's Impact on Climate), *Inadvertent climate modification*. Report of the Study of Man's Impact on Climate. Cambridge: MIT Press 1971.

Magalhaes, A.R. 1998. Planning for sustainable development in the context of global change. *Global Environmental Change* 8:1–10.

Manabe, S., and K. Bryan. 1969. Climate calculations with a combined ocean-atmosphere model. *Journal of Atmospheric Sciences* 26:786–9. Cited in S. Weart, *The discovery of global warming* (Cambridge: Harvard University Press 2004). Available online at http://www.aip.org/history/climate/.

Manabe, S., and R.T. Wetherald. 1975. The effects of doubling the CO_2 concentration on the climate of a general circulation model. *Journal of Atmospheric Sciences* 32:3–15. Cited in M.I. Budyko, *The earth's climate: Past and future*. Vol. 29, International Geophysics Series (New York: Academic Press 1982).

Mann, M.E., C.M. Ammann, R.S. Bradley, K.R. Briffa, T.J. Crowley, M.K. Hughes, P.D. Jones, M. Oppenheimer, T.J. Overpeck, S. Rutherford, K.E. Trenberth, T.M.L. Wigley. 2003. On past temperatures and anomalous late 20th century warmth. *Eos* 84:256–8.

Mann, M.E., R.S. Bradley, and M.K. Hughes. 1999. Northern hemisphere temperatures during the past millennium: Inferences, uncertainties, and limitations. *Geophysical Research Letters* 26:759–62.

Mann, M.E., and P.D. Jones. 2003. Global surface temperatures over the past two millennia. *Geophysical Research Letters* 30 (15):1820. doi:10.1029/2003GL017814.

Mann, M.E., S. Rutherford, R.S. Bradley, M.K. Hughes, and F.T. Keimig. 2003. Optimal surface temperature reconstructions using terrestrial borehole data. *Journal of Geophysical Research* 108 (D7): 4203, doi: 10.1029/2002JD002532

Marland, G., R.A. Pielke Sr, M. Apps, R. Avissar, R.A. Betts, K.J. Davis, P.C. Frumhoff, S.T. Jackson, L.A. Joyce, P. Kauppi, J. Katzenberger, K.G. MacDicken, R.P. Neilson, J.O. Niles, D.S. Niyogi, R.J. Norby, N. Pena, N. Sampson, and Y. Xue. 2003. The climatic impacts of land surface changes and carbon management, and the implications for climate-change mitigation policy. *Climate Policy* 3:149–57.

Martens, P., R.S. Kovats, S. Nijhof, P. de Vries, M.T.J. Livermore, D.J. Bradley, J. Cox, and A.J. McMichael. 1999. Climate change and future populations at risk of malaria. *Global Environmental Change* 9(s1):S89–S107.

McAvaney, B.J., C. Covey, S. Joussaume, V. Kattsov, A. Kitoh, W. Ogana, A.J. Pitman, A.J. Weaver, R.A. Wood, and Z.-C. Zhao. 2001. Model evaluation.

Chap. 8 in *Climate change 2001: The scientific basis. Contribution of Working Group 1 to the third assessment report of the Intergovernmental Panel on Climate Change*, ed. J.T. Houghton, Y. Ding, D.J. Griggs, M. Noguer, P.J. van der Linden, X. Dai, K. Maskell and C.A. Johnson. Cambridge: Cambridge University Press, 471–524.

McCarthy, J.J., O.F. Canziani, N.A. Leary, D.J. Dokken, and K.S. White, eds. 2001a. *Climate change 2001: Impacts, adaptation, and vulnerability. Contribution of Working Group II to the third assessment report of the Intergovernmental Panel on Climate Change.* Cambridge: Cambridge University Press.

– 2001b. Technical summary. In *Climate change 2001: Impacts, adaptation, and vulnerability. Contribution of Working Group II to the third assessment report of the Intergovernmental Panel on Climate Change.* Cambridge: Cambridge University Press.

McIntyre, S., and R. McKitrick. 2003. Corrections to the Mann et. al. (1998) Proxy Data Base and Northern Hemispheric Average Temperature Series. *Energy and Environment* 14:751–71.

– 2005. Hockey sticks, principal components, and spurious significance. *Geophysical Research Letters* 32(3):L03710.

McLean, R.F., A. Tsyban, V. Burkett, J.O. Codignotto, D.L. Forbes, N. Mimura, R.J. Beamish, and V. Ittekkot. 2001. Coastal zones and marine ecosystems. Chap. 6 in *Climate change 2001: Impacts, adaptation, and vulnerability. Contribution of Working Group II to the third assessment report of the Intergovernmental Panel on Climate Change*, ed. J.J. McCarthy, O.F. Canziani, N.A. Leary, D.J. Dokken and K.S. White. Cambridge: Cambridge University Press, 343–80.

McMichael, A., A. Githeko, R. Akhtar, R. Carcavallo, D. Gubler, A. Haines, R.S. Kovats, P. Martens, J. Patz, and A. Sasaki. 2001. Human health. Chap. 9 in *Climate change 2001: Impacts, adaptation, and vulnerability. Contribution of Working Group II to the third assessment report of the Intergovernmental Panel on Climate Change.* Cambridge: Cambridge University Press, 451–86.

MEA (Millennium Ecosystem Assessment). 2005. *Ecosystems and human well-being: Synthesis.* Washington, DC: Island Press.

Meadows, D.H., D.L. Meadows, J. Randers, and W.W. Behrense III. 1972. *The limits to growth.* London : Earth Island Press.

Mearns, L.O., M. Hulme, T.R. Carter, R. Leemans, M. Lal, and P. Whetton. 2001. Climate scenario development. Chap. 13 in *Climate change 2001: The scientific basis. Contribution of Working Group 1 to the third assessment report of the Intergovernmental Panel on Climate Change*, ed. J.T. Houghton, Y. Ding, D.J. Griggs, M. Noguer, P.J. van der Linden, X. Dai, K. Maskell, and C.A. Johnson. Cambridge: Cambridge University Press.

Mearns, L.O., T. Mavromatis, E. Tsvetsinskaya, C. Hays, and W. Easterling. 1999. Comparative response of EPIC and CERES crop models to high and low resolution climate change scenarios. *Journal of Geophysical Research* 104(D6):6623–46.

Meehl, G.A., T.F. Stocker, W.D. Collins, P. Friedlingstein, A.T. Gaye, J.M. Gregory, A. Kitoh, R. Knutti, J.M. Murphy, A. Noda, S.C.B. Raper, I.G. Watterson, A.J. Weaver, and Z.-C. Zhao. 2007. Global Climate Projections. In *Climate Change 2007: The Physical Science Basis. Contribution of Working Group I to the fourth assessment report of the Intergovernmental Panel on Climate Change*, ed. S. Solomon, D. Qin, M. Manning, Z. Chen, M. Marquis, K.B. Averyt, M. Tignor, and H.L. Miller. Cambridge: Cambridge University Press, 747–845.

Mendelsohn, R., W. Morrison, M.E. Schlesinger, and N.G. Andronova. 2000. Country-specific market impacts of climate change. *Climatic Change* 45:553–69.

Mendelsohn, R., and J.E. Neumann, eds. 1999. *The impact of climate change on the United States economy*. Cambridge: Cambridge University Press.

Menne, B., and K.L. Ebi, eds. 2006. Climate change and adaptation strategies for human health. World Health Organisation and Springer.

Metz, B., O. Davidson, J.-W. Martens, S. Van Rooijen, and L. Van Wie Mcgrory, eds. 2000. *Methodological and technological issues in technology transfer, 2000. Special report of the Intergovernmental Panel on Climate Change*. Cambridge: Cambridge University Press.

Metz, B., O. Davidson, R. Swart, and J. Pan, eds. 2001. *Climate change 2001: Mitigation. Contribution of Working Group III to the third assessment report of the Intergovernmental Panel on Climate Change*. Cambridge: Cambridge University Press.

Metzger, M.J., M.D.A. Rounsevell, L. Acosta-Michlik, R. Leemans, and D. Schroter. 2006. The vulnerability of ecosystem services to land use change. *Agriculture, Ecosystems and Environment* 114: 69–85.

Michaelowa, A., and K. Michaelowa. 2007. Climate or development: Is ODA diverted from its original purpose? *Climatic Change* 84: 5–21.

Middelkoop, H., K. Daamen, D. Gellens, W. Grabs, J.C.J. Kwadijk, H. Lang, B.W.A.H. Parmet, B. Schädler, J. Schulla, and K. Wilke. 2001. Impact of climate change on hydrological regimes and water resources management in the Rhine basin. *Climatic Change* 49: 105–28.

Mileti, D. 1999. *Disasters by design: A reassessment of natural hazards in the United States*. Washington, DC: National Academy Press.

Millennium Ecosystem Assessment (MEA). 2005. *Ecosystems and human well-being: synthesis*. Washington, DC: Island Press.

Mills, E. 2005. Insurance in a climate of change. *Science* 309:1040–4.

Mitchell, J.F.B., D.J. Karoly, G.C. Hegerl, F.W. Zwiers, M.R. Allen, and J. Marengo. 2001. Detection of climate change and attribution of causes. Chap. 12 in *Climate change 2001: The scientific basis. Contribution of Working Group 1 to the third assessment report of the Intergovernmental Panel on Climate Change*, ed. J.T. Houghton, Y. Ding, D.J. Griggs, M. Noguer, P.J. van der Linden, X. Dai, K. Maskell, and C.A. Johnson. Cambridge: Cambridge University Press, 695–738.

Moberg, A., D.M. Sonechkin, K. Holmgren, N.M. Datsenko, and W. Karlen. 2005. Highly variable Northern Hemisphere temperatures reconstructed from low- and high-resolution proxy data. *Nature* 433:613–17.

Moldan, B., and S. Billharz, eds. 1997. *Sustainability indicators*. Report of the Project on Indicators of Sustainable Development. Scientific Committee on Problems of the Environment (SCOPE). No. 58. London: Wiley.

Moomaw, W.R., J.R. Moreira, K. Blok, D.L. Greene, K. Gregory, T. Jaszay, T. Kashiwagi, M. Levine, M. McFarland, N. Siva Prasad, L. Price, H.-H. Rogner, R. Sims, F. Zhou, and P. Zhou. 2001. Technological and economic potential of greenhouse gas emissions reduction. Chap. 3 in *Climate change 2001: Mitigation. Contribution of Working Group III to the third assessment report of the Intergovernmental Panel on Climate Change*, ed. B. Metz, O. Davidson, R. Swart, and J. Pan. Cambridge: Cambridge University Press, 167–277.

Morgan, M.G., and H. Dowlatabadi. 1996. Learning from integrated assessment of climate change. *Climatic Change* 34:337–68.

Morrison, J., M.C. Quick, and M.G.G. Foreman. 2002. Climate change in the Fraser River watershed: Flow and temperature projections. *Journal of Hydrology* 263:230–44.

Mortsch, L., H. Hengeveld, M. Lister, B. Lofgren, F. Quinn, M. Silvitzky, and L. Wenger. 2000. Climate change impacts on the hydrology of the Great Lakes–St. Lawrence system. *Canadian Water Resources Journal* 25:153–79.

Moser, S. 2004. Climate change and the sustainability transition: The role of communication and social change. *IHDP Newsletter* 4:18–19.

Moser, S.C., and L. Dilling. 2004. Making climate hot: Communicating the urgency and challenge of global climate change. *Environment* 46(10): 32–46.

Munasinghe, M. 1992. *Environmental economics and sustainable development*. Washington: World Bank.

Munasinghe, M., and R. Swart. 2005. *Primer on climate change and sustainable development.* Cambridge: Cambridge University Press.

Munich Re Group. 2007. *Topics geo: Natural Catastrophes 2006 analyses, assessments, positions.* Münchener Rück-Munich Re Group, Munich. Available online at http://www.munichre.com.

Nakicenovic, N., and R. Swart, eds. 2000. *Emission scenarios. A special report of working group III of the Intergovernmental Panel on Climate Change.* Cambridge: Cambridge University Press.

NAS (National Academy of Sciences). 1979. *Carbon dioxide and climate: A scientific assessment.* Jules Charney, Chair. Washington, DC: National Academy of Sciences.

– 1982. *Carbon dioxide and climate: A second assessment.* Washington, DC: National Academy Press.

– 2001. *Climate change science: An analysis of some key questions.* Washington, DC: National Academy Press.

National Climate Change Process. 1999. *Sinks table options paper: Land-use, land-use change, and forestry in Canada and the Kyoto Protocol.* Available online at http://www.nccp.ca.

National Defense University. 1978. *Climate change to the year 2000: A survey of expert opinion.* Washington, DC: National Defense University.

National Snow and Ice Data Center (NSIDC) Notes, 2007. NSIDC Tracks Record Shattering Summer for Arctic Sea Ice. *NSIDC Notes*, 61:1. Boulder: University of Colorado.

Neilsen, D., W. Koch, W. Merritt, G. Frank, S. Smith, Y. Alila, J. Carmichael, T. Neale, and R. Welbourn. 2004. Risk assessment and vulnerability: Case studies of water supply and demand. In *Expanding the dialogue on climate change & water management in the Okanagan Basin, British Columbia, final report,* ed. S. Cohen, D. Neilsen, and R. Welbourn. Vancouver: Government of Canada and University of British Columbia. Final report, Project A463/433, submitted to Climate Change Action Fund, Natural Resources Canada, Ottawa.

Newell, R.E., and T.G. Dopplick. 1979. Questions concerning the possible influence of anthropogenic CO_2 on atmospheric temperature. *Journal of Applied Meteorology* 18:822–5.

– 1981. Reply to Robert G. Watts' discussion of *questions concerning the Possible Influence of Anthropogenic CO_2 on Atmospheric Temperature. Journal of Applied Meteorology* 20:114.

Nijssen, B., G.M. O'Donnell, A.F. Hamlet, and D.P. Lettenmaier. 2001. Hydrologic sensitivity of global rivers to climate change. *Climatic Change* 50:143–75.

Nohara, D., A. Kitoh, M. Hosaka, and T. Oki. 2006. Impact of climate change on river discharge projected by multimodel ensemble. *Journal of Hydrometeorology* 7: 1076–89.

Nordhaus, W.D., ed. 1998. *Economics and policy issues in climate change.* Washington, DC: Resources for the Future.

Nordhaus, W. 2007. Critical assumptions in the Stern Review on climate change. *Science* 317: 201–2.

Nordhaus, W., and J. Boyer. 2000. *Warming the world: Economic models of climate change.* Cambridge: MIT Press.

Oberndorfer, E., J. Lundholm, B. Bass, R.R. Coffman, H. Doshi, N. Dunnett, S. Gaffin, M. Köhler, K.K.Y. Liu, and B. Rowe. 2007. Green roofs as urban ecosystems: Ecological structures, functions, and services. *Bioscience* 57: 823–33.

Oberthür, S., and H.E. Ott. 1999. *The Kyoto Protocol: International climate policy for the 21st century.* Berlin: Springer.

Okanagan Water Stewardship Council. 2008. Okanagan Sustainable Water Strategy, Action Plan 1.0. Kelowna: Okanagan Basin Water Board.

Oke, T.R. 1978. *Boundary layer climates.* London and New York: Methuen and John Wiley.

Oliver, H.R., and S.A. Oliver, eds. 1995. *The role of water and the hydrological cycle in global change.* Vol. 31, NATO ASI *Series I: Global Environmental Change.* Berlin: Springer-Verlag.

Oreskes, N. 2004. The scientific consensus on climate change. *Science* 306:1686.

Ott, H.E., H. Winkler, B. Brouns, S. Kartha, M. Mace, S. Huq, Y. Kameyama, A.P. Sari, J. Pan, Y. Sokona, P.M. Bhandari, A. Kassenberg, E.L. LaRovere, and A. Rahman. 2004. *South-north dialogue on equity in the greenhouse: A proposal for an adequate and equitable global climate agreement.* Eschborn: Deutsche Gesellschaft für Technische Zusammenarbeit (GTZ).

Parmesan, C., and G. Yohe. 2003. A globally coherent fingerprint of climate change impacts across natural systems. *Nature* 421:37–42.

Parry, M., and T. Carter. 1998. *Climate impact and adaptation assessment.* London: Earthscan Publications.

Parry, M., C. Rosenzweig, A. Iglesias, G. Fischer, and M. Livermore. 1999. Climate change and world food security: A new assessment. *Global Environmental Change* 9:S51–S67.

Payne, J.T., A.W. Wood, A.F. Hamlet, R.N. Palmer, and D.P. Lettenmaier. 2004. Mitigating the effects of climatic change on the water resources of the Columbia River Basin. *Climatic Change* 62:233–56.

Pearce, D.W., W.R. Cline, A.N. Achanta, S. Fankhauser, R.K. Pauchauri, R.S.J. Tol, and P. Vellinga. 1996. The social costs of climatic change: Greenhouse damage and the benefits of control. Chap. 6 in *Climate change 1995: Economic and social dimensions of climatic change. Contribution of Working Group III to the second assessment report of the Intergovernmental*

Panel on Climate Change, ed. J.P. Bruce, H. Lee, and E.F. Haites. Cambridge: Cambridge University Press, 179–224.

Pearson, B. 2005. The CDM is failing. *Tiempo climate newswatch*. Norwich: University of East Anglia, 56: 12–16.

Peterson, T.C., K.P. Gallo, J. Lawrimore, T.W. Owen, A. Huang, and D.A. McKittrick. 1999. Global rural temperature trends. *Geophysical Research Letters* 26(3):329–32.

Peterson, T.C., W.M. Connolley, and J. Fleck. 2008. The myth of the 1970s global cooling scientific consensus. *Bulletin of the American Meteorological Society*. 89:1325–37.

Pimentel, D., and M. Pimentel. 1990. Comment: Adverse environmental consequences of the Green Revolution. *Population and Development Review, Supplement: Resources Environment and Population: Present Knowledge and Future Options* 16:329–32.

Pitman, A.J., A. Henderson-Sellers, C.E. Desborough, Z.-L. Yang, F. Abramopoulos, A. Boone, R.E. Dickinson, N. Gedney, R. Koster, E. Kowalczyk, D. Lettenmaier, X. Liang, J.-F. Mahfouf, J. Noilhan, J. Polcher, W. Qu, A. Robock, C. Rosenzweig, C.A. Schlosser, A.B. Shmakin, J. Smith, M. Suarez, D. Verseghy, P. Wetzel, E. Wood, and Y. Xue. 1999. Key results and implications from phase 1(c) of the Project for Intercomparison of Land-surface Parameterization Schemes. *Climate Dynamics* 15:673–84.

Plummer D., D. Caya, H. Côté, A. Frigon, S. Biner, M. Giguère, D. Paquin, R. Harvey, and R. De Elía, 2006: Climate and climate change over North America as simulated by the Canadian Regional Climate Model. *Journal of Climate*, 19 (13):3112–32.

Ponte, L. 1976. *The cooling*. Englewood Cliffs, NJ: Prentice-Hall. Cited in S. Weart, *The discovery of global warming* (Cambridge: Harvard University Press 2004). Available online at http://www.aip.org/history/climate/.

Portney, P.R. 1998. Applicability of cost-benefit analysis to climatic change. In *Economics and policy issues in climate change*, ed. W.D. Nordhaus. Washington, DC. Resources for the Future, 111–28.

Portney – Concise Encyclopedia of Economics [http://www.econlib.org].

Prentice, C., G.D. Farquhar, M.J.R. Fasham, M.L. Goulden, M. Heimann, V.J. Jaramillo, H.S. Kheshgi, C. Le Quéré, R.J. Scholes, and D.W.R. Wallace. 2001. The carbon cycle and atmospheric carbon dioxide. Chap. 3 in *Climate change 2001: The scientific basis. Contribution of Working Group 1 to the third assessment report of the Intergovernmental Panel on Climate Change*, ed. J.T. Houghton, Y. Ding, D.J. Griggs, M. Noguer, P.J. van der Linden, X. Dai, K. Maskell, and C.A. Johnson. Cambridge: Cambridge University Press, 183–238.

President of COP 6. No date. New Proposals by the President of COP 6. Available at [http://www.unfccc.int].

Ramaswamy, V., O. Boucher, J. Haigh, D. Hauglustaine, J. Haywood, G. Myhre, T. Nakajima, G.Y. Shi, and S. Solomon. 2001. Radiative forcing of climate change. Chap. 6 in *Climate change 2001: The scientific basis. Contribution of Working Group 1 to the Third Assessment Report of the Intergovernmental Panel on Climate Change*, ed. J.T. Houghton, Y. Ding, D.J. Griggs, M. Noguer, P.J. van der Linden, X. Dai, K. Maskell, and C.A. Johnson. Cambridge: Cambridge University Press, 349–416.

Randall, D.A., R.A. Wood, S. Bony, R. Colman, T. Fichefet, J. Fyfe, V. Kattsov, A. Pitman, J. Shukla, J. Srinivasan, R.J. Stouffer, A. Sumi, and K.E. Taylor, 2007. Climate Models and Their Evaluation. In *Climate Change 2007: The Physical Science Basis. Contribution of Working Group 1 to the fourth assessment report of the Intergovernmental Panel on Climate Change*, ed. S. Solomon, D. Qin, M. Manning, Z. Chen, M. Marquis, K.B. Averyt, M. Tignor, and H.L. Miller. Cambridge: Cambridge University Press, 589–662.

Rao, P.K. 2000. *Economics of global climatic change*. Armonk, NY: M.E. Sharpe.

Rayner, S., and E.L. Malone. 1998. Social science insights into climate change. In *What have we learned?* Vol. 4 of *Human Choice & Climate Change*, ed. S. Rayner and E.L. Malone. Columbus, OH: Batelle Press.

Revelle, R., and H. Suess. 1957. Carbon dioxide exchange between atmosphere and ocean and the question of an increase of atmospheric CO_2 during the past decades. *Tellus* 9:18–27. Cited in S. Weart, *The discovery of global warming* (Cambridge, MA: Harvard University Press 2004). Available online at http://www.aip.org/history/climate/.

Robinson, J. 2004. Squaring the circle? Some thoughts on the idea of sustainable development. *Ecological Economics* 48:369–84.

Robinson, J.B., and D. Herbert. 2001. Integrating climate change and sustainable development. *International Journal of Global Environmental Issues* 1(2):130–49.

Rosenberg, N.J., ed. 1993. Towards an integrated assessment of climate change: The MINK study. *Climatic Change* 24(1–2):1–173.

Rosenzweig, C., and D. Hillel. 1998. *Climate change and the global harvest*. New York: Oxford University Press.

Rosenzweig, C., J. Phillips, R. Goldberg, J. Carroll, and T. Hodges. 1996. Potential impacts of climate change on citrus and potato production in the US. *Agricultural Systems* 52, 455–79.

Rotmans, J. 1998. Methods for IA: The challenges and opportunities ahead. *Environmental Modeling and Assessment* 3:155–79.

Rotmans, J., and B. de Vries, eds. 1997. *Perspectives on global change: The TARGETS approach*. Cambridge: Cambridge University Press.

Rotmans, J., and M. van Asselt. 1996. Integrated assessment: A growing child on its way to maturity. *Climatic Change* 34:327–36.

Ruosteenoja, K., T.R. Carter, K. Jylhä, and H. Tuomenvirta. 2003. Future climate in world regions: An intercomparison of model-based projections for the new IPCC emissions scenarios. The Finnish Environment 644. Helsinki: Finnish Environment Institute.

Santer, B.D., T.M.L. Wigley, T.P. Barnett, and E. Anyamba. 1995. Detection of climate change and attribution of causes. Chap. 8 in *Climate change 1995: The science of climate change. Contribution of Working Group 1 to the second assessment report of the Intergovernmental Panel on Climate Change*, ed. J.T. Houghton, L.G. Meira Filho, B.A. Callandar, N. Harris, A. Kattenberg, and K. Maskell. Cambridge: Cambridge University Press, 407–43.

Sathaye, J., A. Najam, C. Cocklin, T. Heller, F. Lecocq, J. Llanes-Regueiro, J. Pan, G. Petschel-Held , S. Rayner, J. Robinson, R. Schaeffer, Y. Sokona, R. Swart, and H. Winkler. 2007. Sustainable Development and Mitigation. In *Climate Change 2007. Mitigation. Contribution of Working Group III to the fourth assessment report of the Intergovernmental Panel on Climate Change*, ed. B. Metz, O.R. Davidson, P.R. Bosch, R. Dave, L.A. Meyer. Cambridge: Cambridge University Press, 691–743.

Schimel, D., D. Alves, I. Enting, M. Heimann, F. Joos, D. Raynaud, and T. Wigley. 1995. CO_2 and the carbon cycle. Chap. 2.1 in *Climate change 1995: The science of climate change. Contribution of Working Group 1 to the second assessment report of the Intergovernmental Panel on Climate Change*, ed. J.T. Houghton, L.G. Meira Filho, B.A. Callander, N. Harris, A. Kattenberg, and K. Maskell. Cambridge: Cambridge University Press.

Schipper, E.L.F. 2006. Conceptual history of adaptation in the UNFCCC process. *Review of European Community and International Environmental Law* 15:82–92.

Schneider, S.H., and L.E. Mesirow. 1975. *The genesis strategy: Climate and global survival*. New York: Plenum Press.

Schneider, S.H., W.E. Easterling, and L.O. Mearns. 2000. Adaptation: Sensitivity to natural variability, agent assumptions, and dynamic climate changes. *Climatic Change* 45:203–21.

Schneider, S.H., S. Semenov, A. Patwardhan, I. Burton, C.H.D. Magadza, M. Oppenheimer, A.B. Pittock, A. Rahman, J.B. Smith, A. Suarez, and F. Yamin. 2007. Assessing key vulnerabilities and the risk from climate change. In *Climate change 2007: Impacts, adaptation, and vulnerability. Contribution of Working Group II to the fourth assessment report of the Intergovernmental*

Panel on Climate Change, ed. M.L. Parry, O. Canziani, J.P. Palutikof, P.J. van der Linden, and C.E. Hanson. Cambridge: Cambridge University Press, 779–810.

Schröter, D., L. Acosta-Michlik, P. Reidsma, M. Metzger, and R.J.T. Klein. 2003. Modelling the vulnerability of eco-social systems to global change: Human adaptive capacity to changes in ecosystem service provision. Presented at the Open Meeting of the Human Dimensions of Global Environmental Change, Montreal, 16–18 October, 2003.

Scott, D., J. Malcolm, and C. Lemieux. 2002. Climate change and biome representation in Canada's national park system: Implications for system planning and park mandates. *Global Ecology and Biogeography* 11:475–84.

Scott, D.S., and R. Suffling, eds. 2000. *Climate change and Canada's national park system: A screening level assessment*. Report prepared for Parks Canada by the Adaptation and Impacts Research Group, Environment Canada, and the Faculty of Environmental Studies, University of Waterloo.

Secretariat of the Convention on Biological Diversity (SCBD). 2003. *Interlinkages between biological diversity and climate change: Advice on the integration of biodiversity considerations into the implementation of the United Nations Framework Convention on Climate Change and its Kyoto Protocol*. CBD Technical Series No. 10. Montreal: SCBD.

Seidel, S., and D. Keyes. 1983. *Can we delay a greenhouse warming?* 2d ed. Washington, DC: Environmental Protection Agency.

Shaw, A. 2005. Imbued meaning: Science-policy interactions in the Intergovernmental Panel on Climate Change. PHD dissertation, University of British Columbia.

Sheppard, S.R.J. 2005. Landscape visualisation and climate change: The potential for influencing perceptions and behaviour. *Environmental Science and Policy* 8:637–54.

Shukla, P.R. 1999. Justice, equity, and efficiency in climate change: A developing country perspective. In *Fair weather? Equity concerns in climate change*, ed. F.L. Toth. London: Earthscan Publications.

Sims, R.E.H., R.N. Schock, A. Adegbululgbe, J. Fenhann, I. Konstantinaviciute, W. Moomaw, H.B. Nimir, B. Schlamadinger, J. Torres-Martínez, C. Turner, Y. Uchiyama, S.J.V. Vuori, N. Wamukonya, and X. Zhang. 2007. Energy supply. In *Climate change 2007: Mitigation. Contribution of Working Group III to the fourth assessment report of the Intergovernmental Panel on Climate Change*, ed. B. Metz, O.R. Davidson, P.R. Bosch, R. Dave, and L.A. Meyer. Cambridge: Cambridge University Press, 251–322.

Slater, L.E., and S.K. Levin. 1981. *Climate's impact on food supplies: Strategies and technologies for climate-defensive food production*. AAAS Selected

Symposium 62, American Association for the Advancement of Science, Boulder, CO: Westview Press.

SMIC (Study of Man's Impact on Climate). 1971. *Inadvertent climate modification.* Report of the Study of Man's Impact on Climate. Cambridge: MIT Press.

Smit, B., O. Pilifosova, I. Burton, B. Challenger, S. Huq, R.J.T. Klein, and G. Yohe. 2001. Adaptation to climate change in the context of sustainable development and equity. In *Climate change 2001: Impacts, adaptation, and vulnerability. Contribution of Working Group II to the third assessment report of the Intergovernmental Panel on Climate Change,* ed. J.J. McCarthy, O.F. Canziani, N.A. Leary, D.J. Dokken, and K.S. White. Cambridge: Cambridge University Press, 877–912.

– 2003. From adaptation to adaptive capacity and vulnerability reduction. In *Climate change, adaptive capacity, and development,* ed. J.B. Smith, R.J.T. Klein, and S. Huq. London: Imperial College Press.

Smit, B., and J. Wandel. 2006. Adaptation, adaptive capacity and vulnerability. *Global Environmental Change* 16, 282–92.

Smith, C.D., and M. Parry, eds. 1981. *Consequences of climatic change.* Nottingham: Department of Geography, University of Nottingham.

Smith, G.S., and D.G. Victor. 2004. *Beyond Kyoto?* In *Hard choices: Climate change in Canada,* ed. H. Coward and A.J. Weaver. Waterloo: Wilfrid Laurier University Press.

Smith, J.B., H.-J. Schellnhuber, M.M.Q. Mirza, S. Fankhauser, R. Leemans, L. Erda, L. Ogallo, B. Pittock, R. Richels, C. Rosenzweig, U. Safriel, R.S.J. Tol, J. Weyant, and G. Yohe. 2001. Vulnerability to climate change and reasons for concern: A synthesis. Chap. 19 in *Climate change 2001: Impacts, adaptation, and vulnerability. Contribution of Working Group II to the third assessment report of the Intergovernmental Panel on Climate Change,* ed. J.J. McCarthy, O.F. Canziani, N.A. Leary, D.J. Dokken, and K.S. White. Cambridge: Cambridge University Press.

Smith, W.N., R.L. Desjardins, and E. Pattey. 2000. The net flux of carbon from agricultural soils in Canada, 1970–2010. *Global Change Biology* 6:557–68.

Smol, J.P., and M.S.V. Douglas. 2007. From controversy to consensus: making the case for recent climate change in the Arctic using lake sediments. *Frontiers in Ecology and the Environment* 5, 466–74, doi:10.1890/060162.

Snover, A.K., L. Whitely Binder, J. Lopez, E. Willmott, J. Kay, D. Howell, and J. Simmonds. 2007. *Preparing for Climate Change: A Guidebook for Local, Regional, and State Governments.* Oakland: ICLEI – Local Government for Sustainability.

Stanton, B., J. Eaton, J. Johnson, D. Rice, B. Schuette, and B. Moser. 2002. Hybrid poplar in the Pacific Northwest. *Journal of Forestry* 100(4):28–33.

Stehr, H., H. von Storch, and M. Flügel. 1995. *The 19ᵗʰ century discussion of climate variability and climate change: Analogies for present debate?* Report No. 157. Hamburg: Max-Planck Institut für Meteorologie.

Stern, N. 2007. The Economics of Climate Change. The Stern Review. Cambridge: Cambridge University Press.

Stern, N., and C. Taylor. 2007. Climate change: Risk, ethics, and the Stern Review. *Science* 317:203–4.

Stocker, T.F., G.K.C. Clarke, H. Le Treut, R.S. Lindzen, V.P. Meleshko, R.K. Mugara, T.N. Palmer, R.T. Pierrehumbert, P.J. Sellers, K.E. Trenberth, and J. Willebrand. 2001. Physical climate processes and feedbacks. Chap. 7 in *Climate change 2001: The scientific basis. Contribution of Working Group 1 to the third assessment report of the Intergovernmental Panel on Climate Change*, ed. J.T. Houghton, Y. Ding, D.J. Griggs, M. Noguer, P.J. van der Linden, X. Dai, K. Maskell, and C.A. Johnson. Cambridge: Cambridge University Press, 417–70.

Stouffer, R.J., S. Manabe, and K. Bryan. 1989. Interhemispheric asymmetry in climate response to a gradual increase of atmospheric carbon dioxide. *Nature* 342:660–2. Cited in F.P. Bretherton, K. Bryan, and J.D. Woods, Time-dependent greenhouse-gas-induced climate change. Chap. 6 in *Climate change: The IPCC scientific assessment. Report prepared for IPCC by Working Group 1*, ed. J.T. Houghton, G.J. Jenkins, and J.J. Ephraums (Cambridge: Cambridge University Press 1990).

Strahler, A.H., and A.S. Strahler. 1997. *Physical geography: Science and systems of the human environment*. New York, NY: John Wiley & Sons.

Summit Environmental Consultants Ltd. 2004. *Trepanier Landscape Unit Water Management Plan final report*. Project 572-02.01. Prepared for Regional District of Central Okanagan, Kelowna, and BC Ministry of Sustainable Resource Management, Kamloops.

Sutter, C., and J.C. Parreño. 2007. Does the current Clean Development Mechanism (CDM) deliver its sustainable development claim? An analysis of officially registered CDM projects. *Climatic Change* 84, 75–90.

Swart, R., J. Robinson, and S.J. Cohen. 2003. Climate change and sustainable development: Expanding the options. *Climate Policy* 3S1:S19–S40.

Swisher, J.N. 1997. Joint implementation under the UN Framework Convention on Climate Change: Technical and institutional challenges. *Mitigation and Adaptation Strategies for Global Change* 2:57–80.

Tansey, J., J. Carmichael, R. van Wynsberghe, and J. Robinson. 2002. The future is not what it used to be: Participatory integrated assessment in the Georgia Basin. *Global Environmental Change* 12:97–104.

Taylor, S.W., and A.L. Carroll. 2004. Disturbance, forest age, and mountain pine beetle outbreak dynamics in BC: A historical perspective. In *Mountain pine beetle symposium: Challenges and solutions, October 30–31, 2003, Kelowna*, ed. T.L. Shore, J.E. Brooks, and J.E. Stone. Information Report BC-X-399, Victoria: Natural Resources Canada, Canadian Forest Service, Pacific Forestry Centre.

Tegart, W.J.McG., G.W. Sheldon, and D.C. Griffiths, eds. 1990. *Climate change. The IPCC impacts assessment report prepared for IPCC by Working Group II.* Canberra: Australian Government Publishing Service.

Tierney, K., and G. Guibert. 2005. Natural Hazards Center recommends independent Katrina review. *Natural Hazards Observer* 30, 2, 4.

Tol, R.S.J. 2000. The marginal costs of greenhouse gas emissions. *Energy Journal* 20:61–81.

– 2002. Estimates of the damage costs of climate change, part 1: Benchmark estimates. *Environmental and Resource Economics* 21:41–73.

Tol, R.S.J., T.E. Downing, O.J. Kuik, and J.B. Smith. 2004. Distributional aspects of climate change impacts. *Global Environmental Change* 14:259–72.

Tol, R.S.J., S. Fankhauser, and D.W. Pearce. 1999. Empirical and ethical arguments in climate change impact valuation and aggregation. In *Fair weather? Equity concerns in climate change*, ed. F.L. Toth. London: Earthscan Publications.

Toronto and Region Conservation Authority. 2004. *Hazel's legacy.* Downsview, ON: Toronto and Region Conservation Authority.

Toth, F.L. 2003. State of the art and future challenges for integrated environmental assessment. *Integrated Assessment* 4:250–64.

Toth, F.L., M. Mwandosya, C. Carraro, J. Christensen, J. Edmonds, B. Flannery, C. Gay-Garcia, H. Lee, K.M. Meyer-Abich, E. Nikitina, A. Rahman, R. Richels, Y. Ruqui, A. Villavicencio, Y. Wake, and J. Weyant. 2001. Decision-making frameworks. In *Climate change 2001: Mitigation. Contribution of Working Group III to the third assessment report of the Intergovernmental Panel on Climate Change*, ed. B. Metz, O. Davidson, R. Swart, and J. Pan. Cambridge: Cambridge University Press, 601–88.

Tubiello, F.N., J.A. Amthor, K. Boote, M. Donatelli, W.E. Easterling, G. Fisher, R. Gifford, M. Howden, J. Reilly, and C. Rosenzweig. 2007. Crop response to elevated CO_2 and world food supply. A comment on "Food for Thought…" by Long et al., *Science* 312 (2006): 1918–21. *European Journal of Agronomy* 26, 215–23.

UNDP (United Nations Development Programme). 2004. *Disaster and risk: A challenge for development (A global report).* UNDP Bureau of Crisis Prevention and Recovery. New York: United Nations Development Programme. Cited in *Drought and water crises: Science, technology, and management issues*, ed. D.A. Wilhite (Boca Raton, FL: CRC Press 2005).

UNEP (United Nations Environment Programme). 1994. *Convention on Climate Change*. Published for the Climate Change Secretariat by UNEP's Information Unit for Conventions. Bonn: Climate Change Secretariat. Available online at http://www.unfccc.int.

UNFCCC (United Nations Framework Convention on Climate Change). 2001. Decision 11/CP.7. *Land use, land-use change and forestry*. Available online at http://unfccc.int.

– 2004. *United Nations Framework Convention on Climate Change: The first ten years*. Bonn: Climate Change Secretariat. Available online at http://www.unfccc.int.

UNFCCC. 2007a. Decision 1/CP.13. *Bali action plan*. Available online at http://unfccc.int.

UNFCCC. 2007b. Decision 1/CMP.3. *Adaptation fund*. Available online at http://unfccc.int.

UNFCCC. 2005. Decision 16/CMP.1. *Land use, land use change and forestry*. Available online at http://unfccc.int.

United Nations. 2004. Progress towards the Millennium Development Goals, 1990–2004. Unofficial working paper, 3 December 2004. Available at http://millenniumindicators.un.org/unsd/mi/mi_coverfinal.htm.

van Asselt, M.B.A., and N. Rijkens-Klomp. 2002. A look in the mirror: Reflection on participation in integrated assessment from a methodological perspective. *Global Environmental Change* 12:167–84.

Vancouver Sun. 1997. Editorial, December.

van de Kerkhof, M. 2004. *Debating climate change: A study of stakeholder participation in an integrated assessment of long-term climate policy in the Netherlands*. Utrecht: Lemma Publishers.

van den Belt, M. 2004. *Mediated modeling: A system dynamics approach to environmental consensus building*. Washington, DC: Island Press.

Victor, D.G. 2001. Collapse of the Kyoto Protocol and the struggle to slow global warming. Princeton: Princeton University Press.

Viner, D., and M. Hulme. 1994. The climate impacts LINK project: Providing climate change scenarios for impacts assessment in the UK. University of East Anglia, Norwich, submitted to UK Department of the Environment, London.

Wara, M. 2007. Is the global carbon market working? *Nature* 445:595–6.

Warrick, R.A. 1980. Drought in the Great Plains: A case study of research on climate and society in the USA. In *Climatic constraints and human activities*, ed. J. Ausubel and A.K. Biswas. New York: Pergamon.

Washington, W.M., and G.A. Meehl. 1989. Climate sensitivity due to increased CO_2: Experiments with a coupled-atmosphere and ocean general-circulation model. *Climate Dynamics* 4:1–38. Cited in F.P. Bretherton, K. Bryan, and

J.D. Woods, Time-dependent greenhouse-gas-induced climate change. Chap. 6 in *Climate change: The IPCC scientific assessment. Report prepared for IPCC by Working Group I*, ed. J.T. Houghton, G.J. Jenkins, and J.J. Ephraums (Cambridge: Cambridge University Press 1990).

Watson, R.T., I.R. Noble, B. Bolin, N.H. Ravindranath, D.J. Verardo, and D.J. Dokken, eds. 2000a. Summary for policymakers. In *Land use, land-use change, and forestry. Special report of the Intergovernmental Panel on Climate Change.* Cambridge: Cambridge University Press.

– 2000b. *Land use, land-use change, and forestry. Special report of the Intergovernmental Panel on Climate Change.* Cambridge: Cambridge University Press.

Watson, R.T., M.C. Zinyowera, and R.H. Moss, eds. 1995. *Climate change 1995: Impacts, adaptations, and mitigation of climate change. Contribution of Working Group II to the second assessment report of the Intergovernmental Panel on Climate Change.* Cambridge: Cambridge University Press.

WBGU (German Advisory Council on Global Change). 2006. The future oceans – warming up, rising high, turning sour. Special Report, available from WBGU, Berlin.

WCED (World Commission on Environment and Development). 1987. *Our Common Future.* Oxford: Oxford University Press.

Weart, S. 2004. *The discovery of global warming.* Cambridge, MA: Harvard University Press. Available online at http://www.aip.org/history/climate/.

Weyant, J. 1996. Integrated assessment of climate change: An overview and comparison of approaches and results. Chap. 10 in *Climate change 1995: Economic and social dimensions of climate change. Contribution of Working Group III to the second assessment of the Intergovernmental Panel on Climate Change*, ed. J.P. Bruce, H. Lee, and E.F. Haites. Cambridge: Cambridge University Press.

Wigley, T.M.L., M.J. Ingram, and G. Farmer, eds. 1981. *Climate and history: Studies in past climates and their impact on man.* Cambridge: Cambridge University Press.

Wigley, T.M.L., R. Richels, and J.A. Edmonds. 1996. Economic and environmental choices in the stabilization of atmospheric CO_2 concentrations. *Nature* 379:240–3.

Wilbanks, T. 2003. Integrating climate change and sustainable development in a place-based context. *Climate Policy* 3S1: S147–S154.

Wilby, R.L., and T.M.L. Wigley. 1997. Downscaling general circulation model output: A review of methods and limitations. *Progress in Physical Geography* 21:530–48.

Wilhite, D.A., ed. 2005. *Drought and water crises: Science, technology, and management issues.* Boca Raton, FL: CRC Press.

Willows, R., and R. Connell, eds. 2003. *Climate adaptation: Risk, uncertainty and decision-making.* UKCIP Technical Report. Oxford: UKCIP.

Winkler, H., R. Spalding-Fecher, S. Mwakasonda, and O. Davidson. 2004. Sustainable development policies and measures: Starting from development to tackle climate change. In *International climate efforts beyond 2012: A survey of approaches*, ed. D. Bodansky, S. Chou, and C. Jorge-Tresolini. Arlington, VA: Pew Center on Global Climate Change. First published in *Building on the Kyoto Protocol: Options for protecting the climate*, ed. K.A. Baumert, O. Blanchard, S. Llosa, and J.R. Perkans (World Resources Institute 2002).

WMO (World Meteorological Organization). 1986. *Report of the international conference on the assessment of the role of carbon dioxide and other greenhouse gases on climate variations and associated impacts.* WMO-No. 661. Geneva: World Meteorological Organization.

– 1989. *The changing atmosphere: Implications for global security.* Conference Proceedings, 27–30 June. 1988, Toronto. WMO–No. 710. Geneva: World Meteorological Organization.

– 2008. WMO Greenhouse Gas Bulletin, No. 4, 14 November 2008. Global Atmosphere Watch programme, WMO, Geneva.

Wood, E.F., Lettenmaier, D.P., Liang, X., Lohmann, D., Boone, A., Chang, S., Chen, F., Dai, Y., Dickinson, R.E., Ek, M., Gusev, Y.M., Habets, F., Irranejad, P., Koster, R., Mitchell, K.E., Nasonova, O.N., Noilhan, J., Schaake, J., Schlosser, C.A., Shao, Y., Schmakin, A.B., Verseghy, D., Warrach, K., Wetzel, P., Xue, Y., Yang, Z.-L., and Zeng, Q.-C. 1998. The project for intercomparison of land-surface parameterisation schemes (PILPS) Phase 2(c) Red-Arkansas River basin experiment: 1 Experiment Description and Summary Intercomparison. *Global and Planetary Change* 19(1–4):115–35.

World Bank. 2003. *Poverty and climate change: Reducing the vulnerability of the poor through adaptation.* Prepared by African Development Bank, Asian Development Bank, Department for International Development (United Kingdom), Directorate General for Development (European Commission), Federal Ministry for Economic Cooperation and Development (Germany), Ministry of Foreign Affairs (The Netherlands), Organization for Economic Cooperation and Development, United Nations Development Programme, United Nations Environment Programme, and The World Bank. Available online at http://povertymap.net/publications/doc/PovertyAndClimateChange _WorldBank.pdf.

Yamin, F., and J. Depledge. 2004. The international climate change regime: A guide to rules, institutions, and procedures. Cambridge: Cambridge University Press.

Yohe, G.W., R.D. Lasco, Q.K. Ahmad, N.W. Arnell, S.J. Cohen, C. Hope, A.C. Janetos, and R.T. Perez. 2007. Perspectives on climate change and sustainability. *Climate Change 2007: Impacts, Adaptation and Vulnerability.*

Contribution of Working Group II *to the fourth assessment report of the Intergovernmental Panel on Climate Change*, ed. M.L. Parry, O.F. Canziani, J.P. Palutikof, P.J. van der Linden, and C.E. Hanson. Cambridge: Cambridge University Press, 811–41.

Yohe, G., J.E. Neumann, and P. Marshall. 1999. The economic damage induced by sea level rise in the United States. In *The impact of climate change on the United States economy*, ed. R. Mendelsohn and J.E. Neumann. Cambridge: Cambridge University Press.

Index